A Boy's Dream —
Ohio State:
The Dennis Bunda Story

by

Dennis Bunda

Published by Pen It! Publications, LLC in the U.S.A.
812-371-4128 www.penitpublications.com

ISBN: 978-1-954868-63-2
Edited by Dina Husseini
Cover Design by Donna Cook

Review by

Brian T. Portlock
December 2020

I grew up in Merrillville, a town in northwest Indiana. This area is affectionately known by locals as "the Region". This name comes from the Calumet Region, which shares a border with Illinois. There are official reasons for the name, but to me it has always meant tough, hard working men and women who love their Bears, Bulls, Cubs and Blackhawks, and who know the meaning of lake effect snow! It also includes US Steel, one of the main employers in the Region. NW Indiana is a place full of union workers, and my father was no exception.

My family life was not a happy one. My parents split when I was 11, and even though in my mind it was the best thing that could have happened, things at home went from bad to worse. My mom raised us. We were four teenagers, and she somehow kept us afloat. Sports was an outlet for me, and I played them all the time.

I met Dennis Bunda, (Denny) in the fall of 1979. We played together on the same Pop Warner football team. He had just moved to Merrillville less than two years earlier and went to a different elementary school. Denny and I were both quarterbacks, and we became quick friends. That season was so much fun, and we laughed a lot! After the season was over, I lost contact with him, temporarily…

Fall of '80 brought on 7th grade and new opportunities. My grade school friends had changed, and I sought new friends. I saw Denny in the cafeteria and sat with him. From then on, Denny and I were good friends. We played basketball and ran track together that year. The next few years were spent playing football, basketball and running track, along with having classes together. We had two of the worst football teams in the history of Harrison Jr High School! We still laugh about that.

Freshman year I started spending time at Denny's home. He had what in mind was the ideal family; dad, mom, one boy and two girls. Everyone got along. It was the opposite of my home; everyone always fighting, mom always working. Denny's parents were so great to me. They treated me like their own. His mom gave me rides home all the time from practices. Denny and I spent ¾ of that summer together and remained great friends all throughout high school as well.

The first thing I noticed about Denny was his Ohio State jersey he wore at football practice. I think he wore one every day that season. He would wear an

Ohio State shirt nearly every single day to school! The first time I spent the night at his house, when we went into his room he has a plate around his light switch that said, "Ohio State turns me on, Michigan turns me off". His walls were covered with Ohio State posters. His bedspread was Ohio State. Denny is truly the #1 Ohio State fan!

As we went off to college, Denny and I drifted for a few years. He went to Ball State for a year, but in my mind I had no doubt he would fulfill his dream of going to The Ohio State University!

Denny and I reconnected while I was in the US Air Force. Every single time I came home, I make a point to see Denny. I always call him on his birthday, and we talk often. I love him like a brother. This book will take you on a journey full of suspense, laughter and sometimes tears. It is a story of determination and dedication, and ultimately victory in life. I know you will enjoy the ride.

Review by

Rick Keneson
December 2020

Martin Luther King once said, "I have a dream." Well Dennis Bunda had a dream and that dream was to attend The Ohio State University.

I met Dennis in the fifth grade. He had just moved to Merrillville from Griffith. We rode the same bus, so we sat together and became friends immediately. We had a similar sense of humor and shared a love of sports which was realized while playing football during recess. I didn't know right away about his love for Ohio State and I didn't really have a favorite college team at the time. I soon became a University of Michigan fan and realized Dennis' love of Ohio State. I quickly learned of the intense rivalry between the two schools and despite that we remained the best of friends except for that one day in November every year. A lot of people lose touch with their friends as they grow older but my friendship with Dennis has grown stronger over a 42-year span. I am proud to call Dennis my best friend and I know our friendship will last a lifetime.

The book you are about to read is filled with stories from our youth like the time we played a Halloween prank on a girl that liked Dennis or the time we snuck into the drive-in or the time we played leapfrog at the library instead of doing our mythology report. The stories in this book will make you laugh, it will make you cry, they will make you remember the fun times you had growing up and they will inspire you to follow your own dreams.

Dedication

To my wonderful parents, Dennis and Gayle Bunda. Thank you for believing that I could accomplish great things in life and allowing me to pursue my dreams as well as goals. You could have easily said "no" or that it couldn't have been done. You allowed a young boy to live out a dream of attending and graduating from The Ohio State University. You never wavered in your belief of me. Thank you, mom and dad!

Acknowledgements

Ohio State… "A Boy's Dream" has been a tremendous effort. I am truly grateful for the many friends, colleagues, and family members who have helped guide me in writing this book. They have offered their advice and guidance while completing this project.

Many thanks to my friends for sharing their stories with me of our childhood while growing up in Merrillville, Indiana.

Special thanks to Steve Pederson for giving me the opportunity to work for the Ohio State football program.

I want to credit Buckeye Sports Bulletin for their great newspaper which has allowed me to look back at special games, players, and events of Ohio State football.

To all my schoolteachers like Ruth Homco, Lafey Armontrout, Tom Peller, Ruth Staniszeski, Miss Onika, John Stefek, Tom Feeney, Bonnie Sanders, and others...Thank you for your guidance and inspiration!! Lastly, to my brother-in-law John Spinks for giving me the idea to write this book.

Table of Contents

Foreword

Michael "D" Demakas
December 2020

This book is written about one of my best friends in the whole world Dennis (Denny) Bunda. What I really mean to say is Denny has been my best friend since the Fall of 1982. I have never called him Dennis, or Denny, so we are not about to start now!

I first remember meeting Bunda during a ninth grade lopsided football game between the only two Junior high schools in Merrillville, IN. I was playing wide receiver for Pierce and Bunda was playing wide receiver for Harrison that night. The score was 68-0 before I remember from the sideline seeing Bunda take a seemingly meaningless fourth quarter punt return back for a touchdown to end the game 68-6. The game was over for everyone….except Bunda!

That was the first time I remember meeting Bunda, but it describes his relentless, competitive attitude that he still carries with him today in his fifties. Fast forward to the next summer and we are now both playing wide receiver for the same High School JV team as sophomores at a new school together. Two a day practices started before school actually started and Bunda and I found each other fast friends now finally playing on the same team. We have been on the same team over the past thirty-eight years and that will never change. Looking back on it now, I needed Bunda more than he needed me. He had what I always dreamed of growing-up; a mom, dad, sisters, and loving grandparents. What I myopically needed was a ride to and from practice and I found it in Bunda along with so much more! Bunda always knew he was going to go to Ohio State for college. He would wear it, talk about it, he truly lived his dream each and every day of his young life...it was more than a dream to Bunda.

I remember Bunda and I being together...kinda like the Bobbsey twins from the first day of two-a-day football practice in high school until today. We played football and ran track and field together for the next three years and so much more together. Every possible moment when we were not in school together; we spent time together. Bunda and I were at practices, football games, track meets and working out at Southlake Nautilus (whirlpool) it seemed like daily.

Bunda and I got together every weekend with the sole purpose of finding girls for me, for him (think Brenna Break-up) or more commonly for both of us. In our quest for girls, we would leave no avenue unturned over the next three years of high school. We were break dancing at GOYA's or Club Soda, cruising Lincolnway, underage drinking all along the way thanks to the combination of Jundale liquors, Illinois State fake IDs, and my mustache at sixteen. Bunda and I did it all! If I were to list all of our serial capers that we pulled-off together, or got caught together (think Gayle and Little Kings), and narrowly escaped prosecution (think screen door kicked-open)...well quite honestly nobody would believe any of them and most importantly we need to protect our kids and spouses' culpability in all of these stories.

The real reason I found Bunda, stayed with Bunda, and to this day love Bunda....he was from day one family to me. He had a family and I needed his mom Gayle at a time when I did not have a mother. His dad...he was a character (think me washing his car so we could take it for the night) and I always remember calling the house phone and Mr. Bunda answering... "Mr. Bunda is Bunda there?" But his dad's connection as Athletic Director was how we were able to use the indoor field house to practice long jumping our senior year that propelled us both to State that year. Being a part of the Bunda family was truly life changing for my success and so much of the person I am today. We truly are helped by so many in our journey through life. I have a couple of quotes that I keep as the cornerstones of success. There is one that sums up the impact of Bunda and I on each other; "¡Dime con quién andas y te diré quien eres!" Literally it means "Tell me who you "hang" with and I will tell you who you are." In other words, "you are known by the company you keep!" Bunda is the best company a friend could ever keep!

Introduction

We all have dreams in life. Maybe it is to do well in school or in a sport. Maybe it is to have a rewarding career and make a lot of money. Maybe it is to take a vacation that we have only read about in travel magazines or on the internet. Maybe it is to meet the person of our dreams. Or, maybe it is to just be happy and live a fulfilling life. Is all of this possible? Can dreams really come true?

As the famous playwright George Bernard Shaw once stated, *"You see things; and you say, 'Why?' But I dream things that never were; and I say, 'Why not?'"*

If dreams really do come true, then, life has been the ultimate experience. This is my own personal quest to fulfill a dream that only a few could have even imagined as being possible. It has been a turbulent ride throughout life. There have been many exciting moments in my journey. There have also been many obstacles and life-changing experiences that could have prevented me from accomplishing my ultimate goal.

This is my story.

Chapter 1
The Start to a Wonderful Experience

I guess my day started out like most days as a child. It would be just like any other normal day. I would wake up, and do my usual routine of eating breakfast, have my two sisters antagonize me, and go outside and play all day long with friends. Just a regular normal day for most children growing up in mainstream America during the 1970's. I grew up with having both my parents around as well as my sibling sisters, Nikki and Erin. We were your regular American family.

Well...almost!

However, I didn't realize that Saturday, November 22nd,1975 would change my life forever. It has been a roller-coaster ride through many ups and downs and the highs and lows of life. Many times, my journey has proved to be not only challenging but full of despair and heartbreak. In other ways, it has been a quest for greatness, success, and accomplishing goals.

Only in life, does one go through many peaks and valleys to get to their own personal destination.

November 22, 1975 was the day that I hoped my dreams would someday become reality. I just didn't know that I would have to endure so much in my life, both good and bad.

My dad grew up in Northwest Indiana but he didn't like living there much. Dad, whose real name is Dennis, named me after him, went to Horace Mann High School in Gary, Indiana. A taste of Arizona dry heat, miles of desert, as well as the view of mountains, changed his mind on where he wanted to live and go to college. Dad loved Arizona's scenery and the slow pace lifestyle. He actually went out there for a short time to go to college at the University of Arizona in the 1960's. It wasn't dad's first college choice. He skipped around from place to place just being young and enjoying life's adventures.

One of his first college experiences was at Culver Stockton College in Canton, Missouri. To hear my dad talk about his early college years was like seeing the movie, *"Animal House"* over and over again. My grandparents paid for my dad on his journey of getting a college education or need I say, enjoy the social aspect of it. During one of his many breaks home from college, he met a beautiful girl named Gayle Maus. She was a graduate of nearby Hammond High School.

As fate would have it, my dad actually came home sick from college with what was known as *"Valley Fever"* when he first met this young woman. Dennis and Gayle would start a romance which would last thirty-nine years. It would be love at first sight, you could say, and change the direction in both of their lives as well as mine.

This love affair would stall dad's college plans for a while.

After all, how could he leave this beautiful girl and go back to college in Arizona?

Dennis and Gayle would marry in November of 1966 in front of family and friends in Northwest Indiana. Gayle Maus would become my mother almost a year later. I was born in September of 1967, and my sister Nikki would arrive in February of 1971. My youngest sister Erin would come along by March of 1972. I was actually shocked to see Erin when she was born as if to think, does this child really belong to our family? I even questioned my parents if Erin was adopted!

To have her tell it now...

Erin believes that she is the most gorgeous and beautiful of us three siblings. We all happen to be the best of friends and siblings now, but that was not always the case growing up in the 1970's and 1980's.

From a blink of an eye, my dad went from a carefree college life and tending for himself, to having a family of five.

Life changes in an instant. We just didn't realize how much it would change.

You need to understand that Nikki, Erin, and I were all born during the height of the Vietnam War or conflict as it has been called. It was a lot different back then than it seems now-a-days as I write this book in 2020. We didn't have a lot of technology, video games, or even multiple TV stations which people enjoy today. We may have been lucky to get a total of 4-5 television stations, and most of those aired soap operas throughout the day.

Needless to say, mom told us to go outside and find something to do without getting into trouble on our off-school days. We had to create our own fun or boredom based on what was going on at the time. Therefore, I don't remember watching much sports on TV prior to 1975.

My dad had a job as an insurance technical representative in 1972 and my mom was a 'stay at home' mother. She always made us breakfast, lunch, and dinner. We had three hot meals each day which might seem like a rarity now for the American family.

In today's world, everything is based on a fast-paced lifestyle, with both parents working, and not having time to spend with each other or their children.

Since my mom didn't drive a car until around 1978, we had to walk most places due to dad being at work or in college.

I started my school education at Eads Elementary School in Munster, Indiana in the fall of 1972 as a kindergartener. Being the only four-year-old, I was younger than most kids, but mom and dad thought I was ready for school. I don't remember much about Eads because I wasn't there very long. Gym was my favorite class due to the fact I really liked to run. It was at this early age that I realized that I was a pretty fast runner compared to most kids my age.

Our life changed one day when dad came home and told my mother that he was taking her out to dinner to discuss their future. It was at dinner that dad told her that he wanted to quit his job, and move to Arizona to finish his college degree. Dad loved the University of Arizona, and his time out there prior to meeting my mother.

It was his dream.

The move would prove to be difficult. After all, he had a wife and three kids to support now. It was a major responsibility to go to school, get a job, and raise a family. I am not sure my mom's parents fully approved of their daughter being taken across the country with three little kids and not a lot of money either. My dad is a true testament of not letting anything step in the way of dreams. I am sure even his own parents questioned why he was taking such a big risk.

As they say...without great risks there are no great rewards. Sometimes you only have one chance to accomplish your dreams in life.

We packed up our belongings and headed west to Tucson, Arizona in 1972 to start our new life in a different state.

I actually had to repeat kindergarten again while in Arizona. I wasn't really ready to take on schoolwork and I was a little hyperactive as a child. Mom always said that I was high energy and a constant motion type of kid. "If he still...he is ill," my parents would say.

Dad would go back to school on the University of Arizona campus to work on a degree in Business Administration. Mom would take the lead role of staying home, and raising Nikki, Erin, and I. She did work outside of the home for a short time in an office job on the University of Arizona campus. Believe it or not...I would get my mom fired for something that I heard her say at home one night. I later repeated her statement while visiting her office one day.

Mom mentioned that she didn't really like her boss, and being young and dumb, I repeated mom's comments at her workplace. Well... mom was removed from her job and went back to being a full-time housewife and mother. We were just counting on my dad's paychecks from a part-time job he was working at a local hotel. In other words, we were in Arizona away from most of our family with very little money.

At a young age, I didn't understand the hardships of what my parents were going through financially as well as raising three young children. As a child, I lived a carefree lifestyle. Didn't really have a care in the world.

Since my dad was now enrolled as a student at the University of Arizona, I would sometimes go with him to see the campus. There were cactus, mountains, and desert everywhere you looked. It was absolutely a beautiful place to live. It definitely was a lot different than what I had experienced living in Northwest Indiana with climate change, especially snow in the wintertime. The wildlife was different too. You had to watch out for black widow spiders, scorpions, rattlesnakes, and tarantulas in Arizona. At the time, it just seemed like the perfect place to live.

The University of Arizona was a big place with a lot of people on its campus. Some looked very bizarre to me because they dressed in funny colors, had necklaces, and long hair. Many of them were part of the 'hippie' movement protesting the Vietnam War. I didn't care though because I was so young and didn't realize what all the fuss was about. I just wanted to be around my dad.

Since my schooling was limited at this point of just being in kindergarten, I wondered if someday I would go to a big school like Arizona. I looked at dad and said, *"Do you think I can go here someday?"*

He smiled. *"Someday."*

I have to admit that since my dad went to college there, I was intrigued by the university, and how someone could go to a school that was so big with so many people. I told him that he must be really smart to go to the university. My elementary school seemed so small compared to the likes of a place such as the University of Arizona. It was on this campus that I would get my first taste of big-time sports.

That didn't mean that I had a favorite sports team or an affinity to any school in the early 1970's, even though dad went to school there. Although, I did know the words to the University of Arizona's fight song, *"Bear Down Arizona"* by heart. Dad would sing the song every time we were in the car going to the campus or going out to eat somewhere.

"Bear down, Arizona- Bear down, red and blue- Bear down, Arizona- Hit 'em hard, let 'em know who's who!"

In some ways, I think dad was hoping that his love for Arizona would rub off on me, and that I would actually go to school there one day.

Who knew?

It seemed like a great place. He even bought Nikki, Erin, and I all matching Arizona Wildcat t-shirts from the campus bookstore. In addition, dad would bring home University of Arizona football players to tutor for extra money.

The one Arizona football player who caught my eye was this guy named Theo Bell. Theo was from Bakersfield, California but played his college football for the Arizona Wildcats. He would walk in our house door and my whole family would just stare at him. Nikki, Erin, and I had never seen anyone that big before who was a star football player! We were all amazed my dad knew him, and that he played sports at Arizona.

Theo really didn't need much tutoring because he was really smart, but it was a chance for my dad to get paid by the university so we could eat. Theo would later go on to play pro football for the NFL Pittsburgh Steelers in 1976. He would win two NFL Super Bowls with the Steelers in 1979 and 1980. My friends always thought I was lying when I said that Theo Bell was in my house growing up, and he was being tutored by my father. I could never convince them that I knew Theo!

Because my dad tutored him, we had some extra money. Not a lot, just enough to put food on the table and pay our family bills. Most of the time in the early 1970's, we would live on food stamps or money that my grandparents would send to us. We never went hungry or without clothes though.

A lot of times, my family would go over to my parents' good friends, Connie and Mike Weiss to eat dinner, or they would come to our house. Every family would make something to eat or drink, and we would all have a shared meal together. There may have been other families there at this communal eating arrangement, but I just don't remember them.

Connie and Mike had two sons named Mike Jr. and Craig. I was friends with both of the boys but I really hit it off with Craig. We were the same age and interested in the same things, mostly GI Joe action figures.

At a young age, he and I really didn't talk about sports because it just wasn't on TV, or advertised like it is now. We did go into his room and stage boxing matches all the time.

Our parents would make us put on football helmets so we wouldn't get hurt too badly. Those were great times! Craig and I would also swim in an in-ground swimming pool that was in the back of our house. If you live in Arizona, you must have a swimming pool due to it being so hot.

When the Weiss family would move to Germantown, Ohio by 1976, I would not see Craig or Mike Jr. until our family went to visit them in 1980.

Just like the day of November 22nd, 1975 would change my life, the weekend of September 19th of 1980 would also prove to be an impactful event.

Like most of the time in the 1970's, it was a carefree world or at least it was to me. The Vietnam War was going on but it didn't impact me personally at the time, mainly because I was just a happy go lucky kid riding on my Schwinn bicycle with a banana seat. If you grew up in the 1970's, you know what I'm talking about.

When we were not eating dinner with other families, dad and mom would take Nikki, Erin, and I to *Farrell's Ice Cream Parlor* located in Tucson to get pizza and ice cream. Dad would also take us to a place known as *"Old Tucson Studios"* to learn about the wild west, cowboy life, and watch actors stage fake gun fights. My mom and dad always wanted us to experience many things in life even with the little money we had.

At this point, I thought that I would always live in Arizona with my family. I was meeting new friends, at a new school, and enjoying the western lifestyle.

It was at Shoemaker Elementary that I met a new friend named Cass. At the time, Cass was one of the few African American students in the school. I always noticed that he sat alone on the playground while the others were playing kickball, basketball, or football. Being young, I could never figure out why the other kids wouldn't want to play with him.

Until one day, when I asked him to play on my kickball team. He and I became instant friends. We had a lot in common, and the color of our skin didn't matter. I just didn't understand the many obstacles of racism and discrimination that Cass faced in life. I remembered being upset when other kids said remarks to him or looked at him the wrong way. We enjoyed each other's friendship and companionship throughout my time at Shoemaker.

Along with a girl named Mardie Allen, Cass became one of my first friends. He is the one friend that I wish I would have kept in contact with throughout the years. When you are so young, a person doesn't realize the many changes that will occur throughout a lifetime. I didn't know that one day I would say 'goodbye' to Cass and never see him again.

By 1975, my dad had his Public Administration degree from the University of Arizona. After he finished, dad realized he didn't want to have a career the rest of his life involving public administration, or wearing a suit & tie. Dad told my mother that he wanted to be a teacher and a coach. Being supportive like she always was, mom allowed dad to once again go back to the University of Arizona to obtain a second degree in education. That would mean a couple more years of struggling financially, and just trying to get by with what little we had. As kids, we didn't know any different.

As long as there was plenty to eat and we had clothes on our back, what else was there?

One of the best years of my life was when I was in the second grade. Dad had to learn to teach school by being a 'student teacher' at Shoemaker Elementary. Now this may not seem like a big deal but it would shape the rest of my life in more ways than one. Due to him not being able to find a permanent teaching job in Arizona once he completed his second degree, we would ironically have to move back to Northwest Indiana.

I don't think anyone at the time realized how the move back to Indiana would change all our lives forever. We were not happy about it, and I know dad really didn't want to leave Tucson, Arizona. He loved living there and everything that came with it, including the great friends we met, the sunny weather, and the slow pace of living. Knowing that he had a wife and three children to support, tutoring football players or working a night job at a local hotel, would not pay the bills. In the back of my dad's mind was giving Nikki, Erin, and I, a college education much like he received at the University of Arizona.

You may be wondering at this point of the book what this all has to do with Saturday, November 22nd, 1975, right??

The day happened six to seven months before we would move back to Northwest, Indiana. Like I said, I really didn't have any affinity with a college or pro team at this point in my young life. I liked the Arizona Wildcats but really didn't follow them that closely. If anything, I followed the California Angels and the Oakland A's professional baseball teams because they were always on the radio before I went to sleep at night. My mom would turn the radio dial to the station that would broadcast the A's or the Angel's games.

My heroes at a young age were Sal Bando, Vida Blue, Rollie Fingers, and Reggie Jackson of the Oakland Athletics. I would fall asleep on summer nights listening to the baseball games play out on the radio. It helped that the Oakland Athletics finished first in the division during 1975, and that their general manager was a man named Charlie Finley. Dad knew of Mr. Finley because he donated baseball uniforms to my dad's high school team back in the 1960's.

November 22nd, 1975, I became glued to one team and one team only, and it would not be the A's or the Angles. It would shape who I am today, and the many people who have impacted my life along the way. Moving back to Northwest Indiana by 1976 would get me closer to that team as well as the school it represented.

I woke up to a normal morning on November 22nd, 1975. I had my breakfast and went outside to play for a while. It was also an unusual day because my dad happened to be home, and not in school or working one of his part-time jobs to help support the family. It wasn't uncommon for me to sit down with dad and watch TV while he was home.

Although, the stations and programming were limited in the 1970's. We usually would watch cowboy movies like the *"High Chaparral"* which was on NBC in the early 1970's. My favorite show was a police drama known as "The *Rookies"* starring Kate Jackson. Other than that, my entertainment was pretty much limited.

It just so happened that on Saturday, November 22nd, 1975, there was a major college football game being televised on one of our five channels. It was on ABC Sports, and it was a game involving two teams from the Midwest. The game started around 9 am in Tucson since the rest of the country was two or three hours ahead of Arizona time. The Arizona Wildcats were playing Utah that day, and won the game 38-14. Arizona was a good football team that year led by Theo Bell, and finished the regular season at 9-2.

We could have gone to the Arizona/Utah game at Arizona Stadium, but watched another one on TV instead that day. That game, or mostly commonly known as "The Game," would be the Ohio State Buckeyes vs. the Michigan Wolverines.

I remember the game just like it was yesterday.

My dad was watching this match as he was always a big football fan. Like most kids growing up, you naturally are interested in a team or school who your dad roots for or seems excited about. I had no idea that he cheered for anybody other than the Arizona Wildcats.

As dad was watching the game, I sat down with him intrigued as to why he was cheering for one team over the other, and why the game didn't include Arizona? I asked him who he was cheering for. He looked over at me without much hesitation and said, *"The team in the white uniforms, gray pants, and silver helmets."*

To say that I knew much about either team, I would be lying to you. Like I stated before, we lived in Arizona, dad tutored the famous Theo Bell, and was supporting our family all based on the University of Arizona. I do know that Ohio State's uniforms caught my eye as well as their football coach, Woody Hayes. I kept thinking who is this crazy coach running up and down the football field yelling at all the players?

It was very amusing.

Almost like watching a cartoon character. Dad seemed to take the game much more seriously than I did. As I sat down with him, Ohio State was getting beat by Michigan by the score of 14-7. At the time, I didn't know anything about Ohio State other than their uniforms and the shiny silver helmets the team wore in the game.

In fact, I didn't know the school existed until I saw dad watching them play football on television that day.

"What is a Buckeye?" I asked.

Dad told me it was a poisonous nut.

Ok... I thought.

We are cheering for a team that has a nickname of a poisonous nut.

Sounds great!

My dad liked the Buckeyes because he was given an Ohio State t-shirt by his high school football coach at Horace Mann High School in 1961. The number on the shirt was #42, which was the number worn by the famous Paul Warfield on the 1961 squad. Dad proceeded to tell me that he liked Ohio State because of Howard 'Hopalong' Cassady, Jim Parker, and Dave Leggett—all members of the 1954 Ohio State National Championship football team who went 10-0, and beat USC in the Rose Bowl.

I looked at him like any other eight-year-old would look at their dad. I just nodded at him as If I knew the names of these players by heart. Not willing to admit that I had no idea what he was talking about nor did I really care at the time. All I cared about was the Ohio State uniforms looked much better than the ones Michigan were wearing that day.

"The Game" as it has been called, looked bleak for Ohio State. Michigan was up 14-7 late in the 4th quarter on this fateful day in November '75.

There are a lot of rivalries in college and pro sports. Oklahoma vs. Texas, Green Bay Packers vs. Chicago Bears, New York Yankees vs. Boston Red Sox, Celtics vs. Lakers, etc...

There is no rivalry like the "The Game" between Ohio State and Michigan. I got my first taste of this rivalry, especially in the 4th quarter of the 1975 version of this famous college game. I was no longer sitting in my chair next to my dad. I was up cheering loudly for the scarlet and gray of Ohio State! Somehow, I knew that I would be very upset if they lost this game.

Why? I asked myself.

I only knew of this team for about a half an hour or so. Why would I even care who won the game? Maybe it was the fact that my dad was cheering for them too.

For whatever reason, I started shouting and jumping up and down with every successful run or pass by the Ohio State Buckeyes. Although, the Buckeyes didn't do much passing back then in the 1970's. Coach Woody Hayes believed that three things could happen to a pass, and two of them were bad: incomplete and interception.

Anyways, the game had about 7 minutes to go, and the Buckeyes could not move the football. It really looked like the first game, and the start of my fandom with Ohio State, would end in defeat. The very same Ohio State team that didn't pass a lot during the game, completed three consecutive throws down the field.

My dad and I were cheering as if we were actually at the stadium that day in Ann Arbor, Michigan. Ohio State had fourth down on the one-yard line.

My dad said, *"This is it! If Ohio State doesn't score a touchdown here, the game is over, and Michigan will win."*

It was as if the world would come to an end that day if the Buckeyes couldn't score the game-winning touchdown. I could feel the intensity by just watching the game on television. I couldn't stand to watch but then again, how could I turn away from our small TV set?

Quarterback Cornelius Greene handed the ball off to fullback Pete Johnson.........

Touchdown!! Ohio State!!!

I never felt so excited in my life! Even more so than listening to the Oakland A's or California Angels on the radio. With the extra point, the score was now 14-14 and only three minutes to go. Understand that college games in the 1970's could end in a tie because there were no overtimes back then.

My dad said that the chances of Ohio State getting the ball back were slim to none. We would have to hold Michigan, and make sure they didn't score in the last three minutes.

He and I started calling Ohio State 'We'.

It was like we were part of the university or team. Did he forget that he actually was a student of the University of Arizona and not Ohio State?

The unthinkable happened.

Michigan's freshman quarterback, Rick Leach, threw an interception to an Ohio State player named Ray Griffin, who took the football inside the five-yard line.

Some moments in life, you always remember where you were at and what you were doing at the time.

I will always look back at the memory of hugging my dad and high-fiving him after the Buckeyes intercepted the football. This started a life-long tradition with my dad. Even though my dad may not be in the same house or in the stadium with me when Ohio State scores, I always call him after every Buckeye touchdown. I realize now how important it is, and it is a bond that my dad and I have even to this day. Through the good times and the bad times, we have always let Ohio State football take us away from the stresses of life.

My dad is 77 years old now, and I realize more than ever, how important it is to reach out to him after Ohio State scores, especially in the Michigan game. I don't want to get sentimental in this part of the book, but I also realize that there will be a point in my life that I will no longer be able to call my dad after Ohio State scores or wins. To this day, the 1975 game against Michigan remains one of my most important memories with my dad.

With the memory etched in my head, Ray Griffin intercepted the Michigan pass, and another Ohio State legend, Pete Johnson took the ball in and scored. The score was now Ohio State 21 and Michigan 14. On the next possession, the Wolverines' Rick Leach threw the deciding interception to Ohio State's Craig Cassady.

Game. Set. Match...Ohio State!

I was hooked after that point. This would be my team. This would be my school. My dad told me that the next time Ohio State would play was going to be in the Rose Bowl on January 1st, 1976. I couldn't wait to see the game. Where was I going to watch it?

My family was going to travel back from Arizona to Northwest Indiana to visit my dad's parents who were my grandparents, Nick and Ivaloo.

I would be watching my first Rose Bowl game during Christmas Break. A new tradition would be starting. I would watch games with my dad and grandfather.

Little did I know, a life-changing tragedy would be right around the corner.

Chapter 2

Overcoming Adversity as a Fan and in Life

By early 1976, we could no longer afford living in our Tucson, Arizona home. Dad had received his Public Administration degree in Business but really wanted to go back to school to become a teacher. We moved to an apartment complex on the other side of Tucson, Arizona known as *Langley Gardens*. It was a small apartment but we really didn't care much. I continued to go to Shoemaker Elementary School even though the move meant that I should have gone to a different school.

By Christmas time prior to our move in 1976, we were off to my grandparent's house in Northwest, Indiana. It would be a place we would call home eventually and still call home today. My friends and family often joked with me that I am a *"Hoosier."*

That is the nickname for people who live in Indiana.

That nickname never caught on with me as I always referred to myself as an Ohio State Buckeye!

We didn't fly out for Christmas in 1975. We actually would drive for three days from our place in Tucson, Arizona to my grandparents' apartment in Griffith, Indiana. Flying on an airplane would have been much faster and easier.

My dad never liked flying on airplanes as he had a bad experience earlier in his life. He prayed to the heavens above that if he landed in one piece, he would never get on an airplane again. Well...he didn't, and everywhere we traveled with my dad, he would drive there. I guess that was good because we got to visit interesting places in the many states on our way to Northwest Indiana.

Going to my grandparents meant that we would spend two weeks with them. My grandparents were known as Nick and Ivaloo Bunda. We didn't call them by their names nor did we call them grandpa and grandma. We simply called them "Papa" and "Grammy."

Nikki, Erin, and I were their only grandchildren since my dad was an only child. Needless to say, we were 'spoiled rotten' by Grammy and Papa. To know them... was to love them.

Growing up, they were very instrumental in my life, and very rarely missed anything that I was involved in with school events or in sports. My grandfather Nick (Papa), was a "Depression Era" kid of the 1920's. He never had much growing up, and came from a very bad home life. Papa would always tell me the story of one of the best Christmas holidays that he had as a child in the late 1920's. He said that he got a red wagon and a bowl of fruit.

Can you imagine being excited to see a red wagon and a bowl of fruit on Christmas Day?

My Papa always had an underlying message to his stories. In other words, it is not what you get for Christmas but to be appreciative that you were receiving something. I really believe that is why he and Grammy provided us with a lot of attention. My Papa wanted me to have things that he didn't get to have as a child growing up in the 1920's.

That Christmas in 1975, Nikki, Erin, and I received a lot of gifts from our grandparents. It would be this Christmas that I would receive one of my first Ohio State jerseys. It was a red (scarlet) mesh jersey with gray stripes on the sleeves with the #77. I would probably wear that a thousand times before mom would wash it. I would learn that my Papa was actually born in Niles, Ohio. Grammy was originally from Lecompton, Kansas.

Lecompton was known as the "Birthplace of the U.S. Civil War."

Being a Buckeye fan due to the great win over the hated Michigan Wolverines in 1975, I was more impressed with the fact that Papa was born in Ohio. Christmas with my grandparents was very special. It would also mean that I would get to watch the famous Rose Bowl with my dad as well as my Papa on January 1st, 1976.

Ohio State would be playing the UCLA Bruins. I remember watching the Rose Bowl Parade with my family and the excitement of the game which was scheduled to be on NBC at 4 pm *Central Standard Time*. Ohio State was ranked #1 at the time, and UCLA was ranked #11.

Archie Griffin had already won his second Heisman Trophy that year with Ohio State as the best player in college football.

Ohio State would come out in their scarlet jerseys while UCLA was wearing their powder blue tops. I could feel the excitement of the game.

The Buckeyes crossed the 50-yard line at the beginning of the game. There was a huge Rose Bowl emblem flower right in the middle of the field. The Rose Bowl stadium was simply beautiful!

No way was Ohio State going to lose this today.

After all, the Buckeyes had players like Archie Griffin, Pete Johnson, Cornelius Greene, and Brian Baschnagel. Not that I really knew much about them. Ohio State also had Woody Hayes as their coach. There he was on the sideline of the Rose Bowl with his red jacket and black hat with the red "Block O" on the front.

To me, he was like a god. I was so mesmerized by Coach Hayes.

Ohio State would score on their first possession with a 43-yard field goal by another one of my Ohio State heroes...Tom Klaban. Tom was a Czechoslovakia immigrant, who became a Buckeye legend the previous year in 1974 by kicking four field goals to beat Michigan 12-10. Tom's kick in the 1976 Rose Bowl would be all the scoring in the first half as Ohio State would lead 3-0. The game would turn for the worse in the second half.

It would be that disastrous third quarter when the UCLA Bruins would score sixteen straight points to take a 16-3 lead into the 4th quarter. My dad and Papa reassured me that there was one more quarter to play, and the Buckeyes were the better team. Ohio State would close the gap to 16-10 with a touchdown by Pete Johnson.

My team would now win the Rose Bowl, I thought!

Craig Cassady, who intercepted a football against Michigan, had done it again. All they had to do was score one more touchdown. The experience and memory would last forever. I would be able to experience an Ohio State National Championship with my father and my grandfather.

In life, things can change instantly in a blink of an eye.

The smiles on our faces would soon disappear as Ohio State quarterback Cornelius Greene would throw an interception a few minutes later.

There are some things in your life that you will never forget…your very first day of school, your first kiss, when you got a driver's license, and when you got married. All those are things that I definitely remember growing up, and I will tell you each and every one throughout the book.

Then, there are memories that are not so great.

By the end of the 1976 Rose Bowl, the sun had faded behind the California mountains as well as Ohio State's hopes of winning. As UCLA started to march down the field again, I started to cry! My team was going to lose the Rose Bowl.

Woody Hayes always used to say that three things can happen with a pass, and two of them are bad. Guess what?!

Ohio State threw another interception with just over four minutes to go in the game. Heartbreak? Yes, you could say that. Even though the game wasn't over yet, my eyes filled with more tears as I sat on my dad's lap. When Wendell Tyler for UCLA scored the decisive touchdown, it was all but over. The game would end with UCLA beating Ohio State 23-10. I was never so dejected in my life. I could see the sorrow in Papa's eyes as well. Even though he was born in Ohio, he really didn't start liking the Buckeyes until I did. He may have been mad that they lost, but he was really upset that I felt bad about the game.

After it had ended, Papa got up, shook his head, and walked away. My dad said nothing as he was in disbelief that Ohio State had just lost the Rose Bowl to a team they had beaten earlier in the year. It would be the start of peaks and valleys of being an Ohio State football fan.

I would leave a day later from my grandparent's house to make the three-day trek back to Tucson, Arizona after I witnessed Ohio State losing the 1976 Rose Bowl. Little did I know or anyone else in my family, that a greater tragedy, than Ohio State losing a football game, would be right around the corner.

Life is so precious, and can be taken away from you at any moment.

Sometimes we forget how important life is, and that sports, including football, are just games which entertain us. I hope this part of the book serves as a reminder to everyone that life has obstacles and setbacks but how you overcome them is what matters. This life-altering event would prove to be just that in my life, too.

As we returned to Tucson, Arizona in January of 1976, I was going to finish my second grade year at Shoemaker Elementary. My dad had to take me to school every day because of the family's move to *Langley Gardens* Apartments. I loved living in *Langley Gardens* Apartments at that time. I met a lot of great friends there but I also seemed to get in some trouble. Nothing major, but just kids being kids.

There was this one time, I had stuck a banana in the tailpipe of a car which belonged to one of my friend's parents. Well, every kid said it was me, and before you knew it...I had about twenty boys running after me trying to beat me up! They never did catch me or have the speed and endurance to do so. My running quickness would prove beneficial when I got into high school.

It was also at *Langley Gardens,* that I imagined myself as Archie Griffin or Cornelius Greene dashing through the Michigan defense on my way to a touchdown. I would get in my mesh red Ohio State t-shirt jersey that I got for Christmas that year and gray pants. I actually cut one of my gray dress pants off at the knees so it looked like football pants. I took a red, white, and black marker to make the Ohio State strip down the side of the pants.

My mom didn't care much. She always said that I had a 'vivid imagination.' I would go outside by myself and run with a football, weaving and juking, as well as pretending to be tackled. I would say, *"Touchdown, Denny Bunda for Ohio State!!"*

I would get up as if the crowd was cheering for me scoring against the Michigan Wolverines! The only problem was that there was no crowd. Just a few of my friends, girls, and neighbors laughing at me as if to think…

Who plays football by themselves?? Is this kid crazy?

I would do that for hours even taking my mom's baking flour to make football yard lines outside the apartment building. This girl named Heidi would tell all the kids that I played football by myself, and fall down on the ground acting like I was being tackled. All of them would just laugh at me, especially if I told them one day I was going to play for Ohio State.

"Isn't that the team that lost to UCLA in the Rose Bowl?" one of them would say.

The teasing about Ohio State would make me angry.

At the time, all the kids my age were playing little league baseball or involved in some kind of sport. For whatever reason, mom and dad would not allow me to play organized sports until I was in the third grade back in Northwest, Indiana.

This may have been a blessing in disguise.

For what I am about to tell you, is still a reminder of how precious life is, and not to take anything or anyone for granted. The purpose of what I am going to disclose is not to say that my tragedy is any greater or more difficult to overcome than what other people have had to go through in life. It is simply my own tragedy and triumph through a major crisis. One that still haunts me to this day but serves as a reminder of overcoming adversity.

I hadn't seen my grandparents since January during the Rose Bowl loss to UCLA. You can understand my joy when I heard that they were coming in May of 1976 for a family vacation to Disneyland in Anaheim, California. Going on vacation with Grammy and Papa was always a special time. It is not like we didn't see the other set of grandparents, who happened to be my mom's parents.

It was just that we spent a lot more time with my dad's parents. We were very close to Grammy and Papa, and always seemed to do a lot of family events with them.

This would be a vacation that would have a tragic ending, and shape who I am today.

The vacation started off well. The entire family went to Disneyland Amusement Park. My sisters, Nikki and Erin, were too small to ride the roller-coasters at the park, but that did not stop Grammy.

She always made sure that we had fun. If I wanted to ride a roller-coaster, Grammy would be the first one to say that she would ride it with me. It was a sunny day at Disneyland, and the whole family had a great day of fun. I really didn't want to leave the amusement park.

As I said earlier in the book, sometimes fate plays a role in life.

We went back to the hotel, which at the time, was called the *"Sheraton Half Moon Hotel"* in San Diego, California.

We were scheduled to go to SeaWorld in San Diego later that afternoon. I really didn't want to go as we had just got done with a busy day at Disneyland, and I was very tired. For whatever reason, I convinced my family not to go on that particular day. How I wish I would not have been so stubborn. We should have gone to SeaWorld.

My Papa and dad left the hotel, and went out to get some lunch during the afternoon. My sister Nikki and I were sitting in the kitchen area of our room of the *Sheraton Half Moon Hotel*. We were eating our snacks with our younger sister, Erin. I think we were drinking Dr. Pepper sodas and having potato chips.

Grammy had gone outside to sit on the porch of the hotel. My grandparents smoked cigarettes, so, she was outside relaxing and enjoying a cigarette in the California sun. In a second, my life changed in the blink of an eye.

Nikki was always a fast runner growing up as a child. In later years, she would race some of my best friends in the front yard, and beat them every single time.

In the hotel room, I am glad this is one race Nikki didn't win. As I sat at the table drinking my soda, and enjoying the company of my two sisters, I told Nikki that I would race her to see who would get to Grammy first. Both of us started to get up, and head for the outdoor porch of the hotel where Grammy was sitting. I ran as fast as I could not realizing that the sliding glass door was closed, and Grammy was on the other side of it.

As I approached the door, I knew that I was going to go right through the glass. I covered my face with my hand as glass shattered everywhere. The sound of the breaking glass was just awful. As I laid there in a pool of blood, I looked down and saw that I was hurt really bad. My right hand was cut down to the bone, and my face was dripping with blood. The Mickey Mouse t-shirt that I was wearing went from the color white to completely blood-stained red. The shattering of glass startled Grammy so much that she looked 'white as a ghost.' My mom was the first one at my side while I was lying there bleeding to death.

Since 1976, people have always asked me if it was painful to go through a sliding glass door. Well, what do you think? If I am going to be totally honest, I was in what they call a 'state of shock.' I knew that I was bleeding pretty badly and I was very weak from the loss of blood.

My mom lifted me up, and took me in the bathroom to wrap me up in towels. She was very calm in the moment of adversity.

My sisters screamed, and Grammy yelled, *"Oh my God!! Feller is Hurt! Somebody Pleeease help him!!"* Grammy had always called me "Feller" ever since I was a little kid.

When my dad and Papa arrived back at the hotel, I could hear Grammy telling them what happened, and saying, *"My Feller is hurt really bad. Oh my God, he is hurt! Please help!"*

My head, my hand, and parts of my leg were bleeding really bad at this point. Two paramedics, who happened to be at the hotel, were called to assist. I remember asking them if I was going to die? They said nothing. As they were attending to me, the paramedics knew that time was going to be of the essence. Instead of waiting for an ambulance to arrive at the *Sheraton Half Moon Hotel,* they placed me in the back seat of a police car to go to the hospital.

Most of the next twenty-four hours, I do not remember much. The hospital where I was taken to flew in a plastic surgeon on a helicopter to perform extensive plastic surgery on my hand, foot, and face. Mom would later tell me that, *"He was a real handsome young man,"* who operated on me. The surgeon happened to be playing golf that day in Los Angeles, and they landed a helicopter on the course to bring him to San Diego for my surgery. I do remember waking up halfway through the procedure, and the nurses sticking a big needle through my arm to put me back to sleep again with anesthesia.

When I woke up in the recovery room, I noticed that they were bringing in another patient right next to me. This patient was a sixteen-year-old girl who was involved in a skiing accident earlier in the day. The girl had hit a landing peer, and severed her leg pretty badly. I never saw her again, so, I often wonder if she recovered physically and emotionally from her injuries.

I, on the other hand, was going to go through some extensive rehabilitation, especially to my right hand. I was lucky to be alive. I just didn't know it at the time. I had survived a major accident at such a young age. I didn't realize how this adversity would play an important role in my life.

When I got back home to Tucson shortly after the accident, I would have to go see a hand specialist. My head, hand, and foot were still wrapped in bandages after the surgery. My dad may not remember this...but I sure do! I was sitting in the waiting room after one of my appointments at the rehabilitation center.

I could hear the hand specialist say to my father that Denny may not have full mobility of his hand. He may not be able to throw a baseball or football like the other kids. Writing may be a tough task as well. People always called me Denny for short, even though my name is Dennis. I always wanted to ask my dad if the office door was open on purpose. I could hear what was being said by the doctor. I just remember having tears run down my face.

Doctor Madden or as he called himself, *"The Mad Madden,"* said that he was going to do everything he could to make sure that I was going to be able to use my hand again. There were no guarantees.

I was thinking that I would not be able to play organized sports like a lot of my friends, let alone play quarterback some day for the Ohio State Buckeyes. I always had this dream that I would play for them since that Michigan game in 1975. This may seem like a true testament to the human spirit, but I was not going to let anything stand in my way of playing sports or using my hand to write or draw.

Doctor Madden worked with me extensively throughout the summer of 1976. The *"Mad Madden"* would always ask me to bend my fingers a little farther than I did before. I cut all of my tendons in my hand due to the accident. He'd say, *"You can do it, and don't give up on yourself!! Don't feel sorry for yourself!"*

In life, you always need people to give you the confidence to get through obstacles and adversities. I don't know what ever happened to Dr. Madden, but I would simply say...Thank you! It was at the rehabilitation center that I understood the term of 'not giving up.'

While I was in rehabilitation for my hand, I saw this patient in a wheelchair. I asked him what happened? He told me that he got into a bar fight on a Friday night. Of course, at age eight, I had no idea what a bar fight was. I told him that I hoped that he had won the fight. By the looks of it, I would say that he lost. He was there for rehabilitation because he had broken his neck. I guess I started looking at things a little bit differently.

A person is going to go through major adversities in their lifetime. There have been a lot of peaks and valleys in my own personal life. I will address a lot more of them in the book.

I always look back to my almost fatal accident in May of 1976 as a watershed moment. If I go through troubling times, I always tell myself that I will pull through it. After all, I went through a sliding glass door and lived to talk about it. The obstacles that lied ahead would prove to be just as challenging as my accident.

Life was about to get a little more interesting.

Chapter 3
Moving Back to Indiana

By the summer of 1976, I had gone through my first real major setback in my life with a near death experience. Dad had finished his second college degree in education but was unable to find a teaching job in Arizona.

With no money or a career, and three kids and a wife to support, he decided to move us back to Northwest Indiana by July of 1976. This would mean that I would be starting the third grade at my third school since kindergarten. My sister Nikki would be starting her education in 1976, and Erin would still be at home with mom.

We would move to the town of Griffith where my grandparents lived in Northwest Indiana. I would get to see Grammy and Papa a whole lot more than I did living in Tucson. With the move back to Indiana, they would become very instrumental in my life. I want you to understand that my mom's parents were part of my life, too.

Actually, my mom's mother, her name was Dorothy Fehring, paid for a lot of things that I needed throughout my childhood. Looking back now, I just wish that I would have said, "thank you" to her. I never did, however. There are moments that you never get back. I wish I could have gone back in time, and told my "other" grandmother (Dorothy) how much that I appreciated her and how much I loved her.

The move to Griffith, Indiana meant a lot of changes for the family. We would live in a ranch house on Pine Street not far from

Griffith High School. It was a very small house with three bedrooms. Nikki and I would now be going to a new school known as Beiriger Elementary down the road from our house. Mom would walk us just past the local high school, and Nikki and I would walk the rest of the way to our elementary school. We were starting all over again, with no friends, a new school, and a lot of uncertainty.

Dad was doing some substitute teaching to gain experience so he could land a job as a permanent schoolteacher. That meant that he wouldn't have a steady paycheck for a while. There were no guarantees for him to land a teaching job in Indiana either. He would not give up on another dream of becoming a full-time teacher someday. I always admired him. Dad always seemed to overcome his own struggles. He has taught me a lot about overcoming obstacles in life.

The fall of 1976, I would be in Mrs. Henrie's 3rd grade class at Beiriger. It also meant the start of the 1976 Ohio State football season. Most of my classmates in school were fans of the Indiana Hoosiers, Purdue Boilermakers, and the Notre Dame Fighting Irish.

In other words, I pretty much stood alone as an Ohio State Buckeye fan living in Northwest Indiana. When the Buckeyes lost, no matter who they were playing, or what the score was, I heard it from fellow students and teachers alike.

Just like in 1975, college football teams were only on television 3-4 times a season, usually on ABC or NBC. It wasn't like modern day, where Ohio State is on every single Saturday plus replays on the Big Ten Network or on ESPN. Back in the 1970's, we didn't tape games on a VCR or on a television's DVR. *You had to make sure that you were home watching it live in front of your television.*

Fortunately for me, dad always reminded me when Ohio State was on a TV station. It never entered my mind that someday my dad would take me to an Ohio State game. Maybe it was because we didn't have a lot of money or my dad and mom didn't realize that eventually I would cheer for one team and only one team.

Sure, I liked other teams, especially major league baseball. I was also a fan of the NFL pro team, the Dallas Cowboys. Watching Ohio

State play on television was different. I never wanted to miss one second that they were playing in a game.

Ohio State would have a 9-2-1 record during our first year back living in the Midwest. I watched all four televised games on TV, including a heart-breaking loss to Michigan by the score of 22-0. The Buckeyes no longer had football stars Archie Griffin nor Cornelius Greene on the team. Both of them had graduated from college. They were now replaced by Rod Gerald at quarterback and Jeff Logan at tailback.

I remember the 1976 Michigan game like it was yesterday. Ohio State was tied with the Wolverines at halftime, and then Michigan scored 22 points in the second half. It was then that I knew that I would hate the Wolverines! The year before, Ohio State had beaten Michigan 21-14, so the hatred was not there.

A fan usually builds up a dislike for another school or team when they beat your own school or team. Even to this day, if Michigan beats the Buckeyes in football, it is not a very good year.

Michigan became the villain, and I didn't want anything to do with that school or anyone who was a fan of them. I didn't know at the time that I would someday come face-to-face with someone who liked them.

My dad would always try to calm me down after an Ohio State loss which is something he still tries to do to this day.

He would say, *"The players don't even take it as seriously as you do."* Dad would also comment, *"That is part of being a fan, you take the good moments with the bad. Ohio State isn't going to win all the time."*

Well, when you are a 9-year-old boy, there are no words that would make you feel any better when your favorite team loses a game, especially one to Michigan. Maybe I was upset that they lost but also because I knew what was coming my way following the game at school on Monday.

It would be at Beiriger Elementary School where my fellow students started teasing me about Ohio State. A lot of the kids didn't really care because most of them followed the Indiana University Hoosiers basketball team and Coach Bobby Knight. There was another side to it as well. Most kids growing up in the 1970's would actually follow the local high school team more so than a college football team. If my friends were watching football on television, it was usually a professional NFL team.

The Chicago Bears were not very good in the 1970's, so most of them at my elementary school followed the Denver Broncos, Dallas Cowboys, or the Minnesota Vikings.

If there is one thing that I have learned in life, it is that a lot of people like following winning teams.

In the mid-1970's, every school-boy kid in Griffith, Indiana was following the local high school team, the *Griffith Panthers*. Since we lived down the street from the high school, my dad would take me to a lot of the Panther 'home games' on Friday nights. I was like every other kid in town by 1977.

We all had the same hero, the local Griffith star, Craig Buzea. Craig was a player on the GHS football team and was idolized by everyone in Griffith. I would walk home from school every day, and watch football practice from the fence. I wanted to see the famous Craig Buzea.

To me, Craig was the high school version of the Ohio State tailback, Jeff Logan. Both Craig and Jeff were not the biggest players in the world, but they were exciting to watch. As I stood by the fence at their practices or watching their games, it was my dream to one day play for the Griffith Panthers High School football team. I thought that if I could be like Craig Buzea, then someday I would have a chance to go to college, and play for the Buckeyes.

At Beiriger Elementary, I would go out at recess time, and pretend that I was either Craig or Jeff playing football with all my friends. At the time, some of my friends were involved in a youth league Pop Warner football program. I don't think that I ever asked my parents to put me in a football league. I was on the small side and not very tall either.

As I watched all those Griffith High School practices from the fence, I also wondered what it was like to be tackled by another player.

I knew that I was fast because I could out-run every kid on the playground. I had to run for my life a year earlier from the kids at *Langley Gardens* who blamed me for putting a banana in the tailpipe of a car.

If they caught me, they were going to beat me up. Like I said earlier, I knew they weren't going to catch me though.

As Griffith would wrap up practice, the players would run right past the fence on their way to the school's locker room. One of the players patted me on the head as he ran by me.

He said, *"Someday you can play football at Griffith just like us."*

Exciting!! I sprinted all the way home to tell mom that I watched Griffith football practice. *"Wow, that is neat,"* mom would say.

I am not sure mom cared. She was just happy that I was excited about something, and I was starting to get over my emotional and physical distress due to the accident in May.

During that year, Ohio State wrapped up the 1976 season with a victory over the Colorado Buffaloes in the 1977 Orange Bowl. The Buckeyes would win by the score of 27-10. The Orange Bowl would become my second favorite bowl to the Rose Bowl. There being a big *"Orange"* painted in the middle of the field with a crown on its head. I thought that was pretty cool. I thought it was even cooler that Ohio State won the game.

It became apparent that beating Michigan would always be the benchmark to a great season. My gym teacher in elementary school telling me that the game with Michigan was the only thing that mattered to Ohio State. I am not sure if he was from Ohio or Michigan but he knew about the rivalry between the two schools.

In that 1977 Orange Bowl, Colorado took a 10-0 lead over the Buckeyes, stomping off to my room and slamming the door. I sat there in my room playing with my model train that my dad set up for me. It was actually his model train set that he had as a kid, but we put it in my bedroom.

I was not going to sit in the living room watching my team lose again. It was enough seeing them get beat by Michigan earlier in

November. My dad would come in and get me, saying his famous words whenever Ohio State was winning or in this case...losing.

He said, *"Relax, it's early in the game!"*

I came out of my room to see my hero Jeff Logan rip through the Colorado line for a touchdown. It seemed that every time Jeff carried the football, he would break through the line for a big run against Colorado. Ohio State quarterback Rod Gerald would score the final touchdown of the night and the Buckeyes would win. This would be the last time Ohio State won the Orange Bowl since writing this book.

After the Orange Bowl win, I started playing organized sports by the spring of 1977 for the first time. I would be participating in Griffith Little League Baseball. I had never been on a team before that year so this was a big deal for me to play organized youth sports. Most of my time playing sports was going out on the school playground with my friends, or just going outside playing football by myself.

I would throw the football to myself and catch it, pretending to be a star player for the Ohio State Buckeyes or the Griffith Panthers. The kids in Griffith thought I was weird just like my friends back in Arizona. They didn't realize that I had a vivid imagination and a dream of being a football star at Griffith and later at Ohio State.

Keep in mind that back in 1977, a lot of my friends had already played a few years of organized sports. I didn't know what it was like playing for a team or to have a 'real' coach. I didn't possess the skills of my classmates. They had the experience of playing sports for a few years before I even started. This was a brand new experience for me.

I played for a little league team named the "Crows." The Crows were sponsored by a company known as the *American Chemical Service* in Griffith. I was so excited to be playing on a team and wearing a uniform. I must have worn my little league hat everywhere that I went and even to bed at night.

After my accident at the *Half Moon Hotel* in 1976, I don't think there were too many people that thought I would be playing on a little league baseball team. No one said anything to me about not being able to play. My hand had healed to the point that I could now throw a baseball. That didn't stop the teasing from kids at my new school in Griffith about the scars that the accident had left behind.

The kids would yell: *"Scarface"! "Freak"! "Railroad face"!*

This would happen at school or on the playground. I didn't think it would affect me that much until the whole girl scene entered the picture. When you hear other kids making fun of you, and calling you names, it really cuts to the emotional core. The kids at Beiriger Elementary would ask me what happened to my face and right hand. If I told them the truth about going through a sliding glass door, they would simply laugh and call me stupid.

"Who would run through a sliding glass door?" they would say.

Sports became my escape from the teasing and sometimes the reality of life. I was good at sports, too. That is not to say that I am bragging about my abilities but just to say that I used it as motivation to overcome adversity in my life.

In the 1977 little league season, I played for Coach Adams. He was my first real coach and I will always remember him for that as well as the lessons he taught me in my initial season. His son, Brian, was a friend of mine, and in the same third grade class. I never thought that I would be a starting player in the 1977 little league season but that is exactly what happened. I played 2nd base, and really never came out of the game.

Well...there was this one time…

We were playing a game that would be decided in the final inning. I was running really fast around the bases to home plate for the winning run, slid to beat the tag by the catcher, and I was called out! I immediately hit the catcher in the chest protector with my closed fist, and was thrown out of the game for punching him. I am so glad that my dad was not there to see what I had just done.

Coach Adams screamed at me, up one side and down the other, and rightfully so! I didn't like being yelled at, as I thought I was safe. Coach Adams wasn't mad at me for being called out at home plate. He was upset with me for punching the catcher with my fist.

I learned a hard lesson that day about sportsmanship. It wouldn't be the last time either. I would get another dose of reality in my high school years.

Needless to say, I didn't play in the next game. I had a nice seat on the bench right next to Coach Adams. I didn't understand then...but I do now.

He taught me that things may not always go your way but it is how you react to certain situations that will make you a better player as well as person. If I ran into Coach Adams today, I would say thank you for the guidance and teaching me that not everything is going to go well in life and in sports.

You have to always keep working hard to fulfill your dreams.

In the fall of 1977, my parents still didn't let me play organized football. I really wanted to play like all my friends did at Beiriger. There were other reasons that I wanted to play football. The girls always liked the boys in school who played organized sports, especially football. The sport of football was very popular in the town of Griffith.

Many of the girls at my school were cheerleaders at the youth league football games. Even in the 4th grade, there were cliques starting to form between the students.

You either were popular or you were not popular. It was just that simple.

A lot of it was based on if you were good-looking or if you played sports, like football or baseball. I kind of fit into the middle group. I wasn't popular but I also wasn't on the lower end either.

Girls didn't really pay attention to me that much, mainly because I was new to the school. I also wasn't a very good student. I struggled with paying attention and doing my schoolwork. On one of my report cards, my third grade teacher Mrs. Henrie commented, *"Denny is becoming too careless. I would like to see the reading come back up. The poor social studies and science grades are from not listening."*

Yikes!

Not exactly what my parents wanted to hear about their son's school performance. It didn't help matters much since my dad was a schoolteacher. He never did say but it may have been embarrassing for a teacher's son to get poor grades. I just don't think I cared how I did in school. Daydreaming about someday playing football for my favorite team and impressing all the girls at my school was really all that mattered. There were many times that Mrs. Henrie would call on me for an answer to a question, but I was too busy daydreaming about football and girls. She would just shake her head at me.

By this time, my dad had received his first permanent teaching job at Grissom Elementary School in Gary, Indiana. It would mean that he would have a steady income, and we could afford to have more things in life. He would eventually start coaching football at Calumet High School to go along with his teaching job.

Even though my dad loved football and was now coaching the sport, he thought I was too small and not mature enough to play in an organized league at the time. A lot of my heroics were still on the playground at Beiriger or in our backyard on Pine Street. I still pretended that I was Craig Buzea of Griffith High School or Jeff Logan for the Buckeyes.

In 1977, it would mark the third year that I was a fan of Ohio State football. At that point, I still didn't go to any games. They weren't on TV much in 1977, but the one time they were on ABC sports in September, I couldn't watch the game.

We had to go see my Uncle Ross at a Glenbard North High School football game in Illinois. My Uncle Ross didn't coach the team but we were on the high school sidelines with him that Saturday, September 24th, 1977. He was part of what was called the "chain gang" that spotted the football, and if the team had a first down or not. It's funny that I remember that.

Uncle Ross wasn't really my uncle either. He is actually my dad's cousin. We always referred to him as *Uncle Ross*. I remember that specifically because Ohio State was supposed to play Oklahoma that day.

The Buckeyes were ranked #4 in the country and the Oklahoma Sooners were ranked #3. Instead of being able to watch my Buckeye heroes on TV, I was stuck watching Glenbard North play Glenbard South in a high school football game. I had no idea what was going on with Ohio State that day. You couldn't stream the game live from a mobile device like you can nowadays. In fact, there were no cell phones back then, either. All we had was a car radio which aired the game.

After the high school game was over, dad and I hurried to the car to catch the last few minutes of the tilt between Ohio State and Oklahoma. I am not even sure who won the battle between the two Glenbard high schools nor did I care.

If you ever listen to a game on the radio, it is way more dramatic than watching it on TV.

Ohio State held a 28-20 lead in the fourth quarter of the game, and looked like they would pull off another exciting victory much like they did in Ann Arbor, Michigan when I first started liking Ohio State in 1975.

There is this old saying known as Murphy's Law... *"Anything that can go wrong will go wrong."*

Well, Ohio State quarterback Greg Castignola would fumble the football towards the end of the game running an option play to the right side. Oklahoma would now have the ball for a chance at a touchdown, and to possibly tie the game with the two point conversion. The Sooners drove down to the twelve-yard line. All Ohio State had to do was stop Oklahoma on one play, and the game would be over.

My dad and I sat in the car listening to the end of the game as we drove to my Uncle Ross' house. Again, listening to the radio broadcast was more nerve-racking because you couldn't see what was going on. You just had to visualize it in your mind.

As Oklahoma was going for it on fourth down, I could hear the roar of the crowd on the radio, and the announcer saying that Ohio State stopped Oklahoma short of the first down. I was going crazy in the car! Dad told me to settle down or he would crash. (He was driving as the final minutes of the game were going on) Ohio State was going to win a thrilling game much like they did in the 1975 Michigan game!

Wouldn't you know it... there was a penalty on the play, and Ohio State was called for off-sides. Oklahoma would get a second chance. Once again, Oklahoma would have 4th down inside the two yard line. All Ohio State had to do was stop them one more time! I was screaming at the radio, and saying... *'PLEASE don't jump offsides!'* as if the Ohio State players could hear me. On that 4th down play, Oklahoma would score the touchdown. The Sooners would then go for two points to tie the game but were stopped short.

Ohio State led 28-26 with about a minute to go in the game. The Sooners would try an on-side kick in hopes that Ohio State would fumble the ball. It couldn't happen, could it? It was during this game that I realized I would go through a lot of heartaches as a Buckeye fan.

You could say that it was just a game.

Most people would say that football is fun, and it's just entertainment. It became a way of life, to me. This was my team. This was my school. Scarlet and Gray were my colors. I hurt emotionally every time Ohio State lost a game. It would absolutely ruin my entire weekend. All my friends started associating me with Ohio State.

Years later, my classmate from high school named Katie, told me at a reunion that every time Ohio State was on TV, she would think of me. Through the years, I have had a lot of people tell me that. I was such an OSU football fanatic. It was as if nothing else really mattered in my life. Like I said, my classmates would laugh at me when Ohio State lost.

Going to school on Mondays was absolutely terrible. Most of the other kids would say, *"What happened to Ohio State?"* As if they didn't know. Most of them really didn't care but they knew that I did. The more my fandom grew with Ohio State, the more I got heckled by my classmates when they lost.

What happened next in the Oklahoma game was something that I would never forget. Oklahoma went for the on-side kick, and recovered the football. My dad once again tried to calm me down in this tight situation.

He just said, *"Relax! Ohio State just needs to stop them, and force them into a long field goal."*

Oklahoma had a great kicker that year named Ewe von Schamann. Ewe would come on to attempt a 41-yard field goal to try to win the game. I can still picture in my mind the announcer on the radio saying, *"The kick is up... (Long Pause) and the kick is good!!"*

I sat still in my dad's car dejected. There was only three seconds left, and Ohio State had very little chance to win. The Buckeyes had one play left but Ohio State's quarterback, Greg Castignola would be stopped. I sat in my seat stunned and paralyzed to a point I couldn't move.

It was as if my life was about ready to end.

Dad told me to get out of the car and go have fun with my cousins Brian and Brett who were Uncle Ross' kids. I must have sat in that car for a half an hour before I moved. My dad would say... *"There will be other Ohio State games."*

Obviously, there would be other games as exciting and thrilling as that one in 1977.

I often look at the program from that Ohio State/Oklahoma game and wonder back to the time we were listening on the radio. I had acquired that game program years later. The game may have had a dramatic ending and will be remembered as one of the best games ever in the famous Ohio Stadium that September of 1977.

I remember it for another reason. I got to share that moment of Ohio State football with my dad.

In 1977, I was in the 4th grade at Beiriger Elementary School. I had a great teacher that year in Mrs. Bell. The problem was that Mrs. Bell was a Purdue graduate and big time football fan. Purdue wasn't really a threat to Ohio State football at that point so when she said, *"Go Boilermakers!"* it didn't really bother me.

I would always threaten to change her pull down maps in the classroom to the state of Ohio. She would laugh but Mrs. Bell could never understand my love for Ohio or for the Buckeyes. She would tell me that I live in Indiana, and should cheer for an Indiana school like Purdue or IU. I could never do that.

Besides my grandfather being born there (Papa), I really didn't have any affiliation with the state of Ohio. There were many times that I was late coming back from lunch to Mrs. Bell's 4th grade class. I was too busy pretending that I was Jeff Logan or another Ohio State Buckeye great on the Beiriger playground weaving and dodging my childhood classmates.

She would just shake her head at me and say, *"Denny Bunda, what are we going to do with you? Quit day-dreaming!"*

I told her that I would someday play for Ohio State and beat her Purdue Boilermakers. She would just smile and shake her head at me. The kids in the class would all look back at me and smile. Although, it wasn't a confident smile. It was more of a smirk as if to think... 'Is this kid for real?'

Hey... a person can dream, can't they?

In late November of 1977, Ohio State would once again be on TV as they faced the Michigan Wolverines. It would be up in Ann Arbor as it was two years previously when the Buckeyes won. My mom had my lunch ready to go before the big game. Dad and I always ate on TV trays in front of the set when there was a big game on or a program we enjoyed watching together.

There was one problem though.

The Ohio State vs. Michigan football game was not on TV because of some foreign leader visiting Israel. I want to say it was Anwar Sadat who was the president of Egypt. I don't want to diminish who this person was or the impact of him visiting Israel in 1977. It just happened to coincide with the biggest football game of the year.

Being ten years old, I was not interested in world affairs or leaders visiting places around the globe. All I knew was that it was interrupting the Ohio State vs. Michigan game!

When the game finally came on, it was about midway through the first quarter. That afternoon, the Buckeyes would lose another tough game to the Michigan Wolverines by the score of 14-6. Ohio State actually outplayed them that day in a losing effort.

The Buckeyes had the ball in Michigan territory ready to score a touchdown towards the end of the game. Rod Gerald would run an option play to the right side, and fumble the ball away to Michigan. Coach Woody Hayes slammed down his headset in disgust. I did find that very amusing even though the game would end in defeat. He was as interesting to watch as the game itself. I wondered what it would be like to play for Coach Hayes. Maybe someday I would get that chance.

After reading the many articles and documents on Coach Hayes, he stated that the 1977 game was one that Ohio State should have won. Ohio State now had lost two years in a row to Michigan. I kept thinking to myself that as long as Rick Leach was the quarterback of the Wolverines, Ohio State would not beat them. Rick was an unbelievable player for Michigan, and he was difficult to stop in big games. There was another problem...we would have to face him again in the 1978 game.

On January 2nd, 1978, Ohio State was going to play the Alabama Crimson Tide in the Sugar Bowl at the Superdome in New Orleans, Louisiana. I knew that Alabama had a famous coach named Paul "Bear" Bryant. He was the equivalent of Woody Hayes of Ohio State. The Buckeyes were coming off that stinging loss to Michigan.

I had faith that the Buckeyes would come through and win the game. After all, Ohio State couldn't lose twice in a row, could they? The game was to air on television around 1 pm the day after New Year's Day. As luck would have it, I wouldn't be watching the game at home. My parents had a lot of friends and associates, even when we moved back to Northwest Indiana.

That particular day, we were going to my dad's friend, Louie Zatorski's house. Louie was a local pharmacist in a neighboring town of Munster. Dad always would take me to his store to get penicillin when I was sick, especially with a sore throat. I remember Louie always mixing in this orange flavor so the penicillin medicine would taste a little better. Those of you that grew up in the 1970's know what I am talking about with the taste of penicillin.

It was awful!

I wouldn't take the penicillin unless it was Louie who made it for me. He would also give me a hand full of those *Dum Dum suckers* to take home to make everything better. It wasn't until later in life that I realized that *Dum Dum suckers* originated in the state of Ohio. I now know why I liked them so much.

Louie also happened to be the Godfather to my sister, Erin. Anyways, it always seemed like we were going somewhere for New Year's Eve or New Year's Day. This particular year, Ohio State played on Monday, January 2nd.

Louie had this old Zenith TV that looked like a piece of furniture. We didn't have those big flat screen TV's that people have now-a-days. I remember sitting close to Louie's TV set so I would be able to watch the Buckeyes. Ohio State was wearing their 'white' jerseys that day along with their silver helmets and gray pants.

Louie wanted to change the station to another game but I wouldn't let him even though it was his television. I just had to watch Ohio State! The game turned out to be a blowout, and not in a good way. The Buckeyes lost to Alabama by the score of 35-6.

Ohio State's only touchdown in the Sugar Bowl game was a pass to wide receiver, #11 Jim Harrell. Rod Gerald, the OSU quarterback, would throw three interceptions in the game, and "my team" would once again lose.

As a young kid, I just couldn't handle defeat very well, either watching my team play or playing sports myself. When I played games with my dad, he never let me win at anything. He was trying to teach me how to be competitive and have a strong work ethic.

At the time, I couldn't see what he was trying to teach me in terms of winning and losing. I don't care if it was playing air hockey, shooting basketball, or a board game. It just seemed as if my dad would always win. You would have thought that he would at least let me win

45

once in a while. Nothing in life should come easy. You need to work for it.

I would stomp off out of a room, throw things, cry, tear up my room, etc. I was a very 'poor sport' as a kid and had a very bad temper. Dad's inner teachings taught me that if I hated to lose, I would have to work hard to achieve success.

Oh, I still hate to lose but I never give up.

Many times, people give up on their aspirations, goals, and dreams. I see little league kids quit today because they didn't get their way or someone on their team was better than them. For me...I just tried harder and used losing as motivation. Ohio State lost to Alabama in the 1978 Sugar Bowl.

So, what, right??

I remember saying to my dad at Louie Zatorski's house that day… *"I am done being an Ohio State fan!"*

My dad searching for his words simply said, *"If you can't accept the fact that Ohio State is going to lose sometimes, then you are not a real fan anyways."*

Boy… that really upset me. You know what? It is amazing what we remember as kids that we carry into our adult lives.

It wasn't the 35-6 thrashing that Alabama gave "my team" that day. It was what my dad said to me that hit to the core, and it wouldn't be the last time either. I don't know how many times that I told my dad that I hated Ohio State for losing, and that I would never watch them again.

That I was done being an Ohio State fan!

Dad would also say, *"When the Buckeyes win it all, you can't say that you were a real fan, if you don't take the good with the bad."*

I know deep down that he didn't like it when Ohio State lost either but he never showed his emotions. You learn a lot from sports and how it translates into "real" life situations. I just couldn't see it then as a ten year old kid.

In the Spring of 1978, I was once again playing little league baseball. This time, it was my dad who was the head coach of my little league team, the "Crows." Dad had me play shortstop that year, and he would always have me steal second base. No one believes me now or is willing to care, but I stole 72 bases in the 1978 little league season! I guess my dad realized how fast I was as well.

Under his direction, the "Crows" went 17-2 that summer of 1978. You would think that I would remember how great that season was playing for my dad, and all the friends I had on the team, right? Well… it would be the two losses that would stick out the most during that little league season. We went undefeated most of the year. However, we were set to play the "Gulls" after a rainy morning in June. That day, I asked my dad if we were going to play the game that afternoon against the Gulls?

I had begged him to let me pitch in the game. I had a way of always nagging my parents until they gave in to me on my demands. He told me that one of my friends, Mike Carlson, was going to be the pitcher that day. I was confident in my abilities to win the game as the starting pitcher. I kept bothering him to pitch me in this little league game. Finally, dad said that he would play me at pitcher, and Mike Carlson would play my position at shortstop. I should have listened to my dad that day. Another life lesson was about to happen.

Before the game, all the coaches who were at the little league complex that day, helped get the playing field ready to go. It was really muddy due to all the rain we got in the morning. How they got the field ready really surprised me. I couldn't believe my eyes but it did in fact happen! I saw all the coaches dumping gasoline on the muddy infield. They lit a match, and torched the playing surface. They actually lit the field on fire!

You see some strange things in life, but this happened to be one of the oddest things I have ever seen in sports.

My dad told me it was a way to dry up the muddy field. Believe it or not, we did play the game that day against the Gulls. I was the starting pitcher, and it may have been the last time I was a starting pitcher ever again. It seemed as if every batter I faced either walked or got on base with a hit.

Did my dad take me out of the game? Nope!

47

He let me stay in there as long as possible to teach me another lesson. We absolutely got crushed that day in the little league game. By the fifth inning, he finally took me out and put in…you guessed it…Mike Carlson.

Mike was a great little league player and much better pitcher than I was that year. I just didn't want to admit it until now. I pretty much sat on the bench the rest of the game watching my little league team play and get beat by the Gulls.

Dad didn't have to say much to me after the game nor did my teammates. If we would have pitched Mike Carlson the entire game, we would have won. The message came through loud and clear. In team sports, everyone has a role to play, and it is better to listen to the coach.

Oh…and the second lost that year?

There wasn't supposed to be a championship game. The Griffith Little League was going to give us the championship trophies, with the words, "Crows" written on them. It was up to the teams to decide if we wanted an All-Star game or a Championship game.

As members of the Crows that year, we all chose to play in a championship game. It would have been easy to just play an All-Star game, but we wanted to say that we were the 'real' champions of the Griffith Little League.

Once again, on a rainy day in late June, we lost.

The game was actually cancelled after the 4th inning due to thunder and lightning. What I remember most was the tears and sad faces in the dugout by all my teammates and friends. Most of them, I would never see again. Players like Brett Dines, Mike Carlson, and Mark Wimmer were some of my closest friends on the team.

I often wonder what has happened to those three friends, and how their lives have turned out.

As for me, life was about to change again, as well as the names and places in my life. This would also be true for the Ohio State Buckeyes as the fall of 1978 approached.

Chapter 4
Life Transitions Again

My mom and dad decided to move from Griffith to another local town known as Merrillville by the end of the summer of 1978. My parents believed that we needed a bigger house due to the fact we started to accumulate a lot of household items. I really didn't want to move again because it meant that I would have to start over at a new school, make new friends, and play on new sports teams. I would be entering the fifth grade, and again not knowing anyone at my new school. The older I got in age; it was more difficult to transition into another school. Most kids entering the 5th grade already had established friends or need I say...cliques.

We moved to a house on Johnson Street in a subdivision known as Meadowdale. My family would live there from 1978 until 1988, and it would be where most of my childhood memories were created growing up as a kid.

It is often stated that when one door closes, another one is about to open. The transition would prove not to be an easy one.

By this time, both my sisters, Nikki and Erin, were of school-age, and starting a new school along with me. We met a lot of new people that summer on Johnson Street. You could walk out your door, and there would be kids everywhere playing and having fun.

I often comment that growing up in the 1970's and the 1980's was a lot different than it is today. Kids were always outside playing different games and hanging out.

We would play whiffle ball or football in the yard every day, and you didn't have to look very far to find someone who wanted to join in on the fun. My new friends on the block were Daenan and Tommy. If they were not available to go out and play, you could always find someone else on Johnson Street.

Starting the school year in Merrillville proved to be a little more difficult than the move back from Arizona to Beiriger Elementary in Griffith. My new school in Merrillville was called Miller Elementary, and my fifth-grade teacher was Mrs. Ruth Staniszeski. The first few months of fifth grade were rough and oftentimes very lonely. I had no friends and would sit at the lunch table by myself. No one really talked to me.

I would even crack a few jokes with my classmates but no one seemed interested in being friends with me. There was one other kid at my lunch table but I learned quickly that no one talked to him either. I would think back to my times at Shoemaker and Beiriger Elementary schools, and wish I was at one or the other. At least I had friends at those schools. Miller school seemed different. A lot of the kids seemed mean and arrogant. One day, I sat my lunch tray down at the table to go the bathroom, only to come back to see chocolate milk spilled all over my pizza, vegetables, and dessert. I could see a table of boys laughing at me. Why couldn't my parents have stopped moving around? It was really tough making new friends.

Another day, I was sitting on the playground with no one to talk to, or play with, during recess. I was staring out at the fifth graders playing football in the open field across from the playground. I asked myself why no one was interested in playing games with me at recess or *wanting to be my friend? Was it because I was the 'new kid' or was it the scar on my face due to the terrible accident I had in 1976? I wondered if this is how Cass felt sitting on the playground by himself back at Shoemaker?* I wasn't about to ask or find out from this group of fifth graders who never let me play football with them at lunch recess.

I decided to take matters into my own hands. I hopped off the swing, and went right up to them in the open field. I told them that I wanted to play football!! One of the boys looked at me and said, *"We already have teams made. Maybe some other day, kid."*

I looked at them with a glare and said to all of them, *"Let me tell you what. I will take all of you on in a game of football, and I'll just take one other person on my team!"* I pointed to one of the shortest 5th grade kids at Miller Elementary School and said, *"I'll take him on my team!"*

His name was Bobby, and he really wasn't that good of a player.

At the time, I thought this was the biggest risk in my life. If I didn't show them that I could play football, then I would probably be alone again on the playground. Bobby and I took on about 32 fifth graders in a tag football game at the field in back of Miller school.

We got the ball first to start the game. I told him to just snap the football to me, and I would do the rest. Would you believe that not one fifth grader was able to catch me on my way to the end zone which was actually the edge of the playground?

Every time we had the football, Bobby would snap the ball to me, and I would just run as fast as I could away from the other fifth graders. This brought me back to a time when I pretended to be Jeff Logan from Ohio State, or the great Craig Buzea from Griffith High School.

That moment has always been etched in my memory as the day I made friends at Miller Elementary School.

By the way, Bobby and I won the game that day by beating 32 other kids in a two-hand touch football game.

With that being said, my parents still didn't let me play in the organized Pop Warner Youth Football League. I have to admit that there was still a part of me that really didn't want to play football. I saw how players got tackled at the high school level, or even watching the Buckeyes play on television. Did I really want to get hurt during a practice or in a game? Playing 'real' football looked dangerous. However, I knew the girls liked boys who played football.

I received news one day about an after school football club run by our art teacher at Miller Elementary School. It was a flag football team made up of 4th through 6th graders. I loved playing flag football after school, mainly because I knew that I wasn't going to be tackled by larger kids.

It was playing flag football in the fall of 1978 that I knew someday I wanted to play high school as well as college football. The dream of playing for the Griffith High School Panthers like my boyhood hero, Craig Buzea, quickly faded to playing for the Merrillville Pirates high school team led by Coach Ken Haupt. Coach Haupt had won a football state championship at Merrillville in 1976, so the school was well-known for the sport.

In the classroom, I was struggling to keep up with the other students. I didn't realize at the time how far I was behind academically as a fifth grader at Miller. It would be Mrs. Staniszeski who would have the biggest impact on me in the classroom that year.

She was a young and very attractive teacher. Mrs. "S" as I would call her, would sit with me for hours and make sure that I was caught up in all my subjects, especially in math. I was an absolutely terrible math student! There were many times that I would bring my lunch into her classroom so she could help me with my homework.

It was during this year that I really discovered all the attractive girls in my class as well. There was this one girl named Kelli who sat across from me in Mrs. Staniszeski's room. She had short blonde hair with braces on her teeth. For whatever reason, I thought girls with braces were attractive. In this case, Kelli was a pretty girl and very smart too.

So, you could say that my total focus wasn't just on Ohio State football that year, but girls as well.

Kelli became my first 'real girlfriend' during my elementary school years. I was scared to death of her. It would take me an hour just to call her on the phone. I must have tried to dial her number a dozen times before I actually completed the phone call.

In school, I would just sit and stare at her while Mrs. Staniszeski was teaching the class. Kelli had a great smile and was very personable. I know Mrs. Staniszeski could tell that I had a "crush" on Kelli. This could have been another reason why I had to stay in at lunch to catch up on my studies. It was there that Mrs. Staniszeski told me that she was a Purdue University graduate.

Oh great, I thought! *Another Purdue fan!*

Ohio State was scheduled to play the Boilermakers that year at Ross-Ade Stadium in West Lafayette, Indiana in October. Just like Mrs. Bell, who was my 4th grade teacher, I am not sure Mrs. Staniszeski understood my fandom with Ohio State. It would also be the year that my all-time favorite player started at quarterback for the Buckeyes.

He is still my all-time favorite player at Ohio State to this day.

Ohio State football was about to go through major changes both good and bad in 1978. The day of September 16th would be a whole new level of my fandom with Ohio State. The Buckeyes were scheduled to play Penn State that day on ABC TV. Penn State was another one of those strong powerhouse programs in college football during the 1970's.

Like most Ohio State football seasons, I was ready for this one! The game between Ohio State vs. Penn State was scheduled for 12:30 pm central time that day, and one of my dad's friends happened to be there to watch the game with us. His name was Bob Mizura but my dad called him, "Beero." I believe he got that nickname for his love for drinking beer. He was a fellow teacher with my dad in the Lake Ridge School Corporation.

Bob taught high school science and coached football. I really never called him Bob or Mr. Mizura, it was just simply, "Beero." Bob was a Vietnam veteran and became a great family friend. He always seemed to be over our house to visit. Oftentimes, just to talk about football with me and my dad.

As Ohio State was about to start the game with Penn State, there were two quarterbacks standing next to Coach Woody Hayes on the sidelines. I had heard from my dad, as well as reading the local newspapers, that Ohio State had a freshman quarterback who set all kinds of high school records in Ohio. Rod Gerald had started as the Ohio State quarterback the year before and was back for another season in 1978.

53

Would Woody Hayes really start a freshman quarterback over a veteran player?

The answer would come moments later. Both players started trotting out onto the field to start the game. Art went in at quarterback and Rod Gerald at wide receiver. I only knew what I was reading in the local paper or heard from my dad about Art Schlichter. We didn't have the internet back then or publications that covered Ohio State football.

Such publications as the *Buckeye Sports Bulletin* and websites like *Eleven Warriors* or the *Ozone* didn't really exist like they do now. Art went on the field to the roar of the crowd in Ohio Stadium, and I was cheering loudly at my home watching the game on TV.

Although I didn't know much about him at the time, Art would become my all-time favorite player. Art's first pass as an Ohio State player was completed to a receiver named Doug Donley for a 6 yard gain. As the game was going on, I had mentioned to my dad and "Beero" that I someday wanted to play quarterback and be like Art Schlichter.

"Beero" started showing me 'quarterback moves' in our basement as the game was going on and explaining how to play the position. He was showing me the right way to grip a football and how to drop back, and make a pass.

As stated before, I was a fast runner. I just couldn't throw a football very well.

Bob "Beero" Mizura as well as my dad, gave me my first lessons on how to play quarterback right down in our basement on Johnson Street. They pointed out everything Art was doing right as well as doing wrong in the football game against Penn State. That day, Art may have done more wrong than he did right. He went on to throw five interceptions, and Ohio State lost to Penn State by the score of 19-0. I knew there would be better days ahead for Ohio State as well as for Art Schlichter.

Later in October, Ohio State would lose again, and this time it would be to Mrs. Staniszeski school...the Purdue Boilermakers. I listened to that game on the radio in my bedroom. The game wasn't on TV but since I lived in Indiana, I could get the Purdue University football network on my radio. On Monday, I didn't wear anything Ohio State, and I was hoping that no one mentioned the 27-16 loss to the Boilermakers.

Fat chance that was going to happen!

I believe Mrs. Staniszeski said something to the effect of *"Hail Purdue"* or *"Go Purdue!"* All the kids in the class started cheering along with Mrs. "S" at the fact that the Buckeyes lost to Purdue.

Any time Ohio State lost in football to an Indiana school like IU or Purdue, it was even harder to face students and teachers after the weekend. The kids would wear their Indiana or Purdue t-shirts and jerseys to school just to *'rub it in,'* I thought.

My dad would always tell me not to say anything to the teachers or students about Ohio State losing but I couldn't resist. It just seemed like everyone was against the Buckeyes. To ease my anger with Ohio State losing, I could always focus on the girl situation at school.

I had my first real 'girl crush' in grade school with Kelli. My parents really liked her too, especially my dad. My parents would take Kelli to my little league games that first summer living in Merrillville to watch me play baseball. Most of the season, I would strike out at bat because my concentration wasn't on the game... it was on Kelli. I was really mesmerized by her.

Dad and mom would take us to the local Dairy Queen after those baseball games to get ice cream. Dad would often joke around with Kelli, and tell her that he couldn't afford to buy her an ice cream cone because he was a schoolteacher.

Dad would tell her that she would have to settle for ice cream on a napkin. She always found that very amusing. I envisioned that my relationship with Kelli would last forever. In life as well in sports, good moments sometimes don't last, and become distant memories.

Ohio State would go on to lose a third straight year to the Michigan Wolverines in 1978 by the score of 14-3. What I remember about the game was that it wasn't as close as the score indicated. Art

Schlichter was still going through growing pains as Ohio State's starting quarterback. He had thrown nineteen interceptions going into that 1978 game with the Wolverines.

I was mad that Ohio State lost, but I knew that the Buckeyes would not have to face Rick Leach ever again as the Michigan quarterback.

Rick was a senior, and would be moving on to a pro baseball career with the Detroit Tigers and later the Toronto Blue Jays. Due to the loss to the Wolverines in 1978, Ohio State would have to settle for going to a Gator Bowl.

Ohio State would play Clemson on December 29th, 1978 a little over after a month after the Michigan defeat. The game would be played on a Friday night with most fans at the game cheering for Clemson. I remember the TV broadcast scanning the crowd to a sea of people wearing orange shirts. This could have been due to the fact that Ohio State lost again to Michigan, and the Gator Bowl didn't seem as important to Buckeye fans. I was not going to let the bad season by Ohio State standards deter me from watching the game.

The Buckeyes had a chance to win at the end with a field goal. They only trailed Clemson 17-15 in the 4th quarter when the unthinkable happened. Coach Woody Hayes went against his conventional wisdom and called a 'pass play.'

From all the interviews and research that I have done on the subject, Coach Hayes had told Art Schlichter not to throw the ball if the receiver was not open. Well, every Buckeye fan knows what happens next in this part of the story.

Clemson player Charlie Bauman, who's #58, picked off the pass, and headed right towards the Ohio State sidelines. After Charlie was tackled, he got up, and was punched by Coach Hayes. The announcers may not have seen what had happened but I saw it live on TV.

Did that just happen? The coach that I grew up loving just slugged a player from the opposite team?

There has been a lot of debate of what happened that December night in the Gator Bowl. Some say that Coach Hayes was suffering from diabetes and didn't properly take his medication. Others say that he went through another bad season by Ohio State standards, and had endured his third straight loss to Michigan.

I have never met Coach Hayes. I only saw him once while I was at a football camp at Ohio State in the 1980's. I have read every book on Woody Hayes over and over again. I have also listened to the many interviews and stories by former coaches and players about him.

To me, Coach Hayes will always be one of the greatest coaches and people of all time. I find myself always justifying his actions to other fans or people who didn't know what happened that night in the Gator Bowl. If others only knew of all the great things Coach Hayes did and the many people that he had impacted throughout his career, they wouldn't be as quick to judge him.

I have heard stories about him going up to Children's Hospital to visit kids with terminal illness, or visiting grown adults who were about ready to die. He would even leave an Ohio State practice to be with former players who were going through their own personal tragedies.

Coach Hayes used the line... *"You Win with People."*

He was always there for his players, Ohio State University, the state of Ohio, and people in general. Time really didn't matter to Woody. He always had time to make an impact on people's lives.

Years later, I would have breakfast at the old Holiday Inn on Lane Avenue on the Ohio State campus listening to former players talk about Woody Hayes and the impact he had on their lives. Not one player ever said any negative comments about him!

I was crushed the next day when I found out that Woody Hayes was relieved (fired) from his coaching responsibilities at Ohio State. Coach Hayes was always this iconic figure in my life. He was Ohio State football.

I remember getting this painted picture of Woody Hayes from my Grandma Lorraine. Grandma Lorraine was married to my grandfather on my mom's side. Even though my mother really didn't refer to Grandma Lorraine as her step-mom, she technically was.

She painted this portrait of Woody Hayes holding a pennant that said, *"1978 is our year!"*

Of all the memorabilia that I have of Ohio State, that is one item that I wish I would have kept. It is often debated whether Woody Hayes actually resigned or was fired by the university that December of 1978.

The athletic director at the time was former Buckeye assistant coach Hugh Hindman. I can't imagine the tough spot Mr. Hindman was put in to relieve Woody Hayes after his twenty-eight years as coach of Ohio State.

He is one of the many reasons that I started loving Buckeye football in the first place. All I heard from my fellow students and teachers was that Coach Hayes slugged a Clemson player, and that he was a bad person.

Another thing my friends and classmates would say, *"Oh, you like Ohio State? That is the coach who hit an opposing player!"* It would make me so angry at times.

Woody amassed a record of 205-61-10 at Ohio State, and won 13-Big Ten Conference titles. I was around for three of those titles when I started becoming a Buckeye fan in 1975. I have always been proud of that fact.

As 1978 faded in the distance, things were about to change in my life as well. A lot of people always say that things never stay the same. Life is a constant and evolving chain of events that shaped who we are as people. I didn't realize how much that was going to become reality.

I was going to get my wish, finally.

Chapter 5
Two New Careers Start

As the summer turned to the fall of 1979, I finally got to do some of the things I wanted to do at a young age. I still had a crush on Kelli as we started the 6th grade that August. When you are that young, you think that this will be the person who you marry, have kids with, and live in a big house.

Hey... a guy can dream, right?

She was beautiful as 6th graders go, and we had a lot in common. My parents also finally agreed to sign me up for the Merrillville Pop Warner Football League. At that point, the only organized sport I played was little league baseball. I was going to finally play tackle football with a real helmet and shoulder pads. This would be a far cry from playing flag football on Miller Elementary School front lawn with my art teacher. I would have a football coach with practices and real games.

Kelli would surely come see me play in the fall. I know girls have always liked boys who played football at least back in the late 1970's and early 1980's. I knew I could run fast and score touchdowns just like I did against all those 5th graders the year before when I started school at Miller Elementary. I wanted to be like Archie Griffin, Jeff Logan, and now Art Schlichter of Ohio State. I wanted to be a star player, and do some of the things that I saw them do on television.

I was picked to play on a 'purple' Merrillville Pirates team led by Coach Andy Tancos. In our first football meeting, in his loud booming voice, he asked how many of us had played organized football before? I was the only kid who didn't raise my hand.

A few of the kids looked back at me as if to think, *"Are you for real?"*

Most of them had already played a season or two of organized football. When Andy started assigning us positions, he looked at me.

"What position are you most comfortable playing?"

Not ever playing organized football before besides the flag version at Miller Elementary, I told him that I wanted to be the quarterback.

"Are you freaking kidding me!?" he said.

That was the most important position, and usually reserved for players who had already played football. I was also smaller than most of the kids on the team. Coach Tancos just smiled, and told me that I had a lot to learn. Andy had to be about mid-twenties at the time, and always wore these construction boots to football practice. We would practice behind a school known as Harrison Junior High, not far from my house. I would sometimes ride my ten speed bike to practice, while other times my dad would take me there.

I am sure dad wanted to see if he made the right choice on putting me on a youth league football team. He was proud that I was now playing a sport he loved as well as coached. Not that there was anything wrong with playing baseball or basketball, but football always was the main sport we watched in our household along with Chicago Blackhawk Hockey.

The first couple of practices that fall of 1979, I felt out of place. First, none of my friends who went to Miller Elementary, were on my Pop Warner football team. Second, I had no idea what I was doing in practice. Coach Tancos told me that if he called a "24 Play" to hand the football off to the running back to the right side. If he called a "25 Play" I was to hand the ball off to the left side.

"Even numbers the ball is going to the right side, and odd numbers are going to the left... got it, Bunda?" he would shout.

It sounded simple but I can't tell you how many times I turned the wrong way to hand-off the football. The more I messed up the play, the angrier Coach Tancos would get. He was a perfectionist, and wanted to win much like Woody Hayes did at Ohio State. He wasn't going to stand for anything but your best in practice or in a game. It seemed like most of the practices were spent yelling at me to run the right play. I know he was just trying to make me a better player. It just didn't seem like that at the time.

For whatever reason, I also seemed to upset some of the players on my team. Maybe it was because I was still the 'new kid' in Merrillville or maybe because of the many mistakes I made in practice which made the team look bad. There was this one kid named John who always wanted to pick a fight with me after practice. I have no idea why because I never bothered or said anything to him.

He would just come up to me after football practice and say things like, *"You want to fight me now?"*

It was the oddest thing. I told him that I didn't want to fight him or had no reason to do so. If he made me mad enough, I wasn't going to hold back. I didn't get involved in too many fights during this time of my life, but I wasn't afraid of him either. I did meet one of my life-long best friends that year in youth league football. His name was Brian Portlock, and he went to another elementary school in the district known as Salk. Brian became a really good friend. We would go on to play both junior high as well as high school sports together.

I really liked Coach Tancos even though he was intimidating and very tough on me. He taught me discipline, hard work, as well as the game of football. We didn't have practice jerseys back then, so we just wore whatever could fit over our shoulder pads in practice.

I, of course, wore an Ohio State jersey that my dad bought me at the old *Sportmart* store in Merrillville. I wore that jersey to practice on most days. It was a #24 jersey that was worn by another Buckeye great named Jeff Cisco in the 1970's. I wasn't the only quarterback on the roster.

Brian Portlock and another elementary school kid named Chuck Collins, also played the position. They were both smarter, and knew the plays a lot better than I did. I never thought that I would ever get a chance to play in a game.

Practices under Coach Tancos were very tough. Every time that we made a mistake, the team would have to run around the fields in the back of Harrison Junior High School until he told us to stop. A lot of my teammates would fall to the ground due to exhaustion. There is one practice that I remember very well. I was playing quarterback, and Coach Tancos yelled at me to run play number '24.'

Like I said before, even numbers the play goes to the right, and odd numbers the play was going to the left.

"Got it, Coach!" I said.

I was supposed to turn to my right and hand off to a running back named Freddy. I turned the wrong way, and got crushed by a defensive player named Joe Casper. Joe was just a great youth league football player. Coach Tancos probably said every nasty word in the book at me. He said that I may have been the dumbest quarterback he had ever coached! I mean, he really let me have it. Of course, wearing an Ohio State jersey to practice didn't help matter much either.

He would say, *"Ohio State!? There is no way you can play there if you can't hand off the (bleep!) ball the right way in a youth league practice!!!"*

It's a warm memory now but it wasn't back then. I got to the car and said to my dad, *"Did you hear what Coach Tancos said to me!?"*

My dad who was sitting on the hood of his car simply said, *"Turn the right way next time, and Coach won't get mad at you."*

All I thought was...*Geez, thanks dad!!*

One of our first games that year was against the Hobart Pop Warner League. I didn't start the game as Chuck and Brian were obviously much better quarterbacks than I was at the time. As I stood there by Coach Tancos, he put his arm around me, and told me to get in the game at quarterback.

What!? Was I really ready for this moment?

After all, I couldn't even run the right plays in practice. Coach Tancos believed in me, and I went into the game, and actually played pretty well. My watershed moment that first season of playing organized football was against a team from the town of Portage. The game was tied at the time by the score of zero to zero. Nobody really scored a lot of points back then so it usually came down to a last minute touchdown. There was about twenty seconds left in the game, and Coach Tancos sent Freddy in with a play.

Freddy got into the huddle and told me the play is going to be *"Pop Pass at 8."* I am supposed to drop back and throw the football to him over the middle of the field.

Sounds easy, right?

My team breaks the huddle, and I grab Freddy by the shoulder pads. I told him that I am not throwing the football to him. Instead, I'm going to try to run the ball for the score. Freddy glanced at me with a startled look as if to think who would go against Coach Tancos' play?

We had about sixty-five yards to go for a touchdown, and there was no way I was going to throw the football.

I remembered what Coach Woody Hayes used to say about passing the football. Three things could happen and two of them were bad… incomplete or interception. I guess watching all those Ohio State football games and seeing Archie Griffin, Jeff Logan, Cornelius Green(e), as well as Rod Gerald run the football stuck in my head. I was going to run the football alright! Our center snapped me the ball, and I took off around the right end.

I eluded the first set of defenders who were trying to bring me down, made a couple of moves, and was off to the endzone. I could see the scoreboard in my sight as the clock started counting down the last remaining seconds of the game. I started getting closer to the winning score.

For a split second, I wasn't trying to score for Merrillville Pop Warner but for the Ohio State Buckeyes! It was as if the Michigan Wolverines were chasing me and not the Portage youth team.

When I got to the endzone, I looked up at the stands, and saw all these people cheering for me! Of course, in that crowd that day, were both mom and dad. I could tell that my dad was very proud.

These are moments that you never forget but often fade away as a distant memory as time goes by in your life.

As my team mobbed me with cheers and pats on the back, Coach Tancos had all my teammates stand in a line, and shake my hand. *I had won the game!* Our team had beaten the Portage team by the score of 6-0. Was I thinking at the time that I would be the next Art Schlichter at Ohio State? Maybe.

There would be one person missing from watching me play that day, and it was my elementary school girlfriend, Kelli. Like a lot of young relationships, it really doesn't last forever.

There was a new boy who moved into Merrillville and Miller Elementary School that year. His name was Kevin. For whatever reason, the girls always liked the "new" kid who moved into the school. Kelli started liking Kevin and as they would say... I was history.

Now on "cloud nine" with being a football hero. Scoring that winning touchdown in the youth league football game that September of 1979 made me feel like I was invisible. None of my teammates were laughing at me now. I was going to be the main player on the team, or at least that is what I thought.

Our next football game that year would be against a team known as South Haven. I had a great week of practice, and it seemed that everything was going my way. Coach Tancos told me that I was now the starting quarterback of Merrillville Pop Warner.

A football player was born and I was going to someday be a star at Ohio State, just like Art Schlichter. Art had set all kinds of passing records when he was in school at Miami Trace High School in Ohio. I really wanted to wear jersey #10 because that is what Art wore at Ohio State. The only problem was the jersey was too small for me, and went to another player on our youth team. I had to settle for jersey #14 that year but I still dreamed that I was Art Schlichter commanding an offense as the quarterback.

The game against South Haven came down to the last minute just like the week before against Portage. Here we go again! The same scenario and situation presented itself. Coach Tancos called the same play as the week before known as *"Pop Pass at 8."* I told the players in the huddle that I was going to keep the football and run it again for the winning touchdown. Maybe I became too confident or arrogant based on the week before but nothing was going to stop me!

Our center snapped me the football, and I started to go to the left side because I saw a path to the endzone. As I approached this big hole that I was going to run through, a South Haven player hit me on my side, and the football popped straight in the air. I saw another South Haven player grab the football before it could hit the ground, and run towards the other end zone. It was as if the play from the last game was in reverse.

As I sat on the ground, all I could see was the South Haven players celebrating in their end zone, and the fans cheering on their side. The final score was South Haven 12 Merrillville 6. As I went to the sideline to confront Coach Tancos, he gave me an ear full!

I mean he really let me have it about being a team player, and not being selfish, or trying to be a hero. You can just imagine what he said to me. Let's just say the words weren't of the pleasant kind.

Unlike the week before, where every player had to shake my hand, Coach Tancos made me apologize to the entire team for my behavior out on the field. I was really embarrassed.

Needless to say, I don't remember who we played in our next youth league football game after the loss, because I had sat on the bench. It was a life lesson that I would never forget. Coach Tancos taught me that no one was above the team. Football is a team sport, and everyone on the team was important.

As my youth league football career started for the Merrillville "Pirates," another one was starting at Ohio State. Coach Woody Hayes had been fired for hitting the Clemson player on that fateful night that previous December. The Buckeyes would have a new coach in the fall of 1979. His name was Earle Bruce, and he was a head coach

65

previously at Iowa State. I had never heard of him before. I did know that Art Schilchter was coming back as well as wide receiver, Doug Donley for the Buckeyes.

The Buckeyes would open their season on September 8th against the Syracuse Orangemen, and would win by the score of 31-8. Years later, I would acquire the game program from Earle Bruce's first game as coach against Syracuse, and he would sign it for me. I read about the game in our local newspaper known as the *Hammond Times*. There would be a paragraph or two about the game, and a box score of the statistics. I am not sure I cared that much back then because when you are a 6th grade kid, there are more things that take up your time like—friends, family, and playing your own sports. I knew the dates Ohio State was on TV, and I would make sure that I would be home to watch every single game.

As I watched the Ohio State games, I remember looking at everything Art Schlichter did as a quarterback. He became my idol. It would only be later in life did I realize that Art had all these problems, including a major gambling addiction. When his addiction became public news, it really upset me. My classmates would always make fun of me for idolizing an addicted gambler.

To this day, he has remained my favorite Ohio State player of all-time. I know what he did, and I don't agree with a lot of his life choices. I have read every book on Art, and I know his story very well. With that being said, he will always be my favorite player. As a 6th grade kid, you idolize sports figures, especially those who play on your favorite team. Yes, I idolized Archie Griffin, Cornelius Green(e), Rod Gerald, and Jeff Logan as all-time Buckeye greats.

Art just was different to me. I wanted to be like him. He was good-looking, was a quarterback, and played for the Ohio State Buckeyes. I wanted to be all those things that Art represented as a person.

In 1979, a lot of my friends started liking Ohio State as well. One of my friends, Tommy, who lived off of Johnson Street in Merrillville, started saying that the Buckeyes were his favorite team.

It's amazing what winning does, and how many kids want to say that they are "real" fans of a team. When a team starts losing, how many kids quickly change allegiance to another school. I remembered what my dad told me about being a 'real fan' no matter if your team wins or loses. Ohio State was my team and my school.

I still played quarterback the rest of that first year as a youth league player. I learned that when the coach tells you to do something, you listen to what he wants you to do. Oh... I still wanted to be the hero, and try to win the games just like Art Schlichter. I guess you could say that I learned some hard lessons, both playing little league baseball for my dad, and now for Coach Andy Tancos in youth league football.

In terms of the situation at school, Kelli had moved on, and I was looking for a new girlfriend as well.

In the fall of 1979, I was in Mrs. Kosica's 6th grade class, and there was another blonde- haired girl who caught my eye. Her name was Karen, and she had braces on her teeth just like Kelli did.

There was another girl who liked me that year in 6th grade too. Her name was Bess but I looked at her more as a friend. Karen was both smart and pretty. In 1979, it was the year of rolling skating parties at a place simply known as the "Rink."

Every kid in Merrillville went on Friday and Saturday nights to the "Rink." I started getting interested in roller-skating as well. I wanted to fit in with what the other kids at my school were doing at the time.

There was only one problem...I didn't know how to skate! My sisters Nikki and Erin were also both very much interested in skating at the "Rink."

They would have to settle for going on Saturday afternoons as they were much too young to go at night. Roller-skating at night was reserved for kids who were in the 6th through 12th grade. There was another problem. I had no way of getting to the roller-skating rink. My mom didn't really drive and dad was usually busy working a coaching job to go along with his teaching responsibilities.

Mom was about thirty-three years old, and still didn't have her driver's license. She was learning to drive from a family friend, Mrs. Hixon. Karen had told me that she wanted to be boyfriend and girlfriend with me. Great! The "Rink" served more of a purpose than skating by the way. This is where kids went to kiss and make-out with who they were dating.

Even though Kelli was my first girlfriend, I never kissed her. Karen told me she would be at the "Rink" with her friends on Friday night. She passed me a note in school asking if I would be there?

Of course, I said yes!

I asked everyone I knew if they could come pick me up at my house to go to the roller-skating rink that night. It seemed like everyone was going with someone else or had other plans. How was I going to get there? My dad had the answer. He had a friend named Woodrow Feeler. Everyone called him, "Woody."

I thought that was neat because he shared the same nickname as the former Ohio State football coach, Woody Hayes. Woody Feeler was a police officer in Gary, Indiana at the time. My dad knew him because Woody was working part-time as a freshman basketball coach at Calumet High School.

One of Woody's daughters happened to babysit us a lot when Nikki, Erin, and I were younger kids. Dad suggested that Woody and his girlfriend Donna, pick me up to go to the roller-skating rink. Problem solved. I could now go to the skating rink to meet up with Karen on Friday night. This would be the night she was planning on kissing me. It would also be the first chance that I could kiss a girl. There would be no sitting around watching the *Dukes of Hazzard* or the mini-series, *Dallas* on this Friday night! Woody Feeler and his girlfriend Donna would be picking me up to go to the "Rink."

When they arrived at my house on Johnson Street, Woody was not in a normal car. He was driving his police car that he used for his job! I looked at my mom in amazement. *I am going to the roller-skating rink in a police car? What if all my friends saw me including my new girlfriend, Karen??*

Well, it was either to be escorted in a police car or not go at all.

Woody and Donna drove me to the "Rink" that night, and we had a nice conversation. I imagined what it must be like to be a criminal sitting in the back of a police car. I really didn't know either one very well at the time, but it was nice that they were taking me to see Karen at the skating rink.

When we got there on Whitcomb Avenue in Merrillville, there was a line a mile long to go inside. Woody did the unthinkable. As we pulled up to the "Rink," he turned on his siren and his lights to his police car.

You got to be kidding me.

I was never so embarrassed in my life! All these kids turned around to look at what all the commotion was about. As I stepped out of the police car, you could hear a pin drop. Every kid going into the building that night just stared at me. I really just wanted to hide. I was hoping that Karen didn't see me as I tried to go behind the crowd.

Luckily, she was already inside skating with her friends. Unlucky for me, I still didn't know how to skate. For one of the first times in my life, I was outside of my element. I was used to running fast, and playing football and baseball. I was wondering if Art Schlichter could skate? This could be a deal breaker with Karen. Would she want to be with a boyfriend who didn't know how to roller-skate? I don't think scoring a winning touchdown in a pop warner football game impressed her but my ability or inability to skate would.

As I got my roller-skates from the shoe window, Rod Stewart's song, *"Do Ya Think I'm Sexy"* was playing on the speakers at the skating rink. It was a popular song at roller-skating rinks around the country in 1979. I saw all these kids skating by fast, and holding hands with each other, as the song was playing. It looked like everyone could skate really well.

At that point, I still hadn't seen Karen. I thought to myself… here goes nothing! I remember going on the floor with my roller-skates just shuffling around as kids flew past me on their own skates. I fell right into the wall because I didn't know how to use the toe stops on the bottom of the roller-skates. As I tried to get up, there was Karen. She reached down with her hand to offer assistance in helping me off the floor.

How embarrassing!!

Karen and her friend Stacey would teach me how to skate that year. Whenever there was a couple-skate slow song playing at the "Rink," Karen would skate backwards with her hands on my shoulders and mine on her waist. I was the only boy who didn't skate backwards in the couple-skate. It must have looked funny for people to watch me skate while my girlfriend skated backwards with me. Like I said, Karen had told me that we would kiss at the "Rink." I was really nervous to kiss her on the lips. What if I did it wrong? I had never kissed a girl before.

There were certain places you could go inside the skating rink to kiss your girlfriend. I know it wasn't allowed but kids did it anyways. I never did kiss Karen. I know I had my chances but I think I was too afraid. I probably made many excuses on why I couldn't kiss her. As with Kelli, Karen wouldn't last as my girlfriend either during my 6th grade year in elementary school. My "first kiss" would be with another girl that year named Mary Ann.

Mary Ann also attended Miller Elementary School in 1979. I am not sure we really liked one another, but Mary Ann and I were probably just curious as to what it was like to "make-out" and kiss someone else. I was also curious if I would ever see an Ohio State football game in person. That would be answered on November 3rd, 1979 in Champaign, Illinois.

My mom and dad would be celebrating their wedding anniversary that weekend. Most couples would want to spend their anniversary on a cruise, a bed & breakfast, an extended vacation, somewhere warm, etc... I am sure that is what my parents would have preferred to do as well.

On November 3rd, 1979, their destination would be Champaign, Illinois to watch the Ohio State Buckeyes play the University of Illinois "Fighting Illini" in a college football game. They would be taking me with them! Nothing says an anniversary like going to a college football game with your twelve year old son. I would finally get to see the Ohio State Buckeyes in person. All the players that I watched on TV; I would now see live at the game.

Star players that year like Calvin Murray, Ken Fritz, Doug Donley, Jim Laughlin, and especially, Art Schlichter. Those of you that have seen the movie, "Rudy," about the kid who wanted to play for Notre Dame can relate to this part of the book. There is a scene in the movie when Rudy's dad said to the effect that 'this is the best thing these eyes have ever seen' when referring to going inside Notre Dame Stadium.

Well... that is actually what I thought about going to my first Ohio State football game. I couldn't believe that I was actually watching the Ohio State Buckeyes live in person!!

The Buckeyes were undefeated at the time, and ranked fifth in the country. I got one of my first souvenir Ohio State pennants at the game. To this day, it is still on the wall in my house.

I remember the air smelling like hotdogs, hamburgers, bratwurst, and stale beer. Our seats were in the upper deck of Illinois' Memorial Stadium, and we were there from the first play until the final second of the game.

Buckeye punter Tom Orosz kicked the football really high any time Ohio State had to punt. The player I was watching most of the game was my hero, Art Schlichter. I didn't recognize any players on the Illinois team because they just weren't very good in 1979.

The Buckeyes would defeat Illinois that day 44-7 as we would celebrate the win as well as my parent's anniversary. For most fans, this game will not go down as a memorable one in the history of Ohio State football. It will always be remembered as my first game in person, and spending time with mom and dad on their anniversary.

On the way home, mom and I listened to the radio as dad drove us back to our home in Northwest Indiana. We listened to the same song on the radio about a thousand times before we reached home. The song was *"Heartache Tonight"* by the music group, the Eagles. It didn't matter what radio station we turned to, that song was playing! Mom and I just laughed and laughed at that song. My mom enjoyed life more than anyone I knew. She spent most of her life sacrificing and making sure that Nikki, Erin, and I enjoyed our hobbies and interests.

Like dad, she put us three kids above anything else she may have wanted to do or had planned to do for herself. My fondest memory of my mom was years later sitting in a coffee shop known as *Gloria Jean's Coffees*. It wasn't until then that I realized how important life was, and the impact my mom had on me as well as on other people.

As we got our coffee that day, mom started talking to a lady who I thought she knew from earlier in her life. I had gotten a newspaper to read while mom was talking to this unknown person.

After two hours went by, she was still talking to this lady like they were long lost best friends. After I finished reading the newspaper, my mom looked at me, and said she was ready to go.

I asked her, *"Who was that lady? Was that someone you knew back in high school?"*

My mom looked at me and said, *"I have never seen that lady in my life."*

I was startled for a second. What? You spend two hours of your life talking to some stranger?

After a while, I realized that my mom just liked talking to people, and was interested in what they had to say. Whether it was about raising kids, cooking recipes, favorite flowers, or about life in general. My mom made an impact on other people's lives. I know she liked Ohio State football but she really liked the Buckeyes because it made me happy.

The Illinois game of 1979 would not be the last game my mom would go to, or the last game on her and my dad's anniversary, for that matter. The Illinois game in 1979 is one of my fondest memories in my childhood. Thank you mom and dad for sharing that day with me, and celebrating an Ohio State win along with your anniversary.

The rest of Ohio State's 1979 season ended with wins against other conference teams. No game would be more important than the one played in mid-November that year. Ohio State had gone three long years without defeating the University of Michigan. Rick Leach, the great Michigan quarterback had graduated, and moved on to a pro baseball career. Ohio State was 10-0 going into that game against the Wolverines.

ABC sports televised the game with Keith Jackson as the main broadcaster. Like most games that were on TV, my dad and I watched Ohio State football from our basement on Johnson Street in Merrillville. I kept wondering if this would be the year Ohio State would finally beat Michigan.

The Buckeyes would score its first touchdown against Michigan since 1975 when Art Schlichter threw a touchdown pass to Chuck Hunter in the corner of the endzone. Michigan did lead late in the game by the score of 15-12.

The Wolverines had a great wide receiver that year by the name of Anthony Carter. It just seemed that every time that Anthony would touch the football, he would go for a long gain or for a touchdown.

Ohio State would need something special to happen for them to win the game. As luck would have it, that is exactly what happened!

In the 4th quarter, Ohio State would block a punt, and Todd Bell would run in the winning touchdown for the Buckeyes! Marcus Marek intercepted a Michigan pass to end the game. Ohio State would win 18-15.

Ohio State would go to the Rose Bowl on New Year's Day in 1980 to face the USC Trojans. Just like the Rose Bowl four years earlier, it would end in defeat for the Buckeyes. This time by the score of 17-16. Ohio State led in the 4th quarter until Charles White of USC scored the winning touchdown. I remember running up to my parent's bedroom, and shutting the door. I cried and cried for an entire hour. Nothing anyone could say would make me feel any better.

I loved Ohio State, and when they lost, it felt as if the world was coming to an end. I know this bothered a lot of my friends as well as girlfriends because it always seemed like my life revolved around Ohio State. Some girls even told me that they wouldn't go out with me on a date due to my obsession with the Buckeyes. One of the girls I went out with, who shall remain nameless, said that all I talked about was Ohio State football!

What else was there to talk about? Politics? Rock & Roll music? School?

I guess I didn't realize that most people at age twelve or thirteen didn't share the same enthusiasm as I did for the Buckeyes. As 1979 turned to 1980, life was going to change again. I would no longer be at Miller Elementary School.

Back in those days, junior high school was 7th through 9th grade. I would be headed off to Harrison Junior High School with a whole new set of situations coming my way in the fall of 1980. Just like the Ohio State Buckeyes, life would become one big roller-coaster ride.

Chapter 6

Me and Rick
(Game Break)

In February of 1980, I was getting ready to wrap up my year as a 6th grader at Miller, and begin my journey to Harrison Junior High School. Before my final spring in elementary school, I witnessed something special on television with my dad.

It was the famous, *"Miracle on Ice."*

Years later they would make a movie about the 1980 U.S. Hockey Team and its famous coach, Herb Brooks. My dad was always a big hockey fan, especially when it came to the Chicago Blackhawks. Hockey really never caught on with me. I was wrapped up with anything that had to do with Ohio State. I even started liking the Ohio State basketball team. In February of 1980, I got to witness something very special on TV with my dad.

It was February 22, 1980, and the United States was playing the Soviet Union in an Olympic hockey game. Nowadays, a lot of people can see TV replays or YouTube videos of this famous game that they now call, *"Miracle on Ice."* I actually saw it live on television as part of the Olympics coverage that winter. I don't think I fully understood the importance of the moment at the time, but as the years go by, it is something I will always remember watching with my dad.

Why do I bring this up?

It gave me the belief that If you really believe in something, that if you work hard in life... any dream, aspiration, or goal is possible.

Everyone knows the story that the United States wasn't supposed to beat the mighty Soviet Union in hockey during the 1980 Olympics. The Soviet Union was invisible, right? Yet, the United States won 4-3 and earned the Gold Medal in what goes down as one of the greatest victories of any sport throughout time.

The U.S.A. hockey team couldn't have won that year unless there was a real bond between its players. They needed to count on each other. To form relationships as friends as well as hockey players to achieve greatness that year. It is the friends and family members who we share these special moments with in life. They are the ones who mold us and push us to realize dreams. To never let you give up on something that you are passionate about, no matter how great the odds are to obtain your dream.

I am sure it was the same way with that 1980 U.S. Olympic hockey team. To paraphrase what Coach Woody Hayes used to say, *"We all need people to push us."*

For me, a lot of my success in school, in sports, and in life, is due to my parents as well as my friends. I believe it was Benjamin Franklin who said, *"A true friend is the best possession."*

One of the most influential people that I have ever met in my life was my best friend. Let me introduce you to Rick Keneson. Rick has been my friend since the 5th grade at Miller Elementary School. I would like to say we became best friends right away, but that would be a lie. Like most kids at Miller, Rick already had established friends at school. There were other kids like Brian Hixon, Steve Civanich, Tim Bianco, and Scott Otterbacher. All of them would become my friends as well, and I have great memories of all of them.

In life, you will acquire many friends and acquaintances. Some you will keep in touch with for many years and then eventually lose touch. Some will just be your friend based on how popular you are or how you are perceived by others in school. Some friends last long enough until elementary school, junior high, or high school is over, go their separate ways, and you never hear from them again. While other friends are only your friends until you go through a major crisis or situation in your life. They disassociate with you.

None of the above would explain Rick Keneson. He has been my best friend through the good times and the bad times. No matter what, Rick has always been there. I say this now because he will be mentioned throughout the rest of the book. I don't know where I would be without him. Along with Brian Portlock, Rick believed that someday I would realize my dreams. He may not have known of all the problems that I had trying to reach them. How could he? We were about to live through the 'wonder years of our lives.'

Rick grew up in Merrillville, Indiana. He loved everything about his hometown, especially the Merrillville High School "Pirates." They always say that opposites attract in relationships. I could say Rick and I had a lot in common growing up, but that couldn't be further from the truth. Rick cheered for the Chicago Cubs. I eventually cheered for the Chicago White Sox. Rick liked the Chicago Bulls basketball team. I liked the Boston Celtics. Rick loved the Chicago Blackhawks hockey team. I really didn't like hockey at all. Rick was great at math. I was absolutely terrible at math.

So much so, that I changed my math grade with a pen from a D to a B on my report cards. It didn't matter though, my dad always caught me, and he would get mad when I did this. Rick was a good student throughout grade school while I was just 'average' at best. Rick was tall and I wasn't that tall.

I think you get the picture. Oh...I left out one major item. Rick was and still is a MICHIGAN fan!!! Wait a minute...how could I be best friends with someone who likes Ohio State's archrival!!?? I hated Michigan. Besides, the player who ruined Ohio State's season for three years, and made my life miserable during the span of 1976 until 1978, was named Rick. I am talking about Michigan quarterback, Rick Leach. Now, I am best friends with a person named Rick Keneson and he likes Michigan? *Is it true that you keep your friends close but your enemies closer?*

Well, Rick Keneson, has been my best friend for over forty years. I know he doesn't like Ohio State, and he knows that I absolutely hate Michigan. They often say that without Ohio State, there would be no Michigan. Without Michigan, there would be no Ohio State. Without Rick Keneson, there would be no Dennis Bunda.

At least, I wouldn't have had all these great memories, stupid moments, and ridiculous situations that Rick and I always found ourselves in. To this day, he has remained one of the most important people in my life. Just like the 1980 U.S. Hockey team, we have always relied on each other to get through tough times.

As Rick and I approached the junior high school years, we became best friends. We rode and sat on the bus together playing hand-held electronic games like Mattel football or Coleco head-to-head basketball. Most of the time, we were just having fun doing what kids do. It was just creating ways to pass the time on the bus, in school, and on the weekends. We didn't have cell phones or computers in our lives. We didn't have social media outlets like *Instagram, Snapchat,* or *Facebook*.

Rick and I created our own fun back then. A lot of times, it was just making up games or just having fun hanging out. My mom didn't have to worry where we were, or if we were getting into trouble.

I really believe that kids today don't have a lot to do. Maybe it is due to all the social media sites nowadays and being on their cell phones for long periods of time. It also seems like there are a lot more problems with alcohol, vaping, and getting into trouble.

Today, when I walk out my front door during the weekends or in the summertime, it is hard to find kids playing anywhere outside. That was never the case when I was growing up entering my junior high years with Rick Keneson. We were always playing basketball, baseball, or football games. We would go up to a place known as Meadowdale Park, which was a block away from where I lived on Johnson Street. You could always find kids doing some sort of sports activity there.

In the summertime, we would ride our bikes to a community pool simply known as *"Ross Pool."*

We would hold whiffle ball tournaments in my front yard, and play for hours. After a long time of being with our friends, we would ride our bikes to the old *Park it Market* convenience store to buy candy and a soda drink. Yes...times were simple back then. I am sure problems existed but we never really knew about them.

As my elementary school years ended, I would be off to a junior high school known as Harrison. The grades were seventh grade through ninth grade. *Can you imagine that?* A seventh grader going to the same school as someone who was in ninth grade?

All sixth grade kids in the Merrillville school district had to go on an 'orientation field trip' to Harrison Junior High School by the spring of 1980. Walking into that school seemed like a whole new world to me and very intimidating for someone who was that young. I remember sitting in one of the lecture halls listening to Principal Martin talk about all the advantages of Harrison Junior High, and that the students would have to act more mature than they did in elementary school. Principal Martin also told us that Harrison had what was called a 'Grade A' lunch. He just went on and on about how Harrison had these 'Grade A' lunches that no other junior high schools had in their cafeteria.

During the orientation process, Rick and I, along with our fellow classmates, got to spend the whole day at Harrison. We got to visit classrooms and talk with students who were already going to school there. Yes... we would eat the school lunch. As I approached the front of the cafeteria line, I asked the cafeteria workers who were called the *lunch ladies* back then, if I could have a 'Grade A' lunch.

One of them stared at me with this dumbfounded look on her face. She glared back at me and said, *"What is a 'Grade A' lunch?"*

I told her that Principal Martin said that you have 'Grade A' lunches here, and I want one!

She said to me, *"You are holding up the line! What do you want to have for your lunch?"*

I told her again that I wanted what Principal Martin talked to us about in his orientation speech about 'Grade A' lunches.

She said, *"I don't know what you are talking about! We do have pizza, chicken, fries, and a choice of a vanilla or chocolate shake."*

Seeing that my other classmates were laughing at me, but frustrated that I was holding up the line, I told the lunch lady that I would have pizza, fries, and a vanilla shake. Throughout the years, my friends have never let me live that down. I guess what Principal Martin was trying to say was that Harrison had really good lunches! I just thought that all you had to do was ask for a 'Grade A' lunch.

What a way to start my junior high years. It didn't help matters that the current junior high students all looked very intimidating. I accidently bumped into a freshman kid on my way to the bathroom. He said, *"Watch where you are going small fry, or I will kick your butt!"* Not exactly the way to start my junior high years.

Notwithstanding, they would be some of the best years of my life as I spent them with my best friend, Rick. We would never have a dull moment during those wonderful years. Even though Rick loved the Michigan Wolverines, we became best friends during this time and a friendship that has flourished to this day. When you go through life, there are friends like Rick who you make great moments and memories with, and shape who you are as a person. As I write the rest of this book, Rick, my best friend, will be an important part of my journey through time.

Chapter 7
A New Beginning

The summer of 1980 was a great time in my life. I didn't have a care in the world and was ready to embark on my new experiences. I would soon be heading off to Harrison Junior High School in Merrillville, have new friends from other local elementary schools, who would also attend Harrison.

Another Ohio State football season would be underway as well. The Buckeyes would enter the 1980 season ranked #1 in the country. I was looking forward to these new experiences as well as playing another year of youth league football.

I was going to enjoy my last summer before the start of my seventh-grade school year. I played little league baseball and hung out with all my friends before the start of junior high school. They came over and we played basketball in the driveway. Staged whiffle ball tournaments almost every day that summer. I am not sure whiffle ball is popular with kids today, but it sure was back in the early 1980s.

As I journey back to Merrillville nowadays, I don't see many kids playing outside and engaging in the summer games that we enjoyed growing up in the early 1980s. It was also a time of meeting new girls at the local public pool known as Ross Pool. Located a couple of streets over from where I lived on Johnson Street. Every kid around town went to Ross Pool. It was equal to going to the roller-skating rink in Merrillville. We had a pool in our backyard on Johnson Street, and we spend many afternoons that summer swimming in it. On the other hand, there was nothing like going to Ross Pool.

My sisters, Nikki and Erin, always had their little friends come and swim in our backyard pool. When you are going into junior high, the last thing you want to do is hang out with your sisters and their friends! My mom would give me two dollars to head to Ross Pool in the afternoon. Dad had purchased me a used ten-speed bike that year, and I would ride it to the pool with my friends, Daenan and Tommy.

Rick didn't live in the same neighborhood any longer. It was more convenient to go with my neighborhood buddies. It was during this summer that I noticed two girls who were there every day. Their names were Pauline and Patti. Both Pauline and Patti went to a Catholic school known as St. Peter and Paul. They were both entering the seventh grade like I was that coming fall.

At first, they had no idea who I was, or interested in meeting them. I would beg my mom every day to give me the two dollars so I could go see them at the pool. I asked one of their friends to go up to Pauline and Patti to see if they wanted to meet me. I remember liking Patti, because she had blonde hair and was very pretty. She also had braces on her teeth like my previous girlfriends, Kelli and Karen. For me, what attracted me was always girls who had blonde hair and braces on their teeth.

Pauline was a good-looking girl as well. She was really tan and had brunette hair. When my friend Daenan and I finally worked up the nerve to talk to them, it was Pauline who was mostly interested in meeting me. Now when I say that we worked up the nerve to talk to them, I am referring to talking to Pauline and Patti on the phone. They wrote down their telephone numbers to give to us, and we called them the next day. I would talk to Pauline for hours and hours on the phone. Just your typical conversation about school, sports, interests, activities, dating, etc…

The weird thing was that we really didn't see each other in person. We just stared at one other at the pool. Pauline asked if she could ride her bicycle to my house one day and we could just hang out to get to know each other. She had also asked if I was ready to kiss her!

That was really awkward since we never saw each other face to face, I thought!

Of course, I said it was alright for her to come over to my house one afternoon. I think I was more nervous than any baseball or football game that I played in.

I waited outside on Johnson Street for Pauline to come over to the house. I still remember what I was wearing that day. I was wearing my #24 Ohio State jersey that my dad bought me at the local *Sportmart*.

It was the same jersey that I wore in youth league football that Coach Andy Tancos would tease me about when I would make mistakes in practice. I think the jersey gave me confidence, and wearing something that said "Ohio State" would make Pauline like me even more. I am not sure why I thought that, but I felt that all kids should like Ohio State. That couldn't have been further from the truth.

I listened to the song, *"Steal away"* by music artist Robbie Dupree right before Pauline was supposed to come over. It's funny that a person is able to match up songs with the events of their life. The song was often played over the loudspeakers at Ross Pool. Pauline was very attractive. I was scared to death of her. She was absolutely beautiful as far as a thirteen-year-old girl goes. Maybe it was because I thought she was way out of my league in terms of looks, or that I didn't know her that well.

At any rate, she was coming over to see me, and possibly be my girlfriend. I asked myself what Art Schlichter would do? After all, he was the star quarterback at Ohio State, and was dating one of the attractive Buckeye cheerleaders. I thought that if Art Schlichter was good at football as well as with the girls… I could be just like him.

Art was now my hero going into junior high school. He was set to lead the #1 ranked Ohio State Buckeyes that year, and I was set to lead the Merrillville Pop Warner Youth football team. We were both star quarterbacks and going to date beautiful girls.

Well...he was a well-known star quarterback, and I was probably just a 'legend' in my own mind.

I wanted to be just like him. If he liked eating spinach, then so did I. If Art wore his hair a certain way, then so did I! Most importantly, since he was the star quarterback at Ohio State, I had dreams of someday being like him by leading the Buckeyes to a win against the hated Michigan Wolverines.

I saw Pauline riding her bike from a distance as she was approaching Johnson Street. I was sweating and not because it was a hot sunny day! What would I say to her? I mean I talked to her on the phone but this was different. What would happen if she didn't like me once we were finally face-to-face? What if she wanted to kiss me that day? I had a million thoughts racing through my head.

As Pauline was getting closer and closer to my house on her bike, I did what a lot of soon to be junior high kids did... I ran! Pauline didn't see me of course. I ran through the neighborhood yards to get to my friend, Daenan's house. Daenan looked at me kind of strange as if to say, *"You ran from a girl?"*

When you are that young, you really can't explain yourself or your actions. Pauline called me that night, and asked why I wouldn't meet her? Was I afraid to kiss her? I made up some terrible excuse.

You talk about opportunities lost in your life!

Here is this beautiful girl who wants to be my girlfriend, and I ran away from her to a friend's house? Well, that ended the summer of 1980, and Pauline said that she wanted to break up with me. I am not sure we were ever truly ever boyfriend and girlfriend.

Oh well... a new school year was starting as well as another year of Ohio State football. My optimism was high with both of these events ready to start in the fall of 1980. It was my first day as a seventh grader at Harrison Junior High School. I do remember sitting in the cafeteria waiting for the first hour bell to ring.

I had science class with a young teacher named Miss Onika. She quickly became one of my favorite teachers. Not that I was a good science student. I usually got the lowest scores on her tests. One of my new friends, Bucky Randall and I, were always placed in the last row of her class.

Miss Onika would have her seating chart based on how well you did on the science tests. The top students always sat up in the front of the room while the students who did poorly sat in the back of the room. I am not sure that would happen nowadays in school or would be allowed. Nevertheless, I really started to enjoy the subject of science because she was my teacher. I still didn't pass many of her tests though!

I had Mr. Steiner for World Geography during the second hour. I also liked him as a teacher mainly because he looked a lot like my dad. In fact, most of my classes were very interesting. It was just that I wasn't a very good student. Maybe it was because I didn't care or because of all the new girls in the junior high school. There were absolutely girls everywhere! So you could say that my focus wasn't on the academic part of school. I went to my English class, and a girl stared at me the entire hour. Every time I looked at her, she was smiling at me.

I leaned over to one of my friends and said, *"Do I have something on my shirt or is my hair messed up?"*

He shook his head and said, *"No, you dummy! I think that girl likes you!"*

A piece of paper was passed my way by this girl. I opened up the note and it had two boxes. The one box said, *"If you like me, check 'yes.'"* The other box said, *"if you don't like me, check 'no."*

Junior high was definitely going to be a different experience for me than my elementary years. I was too young to play junior high football that year. Harrison football was only reserved for eighth and ninth graders. I was hoping to play another year with Coach Andy Tancos and the Merrillville Youth Pop Warner League. It wouldn't happen.

Instead, I was chosen to play for Coach Harding in the fall of 1980. He knew I was a quarterback, and that I could play the position well. The first practice, Coach Harding had the team do a passing and catching drill.

Being a quarterback, my goal was to complete more passes than the person I was going up against in the drill. He said that the side who completed the most passes wouldn't have to do extra running after practice ended that day. I mean I was really doing a great job. All the coaches were patting me on the back as if I were the next great thing at the youth level, and that maybe I would someday play for Ohio State.

One coach said, *"Wow! Denny can really throw the football!"*

A funny thing happened that afternoon as we were wrapping up the football drill. Another kid named Rod stepped out of his parents' car, and came onto the practice field. Rod told Coach Harding that his parents were running late, and that he was sorry that he missed most of the practice. I had never seen Rod before, but he played the quarterback position, too. I believe Rod may have played for Coach Harding the previous season.

As luck would have it, Coach Harding told me to go to the other side that was losing the contest at the time. Rod stepped into my role, and was completing passes to the kids who were supposed to be on my side! I went to the other group, and completed a lot of passes as well. It just wasn't enough. We came one or two passes short of winning the drill. I thought Coach Harding would applaud me for my efforts, and not make me run since I did well for both groups. Nope! He told me that I was part of the losing side, and I would have to run with that group.

We ran around the practice fields for fifteen minutes without even stopping! Unfair? Yes. Rod became the starting quarterback that year for Coach Harding, and the Merrillville Youth Pop Warner team. The first couple of games that season, I never saw action on the field with the exception of a couple of plays in each game.

It came to a point that I didn't even want to show up to a practice or a game. Most of the kids on the team that year went to the 'other junior high' in Merrillville known as Pierce. I learned how much politics played in sports, and that I didn't attend the popular junior high school in town.

I am not saying that Rod was a bad player or that he couldn't handle the responsibility as a youth league quarterback. He was actually a good player.

When you are growing up, a lot of times it is who you know and not what you know. My dad never wanted me to quit anything. That is the belief that my dad had when playing sports or in anything you do in life. *Don't be a quitter!*

There may have been an exception to that rule because there would be one youth league Pop Warner game that I wouldn't even show up to because I had other plans that day.

In mid-September of 1980, my dad came home with some surprising news. He had just received two tickets to an Ohio State home game on September 20th from a friend of his—Tom Manning.

Tom was a football official in the Big Ten Conference, and was going to work the game. He was a colleague of my dad's at his school. Ohio State was set to play the Minnesota Golden Gophers, and I was going to be there!

This would be my second Ohio State football game in person, but the first time I would travel to Columbus, Ohio to see them in the famous Ohio Stadium. We would travel to see my parent's old friends Connie and Mike Weiss who now lived in Middletown, Ohio.

We hadn't seen them since they moved to Ohio in the mid-1970's. I also hadn't seen my childhood friend Craig going back to those early years growing up in Tucson, Arizona.

It would be an exciting weekend. I would get to see Ohio State and spend time with Craig. I arrived in Middletown on that Friday night to hang out with Craig and his brother Mike Jr. I asked my dad if Craig could go to the Ohio State football game with us the next day. Dad only received two tickets for the game. Seeing Ohio Stadium for the first time was going to be an unbelievable experience.

It was a sunny day on September 20th, of 1980, and the Buckeyes were set to play at 1:30 pm. Dad parked the car in a cow pasture not far from Ohio Stadium. It is now where the Schottenstein Center is located, and where the Ohio State basketball team plays. Dad bought Ohio State hats for us to wear that day prior to the football game against Minnesota. I also received my first Ohio State game program which I still cherish to this day. The game was a blowout as the Buckeyes went on to beat the Minnesota Golden Gophers by the score of 47-0. There were about 87,916 fans there that day.

Dad and I were two of them.

It was my first time to the Ohio State campus but I was hoping it would not be the last time. It was the most beautiful place that my eyes have ever seen. It was also the first time that I saw the Ohio State Marching Band in person. The sight of them marching into the stadium gave me chills up and down my spine.

If you haven't seen the Ohio State band, I highly recommend that you go in person, watch them on TV, or go to YouTube to view their performance.

The marching band's nickname is TBDBITL, which stands for the *Best Damn Band in the Land.* I got to witness *Script Ohio* for the first time, with the Tuba player or better known as the sousaphone player, dotting the "I" in the word OHIO which was spelled out by the band. I can't describe the feeling that was going through me at that moment. Dad just sat there with a big grin on his face. All those years of watching Ohio State on TV, and now I was there to see them in person!

That weekend, I was going to miss my youth league football game back at Merrillville, but I didn't care. After all, I wasn't going to play that much anyways. Coach Harding was going to play Rod at quarterback, and I was going to sit the bench. The Pop Warner game was the furthest from my mind. I was too busy being awe-struck at the sight of the Ohio State Buckeyes team. Even though it wasn't much of a game, I didn't want to leave the stadium that day. As a memory of that special day back on September 20th, 1980, I still have the Coca-Cola cup that dad bought me at the game. My dad's friend, Tom Manning, who officiated the game that afternoon, had Art Schlichter sign my program.

It simply said, *"To Denny Art Schlichter #10." Wow! The Ohio State quarterback actually signed my game program!*

I kind of lied to my friends by saying that Art knew who I was, and that he would be glad to sign my game program for all of them to see. I thought that would impress them as well as all the girls who went to Harrison. I really didn't know Art Schlichter personally but none of them had to know it.

When you are young, you are just trying to fit in with all the other kids in junior high school. I may have looked at that program a thousand times in the last forty years. It never gets old to me and the memories always come back to that day I spent with my dad in Ohio Stadium. There would be another time which would be more significant than my first game at Ohio Stadium in September of 1980. My dad would be at that game as well.

You will see later in the book how incredible that moment was in my life.

As for the rest of the weekend that year, we went back to my dad and mom's friend's house in Middletown, Ohio. I spent a lot of time with Craig when we got back from the game that night. We had a lot in common. It was like we were kids again growing up in Tucson. I just wished that we lived closer to each other or went to the same school.

We did talk about possibly going to Ohio State together someday, even though Craig was a Notre Dame fan. I wouldn't see Craig again after that weekend until he came to visit me in the summer of 1993. He and I always said that we would keep in touch during our junior high as well as high school years. We never did.

You make new friends and get wrapped up in your own life. I missed Craig but I miss him even more today.

The rest of the Ohio State football season provided a 9-3 record. The Buckeyes would lose to UCLA, Michigan, and Penn State. The Penn State loss would be in the Fiesta Bowl. I watched all three of those OSU losses on TV but the one that stung the most was the Michigan game. Losing to the Wolverines is one thing, but hearing it from your best friend, who is a Michigan fan, is another. Rick Keneson and I are best friends with the exception of one day every November when Ohio State plays the Wolverines. I don't call him on the phone and Rick doesn't call me.

We resume our friendship once the game is over. Ohio State lost that November to Michigan by the score of 9-3. The Buckeyes actually had a 3-0 lead but didn't score the rest of the afternoon.

The Wolverines great wide receiver, Anthony Carter, caught the lone touchdown in the game. That was the only score Michigan needed to defeat the Buckeyes. Ohio State followed up that loss with a December 26th defeat in the Fiesta Bowl.

I believe it was one of the few times that the Fiesta Bowl wasn't played on New Year's Day. Even though Ohio State lost the game, that is not what was significant about December of 1980. There would be a tragedy that shook up the country and the music world.

On December 8th, 1980, the music star and a one time member of the famous group known as the *Beatles,* was shot and killed by a crazed fan. His name was John Lennon and his music was still popular in the early 1980's. It happened on a Monday. I was walking home from school on a rainy day when I first learned of his death.

Mom came into my bedroom and told me that he had been assassinated. I couldn't believe something like that could ever happen to someone. I sat in my room stunned. I listened to John Lennon's song, *"Watching the Wheels"* when it was released after his death.

That song played on the radio over and over again. Whenever I hear it today, I think back to the time when my mom entered my room to tell me that John Lennon had been killed. I don't know why that affected me at the time, but it just did.

Of course, I knew that wasn't true based on my own accident back in May of 1976. The rest of my seventh grade year became a nightmare as well. I never did finish out the season in my second year of Merrillville Youth Football in the fall of 1980. It was really the only time I actually quit a sports team. I also was cut from the Harrison Junior High School seventh grade basketball team that November. It was a big deal back then because that was one of the few sports a seventh grader could play at Harrison.

Rick made the basketball squad that year, and played center on the team. I was told by the coach that I didn't make the team because I couldn't dribble with my left hand. That made me really mad. I vowed that I would make the Harrison basketball team the next year as an eighth grader.

I always hated it when someone told me I wasn't good enough or that I couldn't do something that other kids could. It made me want to work even harder to prove them wrong. I just wish that I would have worked harder on my schoolwork at the time.

I practiced the entire winter in my basement dribbling a basketball with my left hand as well as dribbling through my legs. People told me I wouldn't be able to use my right hand after my accident in 1976.

It was my left hand dribbling a basketball that was holding me back. Due to the fact that I didn't make the team as a seventh grader, I was kind of seen as an 'outsider' in school.

Chapter 8

The Wonder Years

It was my first year at Harrison Junior High, and I was no longer seen as a sports person. I hadn't finished my youth football season that year and now I was cut from the basketball team. I was just going to school every day, and coming home on the bus.

Rick was enjoying his first taste of junior high athletics. I wasn't involved in anything school-wise. I tried to fit in with other seventh graders but was often bullied by some other kids. This one kid named Tim would punch me in the arm during choir class every time the teacher wasn't looking.

Another time, in February of that year, I was sitting at the lunch table before school that day. At Harrison, all the students sat in the cafeteria before school started, socializing with their friends and girlfriends. Besides Rick, I really didn't have many friends in the seventh grade. It was like fifth grade all over again.

There I was sitting at the lunch table before school started in February of 1981. I wasn't bothering anyone and was really just minding my own business. I was wearing a red Ohio State stocking cap, mainly because it was cold outside. I hadn't taken it off my head yet.

All of a sudden, this one kid named Mark, who I hung out with a few times, took my Ohio State stocking cap, and threw it up to the ceiling. It actually stuck to the tile above the Harrison Junior High ceiling. I took his hat and tossed it in hopes that it would get stuck to a ceiling tile as well. If Mark was going to take my Ohio State hat, and throw it up to the ceiling, then I was going to do the same thing to his hat.

A lot of the other kids at the table were laughing because he threw my OSU stocking hat up into the ceiling. I had received it as a Christmas gift that winter from my grandparents, Grammy and Papa.

Mark didn't like the fact that I threw his hat up to the ceiling. He got right up from his chair, and started punching me in the head. I had no other choice but to get up, and shove Mark right back. I really should have punched him as I probably could have knocked him out. I believed that I could have due to all the boxing matches that my friend Craig and I staged earlier in our childhood back in Tucson.

But I just shoved him down. Mark got back up again, and I shoved him down again! By this time, the teachers at Harrison broke up the fight, and sent both of us to the office to meet with Principal Martin.

Mr. Martin sat there listening to what the fight was about, and told us that both would receive consequences. I never thought that was fair since Mark started the fight, and threw my Ohio State stocking cap to the ceiling.

I am sure Principal Martin meant well, but it just didn't come across that way. Mark and I were both paddled with a board for getting into a fight. They called it 'corporal punishment' or simple a "swat." It didn't hurt much, but it was embarrassing.

Most kids in school that day knew that both Mark and I got paddled for the fight. The girls just smirked at me and shook their heads. I didn't get in trouble at home because I stood up to bullying at school.

Sometimes you have no other choice than to fight back. I never did talk to Mark again nor did he ever bother me in the future. It is something that I don't regret. I stood up to being bullied by another student in school that day.

Most of the rest of my seventh grade year was a blur. I remember sitting at basketball games that winter watching Rick and the rest of the seventh grade boys play on a team that I thought I was good enough to be part of.

In February of 1981, when we played our rival school, the Pierce Junior High School "Pacers" in basketball, kids would get out at 12 pm from class to watch the game in the gym. Principal Martin gave you a choice to go into the cafeteria for a study hall or go to the main gym to watch the game.

We beat Pierce in an upset that year. The gym was packed with students that day, and my friend Rick got to experience a great victory. As I looked on, I so badly wanted to be part of the team. I vowed that I would play basketball against Pierce Junior School. Maybe basketball would become my main sport. Maybe I put too much emphasis on playing football. Only time would tell if either football or basketball would be my main sport, or maybe it would be neither.

I did go out for the Harrison Junior High Track & Field team that spring of 1981, and made the team. Everyone who came out for Harrison Track & Field made the team. Coach Feeney was our coach, and he made a real impact on my life. He taught me things in track & field that I didn't think I could do.

For example, how to long jump as well as high jump. I also started running sprints. I really liked running track for Coach Feeney. He made the sport fun, and made me feel part of the team. I remember him teaching me how to high jump over this iron bar. We didn't have fiberglass bars like they do nowadays for the high jump. You really had to make it over the crossbar, or you would land with the iron bar on your back. *Ouch!*

Coach Feeney taught me a technique for the high jump known as the *'fosbury flop.'* He would stay late after practice showing me how to do all the events in track & field. Years later, I saw him on a golf course in Merrillville.

I was playing golf with some friends. He had since retired from Merrillville School Corporation and Harrison Junior High School to focus on just enjoying the rest of his life. I thanked him for being part of my own life, and showing interest in me not just as an athlete, but as a person. He made my otherwise turbulent 7th grade year more enjoyable in the end.

Thank you, Coach Feeney!!

Since I no longer was playing little league baseball or youth football, I would now be participating in school sports the following fall at Harrison. The 7th grade year ended in June, and we always had a major tradition in our neighborhood on that last day of school. A lot of my friends would go to the local grocery store known as "Eagle" when the last school bell sounded to signal the start of the summer.

We would go there to buy shaving cream and a carton of eggs. This was not for personal hygiene or to eat, however. We would use both the eggs as well as the shaving cream to spray or throw at each other. Everyone in the neighborhood would have them, and usually we would form teams. We would hide, and then run out when we saw a person from the other team, and douse them with shaving cream or throw eggs at them.

Usually it was boys versus girls. All the kids on Johnson Street as well as the other streets close by, would join in on the fun. We did this tradition all throughout junior high school. It is one of the times in my life that I truly miss. It was a day we always looked forward to that symbolized the start of summer vacation. Even though my seventh grade year didn't go exactly the way I wanted it to, I was looking forward to eighth grade. Maybe things would be different.

I ended the school year with the grades of one B, three C's, and two D's. Not exactly the marks to get into college. At that point, I am not sure I even cared. My attitude about school wasn't exactly a positive one and my chance to someday attend Ohio State looked bleak.

The summer of 1981 was just about hanging out with friends, and getting ready for the 8th grade. Rick would come over, and we would play whiffle ball for hours in the front lawn, or shooting basketball in the driveway.

It may have been the one summer where I didn't have a care in the world. I didn't have a girlfriend to worry about or homework assignments. My day consisted of getting up by ten o'clock in the morning, and playing all day long in the front yard or at a friend's house.

One of my friends, Steve Civanich, would have these neighborhood sleepovers ever so often where all the neighborhood boys would come over to spend the night. We would play flashlight tag, cook marshmallows in his backyard, and have pillow fights before bedtime.

Steve's mom would make this dessert known as apricot tarts. They may have been one of the best desserts that I have ever had in my life! It is the little things in life that you remember the most.

You gain a lot of friends as well as memories that you look back on, and realize that it was truly the wonder years of your life. Nowadays, I often hear young people comment on the fact that they wish they were all-grown up and wanting to be adults. Time goes by too fast!

I believe that it was in the movie, 'Ferris Bueller's Day Off' when actor Mathew Broderick says… *"Life moves pretty fast. If you don't stop and look around once in a while, you could miss it."* As I get older…this quote is one of them that I live by every day.

By the fall of 1981, I would now be in the 8th grade at Harrison Junior High School. Most of my friends were going out for the 8th grade football team, and I was going to do the same. I was hoping the experience was going to be much better than my last year of youth football. Rick didn't play football. He was mostly into basketball. Coach Kobza was our 8th grade football coach. He was a big man, and had a very intimidating voice.

Of course, I thought I was going to be the quarterback of the team due to playing the position before in the youth league. I knew that Coach Kobza was going to go with a popular choice at quarterback with a fellow classmate named Brian Singer.

Brian was a great athlete and very popular with the girls. I still knew that I was one of the fastest kids in my grade, but since I didn't make the basketball team the year before, the coaches really didn't know me. Coach Feeney tried and tried to get me to do cross country that fall since I had a productive spring running on his 7th grade track team.

What Coach Feeney really didn't know was that you were not considered a popular student if you ran on the cross-country team. Nothing against cross country. The students, particularly the girls, didn't really go watch cross country meets. Playing football at Harrison Junior High was a big deal, and the girls in my grade had 'crushes' on the boys who played for the team.

If Brian Singer was to play quarterback that year... what position would I play? Running back? Wide receiver? Defensive back? Nope, none of the above! Coach Kobza asked us in a team meeting one day what position we wanted to play?

He looked at all of us and said, *"Who wants to play offensive tackle?!"*

For whatever reason, I raised my hand proudly in answering his question. Understand that I was probably about one-hundred and thirty pounds in the 8th grade. Coach Kobza never called you by your first name.

He stared at me for a second and said, *"Bunda...you are the starting right tackle on the offensive line! If you mess up playing that position, you will never play for me again and I'll kick you in the butt! Do you understand!?"*

I said, *"Yes, coach!"*

I think Coach Kobza was just excited that I volunteered to play the position. I didn't have to try out for the spot or anything. So from day one, I was practicing and starting on the offensive line at one-hundred and thirty pounds. Because I was now considered an offensive lineman, I started reading more and more about the position, especially about those who played at Ohio State. Jim Lachey and Joe Lukens were two of the players who I looked up to that played for the Buckeyes in 1981.

Even though Art Schlichter was, and still is my favorite player, I wanted now to be like an Ohio State offensive lineman. They always looked bigger than life on TV. I tried to eat a lot more food so I could look like them. Instead of eating three meals a day, I was eating about five to six meals. Mom would go to the Stack & Van Til grocery store to stock up on food.

No matter how much I tried to gain weight, I really couldn't do it. My mom and Grammy were great cooks, and I always had hot meals to eat. I guess that I really just couldn't put on the weight, and that I wasn't really meant to be an offensive-lineman.

Like many of my aspirations in life, I really didn't let anything deter me during my 8th grade year. I was an offensive tackle, and I was going to be the best I could be for the team. I remember getting a neck brace that wrapped around my shoulder pads, and arm guards to cover my forearms.

I didn't need them to play 8th grade football, but it made me look the part as a 'tough' offensive lineman. If you look at the picture section, I am wearing the neck brace while wearing jersey #62.

Coach Kobza ran more of a military boot camp than football practice while I played for him. I did like him as a coach. He always believed in me. I didn't want to mess up in practice to get on his bad side.

Like I said, coach was very intimidating.

Chapter 9

Early Life Lessons

During my 8th grade year, I was also introduced to a person who would become one of my favorite teachers of all-time. Her name was Ruth Homco, and she taught an 8th grade English class at Harrison. Rick and I had the same class together, and Mrs. Homco made the mistake of putting us right next to each other. She was always on my case about doing better, and wanting me to achieve higher goals. I can tell you right now that being a great student was not my priority.

Instead, my goal was to attend Ohio State not as a student, but to play football for the Buckeyes. Since Rick was a Michigan fan, I thought that maybe one of his goals was to be a college student at the University of Michigan. Throughout the years, he never really mentioned it as a goal or dream.

As for me, I dreamed of playing for the Buckeyes, and running out of the tunnel in the historic Ohio Stadium. I guess for most kids at Harrison Junior High growing up in Merrillville Indiana, this would be just considered a "pipe dream." Some kids cheered for them on television as the Buckeyes were a very popular college football team. It was just that kids would usually graduate from high school, and go to Indiana, Purdue, Ball State, Wabash, or another school within the borders of the state of Indiana.

I guess I never thought about going to any other school. The only problem was that I couldn't get the student-part down very well. Ohio State is an academic institution and not just a football school. I just didn't realize that at the time in my eighth grade year.

I had struggled in school mainly because of my early years at Shoemaker Elementary School in Arizona. I was behind academically compared to the other kids at Harrison. I wasn't an "F" student but just a very average or maybe a little below average person going through school.

Kids would often laugh at me when I told them I was going to attend Ohio State. They would laugh even harder when I mentioned that I was going to play football for the Buckeyes.

I think Mrs. Homco saw something in me as a student as well as a person. She was the one teacher in junior high that didn't accept me turning in late work or just going through the motions in her class. She was very tough on me. At first, I had no idea why.

Mrs. "H" once assigned a mythology group project as one of our major assignments in her 8th grade English class. Rick would be my partner for the project. We were assigned to research the *Greek Gods & Goddess*, and their roles in Ancient Greece.

Beyond that, I really couldn't tell you much about the assignment. Probably because Rick and I didn't do much work on the project itself. Mrs. Homco told us that we needed to do research at the old Lake County Library in Merrillville, and to ask the librarian there for help, if we needed it. I don't think we ever saw the librarian in there, and if we did... we surely were not going to ask her for help.

Rick's mom as well as my mom, would drive us to the library to work on this so-called research paper covering the Greek Gods. Most of the time, Rick and I were clowning around playing leap frog in between the rows of books, watching movies on the portable TV's in the basement of the library, or eating at the small cafeteria in the bottom level. We did everything but the Mythology report that Mrs. Homco had assigned to us.

We went to the library many times during the week or weekends to get absolutely nothing done. Both Rick and I received a D- on the Mythology report when it was returned to us the following week.

I wasn't really angry at Mrs. Homco. I guess I didn't care much about doing well or if this report would have any effect on me getting into Ohio State. After all, I was going to Ohio State to play football... not to study about Greek Mythology.

Rick may have been more upset than I was, and probably told me that we should have taken this paper more seriously. I mean, really? Greek Mythology? Did I really care what we got on some dumb paper? As it had often been said by many of my teachers... "You go to school to learn how to learn."

I was about to learn some important lessons in life.

Playing offensive tackle for Coach Kobza probably wasn't going to help my case in becoming an Ohio State football player either. I never came out of the game while playing 8th grade football for him. Our team wasn't very good. We would finish with a 2-6 record in 1981.

The one game I remember most was going up against Pierce. To me, this was equivalent to the Ohio State vs. Michigan game. We didn't like Pierce Junior High and they didn't like us either. We didn't really know many of the kids from Pierce nor did we really have any reason to hate them. I knew a few of them while I played youth football for Coach Tancos and Coach Harding. Rod was the Pierce quarterback that year in 1981.

Yes... the same quarterback that played over me in my second year of youth football during 7th grade.

Right before the game, one of our other coaches at Harrison came into the meeting room, and slammed his fist into the blackboard. His name was Coach Atria. He was one of the most intense coaches that I had ever seen! I believe Coach Atria liked Michigan so naturally he would joke with me about Ohio State. He told us that the game with Pierce was more than just a game...

This was a rivalry!

He told us that we would have to play our best game to beat them. Coach Atria really fired us up as a team. Those years that I went to Harrison Junior High, Pierce was the equivalent to what I thought of Michigan. The game was so intense and we really didn't lose by that many points to them. I also played defensive tackle in the game because one of our other players got hurt. I had to line up against a player named Jim Bittner from Pierce.

I believe Jim's grandfather worked at the same steel mill company that my grandfather (Papa) worked in. Even Papa was teasing me the day before the game on how tough Jim was as a player! Guess what? Jim was a great player and drove me into the ground many times during the game.

I pretended that I was Joe Lukens from Ohio State during the game versus Pierce, and that nothing could stop me. Jim Bittner and the rest of the Pierce team did stop me and the rest of my teammates that night in the Harrison vs. Pierce rivalry game of 1981.

Coach Kobza was really tough on us the rest of the junior high football season. I remember we had this player named Dan who always messed up a play in practice. For whatever reason, Dan kept going the wrong way. Coach Kobza asked him why he continued to mess up the play? Dan just shrugged his shoulders at Coach Kobza. Well, Coach Kobza absolutely started screaming and yelling at Dan.

Coach Kobza said, *"If Dan doesn't know the play then everyone will run the rest of practice around the field!"*

He told us that we were going to run until Dan figured out why he was running the wrong way. Dan never figured it out and so we ran and ran and ran. I did miss playing for Coach Kobza after the season was over. I have to admit, he did have some bizarre ways of teaching us football and making game decisions.

We had these plays called *Choo Choo Right and Choo Choo Left,* when one of our biggest players on the team would run the ball. Another time, he had the 'team vote' during halftime on whether we wanted one of our teammates named Paul to play in the second half of the game. Couldn't Coach Kobza just make the decision? The player wasn't in trouble or anything. Coach Kobza just wanted to see if we wanted him to play or sit the bench.

I often wondered if the Ohio State coaches made decisions like that, or if they had plays called *Choo Choo Right or Choo Choo Left?* Of course, Ohio State was on their way to a much more successful season than the Harrison Junior High team of 1981.

The Ohio State Buckeyes would finish 9-3 in 1981 but who they beat that year became more important to me.

On October 31st, 1981, most kids in Merrillville were gearing up for another year of Halloween and a night of trick or treating throughout the neighborhood. Even kids in the eighth grade were still involved in this ageless tradition that takes place every October. For me, I headed off to Ross-Ade Stadium in West Lafayette, Indiana to watch Ohio State play the Purdue Boilermakers. We would be going with my dad's friend Art Hixon and his son Brian.

Brian's mom actually was the person who taught my mom how to drive a car. My dad and Art Hixon taught together for a while before Art decided to get out of teaching, and enter into the home improvement business. Brian Hixon and I went to school together since our elementary days at Miller.

Our tickets were in the corner of the end zone. Ohio State entered the game with a 5-2 record. They had lost to Florida State and Wisconsin in back-to-back weekends in early October. Any chance that I got to go to an Ohio State game, it really didn't matter what their record was at that point. It was a nice sunny day during the game. Purdue had an identical 5-2 record.

There was a full crowd at Ross-Ade Stadium. The Boilermakers were going for the upset. Purdue had a great quarterback that year named Scott Campbell. Him and Art Schlichter would battle all afternoon to see which quarterback would come out victorious for their team.

Purdue had two players from Merrillville that year... Tim Seneff and Tom Jelesky. Both of them had played on Merrillville High School's state championship squad in 1976. During the game, I would not be cheering for them as they were playing against my team, The Ohio State Buckeyes!

Since a lot of my friends liked Purdue, I really wanted the Buckeyes to win this game. The last time Ohio State played the Boilermakers was when I had Mrs. Staniszeski as a teacher in the 5th grade. Not to bring up bad memories but Ohio State lost that game 27-16. I didn't want the Buckeyes to repeat that performance, and for me to go back home to face my teachers and fellow students.

It appeared that it could end up that way. Purdue took a quick 7-0 lead in the game. The Boilermakers then marched down the field again in the beginning of the second quarter, and seemed like they would score another touchdown. I know I was mad, and telling my dad that I thought Ohio State was going to lose. I kept kicking the seats we were sitting in and saying words that I shouldn't have said.

Once again, dad in his patient voice said, *"Relax, the game is still early."*

When Ohio State's Bob Atha kicked a very long field goal, my dad looked at me, and just smiled. It was as if he knew all along that the Buckeyes were going to come back and win the game. Dad has always had this calming effect about him while it came to watching Ohio State football games. He definitely was the opposite of me when watching a game. I often would scream, throw objects, and storm off to my room.

Dad always knew of ways to calm me down so I could enjoy the rest of the game. Like I have said throughout the book, I love Ohio State. I kept thinking during this game that there was no way I could go back home and face my friends and teachers if Ohio State lost to Purdue.

The Buckeyes would block a punt down near the area where we were sitting when the score was still 7-3. This obnoxious Boilermaker fan sitting to our right side was screaming and yelling! He thought the Purdue punter was interfered with during the blocked punt. He stood up and was shaking his fist in the air. My dad's friend, Art Hixon, took a piece of chewing gum out of his mouth, and put it on the Purdue fan's seat. The fan sat down right on the piece of chewing gum but didn't even know it! I always thought that was kind of funny.

A few plays later, Art Schlichter ran the football in the endzone for an Ohio State touchdown. Even though my friend Brian Hixon wasn't really an Ohio State fan, he was cheering along with me.

Brian was more of an NFL pro football fan, and liked the Minnesota Vikings. He talked about the Vikings and their upcoming game with the Denver Broncos. I acted like I was interested but I really wasn't. Didn't he know that I only cared about Ohio State?

A few minutes later we would be cheering again. When Ohio State got the football back, Art Schlichter threw another touchdown towards the end zone we were sitting in.

Again, my dad looked at me as if to say, *"I told you so!"*

When Tight End John Frank caught a touchdown pass from Art Schlichter at the end of the game, Ohio State would go on to win by the score of 45-33. I would go home happy but not until we went to a smorgasbord restaurant with Art and Brian Hixon. It was my third time seeing Ohio State in person, and each time the Buckeyes came away with the victory.

Dad made it a point since 1979 that we would at least go to one Ohio State game every year. Even though that game with Purdue was important to me, watching high school football with my grandfather (Papa) became more important that year in 1981.

My grandfather would take me to a different high school game every week in the fall of 1981. He worked at Inland Steel in Gary, Indiana. It was a difficult job but he never complained about it. I guess Friday nights were his way of getting away from the hassles & stresses of his job.

More importantly, to spend time with me.

Every week, he would check the local newspaper to see what the so-called 'game of the week' was in Northwest, Indiana. Keep in mind, I was now growing up in Merrillville. Most kids I went to school with were going to their high school games.

I knew Rick would go see Merrillville every Friday night to cheer on the Pirates. I even had a neighbor on Johnson Street who was on the team that year. I wasn't a huge Merrillville Pirates fan even though I lived in the community. I guess I actually cheered against them on most Friday nights because I knew Rick really liked them. I was always cheering against a team who Rick liked just to make him mad.

Some best friend, huh?

Papa and I would select one high school game that we thought would be exciting on Friday night, and attend that one. We did go see Merrillville play that year but sat on the opposing team's bleachers. Can you imagine that? I was a student in the Merrillville school corporation but sat on the opposite side.

I had seen an article in the paper about how good the Portage Indians were, and that they could go undefeated. Believe it or not... I started cheering for one of Merrillville's biggest rivals, the Portage Indians! While all my friends sat on the Merrillville side, Papa and I sat on the Portage side with their parents, students, and fans. Portage lost to Merrillville that night, and I was upset—don't know why.

Maybe it's because I wanted to be different from the other kids at school. Maybe it's because Rick loved Merrillville so much and I wanted another sports rivalry with him. We already had the Ohio State and Michigan debate between us. I have to admit that I would 'rub it' in his face every time the Merrillville Pirates would lose in sports. The funny thing was I knew that I would eventually go to Merrillville High School, and be a Pirate myself.

Papa and I would go to more games during the fall of 1981. I do remember a lot of those games that year, and what teams were playing as well as who won. The most fun were the times after all those high school games when Papa and I would go to the local *Dunkin Donuts* for a treat. This is when I got to spend the most time with my grandfather who I had always known as Papa.

When you are young, you have no idea how important and precious those times are in your life. As the years go by, I wish I could go back to those Friday nights that I spent with him.

My grandfather may have or may not have liked football. He really never said one way or the other. I do know that he loved just spending time with me, and whatever I liked to do in life. My grandfather was one of the nicest people that I have ever met. He didn't have a 'mean bone' in his body.

I am sure that I said thank you to him for every Friday night game we attended that year. As a young person, I don't think you fully understand the magnitude of the moment. I really miss those times with him. Papa and I would never really go to another high school game together again after that season.

Here is a lesson for everyone reading this book: Take the time to be with your parents and grandparents. If I could go back in time, I would have appreciated those Friday nights a little more with Papa. I didn't take them for granted. It's just that I didn't realize how significant those moments were with him.

Thank you, Papa for always being there, and spending those Friday nights with me in the fall of 1981 watching high school football.

As fall turned to wintertime in Northwest Indiana, I once again was going to try out for the Harrison Junior High basketball team. I didn't make the team the year before, so I wanted to work as hard as I could to make the squad. My friends, Rick Keneson and Brian Portlock, were on the 7th grade team and they were definitely going to make the team in the 8th grade. I, on the other hand, had a lot to prove to the 8th grade basketball coach, Mr. Conley.

When he finally called my name as one of the thirteen boys to make the team, I was filled with excitement. I may not have been the best player on the team, but I hustled and gave a lot of effort. I think Coach Conley appreciated that. He wanted players who were not lazy on his team. Making the team was one thing, but playing in a game was another.

My excitement soon turned to resentment and bitterness because Coach Conley really never played me that much in the games.

The game I remember most that season was against Lake Ridge Junior High. They were known as the "Lakers" and coached by Dennis Bunda. Yes...you heard that right. Dennis Bunda, as in, <u>my</u> father!

By 1981, my dad had moved from teaching at an elementary school to teaching and coaching at Lake Ridge Junior High School. He had a great team that year led by a player named Kenny Jones. Coach Conley gathering us in the bleachers in the Harrison gymnasium the day before the game to tell us that if we played great defense, we would beat Lake Ridge with very little problem.

I know this sounds terrible and not very team-like, but I actually wanted my dad's team to beat my school in the basketball game. Maybe it was because I wasn't playing that much or maybe it was because my dad was coaching the other team.

For whatever reason, I sat there listening to Coach Conley talk about how Lake Ridge wasn't that good, and we were the better basketball team. Coach Conley may have believed what he was saying, but I am not sure the rest of the team did. Lake Ridge absolutely demolished us the next night in a home basketball game in front of our students, cheerleaders, and families.

For three quarters of the game, I just sat there watching Lake Ridge run up and down the floor scoring points after points. I sat there silently cheering for my dad's team as the game got out of reach. All of a sudden, Coach Conley looked down the bench, and called my name.

He said, *"Denny, go into the game!"*

I couldn't believe he was now going to send me in the game when we were getting beat by over twenty points! I went into the game, and played the position of guard. I actually made a few points, and I played great defense against one of their top players named Chris Martin.

After the game, I shook my dad's hand as both teams lined up for the customary handshake. Deep down, I wanted to tell my dad that I was cheering for his team. Later that summer, I would go to a basketball camp with a lot of those players on dad's team that year.

I did get into more basketball games after that Lake Ridge game that night. Coach Conley started believing that I wasn't that bad of a player. I never asked him though on what he thought of my basketball skills.

You really never question the coach's intentions on why you weren't playing, back then. Truth to be told, I wasn't that great of a basketball player, but I always tried. In that 8th grade basketball season during the winter of 1982, we would travel for a 12 pm weekday basketball game versus our rival, the Pierce Pacers.

Just like the year before, students got out of school at noon to watch the basketball game in the gym. Unlike last year, this year's game would be played in front of the Pierce Junior High student body. We had lost to them in football, so beating them that winter in basketball became a big deal. During the game, Pierce's student body was right behind our bench. The students were literally a row behind us!

They would say profane words to us, and pound the bleachers with their feet to make noise. They even gave a few of our players 'wedgies.' I am not sure that junior high schools have games in front of the whole student body like they used to in the 1980's.

Even with all the Pierce kids shouting, stomping on the bleachers, and yelling obscenities at our team, we were playing a good game. I didn't think I would get to play because I usually sat on the bench.

Coach Conley looked down at me. *"Denny... you are going into the game."*

What?! Here I am sitting next to my best friend, Rick Keneson on the bench, and Coach Conley wants me to go into the game? I have to admit that before the big game, and had no chance of getting any playing time against Pierce.

Maybe Coach Conley thought I could help the team or he was upset with how the other players were performing against our rival school. For whatever reason, I went into the game in front of a fully packed gymnasium of students. I immediately thought that if the Ohio State Buckeyes could play in front of a lot of people in a 90,000-seat

111

stadium and millions who were watching them on TV, then I could surely play in front of roughly 850 opposing junior high students.

I knew that Art Schlichter was a basketball player during his high school playing days in Ohio, and a star for his team. Once again, I pretended that I was going to save the day for the Harrison Patriots just like my hero, Art Schlichter may have done for his school.

When I got the pass from one of my teammates, I shot it at the basket. I missed but I was fouled on the play. The crowd was really loud and obviously cheering against us. I was going to the free throw line for two shots. How hard could it be?

Therefore, I knew that I could hit both shots, and help my team possibly win. With 850 screaming and extremely loud Pierce students on their feet, I made the first free throw! That should shut all of them up, right? Wrong! It just made them cheer louder as I attempted my second shot. I could actually feel the floor rumbling below my feet. As I stood there at the free throw line, I concentrated on the second shot. I thought I could actually be the hero in this rivalry game versus Pierce!

I bounced the ball off the gym floor a couple of times, and then lifted the basketball up, and attempted the second shot. I would like to tell you that this part of the story had a happy ending. My second free throw shot didn't go in the basket. So much for being a hero, and so much for staying the game.

Coach Conley took me out, and we went on to lose to the Pierce Pacers just like we did in football. There was also a Pierce girl student right behind me on the bench who shouted, *"You suck, Bunda!"* I had no idea who she was or how she knew my name.

Badly, I wanted to beat Pierce. We had always heard how great they were in sports, and all the athletes that came out of their school. I really felt that losing to them was a lot like Ohio State losing to Michigan in football or any other sport for that matter.

Ohio State would close out their 1981 football season with a 14-9 victory over Michigan, and a Big Ten Championship. Unlike me, Art Schlichter would be the hero in his game versus the Wolverines as he ran for the final touchdown to secure the victory. In fact, he scored both of Ohio State's touchdowns that day against the hated Wolverines.

What I remember most was the week leading up to the contest. It seemed like all the students in my school thought Michigan was going to win, and that Ohio State had no shot to pull the upset. I was in gym class that week, and one of the gym assistants named Mike, asked me who I was going to cheer for on Saturday? Didn't he know that I was a big Ohio State fan?

As we were stretching for gym class, I looked at him proudly and said, *"Ohio State is going to beat Michigan in Ann Arbor on Saturday!"*

Mike was a student assistant for our gym teacher, John Stefek. Like Mrs. Homco, Mr. Stefek was another one of my favorite teachers. Mike took a basketball and started bouncing it off my backside as I was stretching.

He kept saying to me, *"Say Michigan is going to win! Say Michigan is going to win!"*

I wasn't going to say that to him or anyone else. Rick Keneson seemed confident too that the Wolverines would beat Ohio State that weekend. I understood that it is not important what people think. It is more important what you are going to do about it. I really believed Ohio State would beat Michigan that Saturday.

As the game started, I realized that Michigan was indeed the favorite to win, and should have had little problem in beating Ohio State.

I believe someone once said, *"That is why you play the game."*

It doesn't matter what people say or who the favorite is in a contest, you still have to go out and play. A win by Michigan that day would have sent them to the Rose Bowl. If truth were to be told, the Wolverines actually should have won the game if I am going to be honest.

Whenever the Wolverines had a chance to pull away from Ohio State, they would make a huge mistake like an interception or fumble. In the end, Ohio State made the plays it needed for the great victory!

Ohio State would then beat the Navy Midshipmen in the Liberty Bowl by the score of 31-28 to end the 1981-82 season. I had to watch the game on a small portable TV in my bedroom because the game was broadcasted on a cable channel. The TV's had antennas on the top, and you had to move them right or left just to get a clear picture. A lot of times, mom had to put aluminum foil on the two antennas just so I could see the picture more clearly. There were many times that I watched sports, TV shows, and the old "Saturday Night Live" show on that old TV.

Most nights, I would fall asleep watching the show, *"The Honeymooners"* starring Jackie Gleason.

The TV was on a rolling cart so mom would also push it into my room on days that I stayed home sick from school or if I just wanted to watch a show after my homework was completed. I appreciated the fact that it was a luxury to watch TV in your room back in the early 1980's.

Chapter 10
Growing Pains

As spring started in 1982, I once again was going to run track & field at Harrison Junior High School. I started coming into my own, and realized that maybe track & field would be another sport I would enjoy, and possibly do well in school. A lot of that was due to Coach Feeney, and making all of us kids feel welcome on his track & field team at Harrison. He suggested one day that maybe I try the long jump.

How hard could it be?

You just run down a runway and jump into sand. I thought to myself that this is a 'piece of cake.' I had excelled for Coach Feeney the previous spring as a sprinter as well as a high jumper, and I could do the same in the long jump. I set my goals that spring to jump sixteen or seventeen feet. I not only wanted to be the best on my team but in the whole conference as well, including beating any kid from our rival school—Pierce!

In late April of 1982, our team was going up against Pierce in a track & field meet. I didn't want to lose to them again like we did in football as well as basketball that year. As the track meet started, Pierce had this one long jumper who seemed really cocky and arrogant. He was a fast kid and could also jump really far. I didn't talk to him much at the track meet that day. He just kind of glared at me as if I really didn't matter, walking past me without saying one word.

He wasn't letting anyone else practice the long jump before the meet started, especially those of us on the Harrison team. This kid seemed to ignore me when I asked him and the other Pierce jumpers if I could practice my jump before the meet started. He really didn't respond to my inquiry. His name was Mike Demakas, and he was one of the top athletes at Pierce. Everyone simply just called him, "D." Well, I won the long jump that day by beating him. He walked away really upset because he lost to a Harrison kid!

If the truth were to be told, I didn't really beat him. His jumps were always further than mine. He was absolutely an extraordinary athlete. I am not proud to say this but I actually cheated to defeat him that day in the long jump. Mike already had his marker in the ground so he knew how many running steps he needed to take before jumping off of the long jump board.

He may or may not know this by now, but I was the one who moved his marker back to throw off his steps to the long jump board. I guess in my mind that was the only way I was going to beat him in the event. I was always very competitive and I didn't want to lose the competition, especially to him or to Pierce Junior High!

The other reason was that he made me mad before the track meet with his junior high school arrogance. It definitely was not the right thing to do, and I knew that I really didn't win the long jump that day. I got the 'blue ribbon' for first place, and really didn't care at the time that I moved his mark.

If he was going to act that way again, I would do the same thing! After all, he was from Pierce, and we couldn't stand those kids from that side of the town. Later on, Mike "D" Demakas would become my teammate in high school. Let's just say that I got to know him pretty well at Merrillville.

In the fall of 1982, I was going into my freshman year in high school. It was during my freshman year at Harrison Junior High, when I really started thinking about playing high school football at one of the area powerhouse programs… the Merrillville Pirates.

I knew that there was no way I was going to be an offensive tackle or play any other position on the offensive line for that matter in high school. At least not at one-hundred and thirty pounds. I turned my attention to either be a quarterback again or a wide receiver who caught the passes. I knew that playing the offensive line was not going to impress the girls.

Throwing or catching touchdown passes would catch their attention. I also knew that if I was going to play for the mighty Merrillville Pirates next year, I would have to develop my skills as an athlete.

With the family's move to Merrillville in 1978, my dreams took a detour, and now I focused on being a Merrillville student-athlete. No offense to Griffith, but Merrillville had won a state championship a few years earlier, and everyone in town wanted to play for Coach Ken Haupt and the Pirates.

Before my freshman football season at Harrison, I had called my good friend Steve Civanich to see if he was going to play on the football team with me. Steve had never played youth football, but was a great baseball player. I used to go over to his house in the summertime to swim and hang out all day long. He lived on 54th Avenue in Merrillville not far from my house on Johnson Street.

Steve was a little league pitcher, and all of us neighborhood kids thought that he would eventually be a professional baseball player. Steve's dad wanted me to come over every day in the summer and play catch with him. His dad would say that he would have to pitch to me for at least an hour before we could do anything else.

Since I was a catcher in my last year of little league, I knew how to catch Steve's pitches. He was very good and my hand usually hurt for hours after I caught many baseballs for him. Steve would often chew tobacco while we were playing catch. I asked him if I could have some chewing tobacco while we practiced his baseball pitching. After a half an hour, I don't think I ever tried chewing tobacco, again.

When I called him on the phone one afternoon, I asked him what position he was thinking about playing for the Harrison Junior

117

High football team. Steve said that he wanted to try playing quarterback. I am not afraid of competition but since Steve could throw a baseball really well, I thought he would be a 'natural' playing quarterback for our team that season. I decided that I was going to try my luck at wide receiver, and catch all of Steve's passes. Harrison Junior High also had another great quarterback that year in Brian Singer.

The team was to report in August for two practices a day. Harrison had a new coach that year. His name was Coach Price. When I first met him he looked just like the former NFL Pittsburgh Steelers quarterback, Terry Bradshaw. He always wore a white baseball hat with a blue "H" on the front of it for Harrison Junior High.

Coach Price made us try out for our positions to see if that is where he was going to put us during the season. This was unlike Coach Kobza from the year before who took volunteers to play positions.

I kept thinking to myself that this is my shot at being a wide receiver when I reached the high school level. There were too many kids who wanted to play quarterback, and I didn't want to take turns playing the position. I knew that as a wide receiver that I wouldn't have to contend with too many kids.

As I was catching all these passes in practice from Coach Price one day, he said, *"Great job, Denny! You want to someday play for Ohio State, huh!?"*

My plans and dreams had changed as far as football goes. I once thought that I would be the next Art Schlichter at Ohio State. I set my sights on another Buckeye hero in wide receiver and tight end, John Frank. John wore #89 for Ohio State. When Coach Price asked me what jersey number I wanted to wear during the freshman season, I naturally said #89.

We had another coach on our freshman team that year by the name of Kevin Keough. Kevin had played high school football at Merrillville but it was his brother Kelly Keough who caught everyone's eye. Kelly Keough had been a star on the 1976 Merrillville state championship football team, and went on to play at Michigan for the legendary coach, Bo Schembechler.

Even though Kelly played for the Wolverines, I was in awe of him. Kelly coached the Harrison 8th grade team while his brother Kevin helped with our freshman team. Kelly actually played with Rick Leach, who was the player from Michigan that I couldn't tolerate, mainly because he always beat Ohio State.

Kelly Keough's presence as a football coach at Harrison Junior High made him an instant celebrity. Here was a person who actually played in the Big Ten Conference, played football for Michigan, and played against Ohio State!

As I was starting my freshman year at Harrison Junior High School, the Ohio State Buckeyes were also going through some major changes as well. Art Schlichter had moved on to the NFL, and was now playing for the Baltimore Colts. The Buckeyes had a young quarterback by the name of Mike Tomczak.

Mike wore #15, and that would be the same number given to my friend Steve Civanich while he played quarterback for Harrison. I highly doubt that Steve chose the number because of Ohio State's Mike Tomczak. Steve liked the Purdue Boilermakers, and would always emphasize the word, PUUURDUUUE!!

Practices were always fun with Coach Price. We may not have taken them seriously. I remember him giving us a demonstration on how to use a piece of football equipment known as a "blocking sled."

We all gathered around him. He hit this sled in an attempt to show all of us how to do it. Coach Price hit the blocking sled so hard that the toupee he was wearing fell right off his head! I didn't realize up until that point that Coach Price was bald, and he was wearing a wig.

We couldn't laugh at him. He would have gotten really angry and probably made us run the rest of the practice. During the season, all we talked about was Coach Price's toupee falling off of his head. We probably should have talked about how we could be a better football team.

After practices, the team would eat their lunch in the Harrison cafeteria, and would be served this delicious orange drink. It came in the same type of carton that schools served their chocolate or white milk in.

My teammates always commented during practice that they could hardly wait until it was over so they could go into the cafeteria to get some of that orange drink. Maybe we should have been more focused on football practice.

When practices did end for the day, one of my friends Oscar Rodriquez and I, would go up to the mini-mart to get more food and hang out there. The mini-mart had video games such as *"Pac-Man."*

1982 was the year that the Pac-Man video game was really popular with teenage kids. The arcade games cost twenty-five cents. I don't know how much money I spent trying to get to the next level of Pac-Man but maybe I should have concentrated more on getting better grades in school.

Ohio State started the 1982 season by beating the likes of Baylor and Michigan State. Neither one of those games were on TV so I had to look at the bottom of the screen while Channel 7 ABC Sports would show the scores. The next three weeks after that may have been one of the worst stretches in Ohio State football history.

It all started on September 25th, 1982.

My mom scheduled a birthday party for me at the house with all my friends. I didn't understand why she would have all of them over on a Saturday. Didn't mom know Ohio State was playing a football game that day? Besides, my birthday was two days later on September 27th.

My dad just said, *"You know your mother!"*

ABC sports was televising the Ohio State versus Stanford game. I begged mom to have the party later on in the day. I was really upset with her for doing this on such an important day. The game was on at 11:30 am, and all my friends were to come over by 1 pm. My mom had scheduled us to go to the movie theater in Merrillville known as the *Cinema.*

We were to see some PG movie that no one cared about watching that day. Most of them just wanted to go to the movies because they knew teenage girls would be there. I couldn't blame them but I was focused on watching my team play on television. This was my team and my school. Most of my friends arrived as Ohio State was beating Stanford 13-0 at halftime.

I kept saying to my mom as well as to my friends, *"Can we go to the movie later on? Can I just watch the rest of the game?"*

My dad said that Ohio State was going to win. He told me to go with my friends on this special day. Dad said there are moments in your life that you will never get back. So, off we went to the theater to see a movie.

When my friends and I got in there, most of us didn't want to see the movie that my mom had chosen for us. I think it was called *Beastmaster*, which was rated PG. I don't think mom realized that we were now freshman, and not little kids anymore wanting to see a PG movie. I really believe that she wanted me to stay young forever. There was another movie that day called the *"Class of 1984"* which came out in the fall of 1982. It was an "R" rated film so a lot of us had to sneak our way into the movie past the usher and ticket taker.

It was a movie about a teacher who had to take on this punk gang of high school students or something like that. I have to admit that the movie took my mind off the Ohio State game that afternoon. Not that the movie was that good. It was just being around my friends doing stupid things. For example, throwing popcorn at older high school girls who sat a row in front of us to get their attention. Well…we got their attention alright! One of the high school girls took my popcorn out of my hands and threw it in the garbage. Hey…I paid money for that! Her response…

"I hate being around children!"

Children, huh? Well, maybe we were trying to stay young just a little while longer. After all, we were still in junior high school.

Like my dad said, Ohio State was going to win anyways so what was the big deal in missing the second half of the game? Wrong! When all of us returned from seeing a movie that we weren't supposed to watch, my dad had some bad news. Ohio State had lost to Stanford by the score of 23-20.

My facial expression told it all. I was absolutely stunned. Even though my friends tried to cheer me up, I was never good company when Ohio State lost. They could tell that my mood had changed quickly that afternoon. We still had birthday cake and ice cream but the day just wasn't the same. I know that Ohio State is going to lose occasionally and they can't win every game. It is just that it always has had an impact on my life.

On Monday, my health teacher and former 8th grade football coach, John Kobza called me to the front of the room.

He said, *"So Bunda, it is your birthday today?"*

I saw him take out a paddle, and he was going to give me a birthday spanking. He asked who my friends were in class. All my buddies in class were shaking their heads as if to say "no" because they knew that they would have to come up and get a paddling as well.

That was Coach Kobza's policy. If it was your birthday, you and your friends got paddled in front of the class. It was just a different time in the 1980's. When I named off all my friends in the class, they each got a whack from Coach Kobza.

When he got to me, the birthday boy, he gave me a light tap. I don't think my friends ever forgave me for that. Coach Kobza was just different.

There were many times that he would pass out a chapter test, and tell us not to cheat. He would leave the classroom, and wouldn't return for the rest of the class period. We all gathered around the smartest kids, and copied all the answers. I think Coach Kobza knew, but I don't think he really cared.

There were other times that he would have us read out-loud in his class. Most of the time I was day-dreaming about Ohio State or girls, so I never paid attention to when it was my time to read to the other students.

Coach Kobza would say, *"Bunda. It is your time to read, you idiot!"*

I would apologize and make up some lame excuse as to why I wasn't paying attention. It was a health class. We were reading a section about the body, how it functions, and how it adapts to change. As I was reading, I came across the word, 'Fatigue.'

While in class at Harrison, this term would often describe me. I mispronounced the word as if to say "FAT-A-Goo" in front of my peers. I looked around and saw all the students laughing at me, especially the girls in the class. I could have just died that day!

It was really embarrassing. Coach Kobza never let me live that down. He would always call me, *"FAT-A-Goo Bunda."*

Was I stupid or did I just not care about learning in school? There were many times that I was writing down Ohio State's starting lineups or trying to memorize all the players on the team, and copy them down in my school notebook. If you were to look at my school papers, it was filled with Ohio State information, but not one note about health class.

My English teacher, Mrs. Homco, took my laziness a little more seriously than Coach Kobza did. I tried to do the same thing in her class by writing the names of all my favorite Ohio State players, their hometowns, positions, and jersey numbers in my notebook.

Mrs. "H" would say, *"Ok, Buckeye! Go to the chalkboard, and put all your Ohio State information in complete sentences, and explain to the class... the noun, pronoun, verb, and adjective in your Ohio State sentence."*

She always called me, *"Buckeye."*

I think Mrs. Homco was trying to use my fandom for Ohio State to teach me English. It actually worked, and I started liking her class because of it. After I wrote the sentences on the board, she told me to go home, and write a paper on Ohio State football using nouns, pronouns, verbs, adverbs, adjectives, etc...

It was her way of getting me to learn English by using Ohio State football as my topic. I did get an (A) on the paper unlike the Mythology project that Rick and I wrote a year earlier for her class while in the 8th grade.

The Buckeyes would go on to drop the next two games against Florida State and Wisconsin. They were now 2-3 on the season, and fans were really upset with Ohio State's coach, Earle Bruce. My Harrison Junior High team wasn't doing much better either. In fact, we were a down- right terrible team. We may have been the worst team in the history of Harrison Junior High School. It seemed every game that we played, our team was getting beat by other junior high opponents.

I did play a lot and scored touchdowns for my school. One of the first games of the year was against a junior high team from Portage. My good friend, Steve Civanich, came into the huddle, and told me he was going to throw me the football on a pass play. Here was my chance at stardom.

I could see Steve drop back to pass and throw the football really far as I raced to catch it. When it fell into my hands, I ran as fast as I could to score the touchdown. I could hear the crowd cheering when I reached the goal line. This was my big chance to be a hero! All of a sudden, the Portage player caught up to me and tackled me to the ground. With the crowd still cheering, I had thought I scored for my team.

I ran all the way to the sideline jumping up and down celebrating my big touchdown with my teammates. As I came off the field, I was greeted by Coach Price.

I said to him, *"How about that touchdown, Coach!!"*

He looked at me and said, *"What the heck are you doing!? You didn't score! You were stopped short of the touchdown at the one-yard line! Get back in there, you idiot!"*

This was another embarrassing moment in my life. We didn't even score a touchdown on the next few plays, and lost the game by the end of the night. The game was played on the Merrillville High School field for some reason, and not on our junior high field.

It was really neat playing on the high school field, and I envisioned myself someday catching touchdowns for the Merrillville Pirates. All my teammates wanted to talk about was the fact that I made a complete fool of myself by thinking I scored when I was actually tackled short of the goal line.

I would forget my embarrassment later on that evening as all the students went out for pizza after the game at a place known as *Noble Roman's*. I would always get these breadsticks and cheese sauce to go with them. My friends and I would talk about the game and how we should have won, even though no one really believed it.

No matter how bad of a junior high football team we were, there were always Noble Roman pizza after our games. Junior high school dances. And, Ohio State football games on Saturday, if they were on TV.

I always had my mind on who Ohio State was playing on Saturday even while I was at those school dances on Friday nights. I never really missed a school dance during my time in junior high. *Why would I?* The main reason was the girls who were at these events. I had a girlfriend named Cheri but she was really just a friend. We had a lot of classes together at Harrison and had a lot in common.

Many of my other friends like Brian Portlock and Rick always told me that Cheri really liked me a lot. Maybe I didn't pay attention because of my other interests in life or the fact that I was always looking at the other girls in school. I could never take a hint really well that Cheri liked me, and wanted me to dance with her at these junior high dances. She would always ask me if I was going to the school dances on Friday night?

"Sure," I said.

Mainly because her friend Kelly Jo was going to be there. There were many times that I would "slow dance" with Kelly Jo. I don't know why but it really never materialized into a boyfriend/girlfriend type of relationship. It was Cheri who really liked me, and wanted to go out on a date. Cheri was very cute but I just considered her a good friend. As I was dancing with Kelly Jo, I could see Cheri looking at us. I just never knew that she liked me that much or I would have asked her to dance.

As the fall of 1982 rolled on, so did the Ohio State Buckeyes. Their 2-3 record started to improve one afternoon when they went to Champaign, Illinois to take on the University of Illinois *"Fighting Illini."* The game was not on TV. I thought Ohio State was going to lose that afternoon anyways so I headed to see my friend, Oscar Rodriquez. We were going to play a pick-up football game at the local church field by his house. Later that evening, I learned the Buckeyes pulled off the upset by the score of 26-21. I was wondering if my junior high team could do the same thing the following week.

As my Harrison Junior High School football career was entering the last game, we were set to play our rival school, the *Pierce Pacers*. I would again get to face my nemesis at the time, Mike Demakas. Mike also played the position of wide receiver just like I did. Our team went into the contest with a record of 0-7.

I also played defensive back against Pierce, so I got to match up against Mike Demakas or "D" as everyone called him. Like I said, I really didn't like him very much at the time. It was also my chance to outplay "D" in the game.

Steve Civanich came from the sideline after talking with Coach Price. Steve said that he was going to throw the football to me just like he did in the Portage game earlier in the year. I faked out the Pierce player who was covering me, and scored a touchdown to make the score 68-6. Our team was going crazy as if we were about to win the Rose Bowl. I looked up at all the students cheering in the bleachers for Harrison that night. All my teammates were hugging me and slapping me on the helmet.

"Way to go!!"

Would Ohio State ever get beat this badly, I thought? All the girls in the front row of the bleachers were waving at me and calling my name. I just couldn't believe that they were so excited about my touchdown catch. Didn't they know that the score was now 68-6? I mean we really got beat bad by Pierce that night but you would have never known it at the time. One of my teammates said that I had 'saved the day.'

From what?

A complete embarrassment of being shut out by the Pierce Pacers? There were a few girls at the game who asked for my telephone number. Maybe I was a hero. If not, they sure did make me feel good about myself. In terms of my junior high team, it was the most dejected that I felt after a game.

What an embarrassment.

The ride home after the Pierce game was complete silence. If there was ever a time that an entire team, as well as their coach, felt totally defeated... this was it. When we got off the bus back at our school, Coach Price asked us to turn in our football gear, and get the heck out of there! I am sure that he had harsher words for us that night.

He was really mad and embarrassed at the same time. He didn't even have us turn in our football equipment to the locker room. We were told to leave it in the gym and the coaches would take care of it. It was like Coach Price and his assistant coach never wanted to see us again. I can't say that I didn't blame them. Pierce Junior High really beat us badly, and at the time, seemed like the worst kind of failure.

My friends and I would again go to the Noble Roman Pizza Place to have our traditional breadsticks and cheese after we turned in our football gear. We didn't talk much about the game but just enjoyed spending time with each other. We didn't realize it, but our junior high football careers had just ended.

The next week in school, Principal Martin called a meeting, and met with all the members of the Harrison football team in a lecture hall. He stood there and stared at us for what seemed like an eternity. I mean what do you say to a bunch of junior high kids that just lost a game by 62 points? What he said next really shocked me.

He asked our team 'if Coach Price should be fired as the football coach at Harrison?'

What!?

A principal is asking a bunch of junior high school teenagers if their coach should be fired? He also told us a story about how he went to Indiana University, and they played against Ohio State in the 1950's.

Principal Martin said that he knew how we felt losing by such a lopsided score. He said that they got crushed by the Buckeyes and Coach Woody Hayes while he was at Indiana. While telling the story, he was looking right at me.

Principal Martin knew, just like everyone else, that I was an Ohio State fan. I just sat there in the Harrison lecture hall listening to him compare our junior high football loss to an Indiana defeat to the Ohio State Buckeyes in the 1950's.

The 1982 junior high football season was about playing the game I loved with my friends like: Brian Portlock, Steve Civanich, Bucky Randall, Oscar Rodriquez, Bob Gustafson, and others. It was definitely the 'wonder years' of our lives. What if our junior high was terrible in football? There were worse things in life after all.

In November of 1982, dad would get tickets to the Ohio State versus Northwestern football game up in Evanston, Illinois. This would be one of many trips that we would see Ohio State play the Northwestern Wildcats. The Buckeyes entered the contest with a 6-3 record after winning four straight games.

Northwestern wasn't very good in 1982 due to the fact that they only won a total of three games. My dad took me below the stadium to watch the Buckeyes come in and out of their locker room. I would pat the players on the shoulder pads and helmets. I kept telling them to 'beat Michigan!' I knew who we played the next week, and what it meant to Ohio State.

It was also special because I got to spend time with dad. He worked a lot by teaching school and coaching a variety of sports. I didn't get to see him that much. Going to Ohio State games was our way of spending time together.

The Buckeyes won that day by the score of 40-28. Ohio State running back Tim Spencer had a great game. It seemed that anytime Ohio State needed a big play, Tim came through for the Buckeyes.

Dad kept saying on the way home that Ohio State would have to play a lot better the following week to beat Michigan.

However, all I could think about was a Spanish test that I had on Monday in Mrs. Sanders' class. Before I could worry about Ohio State beating Michigan, I had to focus on how to do well on the test.

Spanish was literally a foreign language to me, and I lacked effort in that class as well. Mrs. Sanders was a great teacher but her class was very difficult. I would be lucky if I could get a (D). Why did I need to take Spanish anyways?

I wasn't going to college to take Spanish, but instead to play football. I did get a (D) on the test. Mrs. Sanders called my mom to tell her how happy she was that I was giving effort in Spanish class. I appreciated her doing that but I knew the truth.

When you are fifteen years old, there are more important things in life than learning what *"Cómo se llama usted"* means in Spanish. By the way, it means *"What's your name?" Thank you, Mrs. Sanders for teaching me Spanish.* Every day matters in life, and the lessons you learn from them.

Again, I just didn't realize the life lessons that were being taught to me at the time.

November 20th, 1982 was the Saturday that Ohio State was once again going to play Michigan in football. I had freshman basketball practice in the morning the day of this big game. Coach Braggs was my coach that year as I made the junior high basketball team for a second straight year. Rick was told that he couldn't play organized basketball any longer due to a heart murmur.

My mom had told me one day that she had talked to Rick's mom about his heart condition. I felt bad for Rick because I really wanted to play basketball with him. I realized that nothing in life is a given. Take the good moments with the bad moments. There is always going to be adversity in your life. For Rick, it meant that he could no longer be on the team. For me, Rick was always going to be my best friend, whether he could play sports or not. Sometimes a lot of your friends disappear when you are no longer involved in the same sport, club, or organization as them. That would not be the case with Rick and me.

Even though Rick was a Michigan fan, we would always have fun together. There would be only one day a year when he wouldn't be my best friend. On that day, I wouldn't talk or associate with him. It was always the day Ohio State played Michigan. The game in 1982 I would break my own rule. In fact, I called him at the conclusion of the game. It would not be a friendly conversation.

Everyone at school thought Michigan was going to win. Kids were betting on the game and harassing me about how much better Michigan was than Ohio State. They probably were not wrong.

All week long, I heard from the other students who were saying, *"Go Blue!"* and *"Beat Ohio State!"*

I am not sure many of them cheered for either team but they just wanted to harass me about the Buckeyes. Even the girls were in on it that week. How could I face my peers at Harrison if Ohio State lost? The game that weekend was all I could think about.

After the early morning basketball practice, mom had prepared a great breakfast of eggs, bacon, and toast with a glass of orange juice. I sat downstairs in our basement getting ready for the game when she brought me my meal. As she sat my food down on a TV tray, I started to cry. Mom looked at me and said, *"What is wrong, Denny?"*

I kept crying and said to mom, *"Ohio State is going to lose today!"*

I really believed that the Buckeyes had no chance to upset the mighty Michigan Wolverines. Mom always had this calming feeling about her as she told me that everything would be all right. After I ate the breakfast mom prepared for me, I was glued to the TV. I remember watching Ohio State come out of the locker room led by Coach Earle Bruce.

Earle had always been one of my favorite Ohio State coaches. It might have been because he was the coach of Ohio State during my years in junior high and high school. My heart was racing through my chest. Dad was not in my basement watching the game with me that day. Mom said that he was at Calumet working a basketball game or a wrestling match.

As the contest started, it looked more and more that Michigan indeed would win the game. The Wolverines would score first on a run by their great running back, Lawrence Ricks. When Michigan scored, my phone rang but I ignored it. I just knew it was Rick rubbing it in that Michigan was in the lead, and would win the game.

Ohio State fullback Vaughn Broadnax scored Ohio State's first touchdown, and the Buckeyes and Wolverines were now tied at 7-7. I am not sure I sat down the rest of the game. I have a tendency to pace the floor when the Buckeyes are playing, especially in close games. People have always asked me if I truly enjoy watching Ohio State while they're in a close game?

My answer is always that I enjoyed the game more once it is over, and only if Ohio State had won. During the game, I get lost with my emotions.

It has affected me whether Ohio State wins or loses. This game was no different or maybe it was. Like I said, all the kids at school were betting on the Wolverines to win the game. Michigan had many chances in the first half to beat Ohio State. They always seemed to turn the football over in key situations. The Buckeyes would take a 14-7 lead at halftime.

Was Ohio State going to hold on and claim a victory over Michigan? Was the weather going to get worse in Columbus, Ohio and the Buckeyes wouldn't be able to score any more points? These were the thoughts racing through my head at the time.

I knew that Ohio State had just two quarters left to defeat Michigan. How would it end? The Wolverines would tie the game in the 3rd quarter when Michigan quarterback Steve Smith scored, and it was now 14-14. I was all alone in the basement with no one to cheer with me or console me if the Buckeyes were to lose.

I will never forget that final quarter on November 20th, 1982. With the game on the line, Michigan wide receiver Anthony Carter fumbled the football. Tim Spencer would score the go ahead touchdown for the Buckeyes a few plays later.

All Ohio State had to do now was stop Michigan's offense, and run out the clock. Rich Spangler would kick a field goal, and just like that...Ohio State was leading 24-14!

What I remember most were the Ohio State fans running on the field before the game was actually over, and tearing down the goal post. I had tears running down my face as the seconds ticked down on the game clock. 5-4-3-2-1.... Ohio State had pulled off the upset!! I was literally crying my eyes out. I called my best friend Rick on the phone. After a few rings, he answered with a somber, *"hello?"*

I let him have it with all my jubilation and excitement!

I'm not sure exactly what I said to him, but I wanted to make sure he knew who won the game! Of course Rick knew who won the game, as he watched it with the rest of the nation. It is still one of the best Ohio State versus Michigan games in my lifetime. When people ask what games stand out as some of the best throughout my years as a fan, that one always comes up in conversation.

I could hardly wait to see my classmates on Monday, especially Rick.

Rick was still mad that Michigan lost for a second year in a row to the Buckeyes. I, of course, was smiling down the hallways of Harrison Junior High School. Since I was also playing freshman basketball that winter, I was hoping the season would go better than our Harrison football debacle.

We would have to face our rivals, the Pierce Pacers again but this time in basketball. Mike "D" Demakas was on the Pierce team, so I knew that we would get another shot at them. The freshman basketball team was made up of an "A" team and a "B" team that year. I was mostly a "B" team player but did get to play on the "A" team a few times.

During the "A" games, my friend Dave Hrabrich and I would sit on the bench and sing songs since we didn't get in the games that much. We would often sing the song, *"Ebony and Ivory"* by Paul

McCartney and Stevie Wonder. We also sang the song, *"The Girl is Mine"* by Michael Jackson.

Most of the time Dave and I were not paying much attention to what was going on during the basketball games. Coach Braggs came up to us during an all- important game and saying, *"Do you guys want to play or do you want to sing!?"*

I believe Dave responded to his question with, *"I think we would rather sing!"*

I don't think neither Dave or myself got in the game that day nor did we care. Coach Braggs seemed like a good basketball coach. It was just that by the time I was at the midpoint of my freshman year at Harrison, I realized it would be my last season playing basketball. After all, my dream was to someday go to Ohio State and play football for the Buckeyes. Maybe some of my friends thought I was a good basketball player but I knew I wouldn't play in high school. My friend Brian Portlock, signed my school yearbook that year...

"Denny, to a good basketball player and a great friend. I'm glad we got to be best friends, and I hope we can always be that way." Sincerely yours, Brian.

Brian, on the other hand, was a pretty good player. I really believe he would have gone on to be a great player in high school if it wasn't for the coach.

As for what Brian said about me being a great friend? Well, I guess I was a great friend in many ways but sometimes I let the 'girl situation' get in the way of my friendships. When growing up in the 1980's, it was important to be a popular person as well as to have a girlfriend. I had plenty of girls who I called a "girlfriend." However, those girls were simply innocent relationships.

Girls like Kelli, Karen, and Pauline were my first so-called girlfriends but nothing too serious. That all changed my freshman year at Harrison. I got word of a girl who was a year younger than me that wanted to 'date.'

Her friends started coming up to me and saying to *"ask her out."* When a guy wanted to ask a girl out on a date, he simply said to her, *"Will you go with me?"*

I just had one problem. The girl who liked me was actually Brian Portlock's former girlfriend. Her name was Lori. I chose to go out with her even if it may have bothered Brian. Some great friend, huh?

It was the first time that I would actually go out on a 'real date' with a girl. The trips to the local Dairy Queen with Kelli in the 5th grade didn't count. It wouldn't be the last time that I would date a girl who Brian Portlock also previously had dated. Once again, some great friend, huh?

Chapter 11

Harrison Happenings

I would be with Lori every Friday and Saturday night during the winter of 1983. I remember my dad even driving me to Lori's house on Valentine's Day to drop off flowers that I had purchased at a local floral shop. Actually, my parents paid for them. I didn't really have a job yet. It was a Monday night and I had to wait for dad to get home from work.

We sat in the car at Lori's house for what seemed like an hour. I could feel the palms of my hands sweating from nervousness. Dad just smiled at me. He probably knew what I was going through.

Finally, I got out of the car and rang her doorbell. I was searching for the words to say to Lori as I gave her the Valentine's Day flowers. When Lori answered the door, she had a smile on her face. She simply said, *"Thank you, Denny."*

Lori had this great smile with dimples in her cheeks. She had curly blondish-brown hair. Was I finally falling in love with a girl? I mean I am only in the ninth grade! What would Brian think when I told him I was falling in love with his ex-girlfriend? She gave me a kiss on the cheek as I handed her the flowers.

Lori then winked at me and said, *"I will see you on Friday night."*

Back in the car, dad said, *"Like her, huh?"*

Dad didn't even have to ask the question. He already knew the answer. The winter months of 1983 were spent dating Lori during my final semester at Harrison Junior High. She would pass me in the hallways with that smile on her face.

She would always say, *"Hello, Denny. Call me tonight."* As Lori walked away, she would always look over her shoulder and wink at me. I can't explain the feelings that I had for her but they were real.

I would sit in Mrs. Homco's ninth grade English class day-dreaming about Lori, and what we were going to do on the weekend. I think Mrs. Homco knew that I wasn't paying attention. So she would call on me again to go to the chalkboard and diagram an English sentence. She would just shake her head at me, and tell me that I wouldn't be able to go to Ohio State or any other college if I didn't do well in her class.

Mrs. Homco actually sent me down to the office that year for not taking her English class seriously. Can you believe that? She even called my mom on the phone! Didn't she realize that I had more important things to worry about? I wasn't worried about going to Ohio State for academics. I was going to be a football star at Merrillville High School next year, and earn a scholarship to Ohio State.

Mrs. Homco wasn't the only teacher who had concerns about me. I was flunking Mrs. Johnson's Algebra class and was doing just a little better in Mrs. Sanders' Spanish class with a (D.) They were all great freshman teachers and tried to help me out with my schooling.

Mrs. Johnson would even tutor me on her lunch hour because my mom had set it up to get extra help in math. My only concern was the weekend, and what Lori and I were going to do. What were we going to do? I wouldn't have my driver's license for another six months.

We would meet at a mutual friend's house on Friday and Saturday nights that winter of 1983. My mom would drive me and a few friends over to this other girl's house. Her name was also Lori, but a lot of us called her 'Froggy.' Unbeknownst to my mom, Froggy's dad was never home.

We always told my mom that her dad was home, and he would be watching us. That couldn't have been further from the truth. Mom now had her driver's license. She naturally became our chauffeur.

She would also pick us up from this girl's house around 10:30 pm after the night was over. Mom may have known what we were doing but she never really said anything about it. She knew we were teenagers, and were involved with girl relationships.

Lori and I would sneak into Froggy's basement, and *"make-out."* Brian and Bucky were always upstairs talking to the other girls. Froggy really liked my friend Bucky, but I am not sure the feeling was mutual at the time. Bucky's real name was Mike but we have always called him Bucky or simply "Buck."

Rick was never at these so-called junior high parties, partly because I never invited him, but mainly because he was awkwardly shy around girls. Rick may have been my best friend, but just like I said… girls at the time were my priority. My friends understood though. After all, everyone in junior high was discovering relationships, dating, and kissing. Well…almost everyone…

One of my goals was to try to get Rick a girlfriend in this junior high dating scene. I did the unthinkable. We had a school newspaper known as the *"Harrison Happenings."* This school newspaper talked about important events in the school, sporting events coming up, and oh yeah… a section where students could post comments about other students! Around the time that I was dating Lori, Rick told me that he really liked one of our classmates named Suzanne. Everyone just called her 'Suzie' for short.

She had one of the best laughs as well as personalities in our freshman class. There was only one problem…she probably didn't know Rick existed. I did what any best friend would do. I posted in the comment section of the *"Harrison Happenings"* newspaper that he really liked Suzie. I thought Rick would have appreciated my efforts on getting him a girlfriend. I got the opposite response.

After school had ended for the day, I came down to the gym locker room to find that my sports duffle bag had been thrown out of the locker which Rick and I shared that winter. I mean he was really mad at me! I suppose that may have been the wrong approach but I was just trying to introduce my friend to the 'world of dating.' It's a warm memory now but boy was he upset with me about posting his like for Suzie in the school newspaper. I am not sure Suzie saw the comments in the *Harrison Happenings,* or if she did, she didn't say anything about it.

Lori and I continued to date until the springtime at Harrison. I decided to break up with her before the school year was over. I have no idea why either. She was a beautiful girl with a great personality. Maybe I realized that I was going to Merrillville High School next year, and Lori still had one more year left at Harrison Junior High.

It may have been one of the biggest mistakes that I made in my young life. I had no reason to break off the relationship with her because we had a lot in common. After realizing my stupid mistake, I reached out to her friend Froggy to ask if Lori would be interested in dating me again. I was sure that she would say... 'yes.' The answer was quick and to the point.

Lori had moved on. She was now dating one of my friends whose name was Chuck. I was crushed to hear that Chuck was now "making-out" with Lori on Friday and Saturday nights. So much for my first serious relationship as a teenager. I was dejected and needed something to keep my mind off of my former girlfriend, Lori.

Coach Stefek was starting track & field practice at Harrison in March that year in 1983. Coach Feeney was still coaching track, but he was in-charge of the seventh and eighth grade teams. This would be my last attempt at junior high sports before I headed to Merrillville High School.

We didn't have an indoor running track, so Coach Stefek would have us run the hallways in preparation for the season. We would run all the hallways upstairs and the downstairs of the school. I always liked Coach Stefek. He was a tough guy, and always seemed to motivate you to become better than you were in sports and in life.

Coach Stefek served in the Navy during World War II so I always looked up to him. He would have a local park named after him as well as the gym at Pierce Junior High. Coach Stefek also had a medical procedure done to him while I was a student at Harrison. He would sometimes whisper into my ear before practice to let him know if his ostomy bag was leaking.

He would say things like, *"Bunda, make sure that I am not leaking on my pants!"*

I would have done anything for Coach Stefek. If "Coach" said that running through a wall would make me a better athlete, I would have done it! I loved and appreciated the man that much. This was going to be a lasting memory of Harrison and running track for one of my favorite teachers. How quickly life changes.

Coach Stefek walked into practice one day, and said that there was not going to be a freshman track & field season at Harrison in the spring of 1983. I was devastated when I heard the news. I really wanted to leave my mark on Harrison Junior High as a top track & field athlete. The main two reasons for not having a season that spring was because we didn't have enough kids on our team and other local junior high schools didn't offer freshman track & field.

Coach Stefek looked at me and said the season was cancelled. He told all of us on the team that we had a choice. We could take the school bus up to the high school, and run for the Merrillville Pirates as ninth graders, or find something else to do. I asked Coach Stefek who the coach was at the high school? He mentioned the name Lafey Armontrout. I knew right away that I didn't want to run for that person!

We had heard horrible stories that Lafey Armontrout was a mean coach and very intimidating. *'No thank you'* is what I probably told Coach Stefek. Just like that, my sports career at Harrison Junior High School was over. I was going to play football for Merrillville anyways.

Who cared about running track & field? I thought my track career was over.

I was now going to focus my attention on playing football for the great Ken Haupt at Merrillville High School Bye, Bye Harrison Junior High and hello Merrillville High School. The 'wonder years' of my life were ending but a more memorable three years was ahead of me.

Chapter 12

A Summer with the Buckeyes

The summer of 1983 would be another great moment in my life. My mom and dad had signed me up for the Ohio State football camp. I was actually going to be at camp for a whole week with the Ohio State coaches!

Was I going to be there by myself?

None of my friends could go or wanted to spend the money on a football camp. My dad had another idea. He had a quarterback on his Calumet team who was my age. His name was Mike Crain, and he was entering the tenth grade just like I was in 1983.

My dad talked to Mike's parents about camping at Ohio State and the experience of being coached by college level coaches. You can imagine the excitement that I was experiencing as I packed my bags for Ohio State. Grammy and Papa told my parents that they would drive Mike Crain and I to Columbus, Ohio in June of 1983.

My sisters Nikki and Erin would also ride along to Ohio as well. They obviously wanted to take in other sites besides the Ohio State campus. For example, the Columbus Zoo, German Village, Alum Creek Trail, or even a waterpark.

Either way, Grammy and Papa would have to keep them occupied while I was at football camp.

Mike and I would be staying at Blackburn Hall, which was an OSU dorm for college students during the school year. We would be sharing a room with two other high school campers from Cleveland. I could now show off my football skills to Coach Earle Bruce and the rest of the Ohio State staff.

Mike and I would be assigned to a position group headed by a young assistant coach named Jim Tressel. Coach Tressel was in-charge of the wide receivers and quarterbacks at the camp. Helping out at the football camp were two former Buckeye players. When they were introduced by Earle Bruce, I was in shock. It was none other than Art Schlichter and Doug Donley!

My jaw must have hit the ground. I was speechless that my Ohio State heroes were there in person and right in front of me. I still had the program that Art signed at my first Ohio State home game in 1980, and a part of a 'white jersey' that was ripped off of him during a 1981 Ohio State game against the Wisconsin Badgers.

Now I was standing a stone throw away from Art Schlichter and his main wide receiver, Doug Donley. I thought if this was heaven, I was here now! Camp practices were going to be held in three locations: Ohio Stadium, Biggs Athletic Training Facility, and the French Fieldhouse. I would now get to go inside Ohio Stadium, the same stadium that the Buckeyes played in during their fall football games. Keep in mind, that the only other time that I had been in the stadium was when dad took me there in 1980.

I walked up to Ohio Stadium during the camp like it was yesterday. Each camper had to bring his own helmet. Since I hadn't started my football career at Merrillville High School yet, dad gave me a Calumet "red" helmet to wear for the week.

The Ohio State coaches placed us into straight rows for stretching exercises before any drills were to take place. As I was stretching, I kept looking around Ohio Stadium for a couple of different reasons.

First, I was just amazed at the size of the structure, and how many seats there were in the stadium. In 1983, Ohio Stadium held a seating capacity close to 85,000 people. Nowadays, it holds close to 105,000 people due to all the renovations in the past twenty years.

Second, I was wondering which campers were as good, if not better, than me? The answer would come quickly.

As we got done with routine stretching before the actual practice began, Ohio State assistant coach Jim Tressel told the wide receivers to make two lines about forty yards apart from one another. The quarterbacks in camp, like my new friend Mike Crain, were going to throw passes to the wide receiver group. Coach Tressel would tell us what type of pattern or route he wanted us to run like an *"out route."*

This is where the wide receiver runs about ten yards and cuts towards the sidelines. *No big deal* I thought. I was pretty good at catching a football, and here was my chance to impress Coach Tressel as well as Coach Earle Bruce. With them watching, I sprinted forward ten yards and cut towards the sidelines. Mike Crain threw the football perfectly towards me.

As the ball came closer, I put my fingertips and thumbs together to form a triangle to catch the pass. It would have been a perfect moment to show-off my skills to the football staff. One problem... The football bounced off my hands and fell to the Ohio Stadium turf.

As I ran back to the end of the line, Coach Tressel was twirling his whistle. He simply said to me, *"We catch the football here at Ohio State!"*

By dropping the football, I obviously did not make a good first impression. I knew that I would have many more opportunities at camp if I just settled down. As I got back to the line, there was this tall player in front of me. He was about 6'3", and had these long legs. He had a purple & white helmet with an "M" on the side of it that said *"Middies."*

How good is this kid, I wondered? He definitely looked like a good athlete. I had seen him earlier that day checking into Blackburn Hall for the camp. I just didn't realize how famous he would become at the time.

When his turn was next in line, he ran the same pass route that I did a minute earlier. The result was different than mine. He reached up in the air and came down with the football with one hand! He made it look so easy and graceful.

143

As he was coming back into line, I heard one of the Ohio State coaches say, *"Great catch, Cris!"*

Ok... so at least now I knew his first name. When it was my turn again, I thought I could do what Cris had just done. No problem at all! How hard could it be? As I ran my pattern, the football came in a little high, and sailed right through my hands again. As I went back to the line, there was Coach Tressel standing there with his whistle and a stern look on his face. He didn't say anything to me this time.

He just kind of stared at me as if that was the worst attempt at catching a football he had ever seen. I whispered in a dejected tone as I ran past him... *"I know coach, we catch the football here at Ohio State."*

I am not sure whether Coach Tressel heard me or not. With every drill or pass catching session, it seemed as if this Cris kid from Middletown, Ohio didn't drop any footballs. If you were wondering if I eventually caught the football, the answer was... yes.

After the practice was over, we were to be served dinner at a dining facility on campus. The dinner was outstanding but the fruit juices they served us were even better. I kept asking people at my dining table who this Cris kid was from Middletown.

Someone said, *"I think his name is Cris Carter."*

I told people at the table that this kid was really good! Maybe someday he would get a chance to play at Ohio State. *Little did I know.* As we finished up dinner, we went to the old French Fieldhouse on campus to catch more passes and listen to the coaches. After the night was over, all the campers went back to Blackburn Hall to get rest and just hang out to get to know one another.

It was a nice time to get to meet all the campers from different high schools in Ohio as well as other states. I think a lot of them had the same ambition that I did in wanting to play for the Ohio State Buckeyes. It was nice just meeting people from different high schools, hanging out in the dorm, and shooting a game of pool.

The next day, we had another camp practice session at the Biggs Facility. During the practice, we received assistance from former players like Art Schlichter and Doug Donley. Art was actually throwing footballs to the campers. I had made the comment that I came from six hours away to catch a football from Art Schlichter. I was just mesmerized by the presence of him.

I had only seen him on television of course, so you can imagine my excitement to see Art in person. I did accidently step on Doug Donley's towel that he had set on the ground during one of the football drills.

Doug just kind of looked at me and said, *"That is my towel."*

Wow! Doug Donley actually said something to me! It may not have been the most cordial response but a Buckeye player acknowledged me. As the camp continued on, I enjoyed my time at Ohio State. The camp staff let us walk the campus and visit the gift shops that surrounded Ohio State. Grammy and Papa had given me some spending money to buy souvenirs while I was there.

I purchased two items that I still have to this day. I bought a 'black Woody Hayes' hat with the red block "O" on the front. I also purchased my first Ohio State book known as, *"The Best of the Buckeyes"* which was written by the famous sportswriter, Paul Hornung.

Since it was the first Ohio State football book that I owned, I must have read it cover to cover a hundred times. Every time I look at the 'Woody Hayes hat' or that book, I am taken back to my time as a camper at Ohio State.

The other items I received at the camp was a t-shirt that said, *"Earle Bruce Football Camp"* and a camp certificate with Earle Bruce and Jim Tressel's signatures on it. I no longer have the shirt. I probably wore it out by wearing it too many times. I do have the camp certificate hanging on a wall in my house.

Years later, I was re-introduced to Coach Earle Bruce by a friend of mine named Mark Agerter. Mark's brother had been on the Ohio State football staff as a manager for Earle in the early 1980's. As I sat by Coach Bruce in the Woody Hayes Athletic Center, I told him that I went to his football camp at Ohio State back in the summer of 1983. Coach Bruce asked me about the high school I went to and about my football experience.

I said to him, *"You didn't recruit me to play at Ohio State."* I told him that you selected another wide receiver named Cris instead.

He said, *"You mean Cris Carter, don't you?"*

Coach Bruce looked at me with a grin, and simply said, *"Cris was pretty good... wasn't he?"*

Cris Carter would go on to play and start for the Ohio State Buckeyes in the fall of 1984. He would also have a stellar career in the National Football League. Cris is now in the NFL Hall of Fame, and I believe his high school named its football field after him. If I would have only caught those passes in football camp! Cris is still one of the best wide receivers that I have ever seen at Ohio State. He made catches that would defy explanation.

When I returned from football camp, I had other obligations before I started my first year at Merrillville High School in the fall of 1983. I had to take Lou Lindinger's driver's education class in July. Lou was the head football coach at Calumet where my dad was now an assistant under him. I was planning on getting my driver's license in the fall so I could experience real freedom as a high school student. Mr. Lindinger always had a bottle of Tums stomach pain relievers on the dashboard of the car while I was driving. If I made the wrong turn or didn't put on the breaks at the stop sign, a few choice words would come out of his mouth.

He would just shake his head and say, *"I can't believe you are going to have your license in a few months. You are going to get me killed!"*

As the summer of 1983 was coming to an end, I was getting ready to play football for the Merrillville Pirates and start my sophomore year in high school. Like I said before, Merrillville High School was grades tenth through twelfth. This would be the first time that I would be with students from the 'other' junior high. Both Harrison and Piece kids were now going to come together and be Merrillville High School "Pirates."

Chapter 13
Fast Times at Merrillville High

One of my all-time favorite movies came out the year before I went to Merrillville High School. It was called, *"Fast Times at Ridgemont High."* When I first saw the movie, I thought life at Merrillville High was going to be the same way. The movie was about dating, friends, classes, cliques, and the high school culture.

It starred a female actress by the name of Phoebe Cates. All the guys that I knew in my school were in love with her. Naturally, we thought that there would be girls at Merrillville High School who were just as gorgeous as Phoebe. To my surprise, a lot of them were as good-looking as her!

I could hardly wait until school started in the fall, and that I would officially be on the Merrillville High School "Pirate" football team. I was one step closer to possibly playing football for the Ohio State Buckeyes.

High school also brought many other challenges my way like schoolwork and trying to get along with those kids from Pierce. I knew at some point that I would bump into Mike "D" Demakas either in football practice or in one of my classes. I dreaded the fact that I had to see him, and would now have to be football teammates with him as well.

Football practice started on August 4th of 1983. All varsity players grades 10-12 had to report for two practices a day. We would practice two hours in the morning, and two more hours in the late afternoon.

For whatever reason that year, we also had a yoga instructor who would come in at noon, and teach exercises for about an hour. I was mesmerized by the head coach, Ken Haupt. Everyone knew who 'coach' was because he had won a state championship with Merrillville back in 1976.

Seven years later, I am now going to play for him, and the Merrillville Pirates. I was really excited to be on the football team. I have to admit that I was also a little intimidated.

Most sophomores that year were going to play what was called 'junior varsity.' This allowed all newcomers to the high school to get ready to someday play on the varsity team made up mostly of juniors and seniors.

The first two weeks of football practice were tough and almost like an army boot camp. It was hot every day and we had to do all these agility drills. One of the drills required us players to run backwards known as a 'back pedal run.' While doing this drill, I fell right on my rear end. I was hoping none of the Merrillville coaches were watching. No such luck!

One of the assistant coaches, Jeff Yelton, came up to me and said, *"Do you know what happens to Christmas Trees in August?"*

I stared at him as I started to get off the ground. I looked confused and simply said, *"no."* I had no idea what he meant by that statement. *Why would I know this,* I thought?

Coach Yelton glared back at me and said, *"They get cut down, damn it! Now stay low when you backpedal!!"*

I had a hard time understanding the correlation between a Christmas tree and my inability to do a backpedal run.

Welcome to high school football!

Coach Yelton may have been one of the most intense and exciting coaches that I have ever been around. Those two weeks prior to school starting were some of the most difficult as well as challenging practices that I have ever endured as an athlete. There were players throwing up, cramping, and having heat exhaustion from the hot sun. One player named Tom came by me during a break and vomited all over the grass. He looked at me and said,

"Puke and go!"

He went right back into practice after he left all his breakfast on the field. Very bizarre.

We did have these water troughs that were hooked up to a hose to get water during breaks from the drills. The football managers would also come around with water bottles for the players as we were getting ready for the next drill or session.

I kept thinking to myself, *"Do I really want to do this?"*

I wasn't about to give up on a dream to someday play for the Ohio State Buckeyes. If I could handle Merrillville High School football practice, then I could handle anything in life. There would be more hard practices as well as coaches pointing out my many flaws. At the time, I may not have understood their intentions, and often thought they were criticizing my ability as a player.

What I didn't realize was that they were preparing me for life.

As the school year was about the start, there were two major events that were to take place for incoming sophomores at Merrillville. There was a *"Sophomore Orientation Day"* that the school put on for us to learn all about Merrillville High School, and the resources it had to offer. The juniors and seniors acted as "big brothers" and "big sisters" to help the incoming students learn about the high school, where our classes were, clubs that were available to students, and how to get academic help.

They put on a cookout for all the new students that day. We got to meet people who were coming in from Pierce Junior High. Many of them really didn't talk to us kids from Harrison at the cookout. I couldn't imagine being friends with any of these people from the rival junior high, even if they were now my new classmates in high school.

The second function was a back-to-school dance known as the *"Back to School Boogie"* held on Thursday, August 25th. At the dance, I kept telling all my friends, *"Welcome to high school!"* I was determined to make these some of the best years of my life.

I was going to play football at Merrillville, get my driver's license, maybe meet new friends, and see a lot of girls at MHS! What could be better? Rick would always be my best friend but the excitement of meeting new people in high school was intriguing.

I also knew that Ohio State was going to have a great football team in 1983. Dad was planning on what Ohio State football game we were going to go to that year. Yep...life couldn't get any better! Although, major obstacles and devastation were just around the corner.

As I started my first day at Merrillville High School, it was nice to start another chapter in my life. No longer would I have to worry about junior high or the immaturity brought on by some of the younger kids, and that meant more freedom as well as responsibility. I would also have some great teachers waiting for me as I started my first year at Merrillville.

The first day of school was a complete blur. I must have gotten lost a thousand times looking for my classes. I was also worried that I wouldn't have any classes with Rick Keneson, Brian Portlock, Steve Civanich, or Bucky Randall. One of the Pierce kids, Mike "D" Demakas, was now going to the high school with me.

I really didn't like him and there was no way I could ever be friends with him. Maybe it was because he was from Pierce or maybe it was because he played the same sports as I did. I worried that I would have to compete against him. If I didn't have to see him during the school day, I would be fine with that. It is weird how things would eventually turn out. Who knew?

As I went into my first class of the day, I looked around and saw no one who looked familiar. The class was called *Westward Expansion,* and it was taught by Mr. Edgcomb. Mr. Edgcomb would be my first teacher at Merrillville High School. He told us that we would have to read these old western novels from an author known as Louis L'Amour. We would read books like the *"Cherokee Trail"* and *"Hondo."*

I can't say it was the most interesting class in the world, mainly because Mr. Edgcomb would ask us to read certain parts out loud to the class. Most of the time, I was dreaming about Ohio State and thinking back to my football camp experience earlier in the summer. I did like Mr. Edgcomb as a teacher but I just didn't like reading those old western novels.

As my first day of classes wore on, I would have a physical education class taught by Lafey Armontrout. Was this the same person that Coach John Stefek told me about back at Harrison Junior High School? Was this the track & field coach at Merrillville? I now have this intimidating person as my gym teacher! Also in the gym class was Mike "D" Demakas. *Great!* Mike or "D" was also on the Merrillville football team with me. Not only did I have to see him at football practice but now I had to see him in class as well.

After school that day, I had already made up my mind that I was probably not going out for the track & field team in the spring, especially if Lafey Armontrout was the coach. I was also going to ask for a scheduling change to get away from this kid named "D."

As the afternoon approached on that first day of school, the football team was now limited to just one practice. All the sophomores were going to play junior varsity with Coach Braggs and Coach Tom Peller. Coach Braggs had moved up from being the Harrison Junior High basketball coach to now being a football coach at Merrillville. Tom Peller was a super star quarterback at a local high school known as Andrean, and also played his college football at the University of Indianapolis.

Merrillville High School may have been his first teaching job as well as coaching assignment. Coach Peller didn't seem that much older than the students at Merrillville. He was my wide receiver coach all the way through high school and one of my favorite teachers. Just like Coach Yelton on the Merrillville varsity staff, Tom Peller was a very enthusiastic person. Because he was a quarterback in high school as well as in college, Coach Peller would throw the football to us in pass-catching drills. He never called you by your first name.

151

Instead, Coach Peller called you by your first and last name together. If you caught the football while he was throwing it to you in practice... he would say, *"Nice job, Denny Bunda!"* If I missed the football or dropped it in practice, Coach Peller would have this disgusted look on his face and say... *"What are you doing, Denny Bunda!?"*

As if I missed the football catch on purpose. I also had him as a math teacher at Merrillville High School. He would do the same thing in class. One time in class, I answered one of his math questions incorrectly. It was as if the sky had fallen! The chalk that Coach Peller was using to write on the board dropped out of his hand, and he looked at me like I was the stupidest math student he had ever taught.

However, on the football field as well as in the classroom, Coach Peller never gave up on me. Sometimes my hands would be sore from writing all his math problems down, while other times they were sore from catching all the footballs from him in practice.

My sophomore year in football, the coaches assigned me jersey #19. I really wanted to be #89 like I was the year before at Harrison. #89 was worn by John Frank at Ohio State, and I wanted to be like him. However, that number went to a Pierce kid named Chris.

Ok, I'll select #88 because there was an Ohio State wide receiver named Thad Jemison who wore that number. Nope! That number would go to Mike "D" Demakas. Great! That gave me another reason not to like this kid even though he was now my teammate. The coaches told me that I could be #19 because there was a well-known wide receiver from Penn State named Greg Garrity who wore that number in the 1980's.

What!? Didn't the coaches know that I was an Ohio State fan? Greg Garrity was a great wide receiver but he didn't play for Ohio State. I wanted a number that a well-known Ohio State player wore in games. Besides, Penn State had defeated Ohio State in a Fiesta Bowl a few years earlier. I only liked one team and one team only. How could the coaches think that I wanted to wear a number that a Penn State player wore?

With all that being said, I was still issued the #19 for my first year as a Merrillville Pirate football player. What would my purpose be that first year if I couldn't be like one of my favorite Ohio State Buckeye football players? What would be my motivation? The answer would come in week four of our football season during the school year. I didn't realize that the devastating news I was about to receive would be my motivation.

My mom had gone to the doctor earlier in the week for a routine mammogram. Just a regular breast exam check-up. No big deal, right? When she got the follow-up call from her doctor in September, I was at football practice. My two sisters, Nikki and Erin, were in the living room when mom broke the news to them. She was diagnosed with breast cancer. Mom started crying and my sisters started crying as well. Mom had always been the glue that held our family together. She always made our family three meals a day, drove us to our events once she got her license, and was always there to support us. It would now be dad, Nikki, Erin, and I who would have to be there for mom.

I was stunned and frozen when I got the news. This was my mother after all. How could this be happening during the best years of my life in high school at Merrillville? I knew that I would have to be strong not only for my mom, but for my sisters Nikki and Erin as well. Nikki was now in 7th grade at Harrison Junior High, and Erin was a year younger as a 6th grader at Miller Elementary School. It was the word that day which still haunts me... "Cancer."

I had learned from Coach Earle Bruce at the Ohio State football camp earlier that summer... *"When you get knocked down, you get back up again."*

Coach Bruce telling the campers that statement during those five days when I was there with Mike Crain. No words would be truer spoken when I found out that mom had breast cancer. I knew that I went to the Ohio State football camp to learn more than just football. I was also there to learn how to handle and overcome adversity.

I had done it earlier in my life when I had my accident in 1976. I would now have to be there for my mom in 1983 as she went through

153

her own struggles with cancer. There were many days that I cried silently in my bedroom while I thought what life would be like if my mom passed away. I couldn't imagine my life without her. Nikki and Erin needed mom to guide them through their adolescence, and teach them things that only a mother could do.

As I dealt with my own personal high school struggles and the news that mom now had breast cancer, Ohio State football was also going through their ups and downs in 1983. Not that it was in any way more significant than my mom's diagnosis of breast cancer because it really put life into perspective.

Football is just a game.

The game itself has so many valuable lessons. Such as overcoming adversity, and relying on others around you for support. For me, it was my release from my everyday problems and situations of life.

The Ohio State season started with a win over the Oregon Ducks by the score of 31-6. More importantly, it was the week two matchup that season which had everyone excited about the Buckeyes. Ohio State was to travel to Norman, Oklahoma to take on the University of Oklahoma Sooners.

I was really looking forward to this game for a couple of reasons. Firstly, Ohio State had lost to them in 1977 on a last second field goal as I listened to the game on the radio with my dad while we were visiting my Uncle Ross in Illinois. Secondly, during the football camp earlier in the summer, that is all Coach Bruce and the coaching staff talked about to the campers was this 'Oklahoma game.' This would be a game for the ages. Saturday couldn't come soon enough.

It was September 17th, and I had an early morning football practice at Merrillville. The summer heat hadn't cooled yet, so it was really hot that day. After practice was over, I invited Mark Hamilton, who was one of my friends, to come over and watch the game.

This was again a rarity to watch an Ohio State Buckeye game with one of my friends. Mark also played on the Merrillville Junior

Varsity football team with me. His parents had gone to high school with my dad at Horace Mann in the 1960's.

Oklahoma had a great tailback in 1983 by the name of Marcus Dupree. Ohio State had their own version of a great running back in Keith Byars. One of the announcers broadcasting the game that day said the field surface was well over 120 degrees! Mark and I just stared at one another as if to think that our morning football practice wasn't that bad. Keith Byars had a great game but it was John Frank #89 who was the star for the Buckeyes that afternoon.

As the Ohio State/Oklahoma game was in its early stages, John Frank caught a touchdown pass from Mike Tomczak. The Buckeyes were now leading 7-0 against a team that broke my heart in 1977. John would score again in the 2nd quarter and now Ohio State had a 14-0 lead. I kept telling my friend Mark that this was Ohio State's year! The Buckeyes would go on to win the game that day against Oklahoma by the score of 24-14.

The following week would be a different story. The Buckeyes would be taking on the #7 ranked Iowa Hawkeyes from the Big Ten Conference. Once again, my mom scheduled for my friends to come over during an all-important game. Ohio State looked like they would win as they took a 7-3 lead into halftime. As I went outside to play football catch with all my friends during the break, I felt comfortable that they would in fact win.

My dad called all of us back in and told us to hurry downstairs! The Buckeyes had just lost the lead to Iowa.

The Buckeyes would cut into the deficit with a touchdown by fullback Vaughn Broadnax late in the game. Unfortunately, it was all over with twenty-two seconds left in the 4th quarter when Ohio State threw an interception. The game would end with Iowa winning 20-14, and the crowd at the game pouring on the field tearing down one of the goal posts. My friends saw that I was visibly upset and started filing out of my house one by one. Maybe I shouldn't have friends over for my birthday while Ohio State was on television.

I brought a lot of this on myself. The week before, I was telling anyone who would listen to me, that the Ohio State Buckeyes were the best team in college football. Not many of my classmates cared. The Merrillville students were more concerned with what they were going to do on Friday nights, who they were dating, parties, and what activities they were involved in at school. Kids still made fun of me, but not to the extent of when I was in elementary school or junior high school. Besides, the students were more wrapped up in Merrillville athletics and following Pirate football.

I also learned that high school was more about socialization and how you spent your Friday and Saturday nights. For most kids back in 1983, it meant cruising in your car down a long street known as Broadway. Since I wouldn't have my driver's license until October, I had to rely on upperclassmen to 'Cruise' on Friday and Saturday nights.

Mark Hamilton knew a junior named Chip Ashley. Chip became one of my friends as well during my high school years. Cruising meant meeting new people, listening to music in the car, and trying to find girls. There seemed to be a million teenagers on Broadway Street any given Friday or Saturday night.

You would think that the police would not allow this to happen and tell everyone to go home. As long as you obeyed the rules and stuck to the speed limit, you could have a safe and exciting time out on the town of Merrillville. I have to admit that Friday and Saturday nights would take my mind off of Ohio State football as well as my mom's recent diagnosis.

Since my break-up with Lori in my last year at Harrison Junior High, I was in search of a new girlfriend. I really believed that cruising Broadway on Friday and Saturday nights would allow me to enter into a new relationship.

If I was bothered by the Ohio State football loss to Iowa, it didn't last long. The thought of having a new girlfriend and the excitement of high school times quickly diminished my angst. I did ask this senior girl out while cruising Broadway one Friday night with my friends.

She gave me her telephone number but when I called it the next day, it was the number to a 'dry cleaner company.' I guess she didn't want to go out with me after all. If I didn't understand the word 'rejection' before I was quickly learning it in high school. Most of the girls I knew didn't want to date sophomore boys.

My school day was filled with classes and afternoon football practices. The weekends were now filled with going to the varsity football games and cruising Broadway with Chip and Mark on Friday nights. I feel bad now but I never really asked Rick to go with us.

In the beginning of high school, none of the guidance counselors even talked to me about college, or my plans to someday go to Ohio State and play football. I would sit and daydream during the school day about Buckeye football, girls, and anything else that would pass the time. In my Earth Science class, I had this blonde girl who sat directly in front of me. Her name was Lori, and she had come from Pierce. Maybe I had a thing for girls named Lori with blonde hair.

The only problem was that she really didn't know that I existed. When we got to Merrillville High School, there always seemed to be this separation between those who went to Harrison and those who went to Pierce. In time, this social distancing between the two junior highs would end, especially in the later years of high school.

My Earth Science teacher, Mr. Neuliep, would always call on me when I wasn't listening. He had these three by five index cards with every student's name on it.

He would say, *"Bunda... What does the word, Osmosis mean?"*

As if I knew or really cared about what Osmosis was or why it was important to the class. Mr. Neuliep was a great teacher but I had very little time or interest in Earth Science. Why would I even care about Earth Science? I did invite Lori and her friend Michelle over to study for one of Mr. Neuliep's science tests.

I somehow convinced them that I needed help learning about the science terms and definitions, and that I wanted to get a good grade in the class. None of that could have been further from the truth. I just really wanted to have Lori notice me so I could ask her out on a date. I actually knew all the terms and concepts to at least get an average grade on the test. I played dumb so she could go over the information with me at my house.

My two sisters, Nikki and Erin, were walking into the room and bothering us the whole time. I am not sure she liked me and I never got up the nerve to ask her out. What a way to start high school, huh? I still had football to rely on though. I was playing junior varsity for the Merrillville Pirates.

I was now going to play football for a purpose. When mom was diagnosed with breast cancer in the fall of 1983, our family still didn't know much about the disease. We had no idea about cures or medicines that would help her from this terrible illness. The concepts of radiation or chemotherapy were new to all of us.

There was a chance that the cancer could spread to other parts of her body as well. We had no idea how much longer my mom had to live. It was the type of stress that young people shouldn't have to worry about while going through some of the best times of their lives in high school.

I was riding the bus home after one of our junior varsity games against the Munster Mustangs. We lost 13-10, but I just keep thinking of my mom. How would I ever get through high school as well as the rest of my life without her? The bus ride home was silent mainly because we lost a game.

A game we should have won. While the other players may have been thinking about the loss, my thoughts were on mom. Music star, Robert Plant's song, *"The Big Log"* was playing on the bus radio at the time.

There is a part of the song in which the lyrics are... *"they'll come sensing too well, when the journey is done, there is no turning back, no... there is no turning back... on the run."*

To me, the song meant a lot of unanswered questions about life and love. I am not sure that is what Robert Plant was saying while singing his song, but that is what it meant to me. My journey in life now had a lot of unanswered questions.

- *How would my mom get through her breast cancer?*
- *Would I find the love of my life in high school?*
- *Would I become the football star that I thought I would be?*
- *Would I ever get to go to Ohio State as a student?*

Two weeks later, we were scheduled to play a junior varsity home football game against a school known as Michigan City Rogers. No one was there to see me play that night. The rest of my family was with my mom as she was meeting with her oncology doctor in the late afternoon.

I went into the game very upset. I had no idea what the doctor was going to tell her and the rest of my family. I had a million thoughts racing through my head. How could I play a football game while a doctor was meeting with the rest of my family about my mom's health condition?

I could tell you that I had the game of my life, but that would be another lie. I played the game in a very angry mood. I was going to take my frustration out on the other team we were playing that night. Life seemed unfair at this point and I didn't care who stood in my way. There was a situation when one of our players ran for about 35 yards down the field with the football.

The referee had blown his whistle to signify that the play was over. I saw this Michigan City Rogers player standing there, and not paying attention that I was coming right at him full speed! I absolutely hit him as hard as I could and completely knocked him to the ground. While he was lying there hurt, the game official threw the "yellow" penalty flag, and looked at me.

"You are out of the game!"

They kicked me out of the football game! I came running to the sidelines, and Coach Peller looked at me and said, *"What are you doing? Get back in the game, Denny Bunda!"*

I tried to explain to him that the official disqualified me. I'm not sure Coach Peller heard me or maybe he was too wrapped up in the game itself. Anyways, I went back in and played the final minutes in a 14-0 win.

In October of 1983, mom and dad got me a belated birthday present when they bought me a subscription to an Ohio State newspaper known as the *"Buckeye Leaves."* I received my first issue right after Ohio State lost to Illinois 17-13 in Champaign, Illinois on October 15th. It was one of the best gifts that I ever received. The *Buckeye Leaves* magazine was now going to be delivered to my house every week during the football season.

I could keep up with Ohio State football even when they weren't being televised. Even though I read about the 'Illinois game' in my new publication, I actually listened to the football game on the radio while it happened. Illinois hadn't beaten Ohio State since the year I was born in 1967, and the Buckeyes had a 15-game winning streak against them leading up to the 1983 contest.

Ironically, the score in 1967 was also 17-13. I remember sitting in my basement with my earphones on listening to the game as I was reading one of my assignments given by Mr. Edgcomb for Westward Expansion class. The Buckeyes actually had the game won but gave up a last second touchdown to Illinois when Thomas Rooks scored for the "Fighting Illini." The noise coming through my headphones was deafening. The Illinois fans were cheering loudly as Ohio State went down in defeat.

I put my book down that I was reading for class. My dad, who was upstairs, came down and simply told me, *"Ohio State lost to Illinois."* I told him that I already knew the score.

By that time, my first football season wrapped up at Merrillville as a junior varsity player. My team went 5-4 that year but we showed a lot of promise.

I caught some passes in games. Probably nowhere near the amount that Cris Carter had during his 1983 senior high school season.

I had a feeling during the Ohio State football camp that Cris would eventually become a Buckeye. I would be right.

The Merrillville High School varsity team ended with a 6-4 record, and it would be the last year for Head Coach Ken Haupt. He was relieved from his football duties at the conclusion of the season. Coach Haupt came from Ohio, and coached at Cincinnati Elder High School before he arrived at Merrillville in 1975.

I was always impressed that he was from Ohio. I did get to enjoy listening to his pre-game speech prior to the homecoming game versus Portage High School that year. Coach Haupt was a great motivator and coach. I just wished I got to play for him during my junior and senior years of high school. I did go to the homecoming dance that year with a girl who asked me a few weeks earlier.

Her name was Susan but she was more of a friend. Her younger sister Debbie was friends with my sister, Nikki. I knew that she would not be my girlfriend in high school. Would I have multiple girlfriends or just one throughout high school? The answer would come later on in the spring.

As for the rest of the Ohio State season that started out with such high hopes, the Buckeyes would go on to defeat such opponents as Michigan State and Wisconsin after the Illinois loss on October 15th. They showed former Ohio State coach Woody Hayes *"Dotting the I"* in *Script Ohio* during the halftime of the Wisconsin game on television.

On rare occasions, a celebrity will dot the "I" in *Script Ohio*. For Coach Woody Hayes, that moment would come on October 29th, 1983. I didn't see it live because the Ohio State/ Wisconsin game wasn't aired on television that day. I would eventually read about Woody Hayes' great moment when my *Buckeye Leaves* magazine came in the mail the following week. Another surprise would be waiting for me which would be as important as my *Buckeye Leaves* magazine.

Mom and dad would once again surprise me by acquiring Ohio State tickets to the game versus Indiana on November 5th. If mom was having any symptoms or stress about being diagnosed with breast cancer, she sure didn't show it. She was always smiling and an upbeat person. Mom enjoyed the many moments in life.

She really didn't care if it was something she liked to do or not. Mom knew that I loved Ohio State football, and she just wanted to be at the games because that's what I liked doing. It didn't seem to bother her one bit that a lot of the times we went to an Ohio State football game, it happened to fall on my parent's wedding anniversary.

On November 5th, 1983, they would take me to Bloomington, Indiana to watch the Buckeyes take on the Indiana Hoosiers. I was allowed to bring a friend this time to the game. I chose to take my good friend, Bucky Randall.

Bucky and I had been friends since our days at Harrison Junior High School in science class. Even though Bucky was a huge Alabama fan, he agreed to come down to Bloomington with us for the weekend.

I could have chosen Rick Keneson but I didn't think he would go due to the fact that he liked the Michigan Wolverines. I had a lot of friends who wanted to go because they had never seen a college football game before in person. Many of them asked me what it was like to attend a college football game. I didn't realize that many of them didn't have the same opportunity as I did to witness a game. I grew to appreciate the opportunity that my parents gave me to attend college games.

We sat in the corner of the endzone in Memorial Stadium at Indiana that day. I mean the Buckeyes were really beating the Indiana Hoosiers badly. Jim Karsatos, the backup quarterback for Ohio State in 1983, threw a touchdown pass to Doug Smith with just under two minutes to go in the game. Ohio State was leading at the time by the score of 49-10, and really didn't need any more points.

As Jim Karsatos went back to pass, he threw this 63-yard pass in the endzone where we were sitting. As we stood up and cheered...

I said, *"Ohio State is unstoppable! No one can beat them!"*

Bucky tapped me on the shoulder and said, *"They have lost twice this year to Iowa and Illinois."* Nothing like a friend to remind you of the shortcomings of your team. I didn't care though. I was just happy to be at another Ohio State game cheering on my team. The Buckeyes won that day by the score of 56-17.

Later that night, dad and mom took Bucky and I out for dinner, and to a local *Holiday Inn* hotel not far from the Indiana University campus. I remember sitting in the hotel hot tub talking to Bucky about Ohio State, and that someday I wanted to go there as a student. I am not sure he took me seriously. Why should he?

I was an average student. The start of my high school years was a lot like being back at Harrison Junior High. I would day-dream about Ohio State and girls, and not focus on schoolwork. I was also supposed to study for my driver's exam that week of the Indiana game as well...but I didn't. I would learn a hard lesson about preparation and organization.

The next week, mom would take me to get my driver's license at the Bureau of Motor Vehicles. Mom and dad had told me to study the manual the week before in preparation for the driver's test. I was now sixteen and ready to drive. I would no longer have to rely on my friend, Chip Ashley for a ride to go cruising on Broadway during Friday nights.

This also meant that I would be able to go out on dates with girls without my mom and dad picking them up. I took off school that Monday to go get my license. Mom didn't work outside the household, so she was able to take me to the license bureau. There was only one problem...

I failed the written exam that day.

I should have studied. I looked at my mom and asked her what should I do? The driving instructor told us that I would have to wait two weeks before I could try again to obtain my driver's license. What!? How was I going to go back to Merrillville High School and face my friends?

My friends were counting on me to drive to school in the afternoon, and pick them up for a fun evening. It was really embarrassing. It was one thing to fail an earth science or math test, but fail the driver's test? There are no short-cuts in life.

I had a plan on what mom and I were going to do. I said to mom, *"If we change the "F" to a "B" on the driving test, then I would be able to get my license at another license bureau."*

I was surprised when mom went along with my plan! She said to me, *"Do you think it will work?"* I think mom wanted me to get my license as much as I did. She may have been tired of driving me and all my friends around town.

"This driver's permit has been tampered with, and the grade has been changed!"

Even though mom tried to cover for me, the license bureau wasn't going to believe us. My mom said, *"That is impossible! This is the first place we have been to today!"*

Getting back in the car with embarrassment, mom promised she would not tell dad of what we had just done. I would simply have to wait the additional two weeks before I took the test again. Both mom and dad said that I would have to spend the next two weeks preparing for the driver's exam.

No going out with friends and socializing outside of school. It was a rough two weeks. I may have studied harder than I ever did before. At least for something that I really cared about. At the time, school was not that important to me, but getting my driver's license was.

My friends were all laughing that I had failed my driver's test but I was determined not to have that happen again. There was also another extra motivation. I didn't want to explain to girls that I couldn't go on dates with them because I didn't have my license. Who would even consider going on a date with me if I couldn't drive a car? They surely wouldn't go out with me if my parents had to drive us somewhere.

When I finally did pass my driver's license, it seemed like nothing else mattered. Finally! It was as if I had won the lotto. I was going to use the car to go on dates, go to the Southlake Shopping Mall, be with my friends, and oh yeah...going cruising with the car on

Broadway during Friday and Saturday nights. Oh, the memories that I was about to create.

Chapter 14
More Memories at Merrillville

It's amazing how many friends you acquire once you get a driver's license. It always seemed that I had a carload of friends once I was able to drive. The funny thing was not many of them paid for gas. I didn't care though. Spending my Friday and Saturday nights out on the town was what high school was all about.

The week before the annual Ohio State versus Michigan game in 1983, one of my friends suggested that we go to this dance club known simply as the "Goya." In the 1980's, roller-skating rinks were still somewhat popular, but they were now being replaced by all these local dance clubs for teenagers.

The "Goya" was actually a Greek Church in Merrillville which put-on Friday and Saturday night dances from 7 pm until 11:00 pm. We called them "mixers." They played all the popular music from the 1980's. It was also a place to meet girls, not just from Merrillville, but also from the other local high schools. As we were talking about it in school one day, Michael "D" Demakas suggested that maybe we go to this dance club. Mike Demakas?

As in the same person I didn't like back in junior high school? It was amazing how things had changed. Here was this person that I really didn't care about in junior high or even entering high school, and now I was going to hang out with him on the weekends?

Michael "D" Demakas would become one of my life-long best friends. He and I always had a lot in common. We just didn't realize it until we got to know each other in high school.

We both played football and participated in track & field. Had outgoing personalities and seemed to dodge a lot of trouble. That was not to say that we weren't mischievous because we were at times! We had a tendency never to get caught doing some of the dumb things we did in high school.

My relationship with "D" took on a whole different odyssey of adventure. We were always trying to find something interesting to do. That meant that we would convince Rick into coming along with us as well. My hate for "D" grew into a friendship that is as strong as ever.

Just like Rick and Brian Portlock, "D" has had a major impact on my life. He was always this unique individual who came into my life at the right time. Unique may be a mild word to describe him. It was just strange that the person I despised in junior high became one of my best friends. After forming a friendship with "D," you could say there was never a dull moment in high school.

We met a few other friends at Noble Roman's pizza place not far from our old junior high. This was the same place that we all went after football games and dances. Some people didn't want to go to the Goya that night while others did. "D" and I thought that we would check it out that night. It opened our eyes to a whole new world of high school in November of 1983. There were students there from other schools such as Munster, Andrean, Chesterton, Lake Central, Crown Point, etc…

The 1980's was the 'dance craze time.' A new dance known as *"Break Dancing"* was starting to become popular with teenagers. I suppose it was kind of like the teenagers in the 1970's who liked Disco dancing.

There were a lot of Friday and Saturday nights that "D" and I spent at the Goya dances. We met a lot of girls and other friends from local high schools. It was this type of socialization that took my mind off of school or my mom's diagnosis with cancer.

No matter how much fun I had dancing with all the girls at these high school Goya dances, I knew the Buckeyes were set to face Michigan on November 19th, 1983. Mike "D" Demakas' favorite saying was... *"Don't worry about it, Bunda."* That seemed to be his answer to everything.

Ohio State's game against Michigan wasn't going to be aired on television that year.

I have since watched the replay on *YouTube* and old classics played on television. Ohio State would go on to lose to Michigan for the first time in a couple of years by the score of 24-21. The Buckeyes had many chances to win the game but some experts believe that they lost on a "trick play." Can you believe that?

One particular play would cost the Buckeyes the game. There may have been other plays that proved costly, but that "trick play" is the one that people talked about for years, and still talk about to this day.

Quarterback Mike Tomczak was to place the ball on the ground, and the offensive guard by the name of Jim Lachey was supposed to pick the football up and run with it. I read somewhere that Coach Earle Bruce got the idea for the play from something that the Nebraska Cornhuskers used against Oklahoma. Coach Bruce had told the reporters that it worked well in practice.

Well... it didn't work against Michigan, and the Buckeyes would leave Ann Arbor, Michigan with a loss to the Wolverines for the first time since 1980. Of course, my best friend Rick Keneson, was smiling cheek to cheek. I don't think he cared that much because the game wasn't on TV, and therefore nobody could see the outcome.

Ohio State was now scheduled to play the University of Pittsburgh or "Pitt" as they were often called, in the 1984 Fiesta Bowl. That game would be on television on NBC on January 2nd.

After Christmas came and went, I went downstairs to watch Ohio State take on the Pitt Panthers the following day after New

Year's. Ohio State was wearing their traditional white jerseys, gray pants, and silver helmets. Since Ohio State's game against Michigan wasn't on TV that November, I really was excited to watch the Buckeyes play.

My parents and sisters watched the game upstairs on a set in my parent's bedroom. Don't ask me why but for some reason I ended up watching the game alone. Maybe it was because my family knew that I couldn't sit still during a game, and it would be more enjoyable if they watched it in a different room.

Mike Tomczak scored the first touchdown and it looked like the Buckeyes would win the Fiesta Bowl. One of the most exciting plays in the game was when Ohio State's Keith Byars returned a kickoff in the 2nd half 95 yards to break a 14-14 tie.

The last part of the 4th quarter was one of the most exciting quarters ever of Buckeye football, and yet filled with a ton of tension. Pitt had this kicker named Snuffy Everett. He was a straight- on kicker, and not like the soccer-style kickers you see today in college or pro football.

Snuffy hit a field goal, and Pitt was now leading the Fiesta Bowl by a score of 23-21. *That's it! Game is over! Ohio State is no good! I can't believe I like this team!*

Those were some of the phrases that were coming out of my mouth at the time. I did know that there was still time left on the clock.

Could Ohio State pull off a miracle victory?

The finish to the game… Ohio State had over 90 yards to go for a touchdown or at least a field goal to win. With under a minute to play in the game, Tomczak threw a pass to wide receiver Thad Jemison for the winning score!!

As the ball was caught by Thad, I literally jumped in the air, and knocked out a ceiling tile in our basement. I do remember what happened next. I started crying alone in my basement. I mean I was really crying! I kept saying, *"I love you, Ohio State!"*

It was another moment where I really knew I loved Ohio State more than anything else in my life with the exception of my family. Was it possible to like or love a school that much? I came up the stairs to celebrate with my family even though the game wasn't over yet.

My dad looked at me and said, *"Why are you crying? Ohio State just scored a touchdown!"*

My emotions and the moment just overwhelmed me. As I was set to finish the rest of my sophomore year of high school after the great Ohio State win, I had to make some major life decisions. Was I going to run track & field in the spring for Merrillville? Also, I was midway through the school year and I didn't really have a girlfriend either.

Mike "D" Demakas and I were still going to "Goya" dances and learning "Break Dancing." D would always say that this dance would 'never go out of style.' My dad always found humor in that comment made by him. As we were getting closer to spring, I kept putting Coach Armontrout off about joining the track & field team. The man scared me.

I mean there was a reason why I didn't run track for him the previous year while I was still at Harrison. I knew that I would have to take a bus to the high school. The real reason was that he was a tough and an intimidating individual. Even my dad's friend, Bob "Beero" Mizura, who played football for Coach Armontrout while he was at Merrillville, said that he was just a tough guy. When he approached me again about running track & field, I simply said that I was more interested in playing football for the Pirates.

I knew that Coach Haupt wasn't returning to Merrillville for my last two years of high school, but I still had dreams of making it as a star player for the football team. Coach Armontrout looked at me with this stern glare and said, *"Bull! You can run track and also play football. They are different seasons!"* Coach Armontrout had a way of persuading you to do something. I finally said "ok" to him but under the condition that I would run the 100 and 200 meter dashes.

Wrong again!

Coach "A" as we called him, said that he was going to make me a 400-meter runner. What was I going to say? After all, he had me convinced that track & field would make me faster for football. Besides, Mike "D" Demakas was also going to run track for Merrillville. With two other sophomores named Freddy Summers and Brad Curcio, we were going to be a great track & field program.

We started conditioning for the season in January of 1984. Coach Armontrout never cancelled practices. It could be a blizzard outside or raining terribly, and we would still have practice. I learned real quickly that Coach Armontrout loved track & field, and he was going to get the most out of his athletes. He was going to push me harder than any previous coach had ever before. His practices were hard and very demanding.

Coach "A" never cancelled. I didn't realize it at the time, but I was running for a coach who was considered an "icon" not only in Northwest Indiana but the entire state. It seemed like everywhere we went with Coach Armontrout, people knew him. For me, he took on the same persona as Coach Woody Hayes did while he was coaching at Ohio State.

Tough, fair, detailed, competitive, and always doing things the right way. No shortcuts in sports or in life! That personified Coach Hayes as well as Coach Armontrout. I would be a recipient of some of Coach Armontrout's 'tough love' and his demanding ways throughout my high school years. There were many days that I just didn't think he liked me. I just didn't realize his master plan. Not that he was going to tell me, however.

The track & field team would have to do a grueling 2 ½ mile run every practice around the school and the bus barns. The bus barns were in the far back of Merrillville High School, and this where the school housed the buses when they were not in use. A lot of kids would hide behind the bus barns so Coach Armontrout didn't see them cheating on the workout of the full 2 ½ mile easy run. He knew if you were doing the workout or not. It was really difficult to fool Coach "A."

He told me one time that if I put in the hard work and extra effort, that I would be a good athlete here at Merrillville High School. I did say the one word that Coach Armontrout despised more than any other word in the English dictionary. I told him one time that I can't do this certain workout. You never said the word, 'Can't' to Coach Armontrout. Coach looked at me and simply said, *"Can't never did anything! If you say you can, then you have a chance!"*

Even to this day, I still remember that phrase whenever I don't think I can do something, or if life gets too tough. It was kind of like what Earle Bruce told us at the Ohio State football camp in the summer. If you get knocked down, you get back up again. Coach Armontrout was the same way. He made you believe that you could do things even if you thought you couldn't.

No shortcuts or excuses.

Ok, I thought... I am going to run track for this man at Merrillville High School. He might be crazy, tough, and mean, but I am going to be one of his athletes. I still didn't go to all the so-called demanding conditioning practices in January and February that year.

Sometimes he would search me out in school to ask why I wasn't at practice. Like I said, there were many times that I thought the man hated me. I was too blind to realize that he was instilling work ethic qualities that I would need later in life.

If I had thought my youth football coach Andy Tancos was tough on me, then I hadn't seen anything yet. Coach Armontrout was on a whole different level. He was very persistent with me on doing things the right way.

I have to be honest about something. With the evolution of practice facilities as well as field houses, high school athletes nowadays can practice indoors when the weather gets bad.

In the 1980's, we really didn't have that luxury. The only exception was that if it was raining hard, and only then would we run in the hallways at Merrillville. That's if it was raining really hard and there were tornado watches in the area.

173

Other than that, Coach "A" had us outside practicing track & field in the coldest of elements, and running on hard asphalt or concrete. We would also do these crazy warmup exercises that no one ever heard of like 'twirl-arounds' and 'hop-swings.'

We would always ask Coach if we had to do these in front of other teams at track meets? Our warm-up routine was very odd-looking, and sometimes very embarrassing, especially in front of our girl classmates. Coach Armontrout was very 'old-school' in his approach.

One of my female classmates asked me one time as she walked past practice, *"Denny, what are you guys doing out there to warm-up for track? It looks pretty silly!"* Regardless, Coach had his reasons and it did seem to make us a better team.

As the track season was ready to begin in March, Coach Armontrout was also conducting Saturday morning practices. The week before our first track meet at Bloom Trail High School in Illinois, he told all of us that we would have an early Saturday morning practice. I would not be there.

There were two things that were tugging at my heart. One was that I had never seen an Ohio State basketball game in person. Also, I would be spending time with my grandfather at a college basketball game. Papa always liked going to those high school football games on Friday nights while I was in junior high school. We really didn't do many things together (just he and I) once I got into high school and started driving a car.

To my surprise, Coach Armontrout told me to go ahead and go to the Ohio State game with my grandfather. Either Coach understood how much I loved Ohio State, or he understood the importance of spending time with my grandfather.

With that, Papa and I were off to West Lafayette, Indiana to watch Ohio State take on the Purdue Boilermakers in a basketball game. I remember it was a sunny day driving there. The whole way to the game, my grandfather told stories. We also talked about life, school, as well as girls. It was a very memorable afternoon with the exception of Ohio State losing to the Boilermakers by the score of 85-63.

The Buckeyes had two great players on the team that I really liked—Ron Stokes and Troy Taylor. I am sure I was upset that Ohio State lost the game, but I didn't show it. I was just grateful my grandfather had received the tickets and that we went to a game together. It wouldn't be the last time I would go to Purdue for a sporting event that year with Papa either. We would return again in the fall of 1984 to watch Ohio State play Purdue in football. Would that game prove to be memorable?

My track & field season started a week later when we went to a meet at Bloom Trail High School in Illinois. I was amazed at how different it was competing in high school compared to running at the junior high level for Coach Feeney or Coach Stefek. Everyone seemed so much faster or could jump a lot further. I was surprised when I saw that Coach Armontrout put me in the lineup as a varsity runner and long jumper. It was my first experience as a varsity athlete at Merrillville High School.

I was going against top athletes from different schools in Illinois as well as from Indiana. I can't say that I did well because most of the kids in the track meet were experienced juniors and seniors. When I got home from the meet that night, I was surprised by what my dad and Papa did to my bedroom. I now know why they didn't come to my track & field meet that day…

While I was gone at the track meet, Papa and dad had put Ohio State wallpaper up, and put shelves in my room to display all the Buckeye memorabilia that I had collected over the years. They had also laid down red carpeting in the room. Mom had bought an Ohio State bedspread to go with the design of the room as well. I guess the other people in my family started realizing that I was a big Ohio State fan. This was not just going to be a passing obsession or love for a team which lasted a year or two.

I couldn't even tell you the academic entrance requirements to get into The Ohio State University during my sophomore year in high school. I am not sure any of my friends believed me either when I said I was going to go there as a student. Most of the kids I went to school with at Merrillville were also mature enough to realize that they were going to pick a school to go to base on academics and what they wanted to explore in terms of a career field. They were not really picking colleges because of how good the school was in football or basketball.

Sure, there were other kids at Merrillville who liked watching Ohio State on TV. They never gave it much thought about going to school there as a student. I, on the hand, felt that if I loved the school that much as a fan, why not go there and experience everything that Ohio State had to offer? There was still that one problem. Like I said...

I wasn't a very good student. I mean I could have been a better student if I would have tried a little bit harder at studying, organizing, and preparing. I also was more concerned with who was going to be my high school girlfriend. I hadn't had a steady relationship since the last part of my freshman year at Harrison when I dated Lori.

Of course, there was the "new" Lori from Pierce that I liked but she really didn't take me seriously. The 'girl question' would once again be answered later in the spring of 1984.

First, I had to go into the Merrillville High School main office and talk with my guidance counselor about my plans to attend Ohio State. Maybe she would take me seriously about my quest to be a student there. I just didn't realize what she was about to say...

On Monday morning, after a weekend filled with going to my first high school track meet, as well as Papa and dad remodeling my room with Ohio State wallpaper, I went in to see Mrs. "M," who was my guidance counselor at Merrillville.

She pulled open a filing cabinet drawer which was filled with personalized folders of every student's academic records she was in-charge of at Merrillville High School. As Mrs. "M" opened up my own file, she stared at it for what seemed to be like an eternity. She kept shaking her head back and forth like it was the worst thing she ever seen.

She put her glasses to the tip of her nose, and looked up at me to say, *"You have a lot of work to do if you want to go to Ohio State."* She followed that statement with a sigh and another disappointing head shake.

She asked me if I had researched the university and if I knew what the requirements were to get into such a prestigious school?

"Uh no," I told her.

I could probably tell Mrs. "M" how many passing yards Buckeye quarterback Mike Tomczak had that year, or that John Frank had an unbelievable game against Oklahoma in 1983. I could also tell her that I went to football camp at Ohio State, and that Coach Earle Bruce taught me a lot about football.

She asked me about Ohio State's business program. What about their engineering program? I had no clue. She asked me if I walked around the campus and looked at all the buildings? She did inquire if I researched other schools. What kind of question was that? Of course I didn't research other schools! Why would I do that? In my mind, there was only one school that existed.

When you are sixteen years old, I am not sure that a guidance counselor's advice is going to completely register with you. Besides, I had a track & field season to worry about and more importantly, finding a girlfriend. I couldn't go completely through my sophomore year at Merrillville without finding a girlfriend, could I? A difficult decision was about to happen.

As Merrillville started having outdoor track meets later in the spring of 1984, Mike "D" Demakas and I started learning the event known as the long jump. We both did the long jump in junior high but didn't know how detailed and complicated it was to learn the event. "D" and I had the luxury of learning from an upperclassman named Chris Massa. Chris was an unbelievable athlete at Merrillville.

He taught Mike and I a lot that first year of track & field in high school. We would also read about Carl Lewis, who was this world-class Olympic athlete, and a long jumper. It seemed that Mike "D" and I would be the long jump tandem for the rest of our high school years together. I was still afraid of Coach Armontrout.

The seniors once told us young underclassmen that with Coach "A", 'you feared him as a sophomore, respected him as a junior, and tolerated him as a senior.' Great advice! He was definitely one of a kind. We only lost two track meets that year, and had a lot of great athletes on the team. I have to admit that I wasn't solely focused on track once a certain girl caught my eye that spring.

Leave it to a girl to shift my focus away from school, sports, or Ohio State.

Chapter 15
High School Love and Romance

Her name was Anne. She would be my first girlfriend once I reached high school. There was just one problem though. Anne didn't go to Merrillville High School. In fact, she wasn't in high school at all. Anne was still at Harrison Junior High School as an 8th grader. In other words, she was two years younger than me. Two girls who liked me that spring. Anne was one of them.

The other was a girl named Amy. I met both of them through mutual friends who were also dating younger girls. My friend, Brian Portlock, would also start dating this girl named Jan. She happened to be one of Anne's best friends. I have to admit that I felt a little weird about dating a girl who was still in junior high school. I think my parents probably felt it was strange too. After all, my sister Nikki was going to the same junior high school as Anne.

Amy was beautiful as well but I didn't think that relationship would last. Amy liked a lot of boys, so I knew it would be a short-term fling if I were to date her. Anne was different. I knew my relationship with her would last, and maybe even beyond high school.

I actually met Anne at a Harrison Junior High dance. I am not sure why I was there other than the fact that a lot of my friends would show up at junior high dances. Were we not past that point in our lives?

Why were we hanging out at Harrison Junior High dances and why would the principal of the school let us in? Well, I am not sure he knew that we snuck into these dances reserved just for the kids who attended Harrison. They definitely were not intended for high school students.

Anne and I danced to slow music that night and exchanged phone numbers. We would often double-date to the movies. Anne's parents wouldn't always let her go out with me however, mainly because of our age difference.

I do believe that her parents liked me and thought that I was a nice person. Well... I am not sure her dad liked me that much. Anne's dad was a Michigan football fan and liked Wolverines' coach, Bo Schembechler. Anne wasn't caught up in sports allegiance. She was more interested in falling in love with me. I was also interested in falling in love with her. I even skipped out early from a track meet to be with Anne. If Coach Armontrout only knew the truth.

Our team was scheduled to go to the Griffith Relays in late April. It was held at Griffith High School, the same school that I lived by before I moved to Merrillville in 1978. It was really neat going back and seeing some of the Griffith kids who I grew up with before I changed residence.

I really wanted to be with Anne. Coach Armontrout had put me in four different track events that night. I had to come up with a story. I told him that I had a wedding to go to later that evening and I couldn't stay for the whole track meet. Coach A actually bought my lie! Who would take my place in the other events? The answer would be... Mike "D" Demakas. I hated to lie to Coach "A" but I had to do what I needed to do. I wanted to spend the evening with Anne.

Coach told Mike that he would have to run in my place for some of the events, like a distance medley relay. "D" looked at Coach Armontrout like he was speaking a foreign language. *"What!? Noooooo way, Coach!"*

Those were the words uttered by "D" when he found out that I was leaving the track meet early to attend a wedding. I really wasn't attending a wedding. To this day, I am not sure "D" knew the real reason why I was leaving the meet.

Love does strange things to people.

I wanted to be with Anne more than I wanted to be at the Griffith Track & Field Relays. Even though I really thought I was in love with Lori back in my Harrison Junior High School days, or even my innocent crush with Kelli back when I was at Miller Elementary, Anne became my first 'true love.'

I would often sneak into her house so we could go somewhere to kiss. I believe she was the first girl that uttered the words, *"I love you."*

Anne may have also been the first girl to tolerate my obsession with Ohio State. I am not sure if Anne cared about Buckeye football. I knew that she was younger than me and would still have a couple of years left of high school once I graduated from Merrillville. Would the relationship with her last? Would there be other girls in high school?

I was hoping that was not the case. I was really falling in love with her. One of my friends asked me how the Buckeyes were going to do in the 1984 season. I don't think I really knew. All I cared about was my new girlfriend relationship.

My summer of 1984 was filled with spending time with Anne, going out with my friends to the old Y&W drive-in movie theater in Merrillville, and playing golf at Turkey Creek Golf Course with Rick. The Y& W drive-in was an outdoor movie theater that high school kids went to watch movies and just hang-out as teenagers. A lot of times, I would sneak my friends in the trunk of my car so they wouldn't have to pay the admission price to the drive-in. It was also a place that you took your girlfriend on Friday and Saturday nights to kiss and make-out.

As the fall of 1984 was getting started, I was ready for another season of high school football at Merrillville as well as watching the Ohio State Buckeyes. I was now going to be on the varsity football team and I have a new football coach. Coach Haupt had left Merrillville and was now coaching at Southport High School near Indianapolis.

I'm not going to say the new coach was bad, but he just wasn't Coach Haupt. I also received some bad news that Ohio State's starting quarterback, Mike Tomczak had suffered a double fracture in his right leg in the spring game scrimmage

With him being out of the lineup, how was Ohio State now going to beat Michigan and go to the Rose Bowl? I knew the Buckeyes were going to have a great team in 1984 but they really needed to have Mike Tomczak play in games.

In my bedroom that dad and Papa remodeled for me with Ohio State wallpaper, was a poster of Mike Tomczak. I still held out hope that he was going to play in the 1984 season. I even wrote a letter to the paper I subscribed to known as the *"Buckeye Leaves."*

I wrote the following which was published in the OSU newspaper that August of 1984:

Dear Buckeye Leaves,

"I am very excited about the upcoming football season. The Buckeyes could have one of the best football teams in the country this fall, led by Mike Tomczak and Keith Byars. Though everyone knows how powerful the Ohio State offense is, the Bucks seem to lack a strong defensive backfield- even in the past few years with names like Garcia Lane and Shaun Gayle. I would like to have the Buckeyes undefeated and national and Rose Bowl Champs. (we can do it) Go Bucks. Beat the Blue bad!"

Sincerely,

Denny "Buckeye" Bunda

Merrillville, IN

When I got the preview issue the following week, I looked at the Reader's Viewpoint section of the *Buckeye Leaves* and there were my comments! Of all the people that subscribed to the magazine, they decided to publish my remarks. I was also encouraged to see a picture of Mike Tomczak on the front page of the issue signing autographs for fans at Ohio State's media day.

Coach Earle Bruce's comment in the newspaper stated that he was very optimistic to have Tomczak back for the season as well. I was set to start two- a-day practices at Merrillville High School in the hot

August sun. We were also required to stay at the school in-between practices to meet with our coaches about football plays, drills, tackling, and blocking.

I didn't attend the Ohio State football camp in the summer. Having a girlfriend and spending time with friends took up my days as well as nights. When mandatory football practices started, that would consume most of my time. Anne wanted me to come over to her house after practices ended, but I told her I was too tired from the heat and all the football drills during the day.

Every day I would come home exhausted from those practices. My mom would come into my bedroom and say, *"Anne called. She wants you to call her when you have time."*

I would always ignore her phone calls because I was too tired. I was placing emphasis on playing football for Merrillville above her as my girlfriend. I ate, drank, and slept football. I was really focused on being a great player for Merrillville.

The problem was that I ended up not being such a great boyfriend. I knew it was unfair to treat her that way, but I thought Anne would understand. Until I got another phone call from her one day. Her words left me frozen and shocked. I sat still in my chair as I talked to her on the telephone.

Anne told me that she was breaking up with me. She really didn't give me an explanation but I knew why, or at least I thought I did. I thought that her and I were really meant to be as far as being boyfriend and girlfriend.

She was the first girl I said the magic words of "I love you." I could tell that her voice was cracking while she gave me the bad news, but I kept pleading with her to give our relationship a second chance. Anne finally hung up the phone on me.

Why did I put playing or watching football above her? Could another boy like or love her as much as I did? The answer would come quickly. It is not what I wanted to hear. When I got to football practice the next day, I was very depressed about the situation.

Could one girl really affect my football season, my attitude, and my life?

My friends on the team, Brian Portlock and Bucky Randall, tried to cheer me up. To no avail, I may have had one of the worst practices of my time at Merrillville. Brian said that I needed to call her and work things out.

Coach Peller, who was my wide receiver coach, was probably yelling the words, *"Denny Bunda, what are you doing!?!"* I didn't care though. I wanted to get home and call Anne on the phone. We didn't have cell phones back then, so I am sure I probably made it home in about five minutes going over the speed limit.

For two days straight, I begged and pleaded for Anne to take me back. When she agreed to give the relationship a second chance, I promised her that I would make time to see her even with my busy football schedule.

She did go out with another boy while I was at football practice. When I found that to be true, I was absolutely crushed! Would things ever be the same between us? She was my first 'real love' and wanted to find this 'other' boy to fight with him.

As I took all my friends' home from football practice, one day, we saw him walking on the side of the road. I completely spun my car around, going after him. Seeing that I was chasing him, he ran as fast as he could to get away from my car—absolutely crazed rage that day.

Chapter 16
Life Isn't Always Fair

The school year started on August 30th, 1984. I was set to start a new football season, a new school year, and the Buckeyes would be on TV during Saturdays. Anne was still at Harrison Junior High entering her freshman year so I wouldn't get to see her, or know what boy she was talking to in school. At my high school, things got very interesting that fall of 1984. In the high school, there was an undercover cop disguised as a MHS student, who was part of a drug investigation.

Little did we know at the time, but the result of the investigation prompted Merrillville school officials to close its campus for school lunches. Prior to that, the MHS students could go out to eat during their lunch hour. We would go to the Dairy Queen which was not that far from the high school. All that may have been true about a drug investigation but I think Merrillville wanted to make more money off of their school lunches. The undercover police officer was actually a girl. She looked and acted like a teenager. I had a few friends that even befriended her. She was fairly good-looking and many of my classmates tried to ask her out. Of course, the undercover police officer always said, "no." There was always suspicion that there was a 'drug problem' at the high school. If there was, I didn't know about it. Maybe for the fact that none of my friends did illegal drugs. Many of them just drank beer or wine coolers. It appeared that the fall of 1984 was going to be a lot different than my first year of high school.

In terms of my school schedule, I had some tough classes that year, including English Literature and Geometry. My Geometry teacher was a graduate and fan of the University of Michigan. I guess I needed to keep my mouth shut in that class if I wanted to get a decent grade. If you know me...I didn't though.

My favorite class in my junior year was taught by a lady named Ms. Anderson. Ms. Anderson taught a photography class where she showed the students how to take photos with a professional camera and develop your own pictures. It was the one class that I really looked forward to learning about something that interested me.

Grammy and Papa purchased an expensive camera for me to use in the class. As for the rest of my school schedule, it was boring and/or very difficult. I did have my high school football season to look forward to in 1984. Also, Ohio State's season was about to begin in early September.

We lost our first varsity football game that year to a rival high school known as the Crown Point Bulldogs on our home field. A night or two before the game with them, our football coaches wanted us to practice at night instead of our usual after-school routine. I think they wanted us to get used to playing at night, especially when it came to catching footballs under the lights of our MHS football field known as *"Demaree Field."*

As we were practicing, we noticed a group of about forty kids outside the fence by our south endzone. It was the Crown Point team watching us practice! Coach looked at us and said, *"Go get 'em, boys!!"*

We immediately stopped what we were doing and chased the Crown Point team away from our practice. Even though that made us mad and motivated our team, Crown Point would win the game by the score of 21-14. It was a much better contest than the previous year when we lost to them 24-0.

Two weeks after the Crown Point game, I was coming home from school and football practice feeling more tired than normal. At first, I just shrugged it off as just my days being filled with school, football, and having a girlfriend. There were times that my mom would come into my room to tell me that Anne had called on the phone. I told my mom to tell Anne that I would call her back later in the evening. I had no idea why I felt so tired.

There were many nights when I fell asleep at 7 pm rather than my usual time of 11 pm. A lot of nights, I would never call Anne back or remember to do so. This may have aggravated Anne to a point where she was once again second-guessing our relationship. The answer to my tiredness would come in a few short weeks. It would be devastating news.

Ohio State was opening their football season on September 8th of 1984. My Merrillville team had just beat Michigan City Rogers High School the previous night by the score of 22-6. The Merrillville coaches always had us come in Saturday mornings after the Friday night games so we could watch films of what happened the night before. They would put the team in a large classroom with a TV in front of the room.

The coaches would point out what we did well or not so well in the game. After that, we would go out to the practice field, and run through plays that needed correction or plays that we were going to run against next week's opponent. If time permitted, they would let us swim for a while in the MHS indoor pool.

I knew Ohio State was going to be on TV that day because of the U.S. Supreme Court ruling during the summer which allowed teams to sign television contacts. No longer was Ohio State restricted to three or four games a year on television. I had read in my Ohio State newspaper that the Buckeyes were worried that if more games were televised, people would be less willing to actually go to the game.

Stations like ESPN and Raycom, as well as other cable outlets, were now going to cover college football. I always thought it was funny that the Ohio State athletic administration believed fans wouldn't go to the games if the Buckeyes were on TV every week. For me, there was nothing like being at an Ohio State football game.

Don't get me wrong.

I really liked the fact that Ohio State was now going to be televised a lot more, but there is nothing like being in Ohio Stadium cheering on the Buckeyes during a fall afternoon. However, because dad was a coach himself, and I played high school football, it was tough to go to a lot of games.

Coupled with the fact that Columbus, Ohio was a good five-hour drive from our home in Northwest Indiana. Therefore, we went to a lot of Ohio State games when they played opponents not that far from our house. Trips to Purdue, Northwestern, Illinois, and Indiana were always part of the plan when the Buckeyes were playing in their stadiums.

In 1984, Ohio State football really started to consume me. Due to the fact that my parents had purchased me a subscription to the *Buckeye Leaves* newspaper and Ohio State was televised a lot more, I could really follow my favorite team. I did get a letter in the mail that the *Buckeye Leaves* was no longer going to be a newspaper publication. Instead the *Buckeye Sports Bulletin* would replace my old magazine as a source for my Ohio State information.

I raced home from my morning football practice at Merrillville to turn on the television set. My parents had just signed up for cable television that year so we were getting a lot more stations. Ohio State was set to play the Oregon State Beavers. Mike Tomczak was still recovering from his broken leg, so back-up quarterback Jim Karsatos would get the start for the Buckeyes.

Ohio State also had a young freshman player who had made national headlines by being placed on a 'Wheaties' cereal box that year. His name was Chris Spielman, and he wore jersey #36. He was the first high school football player ever to appear on a Wheaties cereal box. Chris was from Massillon, Ohio. I knew all about him from reading the stories in my *Buckeye Leaves magazine*. I knew that Michigan wanted him to go to school there, and play for the Wolverines.

Mom naturally went to the grocery store and bought a box of Wheaties with Spielman's picture on the front of it. How cool was that, I thought. She was always buying the new cereals on the market in the grocery store. So, after I had my bowl of Wheaties, it was off to the basement to watch the Buckeyes take on Oregon State.

Ohio State was predicted to win the Big Ten Conference in 1984, and had a lot of stars on their team. It was a sunny day in Columbus, Ohio, and the Buckeyes were going to beat Oregon State. I wish it was that simple. Ohio State actually was down 14-3 at halftime to a team who was not even that good.

The Buckeyes were ranked #6 in the country and getting beat by a lesser opponent. Cris Carter was now a freshman playing in his first game for Ohio State. I kept thinking that I went to football camp with this guy back in the summer of 1983. Now he is playing for Ohio State on TV!

Chris Spielman came into the contest for Ohio State at linebacker. He would go on to have ten tackles and forced an Oregon State fumble in his first game as a Buckeye. The Buckeyes went on to win by the score of 22-14. It may not have been Ohio State's best performance but there were a lot of big games to come during the 1984 season.

I still wasn't feeling my greatest, and I probably knew something was physically wrong with me. Again, I just thought that I was suffering from fatigue due to football practice as well as the difficult classes that I was taking during my junior year at Merrillville.

By the end of the following weekend of September 16th, I had a really bad sore throat. The glands on the side of my throat were swollen, and I was coughing terribly. I didn't really want to miss school or football practice that day. Mom said that she thought I had strep throat and was making me an appointment to see our family physician, Doctor Pruitt. Once he took a look at my throat, Dr. Pruitt said he knew what illness had made me feel so sick and tired.

He said that blood tests would confirm it but I had mononucleosis or simply put, *"mono."* They call it the kissing disease but Dr. Pruitt thought that my immune system was worn down due to the strenuous football practices. He told me that I would have to stay home for the rest of the week, and possibly miss 2-3 weeks of school.

What!?

I would miss a couple of football games, assignments from school, and of course, seeing Anne. As we were leaving Doctor Pruitt's office, I looked over at mom and said, *"Life isn't fair!!"* Mom didn't say anything. I think she knew that I would miss a lot of school and the sport I enjoyed playing.

How could this happen to me? I slept the whole way home in the car. She put me in her bedroom so I could watch TV and get some rest. I must have watched one-hundred rerun episodes of: *"The Courtship of Eddie's Father"*. *"The Monkey's"*. *"The Banana Splits"*.

Those were my only choices unless I wanted to watch soap operas like *"All My Children"* or *"General Hospital."* No thank you! We had limited programming back then so that is what I watched on television. I was very miserable sitting there just sleeping, eating, and watching shows.

What were my friends doing in school? How was football practice going? Was Anne talking to another boy? Those were some of the thoughts racing through my head. I was absolutely miserable, frustrated and kept repeating my statement that I made to mom...

"Life Isn't Fair!"

On September 21st, my high school football team traveled to Gary West Side High School to play a varsity football game. I, of course, was home getting over mononucleosis. I actually had to listen to my Merrillville teammates play on the radio. I sat in my bedroom just staring at the walls that my dad and grandfather wallpapered the previous March. When you are as sick as I was, frustration sets in on many levels.

I knew that I would be behind in my schoolwork. My classes were tough that year. I also knew that Dr. Pruitt was not going to let me play football for a couple of weeks until he was completely sure I was over the "mono." I wondered if I could go to the homecoming dance with Anne in a few weeks.

As I listened to the Merrillville game on the radio, which was uneventful because we only won 14-0, it seemed like life was crumbling before my very eyes. My mom was going through her radiation treatments for breast cancer as well. I was really depressed. The Buckeyes were going to be on TV for a third week straight the following day. They were scheduled to play the Iowa Hawkeyes. Maybe that would brighten my spirits.

The next day, I watched Ohio State avenge their loss to Iowa from the previous year by the score of 45-26. What a great game! Iowa had not won in Columbus, Ohio since 1959, and it wouldn't be this day either. Mike Tomczak looked like he was fully recovered from his injuries, and was back in the Ohio State starting lineup. Keith Byars, the Buckeyes tailback, had an unbelievable game.

Early on, Keith ran about 50 yards for a touchdown while he was weaving in and out of Iowa defenders. I thought that Keith really had a great chance to win the Heisman Trophy in 1984, which was given to the top player in all of college football. Byars ran for a touchdown, caught a touchdown, and threw a touchdown all in the same game.

Ohio State was now 3-0 on the season, and things were really looking good for them. As for me, I was set to return to school the following week. That meant that I would be on the sidelines while all the students, cheerleaders, and parents were cheering for all my teammates on the field.

That Friday afternoon, one of my girl classmates saw me in the hallway and said, *"I look forward to seeing you play tonight, Denny! Welcome back!"*

I didn't have the heart to tell her that I wasn't playing but instead holding a clipboard for the coaches. I have to admit that part of the reason I was still playing football was to impress the girls in school, especially Anne. That wouldn't be happening for a while. It was as if life had moved on without me while I was home recovering from my illness.

In school, I was really behind in my academics, especially in my Geometry class. Again, I am not really sure that my teacher liked me much because he was a graduate of Michigan. At least, that is what I used as an excuse for not doing well in his class. I was flunking his class and he was not letting up on the homework. I was also doing poorly in my English Literature class.

At that point, I was just trying to get through the day, and not paying attention to what the teachers were trying to teach. As usual, I would sit at my desk and write down Ohio State football statistics, and try to remember all scores from past games. My Geometry teacher would ask me questions, and of course, I would make up some answer acting like I knew what I was talking about.

My classmates would just laugh at me. One female student uttered the words... *"How could someone be that dumb?"* I didn't care though. Going to Ohio State seemed like a 'pipe dream' now, especially if I couldn't cut it as a student at Merrillville High School.

My dad actually had me research other colleges to see what their academic and entrance requirements were to be accepted. I went to the old *Lake County Library* in Merrillville to look up colleges and see if I could get in with such a low high school grade- point average.

Was I even going to go to college?

I am not sure that was even on my mind. Getting better from my mononucleosis, going back to playing varsity football, and hanging out with friends was on my mind. Oh yeah, there was also my relationship with Anne. I had asked her to our homecoming dance that was going to take place in two weeks.

Anne said 'yes,' and I had to buy a formal suit and tie for the occasion.

I would have to get through another week of school and sit on the bench at our home varsity football game against Valparaiso High School. The coaches handed me my jersey to wear on the sidelines with my jeans. It was the first time that I could recall I was not in full uniform for a football game other than the one I missed the week before while recovering from my illness. It was the day after my birthday when we played the Valparaiso Vikings.

Doctor Pruitt had told me that I was not to exercise or have any physical activity until he released me from being sick from

192

mononucleosis. Supposedly, if you got hit in the spleen, it could enlarge, and kill you. As Merrillville went through warm-ups, I was on the sidelines catching footballs from one of our managers.

I knew I wasn't supposed to do any physical activity according to Doctor Pruitt. I didn't care though. The stands were full that night with spectators because we were playing a good team. I told our manager to throw the ball high so I could leap up and get it, just like I saw Cris Carter do at the Ohio State football camp the year before.

I was trying to impress the crowd even though I wasn't in full uniform or playing that night. It was what happened right before the game which really got me choked up and emotional.

It was announced to the crowd right before the game that a couple of Valparaiso High School students were killed in an automobile/train accident the week before on September 21st, 1984. I was absolutely stunned…

Anytime someone your age is killed in a tragic accident; it really shakes you up. I didn't know the students from VHS, but supposedly one of the girls killed in the accident was a really good high school basketball player.

I think when you are young, a person believes they are invisible. Things like that can't happen. I kept thinking about the car accident that my friends and I were involved in during December of 1983. That could have been us. In my case, thankfully no one was injured or killed.

Before the game started with Valparaiso High School, we had a *'moment of silence'* for those students killed the week before in the crash. I was thinking how precious life was, and that we really don't have a long time to live. We have to take advantage of every moment, and make the most of it. I was thinking of those kids who didn't live out their dreams, goals, and aspirations.

After the announcement and moment of silence, it was as if the football game against Valparaiso really didn't matter. I started thinking about my future and what if my life was to be cut short. Did I accomplish everything that I wanted to at this point in my life? The answer was no. I started thinking about everything that I wanted to do. Merrillville did end up winning the game by the score of 31-27 but football seemed less important to me that night.

The next day, I learned that Ohio State was playing a night game vs. Minnesota in Minneapolis. My mom told me that the game would be on a TV station that we didn't get in our own home. She knew a family friend who had the particular cable station that would be airing the Ohio State/Minnesota football game.

A lot of my friends were planning on going to a teenage nightclub known as *"Club Soda."* There were going to be girls there from other high schools in the area. I was still dating Anne but it seemed that after she broke up with me initially, things started to change with our relationship. I was young and in high school. I couldn't be serious about just one girl, could I? I mean I was too young to have a serious relationship. I have to admit that I still loved Anne.

Anne was two years younger than me, and she wasn't always able to go out on dates. Her parents would put restrictions on our dating. Besides, what she didn't know about me going out with other people wasn't going to hurt her.

Instead of going to my parent's friend's house to watch the Ohio State game, I went with Brian Portlock and some other friends to *Club Soda.* I did feel guilty of not watching Ohio State play that night. The Buckeyes were ranked #3 in the country and looked unstoppable.

I guess I knew they were going to beat the Minnesota Golden Gophers, and it wouldn't be much of a game. I think it shocked my parents that I was going to miss watching them play on television. I lived, ate, drank, and slept... Ohio State football. However, I was my friend's transportation to *Club Soda.* At least that was my excuse for not watching the game.

Chapter 17

Anger Management

We were scheduled to play a rival school for our homecoming game in October of 1984. They were known as the Andrean 59'ers. They got the nickname because they were located on 5959 Broadway in Merrillville—a Catholic school and not far from Merrillville High School.

It became a natural rivalry because they were the 'other school' in town. Besides, we knew a lot of the kids who went to Andrean. Some of them went to Harrison Junior High School with us before electing to attend Andrean instead of Merrillville. There were also former girlfriends who went there like my junior high school girlfriend, Pauline.

The game was known as the *"Battle of Broadway."*

Due to a new school rule, we were not able to have a student assembly or "pep session" during the school day. This was another dumb rule Merrillville decided to impose in addition to not allowing students to leave school during lunch time.

We called homecoming week… *"Spirit Week."*

Each day of the week leading up to the football game was a special theme in our school. On Monday, it was *"inside- out day."* Naturally, we had to wear our clothes inside-out. On Tuesday, it was *"crazy hairdo day!"* On Wednesday, it was *"nerd day,"* and on Thursday it was *"shade day,"* with the pep rally and bonfire during the night.

There was also a parade down Broadway which was the main street in front of the high school with the MHS Marching Band, fire trucks, parade floats, etc... The coaches addressed our student body Thursday night right after practice in Demaree Field. They talked about how important the game was with Andrean and that it would be embarrassing if we lost this homecoming battle to an in-town rival.

It would put a real damper on the homecoming dance the following night as well. With that being said, the game started at 7:30 pm on Friday, and we would win 21-3. Mike "D" Demakas would be the hero of the game that night as he went on to score a touchdown. I felt really happy for him. At the same time, I was on the bench watching the game. I was also told that I would be playing in the junior varsity game the following week.

I thought I worked hard enough to be a varsity player that year. It was not meant to be. Most of the varsity games, I sat there watching from the sidelines. I knew I was one of the faster players on the team and I could do great things that my teammates were doing on the field. It would be a hard lesson for me.

I had read somewhere in one of my Ohio State books that Coach Woody Hayes used to say that *'he wasn't the smartest person around, but he could always out-work people.'* Using Coach Hayes's approach, I knew that I had to work harder. Things were not going to be handed to me in the classroom, on the football field, and more importantly, in life.

I just didn't realize it at the time. I thought I was better than most of my teammates. I was fast and I could catch a football better than them. My friends said that I didn't play a lot during games because of my size and that I was not good at blocking. That couldn't be further from the truth.

I ran into a Merrillville teammate years later, and he said that the other players didn't want to defend me in practice because I was fast. He told me it was like 'tackling air.' That was a great compliment years later but it did me no good during the 1984 football season.

I had a lot of anger inside of me for many reasons. I knew that another guy liked Anne during the early part of the football season, I had mononucleosis, my mom was diagnosed with breast cancer, and my grades were suffering in school. Along with that, I started getting a bad attitude.

If you would have asked me if I was excited about Merrillville winning the homecoming game that year against Andrean, I could have cared less. I was more concerned with getting the game over that night and getting on to the next day. Papa was going to pick me up at my house for the Ohio State game at Purdue. The Boilermakers may not have been ranked in the nation at the time, but it was a big game for me. Growing up mostly in Griffith and Merrillville, there were a lot of Purdue Boilermaker fans around. I was confident that Ohio State would not only win the game, but beat Purdue convincingly.

Papa picked me up early in the morning and we were off to West Lafayette, Indiana. I hadn't been to Purdue's Ross-Ade Stadium since Ohio State defeated the Boilermakers while I was in the 8th grade during the 1981 season. It was another time that I got to spend time with my grandfather. Just he and I going to a football game.

We got to the stadium pretty early in the morning. I was amazed looking around at how many Buckeye fans made the trip from the state of Ohio. Ohio State's fan base always filled a stadium no matter where the Buckeyes played. It didn't seem cold that day either for being October. I was just wearing a gray Ohio State t-shirt. Papa had brought his binoculars so we could see the players up close from our seats. A Purdue fan sat right next to us. We had a pleasant conversation about Ohio State, the players, and how the season was going. He seemed nice.

He was amazed at how much I knew about the Buckeyes, and that I was a fan of them from Northwest Indiana of all places. I guess he didn't realize that not all people from the state of Indiana cheered for Purdue, Indiana, or Notre Dame. Papa bought me a game program for $1.50 which is hardly the price one could expect to pay for a program today.

Nowadays, it is about $10.

I was looking at the program before the start of the game, and noticed that Purdue had a few players on their roster who were from nearby towns close to where I lived. Ohio State's roster was made up mostly of kids who were from the state of Ohio. I knew Ohio was a great football state and produced some unbelievable athletes like Chris Spielman, and of course, Cris Carter.

I was still amazed that I had gone to the Ohio State football camp with Cris. He was now playing for the Ohio State Buckeyes while I was still playing high school football. I really believed the Buckeyes had too many great players to lose to Purdue that day. Plus the Buckeyes has moved up in the rankings to #2 in the nation only to #1 ranked Texas. No way were they going to lose.

Before the game got started, I was watching them warm-up on the field. Ohio State had this team manager who only had one leg. The other managers were throwing him the football as he was running on one leg making all these unbelievable catches. I didn't know who he was at the time, but some of the other Ohio State fans around me said his name was Tim Agerter. I mean he was really unbelievable!

He was just a manager but he was putting on a show for the crowd before the game. Tim was catching the football all the while running on one leg! Tim was from a neighboring town close to Merrillville known as Munster. I couldn't believe that an 'Indiana kid' was actually on the Ohio State staff as a manager. That was awesome! I also didn't realize that years later his brother Mark would become one of my great friends in life.

Purdue actually took an early 7-0 lead but I knew Ohio State was too powerful to not match the Boilermakers in points. Keith Byars seemed unstoppable that day. He would end the game with 191 rushing yards and 102 receiving yards. The Buckeyes led at halftime by the score of 10-7. I didn't seem too worried at the time, but it would be the second half that would be a memory that I would soon want to forget.

The Buckeyes went up 17-7 in the 3rd quarter. Papa and I were cheering and having the time of our lives. I can still see the smile on his face. It wasn't that the Buckeyes were winning that made him smile but just being with his grandson at a football game. The Purdue fans didn't seem to care either because they knew Ohio State was ranked #2 in the nation, and Keith Byars was gashing them every time he ran the football for the Buckeyes.

It was like old times when Papa and I were going to high school football games just a few years earlier while I was in junior high school. It was always a special time being with Papa. Since I was getting older, and in high school, I was spending more time with my friends. You know how the story goes.

Friends and girlfriends start to take center stage in your life. Friday and Saturday nights were filled with going to the Goya dances, Club Soda, high school events, and other places that teenagers would hang out. This day was different. Papa and I were spending the afternoon watching the Buckeyes. We spend time together as a grandfather and grandson, and enjoying every moment. I also had Anne waiting for me at home to take her to the high school homecoming dance later that night. It shaped up like a great memory in more ways than one. I wished it would have ended as a pleasant one.

But Papa would never mention this day, ever again.

In a blink of an eye, Ohio State now trailed Purdue in the 4th quarter by the score of 28-17. Mike Tomczak had thrown an interception to Purdue's defensive back, Rod Woodson. I can still see him in his #26 jersey running to the endzone opposite of where Papa and I were sitting that day. The man that I was sitting next to, who earlier I was cordial with, was now obnoxiously cheering for Purdue!

He kept saying, *"Go Purdue! Beat the Bucks!!"* *"Ohio State sucks!"*

I was so mad at this Purdue fan that I started yelling obscenities at him! I actually had to switch seats with Papa to get away from him! I just couldn't control my anger and the fact that Purdue was about to beat Ohio State.

Cris Carter did catch a touchdown pass with just 2:38 to go in the game to close the gap with the Boilermakers by the score of 28-23. The only problem was that Papa and I didn't see Cris catch the touchdown pass. We were already heading to the parking lot. Tears were filling my eyes. It may have been the only time that I left an Ohio State game early. I was stunned that they were going to lose.

We got into Papa's car and headed back to Northwest Indiana. I had him turn the rest of the game on the radio just to see if Ohio State could somehow pull out the victory. It was pure torture listening to the final minutes of the game. The Buckeyes actually drove down the field and were within scoring range to possibly pull off the miracle comeback.

The only thing I remember was the roar of the crowd coming through the radio. Mike Tomczak actually threw the football out of bounds to try to stop the clock. He didn't realize it was 4th down! I had read a week later in my sports paper that the Purdue scoreboard had said 3rd down, and Mike got confused on what down it actually was.

Papa reached for the radio and turned it off. Not a word was spoken the rest of the way home from West Lafayette until we pulled into my driveway on Johnson Street. What was there really to say? I know Papa felt the pain of the loss as much as I did. We may have stopped to go to the bathroom but I don't remember.

My eyes were filled with tears the whole way home. How was I going to go to the homecoming dance that night? What was I going to tell Anne? How about all the kids at the homecoming dance who were going to make fun of me that Ohio State lost to Purdue? I could just hear my childhood friend Steve Civanich say those words like he did in our junior high days...

Go PUUUUURDUUUE!!

As I came into my house, I headed right for my bedroom. I am not sure that I said thank you or goodbye to Papa. It is terrible to look back now and not realize that the most important thing about the game was spending time with him. Mom came into my bedroom and said that I needed to start getting into my suit and tie for the homecoming dance at Merrillville High School.

Nope!

That was the response to my mom.

There was no way that I was going to the homecoming dance that night. Mom had this glare in her eye like I never saw before. She told me that I had promised Anne, and I would in fact take her to the homecoming dance! No exceptions!

Mom always had this way about getting her point across to Nikki, Erin, and I.

So I got dressed and I headed out to pick up Anne for the dance. At least, I still had my girlfriend. Well... the relationship started falling apart that night as well. Even though Anne and I were still dating, it didn't seem the same as it did the previous spring or summer. We danced that night and even got a homecoming picture taken together. Maybe it was because I was so preoccupied with playing football for Merrillville or that I was too much of an Ohio State fan. She wanted someone that was going to pay attention to her all the time and rightfully so. She was a very beautiful and intelligent girl. That night would end our relationship as boyfriend and girlfriend.

I would take her out on a date one more time during my senior year but nothing too serious. A lot of my friends told me that I really messed up the relationship. She got a new boyfriend and that he treated her really well. Of course, I was jealous and wanted her back as my girlfriend, but it was not meant to be.

In school the next week during Geometry class, I watched people line up outside the gates of our football field. I wondered if they would do the same thing if the weather happened to be bad? My Geometry teacher kept on teaching but I never heard a word he said. Geometry class was the furthest from my mind.

The game against Hobart that night. It was the equivalent of Ohio State playing Michigan. Well... maybe as far as high school games go. I should have been listening to the Geometry lesson that hour but how could I? I was flunking Geometry anyways. We had won six consecutive varsity games, and we were going to try to upset the mighty Hobart team.

Warming up on the field that night, I looked around at all the spectators who were at the game. At the time, it was the biggest football game that I had ever been a part of as a player. As we ran off the field before the game started, I was jumping up and down to get our Merrillville fan section crowd fired up. I was actually leading them in a cheer as we were going back to the locker room for a pre-game speech from our coaches.

One of my teammates said, *"Way to go Denny! Get the crowd fired-up!"*

For whatever reason, I thought I was going to get in the game that night and play against Hobart. This would become another disappointing moment in my life. We lost the game by the score of 28-19 and I didn't play one minute. The coaches told me that I would be playing in the junior varsity game the following week against Hobart's junior varsity team. As a junior in high school, the last thing you want to hear is that you have been regulated as a "JV" player.

It was the equivalent of being a second or third string player on the varsity team. The anger that I had inside of me kept building up. I knew that eventually I would do something that I would regret.

In the junior varsity game against Hobart, I caught a long pass from our quarterback but was tackled from behind by one of their players. My teammates started hugging me and patting me on the helmet for such a good play. My anger enraged with everything that happened to me the previous week—Ohio State had lost to Purdue, things were not going well with Anne, and I was regulated to playing junior varsity football. I should have been happy that I was playing at all due to the fact that I was recovering from mononucleosis.

As the football season was wrapping up, I was playing in another junior varsity game against the LaPorte Slicers. At this time, I wasn't even a 'starting player' on the junior varsity team! Actually, I was splitting time at wide receiver with my great friend, Brian Portlock. He and I should have been playing together but an up and coming sophomore was also getting a lot of playing time at the position. I really believed that I should have been playing more than what the coaches were playing me in the games.

Coach Peller was also the junior varsity coach, and put me in that night against LaPorte. At that point in the game, I hadn't played that much. My attitude was really bad and I could care less who won. If Merrillville lost, so what! Great attitude, huh? However, I wanted to get in the game and do something spectacular to prove that I was better than anyone on the team at wide receiver. Coach Peller called a play from the sidelines for the football to be thrown to me. Here was my chance!

As I went up in the air to catch the ball, I was shoved out of bounds by a LaPorte player. As luck would have it, I dropped the ball as I came down to the ground. When I got up, I pushed the opposing player from LaPorte. This was a similar situation to when I played little league baseball in 1977 for Coach Adams, and the "Crows."

Back then, I hit the catcher in the chest after being thrown out at home plate. In this instance, Coach Peller looked at me and said,

"What are you doing, Denny Bunda!?"

The game official also threw a penalty flag on me for pass interference. Coach Peller told me to go sit on the bench, and that is exactly what I should have done. I did the opposite of what he told me to do. I threw my helmet down at him and yelled, *"I quit!!"*

I stormed off to the Merrillville locker room, while shedding all my football equipment as I left the game field. I could hear my classmates and all the spectators in the football stands yelling at me.

They said such things as:

- *"Quitter!!"*
- *"You are a big baby, Bunda."*
- *"Loser!!"*
- *"You will never make it in life!"*

It didn't matter though. No girlfriend. Bad grades. A football future going nowhere. Well… at least that is how I saw it at the time. I really didn't want to listen to what my family, friends, or coaches had

203

to say to me either. I went in the locker room, got dressed in my regular school clothes, and left before the game was actually over.

My mom was at the game that night watching me throw a tantrum in front of all those people. As my luck would have it, dad happened to be at Calumet High School coaching his football team. When he came home from his game, I told him what I had done. I thought he would have been proud of me for standing up for what I believed in.

Wrong!

A long pause from my dad, disappointed, he didn't raise someone who was going to be a quitter. Dad told me that I had to do the right thing by going in to see the coaches the next day and apologize to them for my behavior. If there was one thing my dad couldn't stand, it was a person who quit a team before the season was over.

The next week in school, I approached Coach Peller. I told him how sorry I was, and that I was just frustrated with what was going on in my life. He understood and listened to everything I had to say. Coach Peller always had the right words to say and offered a message of encouragement. I think that is why he is still one of my favorite teachers to this day. I transferred into the math class he was teaching that year from the other one that I was failing.

He really helped me with my academics. I actually started liking math because of him. In terms of playing in the last football game of the season, that was not going to happen. I would have to do sprints back and forth during practice until I was tired, while my teammates prepared for the Friday night's game. I would also have to sit in the stands for a tournament game against Lake Central, which we lost 27-14. I was not allowed on the sidelines during the game with the teammates as part of my punishment. Rick and I drove to Lake Central to see the game as we cheered on the Merrillville Pirates.

Was my football career at Merrillville officially over? Would I be on the team for my senior year of high school? What about my grades? Would I be able to overcome my situations in life? Would someone be there to help me?

The answer would come from an unlikely source… Coach Lafey Armontrout.

He was the same person I feared while I was still a freshman at Harrison Junior High. The same person who was my gym teacher my first year at Merrillville. Entering my second year, running for him, I received my letterman's jacket as a sophomore for being a varsity track runner.

Still to this day, he has been one of the biggest influences in my life in more ways than one. The second part of my junior year at Merrillville would change who I was as a student, as an athlete, and as a person. Sometimes it takes that one person to make a difference in your life.

For me, that would be Coach Armontrout.

As track & field conditioning was starting up again in November, the Buckeyes were still playing out their football schedule. Don't ask me why Coach Armontrout started track & field conditioning in November when our first meet was actually in the month of March. He may have been one of the most prepared coaches that I have come across in my life and one of the fiercest competitors in terms of sports.

CBS Sports was broadcasting the game with Michigan on television in late November. The Wolverines would enter the game with an unusual 6-4 record and were unranked in the country. This may have been the one Ohio State-Michigan game that I really wasn't nervous about. Ohio State held a 7-0 lead, and it looked like that would be the score going into halftime.

With about 18 seconds to go in the half, Michigan punted the football right to one the Buckeye star players, Mike Lanese. As sure handed as Mike was, he dropped the football. The drop gave Michigan one more chance to score before the end of the first half. The Wolverines would kick a field goal, and now the score was 7-3.

As the game would go into the 4th quarter, it was closer than anyone thought it would be. *Would Ohio State blow it and lose? Would they lose their shot at going to the Rose Bowl?*

The announcers on the television kept saying Ohio State would go to the Rose Bowl "if" they beat Michigan. Something about the word, "if" had me really worried! The crowd seemed to get louder and louder as the game wore on. I was always in awe when Ohio State played in their home stadium known as Ohio Stadium or as some people like to call it, *"The Horseshoe."*

I just couldn't believe that I was on that same field at a football camp a year earlier. I could see myself in Ohio Stadium running down the field or getting yelled at by an assistant coach when I dropped the ball. I was also intrigued to what it would be like to watch an Ohio State versus Michigan game in Ohio Stadium. Would I ever get a chance? Since becoming an Ohio State fan in 1975, I had only seen one game in Ohio Stadium up to that point. I also dreamed of what it would be like to run out of the tunnel in Ohio Stadium, and out on the field with the team. I often shared a lot of these dreams with my friends.

In terms of running out of the tunnel with the Buckeyes... that was never going to happen. Many people at school would just laugh at the idea that I could ever run out on the field with the Ohio State Buckeyes. One classmate in my science class said,

"Dream on, Bunda!!"

In the 4th quarter, Ohio State was just up by a single point at 7-6. Michigan had kicked another field goal and were primed to upset the Buckeyes. It all changed in a moment when Mike Lanese, who was the same player that dropped a punt in the first half, made a spectacular catch for Ohio State. At this moment, I was pacing my downstairs basement and was very nervous. Again, I didn't want to face anyone at school if Ohio State lost, especially Rick. It always seemed to me that it was not a great Ohio State football season if they didn't beat Michigan. Besides, my mom had promised me that I could have a Rose Bowl party with all my friends as well as girls if Ohio State won.

With under ten minutes to go in the game, Keith Byars scored a touchdown, and now Ohio State was up 14-6. As soon as the Buckeyes got the football back on offense, Byars would score again, and just like that, they would win the game 21-6.

I also knew that my Saturday night was going to go a lot better than a month earlier when Ohio State lost to Purdue. I had been inconsolable at the homecoming dance with Anne. However, this Saturday night would be different because Ohio State beat Michigan, and I had met a new girl. Not a bad weekend.

Could this be the girl that I would eventually spend the rest of my life with, or at least my high school years?

Memories Through
Photographs

Author, 2nd grade
Shoemaker
Elementary,
Tucson, Arizona

Author after 1976 accident

Mom and Dad

Dad - Calumet High
School football coach,
1980s

Grandma Dorothy
and Grammy

Grammy and Papa

Author—8th grade
football at Harrison
Junior High

Author and team—Harrison Junior High 8th grade
basketball 1981—1982

Author—Harrison Junior
High 9th grade football

Author— Harrison Junior
High 8th grade basketball

Harrison Junior
High football team
1982.

We never won a
game!

Author—Merrillville High
Sophomore 1983

Author—Merrillville High Sophomore 1984
Track and Field

Author—Merrillville High holding Letterman's
Jacket for becoming a Varsity Runner

Author—Merrillville High
Junior 1985 Track and Field

Author—
Merrillville High
school football

Author with
friends at Camp
Lutherwald
campers—
Summer 1985.

Author and Papa at 1986
high school graduation

Author, Dad, Mark Agerter and Bob Mizura in 1988

Left: Erin, Author
and Nikki

Rick Keneson—
the Michigan fan!

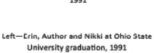

Above: Author and Ms. Kelly Thomas,
1991

Left—Erin, Author and Nikki at Ohio State
University graduation, 1991

Author in Ohio Stadium: "Home of the Buckeyes!"

Author in front of Merrillville, Indiana High School:

"Home of the Pirates!"

Brian
Portlock

Author, Nikki
and Erin

Mom in the
early 1980s

Above: Merrillville Youth football—1979. Author is #14, second row

Above: Harrison Junior High school—Freshman Basketball Team
1982-1983

Left: Brian Portlock, Dave Scott and Bucky Randall

Above: Rick Keneson Merrillville High School Senior picture

Left: Rick in 5th grade at Miller Elementary School

Mike Demakas—Merrillville High School Senior football player

Mike Demakas—Now-a-Days

Left: Steve Civanich—
Playing baseball at
Harrison Junior High

Steve Civanich—All-Star Baseball player

Author and friends at Steve
Civanich's Halloween party—1978

Steve Civanich—
Little League All-Star #11.

Coach Lafey Armontrout—Merrillville High
School, Head Track & Field Coach

Chapter 18

One Big Teenage Roller-Coaster Ride

Christine—from the same town that I lived in prior to my family's move to Merrillville. My good friend Dave Scott and I had met Christine and her friend Andie at a "Goya" mixer dance the night before. Christine knew a lot of the kids who I went to school with at Beiriger Elementary in my younger years living in Griffith. Her father was a local sheriff and worked for the county police department.

Christine was a senior in high school and I was very much attracted to her. She had short curly brunette hair and an unbelievable smile. She was a lot different from those blonde-headed girls who I dated previously. I even did some bizarre things around her so that she would like me.

That Saturday night after the Buckeyes had beat Michigan, Dave and I took Christine and Andie to the local Pizza Hut restaurant in Griffith. When Christine wasn't looking, I went over to the cashier, and told him to stage a fake phone call to me as if I were an important person. The cashier looked at me with this awkward expression.

He said, *"Let me get this straight. You want to pretend that a person is calling you on the phone so you can impress the short- haired brunette girl at the table?"*

"Yes," I said.

He smirked. *"You are nuts, but I will do it."*

The cashier walked away from me muttering something to the effect of, *"What a guy would do to make a girl like him. Crazy!"* I couldn't disagree.

As we were eating our pizza, the cashier came by our table with a telephone and said, *"Dennis Bunda, this phone call is for you."*

Of course, there was no one on the other line. I wanted Christine to think that I was important and not just some ordinary Merrillville kid. Christine looked at me with and smiled. She stated that maybe we ought to start a serious dating relationship.

That night, I asked Christine to the Merrillville High School *"Turnabout Dance."* If you have ever been to a school dance, a turnabout is when the girl is supposed to ask the boy to the formal school dance.

Since Anne and I were broken up again, I really didn't have anyone from Merrillville to go with, or to put it bluntly, no one from my school had asked me to the dance. Therefore, I asked Christine to accompany me to the school dance on December 8th, 1984.

Dave and I would take the girls on a few more dates before the occasion. Christine and I always wanted to kiss or "make-out" on a date. Since Christine's father worked for the sheriff's office, it was not really convenient to go to her house.

Christine's dad always wore his police uniform and his gun around his waist while I was around. He didn't have to say anything but I got the message. Mess with his daughter and I would have to mess with him.

Dave and Andie would go in one car while Christine and I would go in my car. We would go to Miller Elementary School late at night to kiss our new girlfriends.

Of course, Miller Elementary was the same school that I went to when we first moved from Griffith to Merrillville. For whatever reason, Miller school was the place to go if you wanted to make-out with your girlfriend. Sometimes you would see other cars parked there or your friends with their girlfriends.

Would Christine finally be the one girlfriend that I would have a lasting relationship with? Would she be different than Kelli, Lori, and Anne?

Dave really liked Andie. This set the stage for perfect double-dating every Friday and Saturday night. I was also going to invite Christine and Andie to my Rose Bowl party that mom was planning for me later in December prior to the game itself on January 1st. What you plan for doesn't always turn out the way you want it to in life. Disappointment was once again right around the corner.

Dave Scott and I would double-date with Christine and Andie at the annual turnabout dance in the Merrillville High School cafeteria on December 8th, 1984. The night was going really well, and I really liked Christine. We had a strong connection and were very compatible.

As I was slow-dancing with her, I felt a tap on my shoulder. I tried to ignore it. As I turned around, it was my friend Dave Scott. Dave had this somber look on his face, and he asked to speak with me. I looked furiously at him as if to think...

Why would you want to talk with me now? I am dancing with my girlfriend!

Dave said that he really needed to talk with me at that moment. Your friends will always be your friends, and he needed someone to speak to alone. We went over to the side of the cafeteria and he said to me, *"Andie just broke up with me."*

You are kidding me!!

I think that may have been the first words to come out of my mouth. How could that be? I just couldn't believe that this girl would break up with my friend at a school dance! Couldn't she have done it before the dance? What about after the dance? I obviously was concerned for Dave but how was this going to affect the rest of my night with Christine?

The girls wanted to leave the dance, and go to some party at a hotel known as the *Red Roof Inn* put on by their high school classmates in Griffith. The whole way to the party not one word was spoken between Dave and Andie, or Christine and me, for that matter.

As we got to this so-called hotel party, Christine said that maybe we better call it a night. That may have been code for saying that Dave and I needed to leave the party and go somewhere else. I tried to reason with both Christine and Andie on why Dave and I should stay.

We got into my car and drove back to our hometown of Merrillville. I couldn't believe it! Was Christine now breaking up with me as well? Dave and I headed to where kids went when they didn't have a date on the weekends or if a girl had just crushed your heart. What other place could you go but a bowling alley?

It was called the *Stardust* in Merrillville.

As we were shooting a game of pool at the *Stardust*, I looked at Dave and said, *"How in the world did we end up here? We went from a school dance with girls, to a teenage party, and ended up shooting a game of pool at a bowling alley. All in one night!"*

Dave was very upset over the breakup with Andie. It may have been at that moment that I realized how important friends were in my life. Girls will come and go, but you will always have your friends. Besides, I wasn't sure if Christine was breaking up with me. Her and I still could date even if Dave and Andie were no longer a couple, right? Well, the next day confirmed the opposite.

Christine told me that she wanted to move on and date other people. Christine said that she would miss kissing me but didn't want to enter into a long-term serious relationship. Needless to say, that night at the bowling alley wouldn't be the last time that Dave and I would be there.

In fact, there would be a lot of nights that I would spend time at that bowling alley with my other friends like Rick, Brian Portlock, and Mike "D" Demakas after a night of having girl problems. I did have the Rose Bowl party to look forward to that mom was putting on for me.

Right before Christmas break was going to start, mom had said that I could host a teenage party at our home. We were going to celebrate the fact that Ohio State had won the Big Ten Conference in football, and that they were going to play against USC in the Rose Bowl. She said that I could invite all my friends as well as girls to attend the occasion.

I spent one evening making party invitations by individualizing each one for all my guests. Each person invited to my Rose Bowl party was assigned an Ohio State player. I would cut a picture out of the player from my *Buckeye Bulletin* newspaper, and put it on the invitation for each guest. I would also give a description of the player, his position, and what he did to help Ohio State get to the Rose Bowl. Each invitation was also done in scarlet and gray, which are the colors of Ohio State.

I even invited former girlfriends to the Rose Bowl party. Mom went out to the grocery store, and had a cake made especially for the occasion. On the cake it said, *"Ohio State.... Rose Bowl Bound!"*

I was also going to give away party gifts like shirts, buttons, and even an Ohio State practice jersey that I wore during my youth league football years. I didn't mind giving that jersey away even though it was my first one dad bought me at the old *Sport mart*. I guess I didn't care because I knew I was getting a brand-new Ohio State jersey for Christmas.

My mom and dad had purchased my Christmas gift jersey at *Conrad's College Gifts*. It was the same store that dad and I went to when going to my first ever home game in Columbus, Ohio during the 1980 season. I probably snuck into my parent's bedroom about a dozen times to try on that Ohio State jersey before Christmas day. They never really found out that I knew I was getting a jersey for Christmas!

As far as the Rose Bowl party went, it was a complete disaster. There may have been five or six of my friends and one girl at the party. Here I was thinking that all my classmates and closest friends would want to celebrate the excitement of Ohio State going to the Rose Bowl and getting together for a fun time at a high school party.

Wrong again!

I guess if I was still in elementary school or even in junior high, the party may have been more of a success. However, when you are a high school student, having a Rose Bowl party might have been seen as a little weird. Most who came to the party stayed for a little while, and then left to go to dance clubs or other parties which were more suitable for high school-age kids. I felt bad for my parents who spent so much money on food, beverages, and the 'Rose Bowl' cake. Most of it was never eaten at the party.

The night before the Rose Bowl game itself, I had Brian Portlock spend the night for New Year's Eve. It was a tradition that

Brian and I shared throughout junior high as well as into our high school years. He would always come over for New Year's Eve, and we would celebrate the beginning of a new year. We would discuss our new year resolutions and how we would accomplish goals and dreams. I always told Brian that I wanted to go to Ohio State. He was always a great listener. Never once did Brian think that I wasn't capable of accomplishing my dreams and goals. He was the one friend who really encouraged me to try as hard as I could to realize a dream. I think Brian knew and understood.

The game was scheduled to be played at 4 pm *Central Standard Time* in Pasadena, California. I turned on the TV, and saw the beautiful site of the Rose Bowl. It was a sunny day in California unlike where I was watching the game. It was a rainy day in Northwest Indiana on January 1st, 1985, and our basement had just flooded due to all the rain. Our carpet downstairs was soaked with the rainwater that had come in through our basement walls. It didn't matter though. As long as the television worked, I could see Ohio State play in the Rose Bowl.

It started out like Ohio State would win. Cris Carter caught the first pass of the game much like he did in football camp back in 1983. By the third play of the game, Keith Byars ran the football all the way down to about the five yard line. It was like all my problems I was facing during my junior year of high school seemed to disappear once I was watching the Ohio State Buckeyes play in the Rose Bowl. Those issues I had with my mononucleosis, playing football at Merrillville, my grades, and girlfriend relationships, seemed to not matter at this point. Ohio State was my team and my school.

Rich Spangler would set a then Rose Bowl record by hitting a 52-yard field goal in the 3rd quarter of the game. As the sun started to set on the San Gabriel Mountains in Pasadena that day, the Buckeyes' hope of a Rose Bowl win started to fade away into the night.

The Buckeyes would lose 20-17.

Things seemed to settle down after the holidays and the Rose Bowl defeat. I was back to school at Merrillville High School to finish my junior year. Papa also got me my first job making real money. It was at a business simply known as the *Griffith Car Wash*. Papa knew the people who owned the car wash because he got his vehicle washed there every two weeks. It was a family-owned business, and not far from where Grammy and Papa lived in Griffith. I was also set to start my track & field season for Merrillville now as a junior in high school. I had told the owners of the car wash that I probably could only work weekends due to my busy schedule of improving my school grades and the rigors of track practice. Mom was also in remission from her breast cancer due to the fact that she was receiving treatment for her illness.

Every weekend, the Griffith Car Wash had people in a line around the building just waiting to get their car washed. I wasn't allowed to wear anything Ohio State while I worked there. The owners supplied me with two sweatshirts... a red one and a blue one with the words, *Griffith Car Wash* on the back.

I worked there every Saturday and Sunday until May of 1985. There were a few times that I had to tell them that I couldn't work due to an occasional track meet that may have fallen on a Saturday. It also meant that I wouldn't get to see Ohio State play basketball on TV during the weekends due to my job.

There was this one Saturday on January 19th, 1985 when Ohio State was playing the Indiana Hoosiers in basketball. Indiana was one of the top ranked teams in the country and was supposed to beat the Buckeyes that day. The Hoosiers were always considered a basketball school and led by their famous coach, Bobby Knight.

Indiana also had a player on their team who lived not too far from my house on Johnson Street. His name was Dan Dakich. All the neighborhood kids knew who he was. Dan played at the rival high school, Andrean while I was still in junior high.

I really wanted to take off work and not go into the car wash that day. I pleaded with mom but to no avail. She said that I had an obligation to the owners, and that I could find out the outcome of the game when I came home later that night.

As I was drying off car after car at work, all I could think about was this basketball game. So I went into the office, and told the owner that I had to use the phone to make a personal call to my parents about something really important.

Of course, it was about the Ohio State basketball game against Indiana.

My dad told me on the other line that Ohio State actually upset the Indiana Hoosiers by the score of 86-84. I was so excited to hear the news that the Buckeyes won the game, even though I didn't get to see it on television.

When I got off the phone, one of the owners, whose name was Martha, looked at me and said, *"If my husband found out that you made a personal call to learn about the outcome of a basketball game, he could fire you from this job!"* Her husband's name was Ed.

Both he and Martha ran this family business. Who really cares!... is what I thought.

I didn't say that directly to Martha of course. She may not have understood the significance of Ohio State's upset against Indiana in basketball that day. Like that was the biggest event in the world at the time. At least in my mind I thought it was.

I did meet some new friends at the car wash who went to different high schools around the area. One of my new friends there was a guy named Jeff. Although he never went by that name. He actually went by the nickname of "FFEJ." It is actually Jeff spelled backwards.

For whatever reason, he called me "Podge." At the Griffith Car Wash, we simply became known as FFEJ and Podge.

I also had my teenage life at Merrillville High School. My grades started to improve a little bit, and Coach Armontrout was pushing me hard to be a 400 meter runner with the track team. In my spare time, which was very little, I would go workout at this health club known as *Southlake Nautilus*.

Mike "D" Demakas and I joined the health club because Merrillville High School didn't have much of a weight room back then to train for sports. It wasn't like the big fieldhouses, weight rooms, and sports complexes that they have today for high school athletes.

Not only was I getting pushed to be a good track runner by Coach A, but also by the owner of *Southlake Nautilus* health club. His name was Tim. He would write a workout plan for both "D" and myself.

There were many nights after track practice that "D" and I would head over to the nautilus club just sit in the whirlpool. It was located in the health club's locker room. It was there that he and I would talk about track, school, girls, and life ambitions. We would talk about how crazy we thought Coach Armontrout was, and his unorthodox ways of training us during track practices.

I owe a lot to "D" for those years at Merrillville High School. Anyone who has ever played competitive sports in high school or at any level for that matter, understands that you need someone to train with you, to motivate you, and push you harder than you ever thought possible. For me, that was my great friend, Mike "D" Demakas.

The person that I once hated in my junior high years became one of my best friends in high school. Grammy and Papa really liked "D" as well. No one really called him Mike because it just sounded too formal. There were a lot of people named Mike at Merrillville High School but there was only one Mike "D" Demakas.

All of my family, including Grammy and Papa, also called him "D." He was always over at our house. I didn't realize that many of my friends didn't have the same 'home life' that I did. Many of them would tell me that being over at my house was better than anything that they experienced in their own home. At the time, I may not have known the extent of the home situation of some of my friends. In many ways, it was not ideal. Being at my house, with my family, brought happiness to them. I guess I took it for granted that not everyone was as fortunate as I was.

One time that mom said that I could only have two friends spend the night on a particular weekend. Well, "D" had asked me if he could spend the night as well. I asked mom but she stood her ground only allowing me to have two friends spend the night that weekend. I just couldn't leave "D" out as he became a great friend. I did what any normal high school teenager would have done… we snuck him through the downstairs window!

To not get in trouble from my mom, we hid "D" behind a downstairs couch that night. As morning arrived, mom came downstairs to do some laundry and say good morning to the two friends who spent the night. "D" ran into the laundry room to hide so he wouldn't get caught by my mom. As she went into the laundry room, I heard her say, *"D, what are you doing here?"*

He responded by saying that 'he came over for breakfast.'

I don't think my mom ever knew that he spent the night! There were other times that "D," Rick, and other friends of mine, did things that we shouldn't have done in high school. Nothing really too bad though.

Just innocent teenagers being, well… teenagers.

It was during this time in high school that a lot of us started drinking beer or wine coolers. It's not that I condone underage drinking. It was just the thing to do on the weekends. You could say that my friends and I were in the experimental stages of our lives. I am sure dad knew about it because he once found a beer cap in my car. He would always use the line… *"Whatever you do, I've done worse."*

I was usually the designated driver for a lot of my friends who were drinking alcohol on Friday or Saturday nights. I can't say it was one of the smartest things we did in high school. A lot of high school students would drink beer on the weekends at these so-called teenage parties. We knew that girls would be there. No one really stayed home on a Friday or Saturday night during high school. "D" always looked like he was a few years older than the rest of us, mainly because he had a mustache. I was always nervous that we would get caught with alcohol or get pulled over by the police. "D" would simply say, *"Don't worry about it, Bunda."* He never called me Denny but always by my last name. Still to this day he calls me, *"Bunda."*

Chapter 19

Am I Good Enough?

By the time spring rolled around in 1985, a lot of my classmates were starting to take the SAT and ACT college entrance exams. Those were required tests if you planned to someday go to a college or a university. I still had my sights set on attending The Ohio State University but there was no way that I was going to spend my Friday and Saturday nights studying for the SAT or ACT entrance exam.

Many of my classmates were also planning trips to visit some of their college and university choices. Most of them were either visiting Indiana, Purdue, Wabash, or Ball State. Whenever someone asked me where I was going to visit, I always responded, "Ohio State."

I don't know if I really believed it or not. I wanted to be like the rest of my classmates and have a plan to go to college. Unfortunately, I really didn't have much of a plan at all. Maybe my guidance counselor was right. Maybe I wasn't cut out to attend The Ohio State University.

It was at that point that I really started to bring textbooks home to study at night. Believe it or not, I also signed up to take the SAT exam scheduled in March of that year at a local high school known as Gary Lew Wallace. It was about a 4-hour exam that started at 8 am.

Would this exam define me as a student as well as a person? If I didn't score well, would that ruin my chances of realizing a dream?

The day of the test, I remember sitting there thinking that I really don't know any of this stuff! It goes back to the point that I really didn't care enough to prepare for the exam. When I got my test results back, it confirmed what I already knew... I didn't do well. I lied to Rick, Brian, and "D" on what I got on my SAT scores. They all scored really well on the test compared to what I did.

Mrs. "M," my guidance counselor, told me that I would have other opportunities to improve my SAT score to go to college. She then proceeded to give me a list of colleges that looked at other criteria besides the SAT entrance test. She even suggested that I take the ACT test.

She thought it could be a little easier to comprehend for me. I signed up for the ACT test. When I got those scores back, I had similar results to what I had achieved on the SAT. In other words... terrible.

All the while, I kept telling people that I was going to Ohio State and majoring in TV broadcasting. I am sure that all my friends were listening to me but probably not taking me too seriously. Maybe I could get one of those scholarships for a sport? Hey, I had a track & field season coming up and I was training really hard to be a great sprint runner for Coach Armontrout.

My focus shifted on what sport I wanted to concentrate on during my remaining years at Merrillville. It would no longer be the sport that I loved...football. Would I be good enough to get a college scholarship in track & field? Only time would tell...

The track & field season proved to be a great experience for me in 1985. I would win my second varsity letter with the team, and I would be on the Varsity 1600-meter relay team.

Coach A always took us to a lot of track meets that were away from Merrillville and Northwest Indiana. He would take us to this meet called the *Delphi Relays* which was down by West Lafayette, Indiana. It was one of my favorite meets because he made us dress up in a shirt and tie to go to the event. He told us that we represented Merrillville High School, and that we should look nice getting off the bus.

The only problem was that Delphi was out of the 'middle of nowhere' and in the rural part of central Indiana. I'm not sure anyone really cared what we looked like getting off a school bus for a track meet. To Coach Armontrout, it was very important. There was no negotiating with Coach on what we were going to wear to the track & field meet.

As we arrived at the Delphi Relays, we were greeted by a homecoming court made up of a queen and princesses. For a track & field meet? I have heard of schools having homecoming festivities for a varsity football game but never a track meet! Coach Armontrout would tell us to change out of our shirt and tie into our track uniform in the Delphi locker room.

The fellas on the team would always ask me, *"Why does Coach Armontrout make us dress up for a track me*et?"

My response was that he was going to take us out to a fancy steakhouse after the meet was over. Only it wasn't a fancy steakhouse... It was a regular hamburger place. Imagine about 40 Merrillville athletes coming in a hamburger place all dressed up in a shirt & tie. I remember all the customers looking at us in a strange way.

Coach Armontrout made a big deal out of it. I mean he really thought this was a big occasion going out to a hamburger restaurant. Like this was the best hamburger you will ever eat in your life! I can say this now... it wasn't.

I realize years later that Coach Armontrout wasn't trying to impress us with a fancy or a not-so-fancy restaurant but to create memories with our teammates. It is the experiences in life, and the people you are with, that you will always remember and cherish. Even though the Delphi Relays was a nice experience, it was another meet that really made me excited about being a track & field athlete at Merrillville. It wouldn't be in Indiana either. Would I be good enough to compete against the very best?

Coach A told us that he was taking us to Mansfield, Ohio for a meet known as the *Mansfield Mehock Relays*. It would be a two- day trip in April of 1985. That meant that we were released from school on the Friday before the track meet.

He would talk about how significant this meet was, and in the last few years they only cancelled it for a snowstorm. He told us that we would be competing against high schools from Ohio, Michigan, as well as others from Indiana. We would also be competing against high schools from Canada.

I couldn't believe it!

We were going to compete against teams from Canada? I can't tell you how excited I was to go to this meet. Coach Armontrout also handed out brochures of the track meet as well as the hotel arrangements while we were staying in Mansfield. He made it sound like the hotel was one of those big fancy places that you see in New York City like the Ritz-Carlton.

He also mentioned that the Mansfield meet record-holder in the long jump was an athlete from 1976 named Todd Bell. I told Coach A that I knew exactly who that was! Todd Bell played for Ohio State. He actually helped the Buckeyes win against Michigan by scooping up a blocked punt in 1979.

Todd also played his high school football at Middletown High School (Ohio) where Cris Carter was from as well. I just couldn't believe that I would be on the same track as kids from Ohio.

The Mansfield, Ohio trip was about a four hour bus ride from Merrillville. We actually took a school van with Coach A. He only took the athletes from our team that he thought could compete in this big track & field meet.

I talked with a lot of other kids, mainly from the state of Ohio. I told them that I was a big Ohio State fan, and that I was going to school there one day. I got to participate in the 1600 meter relay and the long jump that afternoon. I can't tell you how I did, but I can tell you how one of my teammates did in this 'famous' track meet.

His name was Neil Eubank. He threw the shot put for our team. That day in Mansfield, Neil won his event over the other athletes from all these different states with a throw of 59'10 ½ in the shot put. We were all amazed by Neil and how far he could throw this iron object. He would go on to win the Indiana state high school championship that year in the shot put, and accept a scholarship to Louisiana State University by the end of the season.

With all that being said, what really impressed me was how much Neil could eat. We probably made twelve stops going to Mansfield and another twelve stops going home just so Neil could get something to eat. Coach Armontrout was really mad at him for all the 'eating stops' we had to make. The more upset Coach A got, the more we found amusement in the situation.

I really believe Neil could eat a lot and was hungry, but I think all those food stops were just to get under Coach Armontrout's skin. I mean he was really mad at Neil all the way back to Merrillville! Those are some great memories with my track & field teammates.

The track season ended with me being on one of the best 1600 meter relay teams in Northwest Indiana, and probably in the state at that time. I had received some information from Coach Armontrout about running track in some AAU meets during the summer months.

I knew I had my senior season ahead of me. I was looking to achieve some goals in track & field. I knew that I was good enough to earn a track & field scholarship one day to college. As far as schoolwork in the classroom, I definitely wasn't good enough. With that being said, I was about ready to embark on an odyssey of adventure going into my senior year of high school.

I asked Papa if he would help me train for track & field in the summer of 1985. Also, if he was willing to take me to some of these AAU meets to give me more experience for my senior year. That was the plan anyways. However, a phone call would change that plan and my focus forever.

Chapter 20

A Summer to Remember

In one's lifetime, a person can remember specific events, occurrences, relationships, or special years in their life. For me, it has always been the school year of 1985-1986 that has defined me as the person who I am today. There is nothing like your senior year in high school. It is supposed to be one of the best years of your life.

Many of my classmates were already thinking about the next step in their lives, and what college they may have wanted to attend. I was thinking about that too. Although, I may not have been as serious as some of my peers. I set out to make this the best year of my life.

I still look back at all the fond memories with my friends having fun on the weekends and playing sports. There would be some unexpected situations that I would have to work through as well. People always say that life is the ultimate experience. My journey my senior year in high school would be just that... an experience of a lifetime.

My junior year was officially in the books. I was getting ready to enjoy a summer with my friends at the beach. The Y & W drive-in movie theater, hanging out at teenage night clubs, and running summer track & field. I wanted to be with all my friends like Rick, "D," Brian, Bucky, Dave, Steve, and others.

Yes, it was shaping up to be a great summer of 1985. Plus, I was looking forward to the fall when the Buckeyes would once again be on television.

What game would dad and I go to in 1985? What about the girl situation? All that would have to wait until the summer was over.

On the last day of school, all my friends and I went to this pizza place called *Shakey's* for an 'all you can eat buffet.' We were then headed off to Lake Michigan for a fun day at the beach with all the kids from Merrillville as well as the other local high schools.

I had some news for my friends. I wouldn't be spending the summer at the drive-in movie theater or going to nightclubs on Friday and Saturday nights. I also wouldn't be doing a summer track & field program as I had planned. My mom had told me that our church pastor called and said that there was a camp in Howe, Indiana who needed a teenager for a summer camp counselor position.

I was recommended by Pastor Floyd Trexler from our local church. I had already planned to work at the Griffith Car Wash that summer for extra money. I would have to break the news to Martha and Ed that I would no longer work for them at their business, but instead take a position at this summer camp. I would never see Martha or Ed again or the *Griffith Carwash*.

The decision was made a little easier because my best friend Rick Keneson was due to have surgery on his chest, and would be laid up all summer long. Brian had a steady girlfriend, and "D" was hanging out with some other friends. What the heck, I thought. I told mom to tell Pastor Trexler that I would accept the job at this camp known as *Camp Lutherwald*.

I knew the last day of school would be a long time that I would see any of my friends before our senior year started. I didn't realize this would be a summer to remember even without seeing a lot of my friends. You could say that it was going to be a life-changing experience.

A lot of my friends were also training in the summer for their last football season at Merrillville. I had already decided that I was not going to play football but instead concentrate on my track & field career. I had enough of playing football for Merrillville, and all the problems that I had with the coaches as well as sitting on the bench.

Maybe if I put more time in as a track & field athlete, I could get a scholarship to go to college. I was still seen by many as a dreamer or as they say...'a silly-heart.'

The day at the beach was a memorable one on the last day of school in June of 1985. We played football and volleyball all day long in the hot sand. We had no worries. School was out for the summer, and the teachers hadn't let us know what our final grades were yet. Although, I already knew what my grades were going to look like and they wouldn't be good.

As I was playing football catch with Rick on the beach, I noticed an attractive girl behind him. To get her attention, I was purposely throwing the football over Rick's head, and onto the girl's beach blanket.

I did that for maybe 3 to 4 times before she finally said something to us. I wasn't trying to make her mad but just to get her attention. Not for Rick but for myself. Her response wasn't at all what we expected.

When Rick went over to her blanket to retrieve the football, the attractive girl said,

"This is the only thing a girl would give to you!"

Rick didn't hesitate in his response.

He shouted back at her, *"This is the only thing a guy would want from you!"*

I really thought Rick was going to get into this all-out yelling match with this girl.

He just shook his head at me and said, *"You know dang well you were doing that on purpose!"*

Obviously, I was trying to get her attention, but it did not work.

We all headed to our cars to start summer vacation. The only problem was that I was everyone's designated driver home from the beach. We must have had about eight people in my car driving home that day.

I dropped everyone off to their house one by one. Rick was the last stop for me. He was the only left in the car. We talked about his surgery on his chest, the girl at the beach, and our upcoming senior year of high school at Merrillville.

Rick finally got out of the car. I said to him, *"No camp can hold me down!!"*

I was making reference to my upcoming job at Camp Lutherwald for the summer of 1985. That really would be the last time I saw Rick until August. I was also somewhat seeing a girl named Tracey before I left for work.

We were going out on dates but nothing too serious. I was ready to make a difference in the lives of young kids at this camp anyways. What I didn't realize was the camp would have more of an impact on me than I would have on the kids there. It would be a life-changing job.

I headed out the next day on June 8th for my camp experience at Lutherwald. I didn't really know anyone at the camp or anything about it. My dad had been a camper back in the 1950's at Lutherwald but I had never been there. Every week, we would have a different age group of campers come to the camp. The ages of the campers ranged from five-year old's to kids who were starting high school.

It was a Christian camp run by the Lutheran religion. Every camp counselor had their own cabin with about 8-10 campers. The cabin that I stayed in was called *"Bethany."* Camp Lutherwald taught skill-building, crafts, canoeing, swimming, and religion. At the time, I wouldn't consider myself an over-religious person. Sure, I went to church on Sundays but usually left the service early with dad before it was fully over. I would often day-dream in church when the sermon was given.

Although I have to admit, Pastor Trexler was really interesting to listen to when he gave his messages. Dad and I would usually leave early to get to a restaurant or home to watch some random Sunday NFL football game.

This camp was different though. It really opened my eyes to being focused, living life with a purpose, and setting achievable goals.

The other camp counselors never judged me other than being a regular person.

I was accepted at the camp by others for just being myself. They didn't care that I played football at Merrillville or that I was a rising star on the track & field team. None of that really mattered. Everyone came from different backgrounds and situations. The counselors would often get to know each other on weekends after the campers left on Friday afternoon.

We usually had Friday evenings off until Sunday afternoon when a new group of campers would arrive. There were many times that you could have family members visit you during the weekends as well. Grammy and Papa planned a trip to Lutherwald to visit me in July.

Up until that point, I really didn't have any contact with my family besides the many letters that I would send them through the mail.

I took them on a sailboat ride on the lake that surrounded the camp. It was there that I really opened up to my grandparents about my dreams, goals, and aspirations in life.

I told them that I really wanted to go to Ohio State someday as a student. I also told them that I wanted to meet the girl of my dreams while I was there. Grammy and Papa really took me seriously.

I remember Grammy saying, *"Feller, you can do it! Don't let anything get in your way!"*

At that moment, on a sailboat at Camp Lutherwald with my grandparents, I changed my focus. I knew that I just had to go to Ohio State. Grammy was right...I couldn't let anything stop me from my dream.

The summer at Camp Lutherwald was one of the best summers of my life. I learned a lot about myself. For example, how to get along with others, how to handle tough situations & adversity, coping skills, and time management. It was also there that I learned how to set achievable goals.

I wasn't very good at any of those prior to my job as a camp counselor. I was able to share my experiences with the campers about school, sports, and life. I didn't want them to make some of the same mistakes that I made, especially trying to take the easy way out of school.

For the first time in my own life, I felt that I had a purpose. These kids were really counting on me to give them the right advice and direction in their lives. Many of them had personal struggles and adversity that would be hard to describe to a lot of people. They looked up to me to help them make the right decisions. Achieving greatness in life was no longer about me but how I could help others. I needed to be a role model.

We would often have a football game on the last day of the camp each week between all the boy campers. My cabin was known as the *"Bethany Buckeyes."* The game was played in a grassy area not far from the camp's dining center. The girl campers would sit and watch the game on the grassy hill.

I made some great friends while I was there that summer—like Chris, Paul, Doug, James, Caroline, Jodie, Phil, Deb, and Kristin. Many of them I would never see again once the summer was over. This would also be true for the many campers which I felt I had an impact on during the summer. It would have been nice to have *Facetime, Instagram,* or *Snapchat* in 1985. It just didn't happen.

The memories of the summer of 1985 have stayed with me for a lifetime. The many lessons I learned would prove pivotal for my senior year in high school as well as in the years to come. As the summer came to an end, I came home on a rare weekend in late July.

Most of the time, the camp counselors stayed on campgrounds during the weekends. I arrived to see family and friends as well as what I had been missing by being away from Merrillville. Mom told me that the varsity football coach called, and wanted me to call him right away. I wondered what he wanted.

I wasn't going to play football my senior year. I had already made up my mind. I wasn't going to waste my year sitting on the bench and not playing. He really didn't like me anyways. With our conversation, the football coach said that he would like to have me on the team again and the practices would start in early August.

He said that I would have a chance to play in the games if I worked hard enough. I guess I didn't want my senior year to go by without at least giving football another chance. While at home from camp, I learned that Tracey was going out with Dave Scott.

Dave may have thought that I was mad at him, but I really wasn't upset at all. I liked Tracey but not enough to lose a friendship.

I asked Tracey about the relationship with Dave. She indicated that since I was away at camp, what was she supposed to do?

I went back to Camp Lutherwald to finish up my counselor duties, and get ready for my senior year at Merrillville. Every day I would run up a hill at Camp Lutherwald with a football in my hands. I did this when the campers were boating or swimming, and while I had the time off in the afternoons.

I had seen where the great Chicago Bears running back Walter Payton trained by sprinting up hills. I wanted my senior year to be the best. I wasn't going to let anyone or anything stand in my way.

Running those hills every day while at Camp Lutherwald taught me the skills of hard work and dedication. Grammy and Papa knew my dream of attending Ohio State and graduating from there. Was it eventually going to happen? Did anyone really take me seriously besides my grandparents? The answers would soon be coming my senior year of high school.

Years later, I visited Camp Lutherwald and walked up to the hill that I ran every day during the summer of 1985. I also walked around the camp and remembered all the good times with the camp counselors as well as with the campers. Again, that camp job gave me focus, purpose, and a determination to succeed at anything that I put my mind to in life. I know that I had an impact on all the campers who went through the camp, but I really believe that they impacted me more. I was now driven to succeed at anything that was going to come my way.

This was it...my senior year of high school.

Chapter 21

Senior Rah!

When I got back from Camp Lutherwald, it was early August of 1985. Football practice was ready to start, and I had also renewed my relationship with Anne. She was set to be one of our student trainers for the football team that year. I was back with all my friends as the summer came to a close. Rick had also recovered from his surgery, and was set for his senior year as well.

My friend Brian Portlock was playing football again with me and the rest of our friends. He was still dating Anne's friend; Jan. Brian had dated her throughout most of high school. Like many of us at the time, Brian was also meeting other girls and may not have wanted to stay in a serious relationship with just one girl. Dave Scott and I kind of had a falling out for a while. I don't know why because your friends in high school should always come before a girl relationship. Like I said, I didn't really care that he dated Tracey.

Years later, we would reconcile our friendship. It was a constant reminder not to let years go by without speaking to your friends or being mad at them for something that happened way back in high school. Mike "D" Demakas and I were now as close as two friends could possibly be. I really considered him more like a brother.

We always had a lot in common and he always made me laugh. He had once shared with me that he was actually an Ohio State fan when Art Schlichter played for the Buckeyes in the late 1970's. I never knew!

In one of the first football practices, the coaches had me demonstrate a running drill for the team. I am not sure why they picked me for the demonstration but I think it was to patch-up our differences from the year before. I only blame myself for things that went wrong my junior year at Merrillville. It was my turn to make corrections to everything that happened last year. I seemed to place blame on everyone else.

Ohio State wasn't scheduled to start their season until September 14th. That would be considered a late start by today's standards. It gave me time to focus on my own football season and my time with Anne. When I got back from Camp Lutherwald, I asked her out on a date.

We took things slow because of what happened last time. Anne and I went on date before the school year started to a restaurant known as *Red Lobster* in Merrillville. Staring at her, I noticed how beautiful she actually was.

After our dinner, we went to a private place for a while to kiss. I don't know what it was, but things had changed between us. I think Anne knew that things had changed as well. She looked at me while we were kissing and said,

"What is wrong with you? Your kisses are cold."

I didn't have the heart to tell her. I really wanted to date other girls, and not be tied down to just one during my senior year of high school. With that being said, we dated until I broke it off for good in early October.

As the school year started, we were also told that we would have a new principal at our school named Dr. Rapacz. He was really personable, and wanted to get to know all the students. Dr. Rapacz would often bring us into the school auditorium to give us school information and to talk to us about life situations.

He would also discuss with the students about the dangers of drinking and driving. We knew exactly what he was talking about because a lot of us would have beer and other alcoholic drinks at these so-called high school parties. I took Dr. Rapacz's message seriously, and vowed that I wasn't going to put myself or anyone else in jeopardy by drinking and driving.

Like I said, there were a lot of times where I just simply became the designated driver on Friday and Saturday nights for my friends. Turning 18 in a couple of weeks, I needed to start acting a little more mature.

Our first football game was to be played on August 30th against the Crown Point Bulldogs. They had beaten us the two previous years so this was shaping up to be a big game. We beat them 22-0 in the most memorable game of my high school years. With the score still close, I got in the huddle, and our quarterback called the play, *"99 go/halfback pass."* I knew exactly what that meant. I was going to be on the receiving end of a pass from our running back.

As we broke the huddle, I was thinking to myself, *"Oh no!*
What if I drop the pass? What if I don't make it to the endzone for a touchdown?" *"What will all the Merrillville fans, students, coaches, and teachers think of me?"*

I was looking at the sidelines at all our players and coaches. I was also looking in the fan section of the crowd. Grammy, Papa, and my mom were sitting in the second row of the bleachers staring at me.

For a moment, it was as if time had stopped. I could no longer hear the crowd, the cheerleaders screaming, or even our quarterback yelling out the signals before the snap of the football. Would this be my final chance at being a football star at Merrillville?

As I went out to my wide receiver spot, I saw two Crown Point players line up to guard me so I wouldn't catch the pass. I kept thinking about how average of a person I was at that point. I wasn't the greatest student, the greatest athlete, or even the best friend, that I could have been throughout my school years.

I was always told that I had a lot of potential. A lot of people would tell me to wait my turn or that there would always be next year. I was also told by many that certain kids were just better students or better athletes than I was growing up. Those comments never sat well with me as a person. There wouldn't be a next time or next year. I had to catch the pass to score a touchdown. This was my senior year at Merrillville High School. It would be a defining moment. There was 'dead silence' as the football was snapped. Time stood still.

As I sprinted down the football field, the negative thoughts all disappeared. All I could see was football sail through the air and come right at me. I had dropped quite a few passes at the Ohio State football camp a couple of years before, so it wouldn't have surprised anyone if I dropped this potential game-changing catch.

It was simply my turn as a Merrillville Pirate. There was no way that I was going to drop this football. As I ran past the two Crown Point defenders who were trying to cover me, the football dropped firmly into my hands as I raced to the endzone. The sound of the crowd at the game completely went silent. This time I would not be caught or tackled before I made the touchdown.

As I scored, I could hear the press box announcer shout my name by saying, *"Dennis Bunda!"*

I raised both my hands in the air to signal the touchdown right next to the game official. Today, that would have been considered "unsportsmanlike conduct."

My wide receiver coach Tom Peller was equally as happy for me. He was up in the press box helping call some of the plays. One of our other coaches handed me a headset when I got to the sidelines, and I could hear Coach Peller say,

"Nice catch Denny Bunda... way to go!"

It was as if the touchdown catch that night would define the rest of my senior year of high school. It would be a moment in time that would never be erased from my memory.

As our bus departed that night from Crown Point High School after a great victory, I felt that I was 'walking on air' as all my teammates were hugging me and offering their congratulations.

I put on my Sony Walkman headset to listen to music on the bus ride home. I can tell you exactly what I was listening to that night coming back to Merrillville from the game in Crown Point. It was the theme song from the movie, *St. Elmo's Fire*. It became one of my theme songs my senior year.

After we got our football equipment off in the Merrillville locker, a lot of us headed to the "Goya" dance. I was greeted by classmates, friends, and girls, who all seemed excited that I scored a touchdown that night to beat the Crown Point Bulldogs.

The next week in school, the cheers didn't stop either. As I was walking to my classes, I could hear kids shouting at me,

"Way to go, Denny!" or "That was an unbelievable catch you made against Crown Point!"

A girl named Lisa even ran up to me and gave me a kiss on the cheek. Lisa even told me she loved me!

As I was going to one of my classes, I was smiling all the way. I went into my first class of the day, taught by one of my teachers, Mr. James Wiltshire. He was reading the local newspaper at his desk. He didn't look happy.

He was a Notre Dame graduate and a fan of their football team. As I sat down at my own desk, I said hello to him. Mr. Wiltshire looked up from his newspaper with a somber look on his face and said that he had some bad news for me. Well, it couldn't be the test that I took the week before because he hadn't graded it yet.

What could it be, I thought? Mr. Wiltshire told me that Keith Byars from Ohio State had broken his foot in practice and would be out the first game against Pittsburgh, if not the entire season. Keith was the college football frontrunner for the Heisman Trophy in 1985 and should have probably won it the year before. What was this going to do to Ohio State's season? The other news? Mr. Wiltshire had in fact graded my math test and I received an (A) on it. It was definitely one of the first positive grades I received in a math class.

I had high hopes the Buckeyes would win the Big Ten Conference, beat Michigan, and return to the Rose Bowl. I know the news affected me not only that day but throughout the rest of the week in class as well as in football practice.

I always took negative news about Ohio State football to heart.

246

That Friday night, we ended up beating Chesterton High School by a less than desirable score of 10-3. There were no heroics like the week before against Crown Point. The following week would be a Friday night that I would never forget and it had nothing to do with the game itself.

We called our last year in high school, *"Senior Rah."*

On Friday, September 13th, it would be *"Parent's Night"* at the Merrillville High School football game. All the seniors would be introduced with their parents prior to the start of the game versus the Portage Indians. My dad couldn't attend due to the fact that he was still coaching high school football at Calumet.

We lined up on the track next to the football field. Each senior took his turn being introduced by the press box announcer to the cheers of the crowd. My mom was all smiles that night. I can still see it on her face.

It seemed like mom had finally beaten breast cancer. She was recovering from the surgery two years earlier. Mom had a hold of my arm as we were introduced to the Merrillville crowd. It is a moment in time that I would never forget. She had been a 'mom' not just to me and my sisters, but to all of my friends. She was loved by all who knew her. I still remember hearing my name on the loudspeaker of Merrillville's *Demaree Field*, *"Senior wide receiver Dennis Bunda and his mother, Mrs. Gayle Bunda."*

I really believe my friends in the stands were cheering louder for my mom than they were for me. Mom had that big of an impact on people. I handed mom a flower as we were being introduced. I told her, *"I love you, mom."* Mom's smile would become a distant memory.

Demaree Field has since been torn down at Merrillville, and replaced by a much bigger and updated stadium. There are many times that I pass Merrillville High School, and look out to where Demaree Field once stood. I can still see mom walking down the track near the football field where we were being introduced to the crowd that night in 1985. The years have passed to what seems like a second.

She wasn't happy because it was my senior football season at Merrillville, but simply for the fact that I was her son. We would go on and win the *"Parent's Night"* football game against Portage by the score of 21-6. It didn't really matter—the memory with mom had already been made earlier in the night. I didn't score a touchdown.

I was the punt returner in the game and this player hit me really hard after I caught the football. He said something mean and nasty to me. I don't remember what he said because my ears were still ringing after being tackled by him.

Coach Peller looked at me and said, *"What happened Denny Bunda!?"*

I wish I knew. I was surprised that I wasn't knocked unconscious due to the tackle. Regardless, we won the game and mom was there to see me play in one of my last games as a high school football player.

Senior Rah!

I decided to stay home the following night, and not go out with friends. That was a real rarity for me during my high school years. Most every weekend night, I was going out to the dance clubs, on dates with girlfriends, or just hanging out with my friends. It had nothing to do with being hit hard the night before in the Portage game either.

It was because Ohio State was playing their first game of the season, and it was on television that night. My parents just got done watching a movie together called, *"Romancing the Stone"* starring Kathleen Turner and Michael Douglas.

The game was against the Pittsburgh Panthers. I was curious how Ohio State would do without the services of Keith Byars due to his foot injury. The Buckeyes still had another great tailback that year by the name of John Wooldridge. Mike Tomczak's college career was over and a highly touted player named Jim Karsatos was to take over at quarterback.

I think my friends may have been upset that I was staying home on Saturday night but the Buckeyes were on TV! Besides, I felt guilty missing a night game the year before when Ohio State played

Minnesota. This was different though. This was the first night game ever in Ohio Stadium.

Both my mom and dad sat down to watch the game with me on that Saturday night. I didn't think the game would be a close contest. Mainly because Ohio State was ranked #9 in the country, and Pittsburgh wasn't even that good. The score was only 3-0 in Ohio State's favor going into halftime thanks to Buckeye kicker Rich Spangler's field goal.

I closely watched what Cris Carter did on the football field. I wanted to be able to run like him and catch the football like him. I wanted to take what I learned from Cris, and apply it to what I was doing in practice and in the games on Friday nights.

If I was going to be totally honest, I felt that Pittsburgh had outplayed Ohio State in this game. They had missed a couple of easy field goals in the third quarter.

Therefore, the game remained 3-0 in favor of the Buckeyes going into the 4th quarter.

At some point in the game, I knew Pitt was going to challenge unless Ohio State scored more points. It proved even more difficult when the Panthers took the lead 7-3 on a touchdown pass. With just a few minutes to go in the game, Ohio State had the football around the four-yard line.

They would need a touchdown to win. It came down to just one single play. Who would get the football to win the game? I kept thinking that if Ohio State threw the football, Cris Carter would catch it.

I was screaming at the TV by saying, *"Throw it to Cris Carter!! Throw it to him!"*

It was if the Ohio State coaches could hear me through the television. Cris did catch the football and Ohio State regained the lead, and eventually won 10-7.

Ohio State did go on to win their first three games of the 1985 season against Pittsburgh, Colorado, and Washington State. My

Merrillville team was also on a roll as we had a perfect 4-0 record going into a game against Valparaiso High School.

The game happened to fall on my birthday. I didn't play against them the year before due to my illness with mononucleosis.

"D" and I went to my house after school that day to enjoy cake and ice cream with my family before we headed back to school to catch the bus for Valparaiso.

We would lose to the Vikings by a score of 17-13.

We actually had the football down on the 4-yard line with seconds left to play in the game. It ended with our quarterback being sacked by a Valparaiso linebacker. It was only one loss of course but you could hear a pin drop on the bus ride back to Merrillville.

Many of my teammates blamed the head coach for the defeat. He called a 'pass play' that was intended to be thrown to his own son. The ball should have been thrown to Mike "D" Demakas. Many of my teammates started resenting the head coach and his son. I was one of those people. I just didn't understand why the coach wanted his own son to get 'all the glory' if we won the game. He was a nice kid. It was just unfortunate that he was the son of the head coach, and was put in that difficult situation. Many of my teammates would never see him again after high school ended. A lot of them on that 1985 Merrillville team still talk about how the coach always showed favoritism to his son. We should have won the game that night.

Tracey, who I dated prior to my summer camp job at Lutherwald, invited all of us over to her birthday party in early October. I knew Tracey still liked me. I had told Anne that I was going to a party, and I would pick her up later in the evening. She had just got one of her first high school jobs working at a hamburger place known as *Schoop's*.

The party had a lot of girls there. For the next three hours, I completely forgot about Anne. All my friends were dancing with other girls so I needed to be dancing with someone too. I started talking with this girl named Lisa, who also attended Merrillville High School.

One thing led to another and we were kissing that night. Rick also met a nice girl at the party as well. After the night ended, I drove to pick up Anne from her job. I took her home that night, and it would be the last time that we would be boyfriend/girlfriend. I would never speak to Anne again.

My school grades were really looking good my senior year. There would be a chance I would make the *Merrillville Honor Roll*. For one of the first times in my life, I was really taking my schoolwork seriously. There was the one week in our football season that I didn't think about my grades. It was always the game against the Hobart Brickies.

The Hobart Brickies were one of those high schools that had a lot of tradition and history as far as football goes. Merrillville hadn't beaten them since 1977, and some of the games weren't even close. This would be my last chance to play against them in 1985. I could only imagine what the Ohio State players were going through right before they were set to play Michigan every year.

I felt the same way when we played the Hobart Brickies. All my teammates felt that way too. We didn't like them and they didn't like us. It was the same way between Ohio State and Michigan.

Over the years, I have heard both Ohio State players as well as Michigan players talk about the fact there was mutual respect between both programs. I am sure that was the same way between Merrillville and Hobart but you would never know it.

We did know a lot of their players.

They would hang out at the same teenage night clubs on Friday and Saturday nights that we did. They were undefeated with a perfect 6-0 record. We were pretty good too at 5-1. The game was to be played at the famous Brickie Bowl in Hobart. The "Brickie Bowl" as it was called, always reminded me of Michigan Stadium.

Maybe because both were shaped like a bowl, and they both seemed like really large stadiums. The Brickie Bowl may not have held a capacity of over 100,000 fans like Michigan Stadium did, but it seemed like an intimidating place to play a high school football game.

It was a magical night of high school football in Northwest Indiana on Friday, October 11, 1985. Our football coaches told us that we were going to do warm-ups on our own field before we boarded the busses to Hobart.

What!!??

All my teammates kind of just looked at each other in amazement. I heard one of my teammates question the coaches by asking, *"You mean we are not warming up at the game??"*

They told us to go out to our field and start getting stretched. I kept thinking that we would be late getting to Hobart. It was 6:50 pm and we were still warming up on our own field! The game was to start at 7:30 pm. I kept thinking that the officials would penalize our team if we were late getting to the field.

A few minutes later, the coaches blew a whistle, and told the team to load the busses. We had two buses going to the game that night. One bus was for the offensive players and the other bus was for the defensive players. Brian Portlock and Bucky Randall were defensive players which meant that they would be on a different bus than me.

I sat with Mike "D" Demakas on the offensive bus. There was a Merrillville police car in the front of the buses and another one in the back of them. The Merrillville Police Department was actually giving us an escort to the game! As the police lights as well as sirens came on, we departed our school grounds for Hobart's Brickie Bowl. There was complete silence on the bus. I had never experienced anything like this before in my life. This had to be equivalent to Ohio State playing Michigan.

When we got to the game, it was a little after 7:20 pm. We lined up to the gate of the Brickie Bowl before taking the field as a team. Once our crowd saw us, they absolutely were going crazy and cheering as loud as I ever heard them. Before we charged the field, there was this Hobart elementary-age kid by the fence of the field who was really antagonizing our team.

252

He had this Hobart punch puppet in his hands, and yelling, *"Go Brickies!! Beat Merrillville!"*

One of our players took the puppet out of the kid's hands and ripped off the head to it! He gave the puppet back to the kid in two pieces. The Hobart kid looked absolutely stunned like he was going to cry. In that moment, Merrillville took the field to cheers by our fans and a chorus of boos by the Hobart spectators.

Even though the Hobart players won't admit it to this day… I really believe they grew the grass long and watered it down before they played us that night in the Brickie Bowl. I mean the grass was really tall. We had some fast players on our team and I believe that they tried to slow us down.

I have heard witnesses from both sides say there may have been close to 12,000 fans at the Brickie Bowl that night in 1985. I wish I could tell you there was a happy ending to this game or a miraculous finish by the Merrillville Pirates. There was a miraculous finish but it was by the Hobart Brickies.

In the 4th quarter, the game was tied at 7-7.

With very little time left on the clock, Hobart scored on a long touchdown pass to break the deadlock. The game ended 14-7 in their favor but I always felt that we had outplayed them. I have since run into a lot of their players who played on the Hobart team. They always tell me the scoreboard still reads to this day...

14-7 Hobart.

To this day, it is still one of the most heartbreaking defeats in my time as an athlete. The bus ride home to Merrillville was like a funeral. Our chance to make football history by beating the mighty Brickies had ended. The seniors on the team would never get that opportunity again. Only years later would I realize the 'magnitude of the moment.'

The following week was our homecoming game against the LaPorte Slicers. We won by the score of 5-0 in a driving rainstorm. I remember standing on the sidelines with one of my teammates, Bobby Stewart. We weren't really watching or paying attention to the coaches when we were supposed to go into the game. Bobby and I were talking about how good the food was at the local *Pepe's Mexican Restaurant,* and what we were going to get to eat after the game was over. I could care less if we won or lost.

The rain was coming down really hard, and it was very cold. I just wanted to get out of my football gear, head to the restaurant, and enjoy the rest of the weekend.

The day after the Merrillville homecoming football game, Ohio State would defeat Purdue by the score of 41-27. The game was televised on CBS sports, and I really looked forward to revenge against the Boilermakers.

Papa and I had attended the game the year before which ended in an upset in more ways than one. It was also the return of Ohio State's star player, Keith Byars. It was already the sixth game of the season before Keith made his 1985 debut due to the foot injury. He would score the last two touchdowns of the game to break a 27-27 tie for the Ohio State victory against Purdue.

My high school football career started to come to an end as the regular season was over. We would be heading into the playoffs by the end of October. I would have no idea which game would be my last one in a Merrillville uniform.

My speech teacher my senior year was Mr. Morrow. He actually let me give a class speech on Ohio State. I was to discuss why they were a great football team as well as a great academic school. He had me research the academics at Ohio State and what the school was known for besides sports. I knew a lot about Ohio State football, but didn't know that much about the school itself.

Mr. Morrow wanted me to research the school, and why anyone would go there as a student. It was back to the Lake County Library to research and try to get a good grade on this speech.

It was obviously something that I was interested in unlike the project Rick and I had to do in Mrs. Homco's English class on Greek Mythology years earlier. However, it was one-hundred percent our fault because we didn't try or even care about our grade on Mrs. H's

English project. This time was different. I knew now that I wasn't ever going to play football at Ohio State.

I still wanted to go to college there as a student.

Mr. Morrow sat in the front row listening to my speech about Ohio State, and what a great school it was to attend. He was smiling and nodding at me the whole time. It was as if he knew all along that it was a great institution for higher learning. I really believe Mr. Morrow wanted me to understand that Ohio State was a school, and not just a football powerhouse.

If you were wondering about my grade on the speech… Yes, I got an (A).

Since that day in 1975 when I was introduced to Ohio State by watching them on television, I was the biggest fan of the school. I was meant to go to school there. How could I not go there? My classmates all knew that I loved Ohio State more than anything in the world, outside of my own family.

Even people that didn't know me personally would say, *"Yeah… Denny Bunda, that is the kid who loves Ohio State. I've heard of him."*

It probably cost me a girlfriend or two along the way. All I ever wanted to talk about was Ohio State football. My dad would always say before I went out on a date with a girl, *"Don't talk about Ohio State. Girls don't want to hear about that!"*

I was determined to go there and be an Ohio State Buckeye. My senior year in high school may have been the only time that I brought schoolbooks home every night to study. Many times, I would fall asleep with my government book or math book in my hands. When grades came out after the first semester, I was on the A/B Honor Roll at Merrillville High School. I had never done that before as a student. It is an achievement that I am still proud of to this day. I had worked extremely hard.

As we entered the football playoffs going into November, the Merrillville coaches let us pick one sophomore or junior on the team to tackle one last time before our high school football careers were

255

over. It was a tradition at Merrillville High School for football players to make one last tackle in practice against an underclassman teammate.

We called it... *'Senior Tackle or Senior Rah.'*

I chose Bobby Stewart as the teammate that I wanted to tackle in practice one last time. Bobby was a sophomore on the team, and a great football player. When we came out to practice that Thursday afternoon, he had a piece of tape on the front of his helmet. All my teammates started laughing when they saw what this white piece of tape had written on it.

The tape had the word written across it.... "MICHIGAN."

As my teammates gathered around in a circle for me to take one last tackle hit on Bobby, I envisioned myself as being the Ohio State linebacker, Chris Spielman. I pretended Bobby was this Michigan player who I was going to tackle hard to the ground.

The first time I tried to hit Bobby, I completely missed him. The second chance, I tackled him and immediately helped him off the ground. I thanked my teammates for three great years of playing football at Merrillville. I could have given up playing after my terrible junior year, but I stayed with it. Maybe it was something that my dad said about not giving up in life or the fact that I didn't want to be seen as a quitter.

I knew that after my senior year was over, I would never see many of my high school teammates again. It teaches you to cherish every moment in life because it goes by so quickly. They clapped for me as we headed into the Merrillville locker room after practice was over.

Once in the locker room, I noticed one of my teammates was wearing an "Iowa" t-shirt after he took off his football gear. Iowa was ranked #1 in the country in 1985, and was undefeated. They had beaten Michigan earlier in the season, and now were set to play Ohio State that weekend.

Bill looked at me and said, *"You know Iowa is going to beat Ohio State this weekend, don't you?"*

Of course, I looked at him with amazement. Who would say that to me? I know that I said something back to him in defense of Ohio State. Deep down inside, I was really nervous about the game against the Hawkeyes. I think I was more worried that Ohio State could possibly lose on Saturday than I was about my Merrillville team losing in the high school playoffs.

We were set to play Portage in a rematch game from earlier in the year. There was always that possibility that we could lose, and my football career would be over. The day before our game with Portage and two days before Ohio State would match up against the Iowa Hawkeyes, it was Halloween night in 1985. We had a half day of school that day and a short practice to prepare for Friday's game. We were obviously too old to go trick or treating. We did want to do something fun on Halloween night.

Mike "D" Demakas was dating a girl named Kathy at the time. They had started a serious relationship together. I really wasn't dating anyone since the breakup with Anne. "D" wanted to double date that night. I had to find a girl to go out with me. Rick, and my other friend Jon, wanted to also hang-out on Halloween night.

In other words, no one really wanted to stay home. There was just one problem. Neither Rick nor Jon had girlfriends. There was this girl named Jennifer who really liked me. The feeling wasn't really mutual. I mean it was my senior year of high school. I really didn't want to have a serious relationship with anyone.

I decided that Jennifer and I would go out with "D" and Kathy on Halloween night. I had turned her down on many occasions to go out on a date. Although having a date on Halloween night was better than not having one at all. Rick and Jon would also come along too on the date.

Well… not exactly!

We really wanted to do something bizarre on Halloween like scare our dates. Kind of like the original movie, *"Halloween."* Rick, Jon, "D" and I had planned earlier in the day how we would scare Kathy and Jennifer. After football practice, all four of us drove out to a really scary road outside of the town of Merrillville.

The plan was for Rick and Jon to hide in the bushes next to this dark and scary road that night. "D" and I would act like we were having car trouble, and pull off the side of the road. Rick would then jump on the car and frighten the girls.

Sounds like fun, right?

That night, I dropped off Rick and Jon to the old scary road away from town. "D" and I picked up our dates in my *1980 Mitsubishi Champ* car. The automobile was an old stick shift car that dad had taught me how to drive when I got my license. It was also the car I drove to school during my senior year. I was the only one of my friends who knew how to drive an old stick shift car.

At least, that's what I thought.

Rick and Jon must have been waiting by that old road for at least three hours before "D" and I arrived with the girls. It was due to the fact that Jennifer's family wanted to talk with me about anything and everything, including being an Ohio State fan. I kept looking at "D" as well as my wristwatch knowing that Rick and Jon were really going to be mad at us. I also felt really bad that we were about to play this mean joke on the girls.

I had told them that we were going to a Halloween barn dance party for teenagers. That couldn't have been further from the truth. Jennifer's parents also seemed impressed with me. If they only knew that I was going to play a Halloween prank on their daughter that night.

When we arrived at our destination, we had no idea where Rick and Jon were hiding off to the side of this scary road. I acted like I was having car trouble and stopped on the side of the road. All of a sudden, Rick pulls me out of the car, and drags me off to the side where Jon was hiding behind some trees.

I could hear the girls screaming loudly in the car. At this point, Jon and I were laughing hysterically! Rick then proceeded back to the car, and dove face down on the hood. Jennifer slid over to the driver's side, and started driving the car with Rick still on the hood.

Jon looked at me and said, *'Oh my gosh! Jennifer knows how to drive stick shift! She is going to kill Rick!"*

We had to yell for her to stop the car. Jon and I ran all the way down the old road pleading for her to stop. Rick probably looked like a ghost after he removed himself from the hood of my car! He could have been killed that night because of any innocent teenage prank.

We all had a good laugh about the Halloween joke that night. Also, Jennifer didn't seem to care that we were trying to scare her and Kathy. It seemed to take my mind off of the Friday night rematch game with Portage, and more importantly, the Ohio State game versus Iowa on Saturday.

My high school team would go on to beat the Portage Indians that Friday night by the score of 21-0. However, it was more important what was going to happen the next day...

The game would be on CBS at 1:30 pm. Dad and I sat down to watch history unfold as no one thought Ohio State would win the game. Iowa was loaded with players like Chuck Long, Ronnie Harmon, and Larry Station. Definitely three players who could beat Ohio State.

What I remember most about the game was that it was played in a down pouring rainstorm. It may have been the one time I was glad that I was watching the game at home instead of being there in the stadium. Although I am not sure that is totally true. If dad said we were going to an Ohio State football game, it wouldn't matter what the weather conditions were at the time. It was always more exciting to see the Buckeyes play in person than watching them on TV.

I knew that the Buckeyes were going to pull off this 'magical victory.' I was even praying that if the Buckeyes won, I would attend the church service on Sunday. I hadn't gone to church much that year but said I would if the Buckeyes beat Iowa. Up to that point, Iowa hadn't beaten Ohio State in Ohio Stadium since 1959.

The Buckeyes' defense really played well that day in 1985. It seemed that Chris Spielman was in on every tackle. The superhuman offense that Iowa came in with that day didn't seem as imposing as originally thought. They may have been good but the Ohio State defense was better.

When Iowa lined up to punt the football at the end of the first quarter, Buckeye Sonny Gordon blocked it for a safety, and all of sudden Ohio State was leading 5-0. The crowd really seemed to be electric that day! I wanted to know what that feeling was like to be at a game with everything on the line. Most of the games that dad and I had previously attended were blow-out wins by the Buckeyes.

When John Wooldridge broke free for a 57-yard touchdown run for Ohio State in the second quarter, the game was all but over. John was playing with bruised ribs in the game but you would never know it. He appeared unstoppable.

It also appeared that whenever Iowa's Chuck Long threw a pass, Ohio State was going to intercept it. The Buckeyes went up 15-0 on a Rich Spangler field goal but the Hawkeyes came down the field and scored a touchdown right before halftime.

With the score at 15-7, Iowa still had a chance in the third quarter to make the game close. The one play that all Buckeye fans will remember was a fourth down stop by the Ohio State defense. Iowa's Ronnie Harmon tried to run the football up the middle but was hit hard by Chris Spielman and other Ohio State defenders.

Oh, how I wished I was at the game!

As the game shifted to the fourth quarter, the turf that the game was played on looked more like a sheet of glass. It wasn't like the field turf that college or pro teams play on today. The turf back in the 1980's was like thin carpet and concrete underneath it.

I could tell by watching the game that the players were sliding around on it, and the football was slippery. Freshman Vince Workman would seal the game for the Buckeyes when he scored a touchdown from about the four-yard line.

All I could think about was getting back to Merrillville on Monday. I was going to boast to anyone who was willing to hear that Ohio State had upset the number one ranked Iowa Hawkeyes. I was especially anxious to see my football teammate Bill in the locker room to tell him that he was wrong about his prediction! Iowa did score again but the Buckeyes would still win 22-13.

Ohio State fans ripped down the goal posts at the conclusion of the game. I would always remember it as being one of the biggest upsets in Ohio State's football history.

As promised, the next morning I was at Gloria Dei Lutheran Church listening to one of Pastor Trexler's sermons. His sermons were always uplifting messages. They motivated me to do better in my life.

As the next week approached, my high school team was still in the football playoffs, and Ohio State still had a chance to win the conference as well as go to the Rose Bowl. Sports Illustrated had put a picture of Ohio State beating Iowa in an article of their magazine which came out a week after the game. The title of the article was... *"Splish, Splash, Iowa Took A Bath."* I made sure that I took that article to school, and put it right next to where my teammate Bill sat in the Merrillville locker room. He just shook his head and smiled at me. I am sure he didn't take the game as seriously as I did.

As predicted, my high school team once again beat Crown Point but by a much closer score of 14-7 on Friday, November 8th, 1985.

The next morning, Papa, dad, and I headed out to Evanston, Illinois to watch the Buckeyes play against the Northwestern Wildcats. I brought my Ohio State "Block O" flag to wave at the game, and dad bought me a game program while we were there. The thing I remember most was the thunder and lightning that day. There was this thought that the game might be postponed due to the weather. We had no plans of leaving the game.

Ohio State would take an early 21-0 lead in these less than desirable conditions. Only 26,477 fans apparently showed up for the game. Most of those fans were rooting for the Buckeyes. It is well-known that Ohio State fans could care less if it rains, snows, or if a tornado is located in the area. They will still show up to a game and support the Buckeyes no matter what the weather was like. I am glad to say that Papa, dad, and I were three of those fans in the stadium that day. Ohio State ended up winning the game 35-17.

As we headed to our car after a great Buckeye win, all I could think about was going to the game in Columbus the following weekend against the Wisconsin Badgers. I know this sounds really bad, but I really didn't care if my high school team won or lost the upcoming game with Valparaiso High School. We had just won the Sectional Championship the week before, and now we're heading into another rematch game to a team we lost to earlier in the year.

When a person is young, they don't realize it at the time but there is always a start and a finish to something significant in life. If I had to do it all over again, I would probably have embraced my senior football season a little more than I did back then. I didn't know it at the time, but it would be the final time I would put on football gear for Merrillville High School that week. It would also be the last time that I would play organized football for a team or for a school.

I look back now when my parents started allowing me to play football in elementary school all the way to the final game of my high school season. I thought about playing all those fifth graders at Miller Elementary School just to make friends, or playing youth football for Coach Tancos. I looked back to my days at Harrison Junior High School. Playing football with all my friends even if we were a terrible team. Playing for the Merrillville Pirates. Today, when I look at the field where I scored the touchdown to beat Crown Point in 1985, I can still see Grammy, Papa, and mom in the stands cheering for me. Life goes by so fast not to embrace every moment that you have on this earth.

We would lose that game to Valparaiso by the score of 14-2. My football career was over at Merrillville. Only years later, would I realize how significant that time was in my life.

November 16,1985 started out as a cloudy day in Columbus, Ohio. Ohio State was now 8-1 on the season, and ranked #3 in the country. Dad, mom, and I made the trip to Ohio to see the Buckeyes play the Wisconsin Badgers. For whatever reason, the Badgers were always a tough team for Ohio State to match up against in football.

My parents and I stayed at the old *Holiday Inn Hotel* off of Lane Avenue. From our hotel room window, I could see across the way to the famous Ohio Stadium. It was now the third time that I had been to the Ohio State campus. We would go watch the Ohio State Marching Band do a warmup rehearsal before the game in a gymnasium known as St. John Arena.

I had always watched the band do *Script Ohio* on TV, but it is a lot different when you see them in person. It would be the second time that I got to witness the famous *Script Ohio* in Ohio Stadium.

The thing that wasn't magical that day was the fact Ohio State lost by the score of 12-7. The Buckeyes actually had a 7-6 lead at halftime but just made too many mistakes to win the game. I was devastated when the game came to an end.

Dad, mom, and I left Ohio Stadium in shock. How could Ohio State beat #1 ranked Iowa a couple of weeks earlier, and then lose to a below average Wisconsin team? I remember going back to our hotel room after the game, and riding the elevator up to our floor with the rest of the Buckeye fans who were staying at the *Holiday Inn*.

You could hear a pin drop. It looked like there was a death and everyone was in mourning.

This reminded me of the bus ride home after my high school team lost to Hobart in October. There were actually people crying in the elevator. I not only felt sorry for myself but for all the other Buckeye fans at the game that day. Dad suggested that we go get something to eat that night at Damon's Steakhouse down on Olentangy River Road. I told him that I was in no mood to eat, and I wanted to stay in the hotel room the rest of the night.

As we left Columbus after a long weekend and a devastating loss, I was wondering when would be the next time I would be visiting Ohio State? Would I ever see a game with my family again?

My high school football career had officially ended. I looked forward to my one last chance to make a mark on Merrillville High

School as a track & field athlete coming up in the spring. It was kind of weird going back to school the week after Ohio State lost to Wisconsin. Merrillville had also lost in the football playoffs. There would be no football practice to look forward to or games for that matter. I was working hard on my academics in hopes that I could still go to Ohio State as a student.

The week after my trip to Columbus, I went to talk with my guidance counselor about applying to Ohio State. She indicated that my grade point average was still a little lower than the expected requirements of the university.

She looked at me and said, *"I have an idea.~ You have played sports here at Merrillville High the last three years, but you really don't belong to any clubs. ~ Why don't you join 'Junior Achievement?' ~ They meet every Wednesday night at 7 pm here at Merrillville High School."*

Mrs. "M" told me it was a club to learn about college, how to get ready for a job, financial responsibility, relationships, and contributing to your community. There would be projects to do and hands-on learning activities. A club that meets every Wednesday night? I told Mrs. "M" thanks for the idea and I would think about it.

As I walked out of her office, I confronted Mike "D" Demakas about the possibility of him joining the *Junior Achievement* club with me. "D" and I were ready to start our last track & field season at Merrillville.

I started working really hard on my homework. I would stay up late at night and read the chapters over and over again for each class. I also asked Mrs. Galanis, my government teacher, if I could move to the front of the row of her room so I could listen to everything she had to teach. I hadn't applied to Ohio State yet nor did I really ask my parents if I could go there. I guess I had always assumed that is where I was going to college.

How could I not go there? Like I said, I was the biggest fan in the world, and all my classmates knew that I loved Ohio State. Would I be remembered by them if I went to another university or college? Would it diminish all my dreams and goals in life? Would I look back and regret my decision to at least not give it a try?

Those statements kept repeating themselves in my mind. I was also worried about the upcoming Ohio State game versus Michigan. Ohio State was now 8-2 on the year and had to play the Wolverines up in Ann Arbor, Michigan. I wore Ohio State clothes every day to school that week.

I read as much as I could about the game in my *Buckeye Sports Bulletin* as well as in my local newspaper. I knew that Michigan had a pretty good season in 1985. They had only lost one game to Iowa and tied Illinois. I was pretty confident that the Buckeyes could pull off the upset.

Dad and I would watch the game on TV. CBS was televising the showdown between Ohio State and Michigan. Before the game started, they showed former Coach Woody Hayes in a wheelchair giving a motivational speech to the Ohio State players the day before the game.

I could feel the adrenaline run through my body before the contest even started. It appeared it was going to be a very close contest. In fact, the game was tied 10-10 at halftime. Michigan pulled ahead 20 to 10 after the third quarter. I was still confident that the Buckeyes could rally back, and win against the hated Wolverines. Cris Carter, Chris Spielman, and Keith Byars all played for Ohio State. All three players were superstars.

Keith Byars came back from his foot injury that he suffered in the beginning of the year, and Cris Carter was well… Cris Carter. Chris Spielman also seemed to be making every tackle on the field against Michigan.

When Cris Carter made an amazing catch in the end zone during the four quarter, the game really tightened. The score was now 20-17 with Michigan still leading. Carter made the miraculous catch when Ohio State had fourth down and fifteen yards to go. I believe dad and I were both standing at this point. We pushed back the chairs in the room and stood right next to the television.

We were high-fiving, and cheering as loud as we could. All Ohio State had to do was stop Michigan one time and score a touchdown to win the game. I kept saying, *"We have to win this game! We have to win this game!!"*

Dad and I sat there stunned as to what happened next. Jim Harbaugh, the Michigan quarterback, threw a long touchdown pass to wide receiver John Kolesar, who wore #40 for the Wolverines. I could hear the crowd at the game through my television set. Kolesar raced past the Ohio State defender William White to the end zone.

'Dejected' is the first word that comes to my mind. 'Stunned' would be the second word. My dad just shook his head in disgust. The Buckeyes would lose the game to Michigan by the score of 27-17.

Still to this day, it is one of the most devastating losses I have had as an Ohio State fan. I can still see all the Michigan fans run on the field after the game was over, as the announcer saying, *"Michigan has beaten Ohio State!"*

It probably took me two hours to leave my basement. I just sat there in total disbelief. It wasn't the end of the world. I knew Ohio State would play Michigan again next year—seemed a long time away. Would I be a student at Ohio State by that time, and see them play the Wolverines in person? Only time would tell if the university would accept me as a student. I still had a lot of work to do.

Rick had that smirk on his face when I saw him in school the following week. It was if he already knew Michigan was going to win the game. In my mind, I was counting down the days when Ohio State would play the Wolverines again. I cared how Ohio State did overall, but it was not a good year unless they beat Michigan. The Buckeyes would go on to defeat BYU by the score of 10-7 in the Citrus Bowl three days after Christmas to wrap up their season.

Ohio State would end the season with a 9-3 record. This meant that the Buckeyes had a 9-3 record every year from 1980 to 1985 during the time I was in junior high as well as in high school.

People started calling Ohio State Head Coach Earle Bruce—
"Ol' 9 and 3 Earle." He had a lot of great victories against good
opponents but had some very crushing defeats as well.

After Christmas and New Years were over, it was time to start
my final season of track & field for the coach that I feared during my
earlier years at Merrillville. I just didn't realize the impact he would
have on a decision that would be coming soon. Life is full of surprises.

Chapter 22

It's Over

We started track conditioning right after Christmas break was over in January of 1986. Like I said before, with Coach Armontrout, you knew that you were going to train for track & field rain or shine. In the winter, that also meant in the snow. There was something different about this season. I knew it was my senior year at Merrillville. It would be my last chance competing for Coach Armontrout.

He and I had a great relationship—I didn't think was going to be possible in my earlier years.

I really thought Coach A didn't like me that much. A lot of my teammates would say that I was Coach Armontrout's all-time favorite athlete by the spring of 1986. I asked him one time about that comment. I said, *"Coach, in the many decades that you have been a track coach, I am your favorite athlete!"*

I was expecting him to agree with me.

Coach kind of stared at me for a moment to reflect on what I just said to him. Keep in mind that Coach Armontrout had coached a lot of great athletes at Merrillville as well as other schools during his coaching career. He had coached conference champions, sectional & regional champions, state finalists, and school record-holders.

Coach was also considered a track & field icon in the state of Indiana. He really made you believe that you could achieve anything in life. He continued to stare at me to give a response to my question that I was his 'favorite athlete.'

He had a grin on his face and said, "*Bunda, if you say it enough, you will start to believe it!*" Even with his response, I did believe I was his favorite and so did a lot of my teammates.

For all the young people reading this book, there is a message I would like you to understand. There are certain people who come along who make a major impact in your life. Coach Armontrout was definitely one of those people. It was what he said to me during my sophomore year at Merrillville.

Coach told me that if I put in the hard work, I would be a good athlete at Merrillville High School. There was just one problem with that statement. I didn't just want to be good...I wanted to be a great student-athlete. Notice that I said the term, 'student-athlete.'

This was my chance to do everything that I needed to do and wanted to do, with my remaining days in high school. Soon it would be all over. Coach Armontrout had me sit down and write my goals on a sheet of paper. Some of my goals were to be a conference champion in my events, be a school record holder, and be an Indiana All-State Track & Field student- athlete.

I wasn't going to let anything stop me. I just had one obstacle, and it didn't have anything to do with the sport of track & field or my schoolwork. It was a girl. Her name was Brenna. Brenna didn't go to my high school or even live in my town. She was from Munster High School and was on their school dance team.

I met her through Brian Portlock, who had dated her a few times. Once again...some friend I was! I had already dated a couple of girls who Brian had gone out with in the past. Even when she was dating Brian, Brenna would often stare at me with this beautiful smile. I knew that she liked me and I really liked her too.

I just didn't want to tell Brian that I had feelings for her. Your friends should come before girls, right? I just couldn't take my mind off of her. She was absolutely beautiful. When Brian and Brenna broke off their relationship, it all changed for me. My dad always said she was the most attractive female that I dated in high school, and it wasn't even close.

Not that the other girls weren't pretty but Brenna was different. She could have been a supermodel for a magazine like *Teen Vogue*. I was mesmerized by her because she was so attractive. She had this powerful effect on me. Once I kissed Brenna, I knew I was going to fall completely in love with her. Once again, it would be a girl who would take my focus off of some of my goals and dreams.

Here we go again!

We started to become a serious couple right after the Christmas holidays. When Brenna and I would go out to the movies or somewhere on a date, there would be other teenage boys just staring at her. More times than not, Brenna wouldn't notice these other boys looking her way but I did. In some ways, it made me feel lucky that I had a girlfriend who looked the way she did. In other ways, it made me jealous and insecure that other boys were looking in her direction.

I bought Brenna a *Mizpah necklace* at the local jewelry store to show my affection for her. A *Mizpah* is when you and your girlfriend each wear a necklace to show your token of love. Brenna even asked me if "I *loved her.*"

What was I going to say? Of course, I loved her! - I just never said it to her.

I was absolutely in love with Brenna. My whole family just loved Brenna, especially my mom and dad. For whatever reason, I never told Brenna that I loved her. She would ask me multiple times but I was always afraid to respond. I am not sure why because I had fallen head over heels for this girl. She was one of a kind. Maybe I should have told her those 'magical words.'

As the indoor track & field season started, it was apparent that this would be a season like no other year. I started having a lot of success early on, especially in the 400 meter dash. I knew what the school record was, and who had it at the time. It was Bob Mack from 1972. I also started having a lot of success in a track event that I really enjoyed...the long jump. Mike "D" Demakas and I worked hard together at the event, and really helped each other out.

Early in the season, there were some colleges that were interested in me as a student-athlete. Wow...imagine that! Colleges were actually going to offer me a scholarship for track & field. So with the help of Coach Armontrout, dad set up visits to Franklin College as well as North Central College. It was as if I had completely forgotten about the possibility of going to Ohio State. I was so wrapped up in my success as a student- athlete. Just the thought that I could go to college on a scholarship. Going to Ohio State now seemed more like a dream than a reality.

The visit to Franklin College was a great experience. I visited there in February of 1986. The coaches showed me around the campus. They had academic advisors discuss my options on what areas I would like to study in college. "Red" Faught was the football coach at Franklin College, and seemed really interested in having me play for him. The track & field coaches also said that I would have success right away as part of their program. I must have said something to them about going to school there because in the local paper the next week an article read, *"Bunda to Attend Franklin."*

I told dad that I never indicated to the coaches that I was going to school there. I am not sure what gave them the impression that Franklin College was my future destination. Needless to say, my family was excited that I received my first college offer and decided to throw a 'congratulations party' at my house.

Grammy and Papa would be there as well to celebrate the first college that seemed interested in me as a student- athlete. Besides my dad at the time, no one in my family had really gone to college. I asked my parents if I could surprise Brenna by bringing her back to our house for the big occasion. Since everyone thought this was the girl of my dreams, they all wanted her to be there to celebrate this big event in my life. How I wish I wouldn't have gone to her house that night. If I didn't go see her, I would never know the truth. A night of celebration would soon turn into misery.

271

As my family was ready to celebrate with cake and ice cream, I raced off to Munster to bring Brenna back to our house to share in the joy that I was accepted to Franklin College. She had no idea that I was coming to her house that night in February.

I was so excited to tell her the news that I actually got accepted to Franklin College, and would possibly run track & field and play football for them. Although in my heart, I knew I wasn't going to Franklin College.

When I arrived at Brenna's house, I knocked on the door a few times. At first, no one seemed to be home. Maybe she had a dance competition that night or maybe she was studying with some of her friends? As I started walking back to my car, I noticed that there was a light on in the house.

Somebody had to be home, right?

I approached the door again and proceeded to knock one more time. The door finally opened but it wasn't Brenna. There was another person at her front door. He asked me who I was.

I said, *"I am Brenna's boyfriend."*

He looked at me and stated, *"No, you are not! I am!!"*

As soon as this boy said those words, Brenna appeared right behind his left shoulder. She had this startled look on her face. Brenna asked why I was at her house? Before I could respond, she told me that I needed to leave immediately. We would talk about this the next day.

Who was this guy in the house with her?

As I went back to the car again, I threw my keys across her front lawn. I was upset, hurt, and really angry. How could she do this to me? Why was she with another guy? I thought that Brenna really liked me or possibly loved me! Was it over between us?

When I threw my car keys in the lawn, Brenna and this 'unknown guy' turned off all the lights to the front of the house. It took me a half an hour to find my car keys. All the while, this boy was shouting at me to leave the premises or he would kick my butt.

He never did come out of the house to confront me. There would be another encounter with him soon. Needless to say, the party back at my house came to an uneventful end. I felt bad for all my friends who were there as well as my parents who threw me the party in the first place.

I knew Grammy was upset. She didn't like when someone hurt me, physically or emotionally. I was in no mood to celebrate my first college offer. I wanted to find out why Brenna broke my heart. I was really depressed the following week after the break-up with her. On Monday night, I told my mom that I was going out for a drive in my car to relieve the stress and tension that I was going through at the time.

As I was driving my car, there were a few thoughts that ran through my head on how I could end my life. I never really contemplated suicide before but I was an 'emotional wreck.' I was not in a good mental 'state of mind.' The tears were running down my face. My body was shaking. I know for a fact that there were a couple of 'red lights' that I went through while I was driving my car. I could have been in a bad car accident by simply not paying attention to what I was doing.

This is how it was going to end for me? I no longer had what I thought was the girl of my dreams. It's over.

For whatever reason, I pulled my car into the Merrillville High School parking lot and drove right next to the football field. I got out of my car. I proceeded to walk into *Demaree Field,* and sat in the football field's bleachers for what seemed like hours. It was late at night, pitch dark, cold, and no one was around to talk to about my problems.

As I sat there crying, I was talking to the heavens above. At first, I wanted my life to end right there. I started praying awhile in the bleachers of the stadium. As I was talking to myself, I wanted to make this the best track & field season ever. I was going to accomplish all my goals and dreams with my remaining time at Merrillville.

I also said that I was going to fulfill my dream of going to The Ohio State University. I know no one was there to hear me but it was a chance to be by myself. With that, I took the part of the *Mizpah* necklace that I was wearing around my neck, and threw it on the football field. At that moment, I knew the relationship with Brenna was over.

Although the entire situation surrounding our break-up was still about to unfold. As I got back in my car with tears still filled in my eyes, I turned on my Sony Walkman headset and listened to the Rocky IV theme song, *"Training Montage."*

It is really hard to explain but I felt this overwhelming purpose and focus come over me. As I looked in my car mirror, I had this determined look on my face. I wasn't going to let anything stop me at this point. People always say that there is a reason the front window of a car is larger than the back window.

You always have to look ahead in life.

My teammates, along with Mike "D" Demakas, never saw me so focused in practice or in track meets after the break-up with Brenna. I was winning every drill and every workout for the 400 meter dash. While doing an interview for the *Hammond Times newspaper*, Coach Armontrout would call me a "Fierce Competitor" and one of the best athletes he ever coached.

By Friday that week, I thought I was completely over Brenna. I had found out the 'other' guy's name was Ted. She was now dating him and wanting nothing to do with me.

Our Merrillville varsity basketball team was playing a Sectional playoff game at Calumet High School where my dad worked as a teacher and as a coach. There were about eight different high schools playing games to see who would make it to the Sectional finals on Saturday night.

Before Merrillville was to play against Crown Point in the later game, the school Brenna was from (Munster) was playing their game. It would be an encounter that I would not forget.

She was at the game but refused to talk with me. All I wanted to do was ask her why she wanted to end our relationship. I was still really confused over the break-up.

Brenna kept saying, *"It's over! Leave me alone!"*

I saw Brenna's new boyfriend go into the bathroom during halftime of the basketball game. I didn't know if Ted remembered me that night when I came to Brenna's house or that I was now her ex-boyfriend. I didn't care what he thought of me. I was going to approach him.

I went up to him and simply said, *"Are you Ted?"*

He looked at me with this nervous and startled face. I told him that I was going to fight him right there in the bathroom over Brenna! Who is afraid now? As I was yelling at Ted, my dad happened to walk in the bathroom with a couple of my friends.

Dad was working supervision that night for all the basketball games, and he probably was alerted to what was going on in the bathroom with me wanting to fight this kid from Munster.

Before I knew it, he had Brian Portlock pull me away in the bathroom before I could hit Ted. Brian and Rick kept telling me that Brenna wasn't worth getting in trouble over, especially if Coach Armontrout found out I was involved in some altercation at a basketball game. I guess it is great to have friends look out for your best interests.

With that, I was onto my final track & field season in high school as well as graduating in a few months from Merrillville. I still thought about Brenna and my feelings for her, but if she wanted to be with someone else, then so be it. I would never see or hear from Brenna again. The relationship that I thought would last forever was truly over.

I did take one more college visit to North Central College in Naperville, Illinois in March of 1986. I started having more and more success in track & field, and Coach Armontout was the main reason. He was working me hard to be a school record-holder and a state finalist. North Central College is a beautiful school and was well-known for its track & field program. I met all the coaches as well as the academic advisor.

The school's financial aid department had told my dad that most expenses would be covered for me to attend college there. In other words, my parents wouldn't have to pay much for me to attend North Central College.

On the way back from North Central College, my dad asked how I liked the track coaches? I told him that they were awesome and very nice people. He asked me what I thought of the academic advisors? I told dad how the advisors said I could graduate with a degree in four years. Dad further questioned me about my opinion of the North Central campus. I said it was beautiful. It seemed like a great place to go to college for the next four years.

He looked at me with this grin on his face and said, *"You aren't going there, are you?"*

I just shook my head as if to answer, *"no."* He just told me to be honest with the school and the coaches on my decision. Again, there are moments and years in your life that you will always remember. The spring of 1986 was one of the most memorable times in my life.

I was the *'Most Valuable Athlete'* of two major track & field meets that season. I was the most valuable participant at the *Hobart "Little 5" Relays* as well as the *Griffith Relays*. The Griffith Relays were especially important and memorable to me because I had grown up in the town of Griffith before our family moved to Merrillville in 1978.

I received trophies for both of those meets that I still have to this day. I also defeated one of the top 400-meter runners in the state of Indiana from Gary Roosevelt High School. I set a Merrillville track & field school record in the event while facing the Valparaiso Vikings as well. I would have the 400 meter dash school record until it was broken by a great Merrillville athlete in 2002 who would later go to the Olympics.

His name was David Neville.

Coach Armontrout took us back to Mansfield, Ohio to compete in the *Mehock Relays*. Once again, I would be competing against teams from Indiana, Ohio, Michigan, and Canada. Right before my 400 meter race, I went up to Coach Armontrout and asked him for some last minute advice. He took me down to the starting line of the 400-meter dash.

Coach pointed at the line and said, *"What is that?"*

I replied, *"That is the start & finish line of the 400-meter dash."*

He looked at me without blinking an eye and said, *"You need to cross that finish line before anyone else does at the conclusion of the race!"*

Mike "D" Demakas looked at me and simply said, *"You heard him!"*

I did win my section of the 400-meter dash that day all because of the advice of my coach. Well… it may also had to do with the amount of training Coach Armontrout was putting me through during that season. I once again talked with all the Ohio kids that day on what it was like growing up in the state of Ohio, and being an Ohio State Buckeye fan.

I told many of them that even though I was from Indiana, I too loved Ohio State. I planned to go to school there. I am sure they looked at me as if to think why I had this fascination with Ohio State?

As my senior year was coming to an end, I was voted by all my coaches as well as my teammates as the *Most Valuable Participant as* well as the *Mental Attitude* award winner for the track & field team at Merrillville High School. I had come a long way in my quest of being remembered as a great student-athlete at my school. As far as girls went, I was done with serious high school relationships after the break-up with Brenna.

I did go to the Merrillville High School Prom that year with a girl named Amy who attended Crown Point High School. The Prom was on May 17th and the theme was *"One More Night."*

The song, *"Holding Back the Years"* by the group known as *Simply Red,* was one of the last songs played at the Merrillville Prom that night. I knew that I couldn't hold back the years. It was almost time to move onto the next stage in my life. With only the *Indiana High School Track & Field* meet left as well as the high school graduation ceremony, it was almost time to decide on where I was going to college.

Was I good enough to go to Ohio State? Were my grades going to be sufficient enough? I thought that I had done enough my senior year to go to school there.

Mike "D" Demakas had already made his decision to attend Ball State University in Muncie, Indiana. Rick was going to attend Purdue Calumet University. Brian was heading to Evansville University to play football at the college level. My other friends had made their college plans as well.

North Central College kept calling my house asking if I was still interested in attending their school. I guess they didn't know how to take 'no' for an answer. I wasn't going to run track & field there. I was running out of time. I was hoping my parents would let me apply to Ohio State.

One of my great accomplishments in high school was qualifying for the IHSAA state track meet down in Indianapolis. I didn't do well in the track & field meet itself. I scratched all three times in the long jump that day. I still was able to get a state qualifier patch for my Merrillville letterman's jacket.

The only thing left was the high school graduation ceremony scheduled on Sunday, June 8th, 1986 in the Merrillville High School *"Engelhart Gymnasium."* It was the 60th commencement ceremony at Merrillville, and 433 seniors were graduating from the school that day.

I remember listening to the many students talking about cherishing friendships, as well as the memories and experiences at MHS. As Principal Dr. Rapacz told us to turn our tassels to the other side of our graduation cap, it was time to move on from Merrillville High School. The ceremony came to an end with purple and white balloons falling from the ceiling of the gymnasium. Most of my classmates I would never see again.

High school was over.

Chapter 23

College Go!

The fall of 1986, I was your regular college student at Ball State University. You heard that right...Ball State University! Not, Ohio State University.

When summer ended, I said goodbye to Rick and Brian and headed off to Muncie, Indiana to join Mike "D" Demakas at Ball State. It was one of the few schools I applied to, and got accepted to, as a college student. "D" and I were roommates that first year in college.

Ball State started their school year a little later than most colleges. Dad helped "D" and I pick out bunk beds for our dorm room at *Williams Hall* on the campus. Grammy and Papa came down to help us set up our room as well. Mom and Grammy filling our dorm room refrigerator with juice boxes and snacks.

Once my family said goodbye, "D" and I officially dubbed ourselves, college students.

We got rid of all the juice boxes and snacks in the refrigerator, and filled it with college-type beverages. Ohio State was now a distant memory. I was a Ball State Cardinal, now—wrapped up as a college student, with all the excitement.

But was the dream over? I really loved Ball State University and the campus life. Moreover, I got to share the college experience with one of my best friends, Mike "D" Demakas.

One Saturday, I was heading off to the campus library to study for my classes. I happened to be walking by a large screen TV in the lounge of *Williams Hall*. The Buckeyes were playing that day. I started to walk away. I wasn't interested in Ohio State football anymore. As I headed out the door of *Williams Hall*, I stopped, turned around, and looked at the television one more time.

Wait a second! How could I not watch Ohio State play football?

I had been watching them since they played Michigan way back in 1975. Was I really not a Buckeye fan anymore? I stood there frozen. Something in my mind told me that the library and studying could wait awhile.

I was the only one in the *Williams Hall* lounge that day watching the game. I was clapping every time they made a good play or screamed at the TV when they didn't. It was one of the most exciting times that I watched the Buckeyes.

The only problem was that they lost to the Washington Huskies that day by the score of 40-7. I didn't care though. I could still cheer for Ohio State even though I went to a different college. While walking to the Ball State library after the game was over, my focus shifted once again.

I wasn't just going to study for classes that day to prepare for papers and tests. I was going to the library to prepare to go to Ohio State. I can't tell you how many afternoons and evenings I spent at the Ball State main campus library. I wrote my family the following letter the week after the Ohio State/ Washington game.

Dear Dad, Mom, Nikki and Erin,

Hi!

How are things going with everybody up in M-ville? Things down here could be a little bit better. Classes are classes, the food is terrible almost tastes like your cooking, mom! (just kidding!) One class looks like it might be interesting (Terry).

Terry is a lot like me, she loves to joke around, and she is very good-looking, like myself. She says that I talk about Ohio State football too much but she will be a Buckeye fan like the rest.

Thank God she doesn't like U of M.

The guys on the floor are wild but a great bunch of dudes. I've never studied so hard in all my life. I'm so intense every time I go to the classroom. I'm taking no easy road to Buckeye Country but I assure all of you that I'm getting a chance to get to Ohio State. I'm going to do it just like I've done everything else.

I'm a BUCKEYE not a Cardinal, and when people ask me here, I tell them.

I can't hide it, dad. I am what I am. I miss everybody up in M-ville, especially my sisters because I like talking to them. Nikki and Erin, anytime you want to talk about a problem or a tough situation, just call me up. You know that you have one heck of a brother who will give you some first-class advice.

Tell everyone I said hello, and go tell Rick and Brian... I said college is fun but a lot of work.

Your Son and brother,
Denny

Temptations were always there. Girls. Parties. Fraternities. Hanging out in the *Williams Hall dorm.*

As the letter above indicated, I did meet a girl at Ball State named Terry. She was a great person and we had a lot in common. I just didn't want to be tied down to one girl, especially if I was going to Ohio State the next year.

Was I, though?

After dad read my letter, he said I could apply to Ohio State after the first semester was over, if I still felt strongly about transferring there. He also told me I would have to do well in all my classes if that were to happen.

It was not easy. It took a lot of time, energy, hard work, and effort. Like I said, the temptations of college were always there. My roommate, Mike "D" Demakas could get away with going to parties and hanging out in the dorm. "D" was a very smart student. He did study a lot but probably didn't have to work as hard as I did in school. Some people are just naturally gifted.

That was "D."

As the 1986 Ohio State football team was a few games into their season, it didn't look like they were going to be very good. They started the season losing to both Alabama and Washington. They would have to dig themselves out of a major hole if in fact they were to win games, especially against Michigan.

I started out college poorly. My first college midterm grades weren't very good. After the Washington game, Ohio State started winning game after game after game. Again, the thoughts of Ohio State Head Coach Earle Bruce kept creeping into my head.

"When a person gets knocked down, they need to get back up again."

I needed to take that advice and improve my college grades just liked the Buckeyes were improving their season. You can learn a lot from adversity and how to respond to it.

As the Buckeyes added another win over Illinois by the score of 14-0, it appeared they had a really good shot of overcoming their first two losses of the season. With my first (A) in my Communication class, I thought I had a good chance at applying to Ohio State.

On October 10th, I decided to surprise my family and come home for the weekend. Mike "D" Demakas and I would bring a friend home we met in *Williams Hall.* His name was Dave Alexander. He was from Fort Wayne, Indiana. Dave really didn't have any preference on a college team he cheered for until he met me. He couldn't believe that I was such a big Ohio State fan.

When the Buckeyes were on TV, Dave sat with me in the dorm lounge and watched all the games. Before we went home to Merrillville that weekend, Dave actually helped me with a presentational speech for my Communication class. I brought Dave into my class and dressed him up as an Ohio State Buckeye fan!

I put a jersey on him, a Buckeye necklace around his neck, and an Ohio State hat on his head. We even brought in one of those noise makers into the class. When I was presenting my speech on *"How to dress up for an Ohio State football game"* all the students as well as the professor kind of just looked at us as if we were crazy! The professor said…

"Dennis, if you love Ohio State that much, why don't you go to school there?"

The professor wasn't trying to be mean or sarcastic but simply asked a very good question.

I didn't have the heart to tell her that I really wanted to go to Ohio State but my grades were not good enough yet. I knew that I had three trimesters at Ball State to try to get satisfactory grades so I could apply to Ohio State. Ball State went on what was called the 'quarter system.' This meant that there were three grading periods during the school year and one in the summer. Most colleges nowadays go with a semester plan.

I knew Ohio State would base my application on my first two grading periods at Ball State. What if I didn't get into Ohio State? Could I still be a fan of a school I didn't go to? My parents even mentioned that I could go two years at Ball State and another two years at Ohio State. I didn't want to do that. I knew the longer that I stayed at Ball State, the more I would like it. I would not want to leave.

Ball State was an unbelievable university with great people and a great atmosphere. I was starting to make some really good friends there as well. Even if I was to magically get accepted to Ohio State, leaving Ball State University would prove to be very difficult.

That weekend, Mike "D" Demakas, Dave Alexander, and I went back to Northwest Indiana to see my family and my other friends. Merrillville High School also happened to be playing the Hobart Brickies on Friday night in October of 1986. The same school that beat us three years in a row while I played at Merrillville.

"D" and I kept telling Dave that you have never seen a high school game quite like the Merrillville/Hobart game. Merrillville hadn't beaten Hobart for a very long time, and the game was at *Demaree Field*.

Just like every Merrillville and Hobart game, there were thousands of people there. Rick also came along with us that night. I hadn't seen my best friend since I moved into the dorms at Ball State back in the early fall. The Merrillville Pirates won the game against the Hobart Brickies that night by the score of 13-11.

The crowd rushed onto the playing field. Even Dave Alexander went on the field with us to congratulate the current Merrillville Pirate football players. It was a really exciting night. I hugged my former coach Tom Peller on the great win. It would be one of the last times I visited Merrillville High School. Life just moves on.

The next day, a lot of my high school friends who were still in town, along with Dave Alexander, went to play a pick-up football game at Harrison Junior High. All of them were yelling at me to get out of the car when we arrived to play this pickup football game.

I said to all of them, *"Start the game without me. I'll get out of the car when the Ohio State game is over!"*

While all my friends started playing the game to relive all their glory years, I was still in the car listening to the Ohio State Buckeyes on the radio. Ohio State was playing the Indiana Hoosiers that day in Bloomington. The game wasn't on TV but aired on an Indiana radio station.

As I gazed out the car window to see all my friends play football on the Harrison Junior High field, I was glued to listening to the Buckeye game on the radio station. Ohio State was in a very close battle with the Hoosiers that day. This surprised me because Ohio State hadn't lost to Indiana since 1951.

The Hoosiers almost pulled off the victory that day which would have definitely cost Ohio State a Big Ten Conference title. The Buckeyes won 24-22. Cris Carter had an unbelievable touchdown catch in the game. It was something that I always expected Cris to do in big games.

The weekend came to a close as we all went out for pizza at this famous place known as *Gino's East Pizza* in Chicago, Illinois. It was nice to catch up with a lot of my high school friends that weekend. Watching Merrillville finally beat the Hobart Brickies, and just visiting with my family and friends made it worthwhile to come home to get away from the grind of college life.

As I returned to Ball State after a weekend at home, I continued my quest to get good grades and fulfill the dream of going to Ohio State. Grammy and Papa would come down to see me the following weekend for Ball State *"family day."*

They really wanted to see the Ball State campus that weekend but instead watched every minute of Ohio State's win over Purdue by the score of 39-11 in the *Williams Hall* Lounge. By the time we got to November, Ohio State had a record of 7-2. After the Purdue win, they had also beaten Minnesota as well as Iowa in consecutive weeks.

The whole family picked me up on Friday, November 7th, 1986 for the fun-filled weekend at Ohio State. The Buckeyes were scheduled to play the Northwestern Wildcats in Columbus. Grammy and Papa would also make the trip along with my sisters, Nikki and Erin. When we arrived in Columbus on that Friday, I kept telling my family that I was finally 'home.'

Dad kept asking me if I was sure that I wanted to go to school here? To this day, I really believe that the whole family came to Ohio State that weekend to see where I was possibly going to spend the rest of my college years and fulfill a dream. They never said anything that weekend but they never really had to. I could see it in all of their eyes. I knew that I would have to attend school there not just for me… but for the entire family. I also knew everyone was proud of me for how far I had come in life, and that I was already in college. However, that wasn't the dream or the end goal.

The goal. The dream. The moment—Ohio State!

I kept coming back to the moment in 1975 while watching Ohio State beat Michigan with my dad. It was also the moment I spent with Papa and Grammy at Camp Lutherwald during the summer of 1985 sharing my life's ambitions and dreams. It was all the successes and failures while I was in high school.

It was Coach Armontrout telling me that I needed to chase my dreams. It was finding out that my mom had to overcome her own adversities in life while being diagnosed with breast cancer. It was showing my sisters Nikki and Erin that if you put your faith in something, you can realize and achieve your goals.

It was for my family, coaches, and friends who had supported me throughout the years. It was also for those people who didn't think a Merrillville kid would ever get a chance to go to school there. Ohio State was my school and my university.

The years have passed, but whenever I visit Ohio State, I look up at the second level of that old hotel we stayed at during the weekend of November 1986. It now serves as a resident hall for Ohio State students. It sits quiet after all these years. However, I can still see Papa dancing up there after the game against Northwestern, and the smile on his face. He wasn't smiling because Ohio State won that day.

Papa was smiling because he knew someday he would return to Ohio State.

This time... as a grandparent of an Ohio State student.

This was now a dream that my whole family shared with me. Could this dream possibly come true? I now felt the pressure and the weight of the whole world on my shoulders. I had to do something about it.

As Ohio State was approaching a Big Ten Conference football title, I returned to school to finish classes prior to Thanksgiving Break. The next week, Ohio State was scheduled to play the Wisconsin Badgers on television. I made sure that I set my alarm clock early in my dorm room so I could get down to the lounge before anyone else could claim the TV set. Like there was anything else on television that day?

To my amazement, every seat in the Williams Hall Lounge, not far from the cafeteria, was filled with people getting ready to watch the Ohio State game! What? Ball State may have had a game that day but it seemed that everyone in my dorm was interested in watching the Buckeyes play the Wisconsin Badgers on television.

I also had two friends who were football players on the Ball State team. I never went to see them play. I believe "D" was upset that I woke him up that morning from his partying lifestyle from the night before. Didn't he know the Buckeyes were on television? I am not sure "D" cared.

He went back to sleep by saying, *"Enjoy the game, Bunda. Don't wake me up again."*

I couldn't believe that he wanted to miss this epic showdown with the Wisconsin Badgers! What was he thinking?

To my surprise, everyone in the dorm lounge cheered on the Buckeyes to a 30-17 victory. I am not sure why. It was nice to see everyone in *Williams Hall* cheering for 'my team.' Michigan had lost that day to Minnesota setting up a showdown in Columbus the following week.

I would go home for Thanksgiving break to watch the Ohio State/Michigan game with dad and the rest of my family in November of 1986. It would also be good to see Rick, Brian, and the rest of my friends. The night before the big game, everyone was taunting Rick about how Michigan was going to lose to Ohio State the next day.

The next day, Ohio State was playing the Wolverines for the right to go to the Rose Bowl. Dad and I would take our usual spots in the basement to get ready for the contest. Dad had made me a poster which had Ohio State pictures on it, and about the rivalry between the two schools. There is simply no other game like the one played between Ohio State and Michigan.

In a lot of years, they referred to the Big Ten Conference as the *"Big Two and the Little Eight."* Everyone knew who the Big Two were.... Ohio State and Michigan.

On November 22, 1986, that was surely the mission for Coach Earle Bruce and the Ohio State Buckeyes. Ohio State had rolled to nine straight victories. The winner of this game would of course go to the Rose Bowl. The loser of the contest would get to play Texas A&M in the Cotton Bowl.

The Wolverines were once again led by quarterback Jim Harbaugh and their star tailback, Jamie Morris. It sure looked like Ohio State would win that day. Of course, Jim Harbaugh didn't think so. He had predicted before the game that the Wolverines would beat

Ohio State. I was really mad at his comments. I was hoping that Buckeye linebacker Chris Spielman was going to tackle Harbaugh over and over again. I just didn't realize that Jim Harbaugh's prediction would come true.

Ohio State scored first when Cris Carter caught a touchdown pass over Michigan defender, Erik Campbell. The Wolverines would cut into the lead with a field goal that made the score now 7-3. When Ohio State's Vince Workman scored on a long touchdown run to make it 14-3, I thought the game was over.

I kept yelling at my dad and saying, "*We are going to the Rose Bowl! This game is over!!*" On cue, dad reminded me that it was early in the game, and Ohio State could not relax and take it easy the rest of the way. They would have to try to outscore the Wolverines that day.

In the second half, Michigan was starting to gash the Ohio State defense with big runs by tailback Jamie Morris. The drama of the game really grew when the Wolverines were only trailing 14-13 in the third quarter. When Michigan took the lead and increased it to 26-17 in the 4th quarter, my confidence weakened.

Buckeye Cris Carter made an unbelievable touchdown catch. It was his second of the game, and the Buckeyes had closed the gap to 26-24. I will always remember the time left on the clock when Ohio State had a chance to win this game...1:06.

The Buckeyes had a fourth down and about two yards to go. They could either elect to go for it in hopes of a first down, and try to make the touchdown... or kick a field goal.

Coach Bruce made the decision to kick the field goal that would be over 45 yards. If the kick is good, Ohio State wins the game. If the kick is no good, Ohio State loses the game. It was just that simple. Dad and I were standing right next to the TV. We looked at each other with nervousness and excitement all at the same time.

As the kick sailed through the air, my dad shouted out, "*It's good!*"

The kick was definitely far enough to be good but sailed wide left of the goal post. We sat there stunned. Ohio State would lose to Michigan 26-24.

Through the years, people have always asked me what my favorite memories are of Ohio State football games. I have a lot of great memories. Like my first game in person at Illinois when Ohio State won 44-7 while my parents were celebrating their wedding anniversary.

I also tell people about my first game in Ohio Stadium in 1980 when the Buckeyes beat Minnesota 47-0. I have fond memories of going to games with Papa and watching him dance at a tailgate party afterwards.

The 1986 game will always be stuck in my head as a crushing defeat. It affected me for a while or at least until Ohio State would play again in the Cotton Bowl on New Year's Day. I was really upset about Ohio State's loss to Michigan when I went back to college after Thanksgiving break.

Of course, all my dorm friends at Williams Hall rubbed it in that the Buckeyes lost to Michigan. A lot of them were the same people who cheered on the Buckeyes when they played the Wisconsin Badgers the week before. I needed to stay focused on my grades and going to class though. I also had a couple of friends who were considering joining an on-campus fraternity known as *Sigma Phi Epsilon*.

Chapter 24
A Very Tough Decision

Darren Deboy knew someone in the fraternity who could get us in as pledges. (A pledge is someone who has to go through training and work to join the fraternity.) I didn't know if I would be going to Ohio State or not, so I decided to pledge the fraternity with my good friend, Darren. He had also run track & field with both "D" and I at Merrillville. One of the upperclassmen in the fraternity was also from our high school. His name was Bryant.

If there was ever a time that I took my mind off of possibly going to Ohio State, it was when I decided to join Sigma Phi Epsilon or *Sig Eps* as they were called. Don't get me wrong. I was studying more than I ever did in my life. It was just that the fraternity experience was very exciting.

My pledge class was known as the *"Late Night 15."*

As you could imagine, we had fifteen males who wanted to join the fraternity that December of 1986. All the members gave me the nickname of *"Buddha."* Don't ask me why but they gave all the fraternity pledges nicknames.

Some of the other nicknames of my pledge brothers were: Nomad, Astro, Booger, Serf, Snoopy, Goober, Little Irv, Plow, D-day and Dweezil.

I went to the Ball State University bookstore, and bought everything that had the emblem of Sigma Phi Epsilon fraternity on it. I took great pride that I was going to be a member of this fraternity.

After classes, I would have to go clean the fraternity house and interview all the fraternity brothers to get to know all of them.

There were Friday and Saturday night parties where we got to meet pretty sorority girls as well as just socialize with other college students. My goal was to get Mike "D" Demakas to join the fraternity by the spring. It was like having a whole new set of friends or in this case, fraternity brothers.

Since I really started getting involved with the Sig Ep fraternity, and I was at college with one of my best friends, "D," why would I want to transfer schools? Besides, I didn't know anyone at Ohio State or from the state of Ohio, for that matter. I was also starting to get good grades at Ball State.

I didn't want to tell anyone what I was thinking at the time but my mindset shifted to staying at Ball State. Even when my parents asked me about my future plans, I always told them that I wanted to go to Ohio State.

Was that really true now? I wasn't too sure. "Be happy with who you are and what you have, and you won't have to hunt for happiness."

When I returned home again for Christmas vacation, I thought I would pay a visit to Coach Armontrout. He pushed me to succeed in high school. I now needed his advice on school as well as life.

When I approached him about what I was thinking, Coach Armontrout didn't try to convince me one way or the other about college. He simply said that you have to do what makes you happy. It was his next statement that resonated with me. As I was walking out his office he said,

"Bunda, if you don't chase your dreams...you will never catch them."

Funny thing was that I heard Coach say those words before while I was running track for him at Merrillville. In fact, I heard him say it quite a few times. It was just this time I was actually paying much more attention to him. He smiled at me as if to know what decision I was going to make about my future.

I started my Christmas vacation with my family and friends. I put my 'big decision' on the back-burner. I hadn't even applied to

Ohio State yet, and there was a great chance that I wouldn't even be accepted there. Maybe I wouldn't have to choose between the school that I currently went to and the one that I dreamed about growing up. It would be the next few months that would determine my fate.

It was great seeing all my friends again for Christmas vacation. Even though I went to a different university than Brian and Rick, I was always going to remain close friends with them through the years. Obviously, I saw Mike "D" Demakas a lot due to the fact that we were roommates at Ball State.

It was also nice spending time with my sisters Nikki and Erin. I didn't get to see them that much during the school year. Nikki was now a sophomore at Merrillville High School and Erin was in her last year at Harrison Junior High.

It was tough being away from them because I always want to be that 'big brother' and look out for their best interests. Being away at school, I couldn't monitor what boys they were dating, how they were doing in school, or just being there to offer them 'brotherly advice.' Due to the fact that there were no cell phones back in 1986, it was tough to communicate with them on a regular basis. A lot of times, I would call Nikki and Erin on a phone in the dorm room using what was known as a *"calling card."*

It was also great to see Grammy and Papa again. Just like every other Christmas, we would always go over their house in Griffith to celebrate Christmas Eve.

New Year's Eve was always spent with my friends.

There was this one girl who was there every year named Jennifer. We really didn't have a serious relationship but always hung out at the Radisson together one night every year. We would kiss and hold hands the whole night at the New Year's Eve celebration.

Long-distance relationships are difficult to keep together if you don't see the person frequently. I liked Jennifer but not enough to enter into a relationship where I couldn't see her every day. She was always at the Radisson Hotel New Year's Eve celebration the following year. We would always have a one-night romance. I would later find out how difficult a long-distant relationship could be. Life events happen when you least expect it.

The following day after New Year's Eve, the Buckeyes were on TV against the Texas A&M Aggies in the Cotton Bowl. Ohio State had lost to Michigan in November, so they couldn't go to the Rose Bowl. It would be the first time in Ohio State's football history that they would play in the Cotton Bowl. In fact, it was the first time in Cotton Bowl history that a Big Ten team played in this historic game.

The Buckeyes weren't supposed to win the game either. It also seemed like a Texas A&M home game because the game was played in Dallas, Texas. I did feel confident that Ohio State would win at all. My dad knew someone that could have gotten us tickets to the game.

He said something to me that I still remember to this day. Dad said that we could go to the Cotton Bowl game, but it would mean that it would cost me a year of tuition. In other words, I could go to the Cotton Bowl game or go to Ohio State as a student the following fall. Unbeknownst to dad, I really hadn't made up my mind if I was going to go to Ohio State even if I got accepted there.

When Ohio State took the field that day in January of 1987, Coach Earle Bruce came out in a suit and tie. He usually wore a coaching shirt, with gray pants, and an Ohio State baseball cap. That was Coach Bruce. There was always talk that he didn't have a great image with the university and the athletic department. The Buckeyes would also wear new red Nike football shoes during the game.

I am sure that a lot of the Buckeye fans were getting a little upset with Coach Bruce, mainly because he seemed to finish with a 9-3 record every year. In 1986, he would not finish with a 9-3 record. Instead he would have a 10-3 record. He would beat Texas A&M in the 1987 Cotton Bowl that day by the score of 28-12.

After all these years, I still have the original VHS tape from the Cotton Bowl game that dad and I watched on TV that January 1st, 1987. It was another great moment that we shared together. With Ohio State leading just 7-6 in the 3rd quarter, Chris Spielman made an unbelievable interception for a touchdown to make the game 14-6 in favor of the Buckeyes.

Ohio State would never relinquish the lead in the game and win 28-12. As I sat there watching the postgame celebration, I wondered what it would be like to be part of a university that took so much pride in its football tradition. Until years later, I didn't realize that there were people in the Ohio State administration who wanted to get rid of Coach Bruce.

I also didn't realize that he almost left on his own after the 1987 Cotton Bowl to take a job with the University of Arizona. Obviously, I was familiar with Arizona as I grew up there. My dad also had attended the University of Arizona in the 1970's. I guess Coach Bruce's assistant coaches as well as players talked him out of the Arizona football job. He was going to remain at Ohio State as the coach in the fall of 1987.

I had no idea at the time how big of an industry Ohio State football was in Columbus, Ohio. No matter how good of a football coach Earle Bruce was, he was not going to please everyone. This included both the fans as well as the administration at Ohio State. There are certain expectations at Ohio State, whether good or bad.

First, you have to beat Michigan on a somewhat regular basis. Coach Bruce did that but had lost back to back games in 1985 and 1986 to the Wolverines. Second, is to win the Big Ten Conference or at least contend on a yearly basis for the championship. Third, is to go to the Rose Bowl because that is the *Granddaddy* of all the bowl games watched on television. If you accomplish all those requirements, people love you as the football coach at Ohio State. If you don't… well, they want to get rid of you.

I had read somewhere in one of my *Buckeye Bulletin* papers or another newspaper, Coach Bruce said that when you beat Michigan, you can walk up High Street, which is the main street on the Ohio State campus. If you lose to Michigan, you better take a back alley.

Even though the Buckeyes won the 1987 Cotton Bowl against the Texas A&M Aggies, I still didn't look at the season as being

296

successful because they lost to the Wolverines. By the way, Michigan did lose the Rose Bowl on the same day that Ohio State beat Texas A&M.

They would lose to Arizona State by the score of 22-15. With that being said, I know for a fact that my best friend Rick still saw Michigan's season as being great because they beat Ohio State. I didn't realize at the time the impact of Arizona State's win over Michigan would have on Ohio State football for years to come. It would also have an impact on my own personal life.

Arizona State's win would eventually lead me to one of the most improbable events in my life. I guess you will have to read on to see how another school's victory over Michigan changed who I am today.

I call it... fate.

I went back to Ball State after the holidays were over to complete my freshman year in college. I still hadn't made my mind up whether or not I was going to apply to Ohio State after the winter term. I was enjoying fraternity life at Ball State and all the new friends that I had made at school.

I didn't have a serious girlfriend at the time, but I dated a few girls during that first year at Ball State. I knew the deadline to apply for Ohio State was going to be sometime in March or April. If I didn't apply, I would never know the truth. Whether I could get into school there or not.

I would wonder my entire life if I was really good enough for Ohio State. If I did apply, I would know for sure if I was meant to be a student there. If not, I was very happy at Ball State University. It was just the comment that Coach Armontrout made at Christmas time about 'chasing your dreams' that was still weighing on my mind.

Could I really go to school there? Could I back down on a childhood dream that started back in 1975? How would I be remembered in life?

These were the same constant thoughts going through my head. What the heck, I thought. It couldn't hurt to just apply to Ohio State. So I set out to do my very best at Ball State University and make sure my grades were going to be excellent.

297

During the week, Mike "D" Demakas didn't see me a lot. I was either at the fraternity house doing chores for Sigma Phi Epsilon or I was at the campus library studying for my classes late at night. I was going to do everything in my power to at least try to get accepted to The Ohio State University.

There would be many days when "D" would say, *"Where are you going now, Bunda?"*

I would answer with the same response as I always did… *"I am going back to the campus library to get more studying in."*

I remembered what Woody Hayes used to say about hard work. He would tell people that 'he may not be the smartest person in the world but he could always outwork you.' I took that to heart and applied it to how I was going to excel in college. There were many times that I would look around the Ball State campus library. There wouldn't be many students there, especially on a Friday or Saturday nights.

Most college kids would be at a fraternity party, hitting the campus area bars, going on dates, or hanging out in the dorms. If I wasn't at the library, I was sitting in my room at the desk doing homework or studying. Once again, the temptations of going out were always there—girls, parties, and socializing, which took place on a college campus.

This is not to say that I didn't have my share of fun. I went to the parties and I socialized on campus. Not until I had all my studying and preparation done for my schoolwork. This was it. All the years of being an Ohio State fan, and falling in love with the school that I had wanted to go to since I was a little kid, had reached its final point.

I had never tried so hard at something in my life. I had accomplished a great deal but nothing would be more significant than this. It would all come down to a decision by the admissions department at The Ohio State University.

March 12th, 1987.

I can tell you exactly where I was at the time and what happened on this day. People always ask me how I can remember things like that in life? When you are an Ohio State fan, there are certain dates which always stick out in your mind. When you watched your first Ohio State game on TV, the first game you saw in person, your first game in Ohio Stadium, who you were dating when Ohio State upset number one ranked Iowa in 1985, and the day that Woody Hayes passed away on March 12th, 1987.

Coach Hayes passed away at the age of seventy-four. To me, Woody Hayes was Ohio State Buckeye football. He was one of the main reasons that I started liking the school as well as the team. He coached the Buckeyes for twenty-eight years and had a record of 205 wins, 61 losses, and 10 ties. He had won five national titles and thirteen Big Ten Conference Championships.

Coach Hayes would visit adults and children in the hospital who were terminally ill with cancer, spend time with the soldiers who were in the Vietnam War during the 1960's, help former players who were in need of a job, make sure his players graduated from Ohio State, and talk with students on campus about things that were bothering them. He cared about education.

That his players as well as others needed to obtain a college degree. I have read every book ever written on Woody Hayes over and over again. Through the years, I have studied his career as well as his life. There have been many times when I visit Columbus, Ohio that I have gone to see his grave site. He was, and still is, Ohio State football.

I was getting ready to head to one of my classes when the phone rang in my dorm room at Ball State. It was my dad on the other end. He told me that Woody Hayes had just died of an apparent heart attack. It came as a total shock to me. I would not attend any classes that day.

I sat in the *Williams Hall* dorm contemplating my own life. I think sometimes we believe that our heroes are invincible and nothing could ever happen to them. Stunned, I looked out the window and cried my eyes out for about a half an hour. Woody Hayes used to say that he was a student of the past and enjoyed studying history, but he didn't live in the past.

I couldn't think about my past and the many mistakes that I had made up to this point. I was ready to take the challenge of being the best that I could be in life. The quote of Woody's that I really loved was… *"Nothing that comes easy in this world is worth a damn."*

With that being said, I decided that I was going to apply to The Ohio State University as a student right after Woody Hayes passed away. I got a postcard in the mail that said the Ohio State Admissions Department would render a decision on my academic status in a four-to-six-week time frame. This would be the longest four to six weeks of my life.

I thought about my parents, my sisters, as well as Grammy and Papa. I set out to accomplish the dream of attending Ohio State. When I tell you that I studied harder than any other time in my life, that would not be an exaggeration.

If people thought I was a fierce competitor as a track & field athlete at Merrillville, they hadn't seen anything yet. I know that Rick, Brian, and Mike "D" Demakas knew that I was serious as well. I was doing this for all my coaches who played an impact throughout my life, especially Coach Lafey Armontrout. This was also for all the kids who were younger than me who had similar dreams, goals, and ambitions.

This was it—no turning back now. I was the most focused student that you have ever seen from March until the end of the school year. I was still going to my fraternity house and was initiated as a full-time member of Sigma Phi Epsilon by the spring of 1987. I had kept my secret of applying to Ohio State from all my fraternity brothers.

No one had any idea why I was working so hard at the library or at my dorm room desk. After class, I would go to the *Williams Hall* student mailboxes to see if The Ohio State University had made a decision on whether or not I would be accepted there as a student. Each passing day grew longer and longer. There were many nights that I would be awake in my dorm room staring at the ceiling.

March. April. May. Without a word from Ohio State.

All the while, I was studying, preparing, and staying focused on my goal to go there. I was very nervous that the amount of time, energy, and effort would be lost if I didn't get accepted. I didn't want to think about the admission letter that would be coming in my dorm mailbox soon from Ohio State. I kept thinking negative thoughts. There was no way Ohio State would allow me the opportunity to be a student. At times, the wait was too much to take. I thought about giving up on the dream.

Chapter 25

Finally…Home Again

One of my all-time favorite movies is *"Hitch"* starring Will Smith and Kevin James. There is a quote by Alex "Hitch" Hitchens who is played by actor, Will Smith. He says in the movie, *"Life is not the amount of breaths you take, it's the moments that take your breath away."*

Friday, May 15th would be that day.

It was a sunny day in Muncie, Indiana on the Ball State campus. I had just got done with one of my early afternoon classes. I was on my way back to the Williams Hall dorm to eat my lunch. I stopped by my mailbox at the front desk.

There was a single white envelope with the words, *"The Ohio State University Office of Admissions"* labeled on it. My heart started to race and I was short of breath. I didn't want to open it right away. Should I give it to Mike "D" Demakas to open it for me? Should I wait until later? I was too nervous to open the envelope at that moment.

I ate my lunch but I couldn't tell you what I had to eat. I left Williams Hall to go to the fraternity house with the envelope in my backpack. When I got in the Sigma Phi Epsilon house, there was hardly anyone around.

A lot of my fraternity brothers probably had afternoon classes that day. I went down to the basement of the fraternity house and sat in a chair. I stared at my backpack for a few minutes. I got up out of the chair and paced back and forth for a few more minutes. Once I sat down again, I reached for the Ohio State letter in my backpack. I stared at the envelope knowing that my fate was inside. I opened the envelope as my heart continued to race through my chest. I took out the letter, and started to read it. This had been the moment that I had been waiting for my entire life. It was as if time stood still for that particular moment.

The letter read: *"Dear Dennis: Congratulations! I am pleased to inform you of your admissions to The Ohio State University, Columbus campus for the 1987 autumn quarter."*

(Pause)

The admissions paper started to get smeared with the tears that were running down my face. I did it!!!

I was now going to attend THE Ohio State University in Columbus, Ohio. After I read the letter again a few more times just to make sure it was for real, I ran all the way back to the dorm room to call my parents.

I don't think my feet ever touched the ground on the way back to Williams Hall. Mom was the first to receive my message. I just remember her telling me how proud she was of me. Mom then called my dad at work, and told him that I got accepted to Ohio State. Grammy and Papa received the news next. They called me to offer congratulations on getting accepted to the 'school of my dreams.'

I kept pinching myself to see if I was dreaming or if this was really happening in my life. I remembered all the times that I could have given up or focused on another dream. So many times, people told me that it was just a dream but it was never going to be reality.

However, giving up on the dream was never really an option. If we truly have one life to live, I was going to make sure that I was going to make the most of it. For those of you that have had high goals or dreams in your own life, this is a testament that if you work hard enough, they will come true. Never give up on something that you really want to do, or are passionate about in life.

Many people have dreams but never fulfill them because of the obstacles in their lives. There are others that may have excuses on why they can't fulfill their goals. Whether you have obstacles or excuses, don't let them get in the way of fulfilling the promises that you have made to yourself.

I am living proof of someone who could have given up many times, and settled for less in my life. I could have listened to all the people that told me that I wasn't good enough to go to Ohio State because I was an average student. That Ohio State was too big of a school and only accepted elite students. If I would have listened to all those negative comments, I would have never worked as hard as I did to be accepted to The Ohio State University.

There are many times that I listen to people talk about their dreams and aspirations when they were younger. Only not to achieve them because something stood in their way. A lot of them comment that they wish they could go back in time, and do things over again. In life, very rarely do you get to do things over again or get a second chance to fulfill a dream. This was not going to be the case with me. I knew that I had one shot to fulfill my dream of going to Ohio State.

I would be remiss if I didn't mention how thankful I was to Ball State University. Without Ball State helping me become a better student as well as person, I would not have been able to go to Ohio State. The professors, the support staff, the academic advisors, and students at Ball State, all played a major factor in my success.

I will always be thankful for the experience and guidance they gave me that first year of college. I always tell people that if I had a second favorite school, it would be Ball State University. Go Cardinals! I still had a major problem in May of 1987. It was saying goodbye to all the friends and fraternity brothers that I had made during the school year. Many of them I would never see again.

None of my fraternity brothers at Sigma Phi Epsilon knew until that Sunday night, (May 17th, 1987) when we had our weekly meeting at the fraternity house. There was a ceremony that the fraternity brothers used to do where they shut off all the lights in the basement of the fraternity house. We would gather in a large circle and a gavel, which is a ceremonial mallet made of wood, was passed around from fraternity brother to fraternity brother. When you received the gavel, you could speak what was on your mind about school, girls, life, problems, parties, etc...

I don't think my fraternity brothers knew that I was going to tell them that I was leaving Ball State for another college. The moment was soon approaching... As I sat there listening to the other fraternity brothers talk about what was on their mind, I kept thinking about the words I was going to say once the gavel made its way around to me.

This was not going to be easy. Like I said, I had made a lot of good friends and created a lot of great memories with them. With each passing fraternity brother speaking, I could feel myself sweating. It was getting closer and closer for my turn to talk about what was on my mind. I gathered my thoughts for a second, took a deep breath, and finally told them that I wasn't staying at Ball State. I was going to follow my dream of going to The Ohio State University.

You could have heard a pin drop in the fraternity house.

I could hear one of the fraternity brothers whisper, *"He's leaving us?"*

When the lights came back on, all of them stood there looking at me. One by one they formed a line to shake my hand and congratulate me on my quest. A lot of them hugged me and told me that they would miss me. They said that I would be welcome back to visit if I was ever on the Ball State campus again.

However, I knew that I would never see most of them again. I think that is what bothered me the most. Just like high school, you forge relationships and create memories that last a lifetime. Those fraternity brothers always had a major impact on my life.

I also knew that I wouldn't see Mike "D" Demakas that much anymore once I started college at Ohio State. We had been sports adversaries in junior high, the best of friends in high school, and roommates our first year in college. The college year at Ball State in 1986-1987 would always remain as one of my fondest memories in life.

Once again, one door was about to shut while another door was about to open. A dream was about to be realized as well as some other surprises along the way. I was finally going to my new home...

The Ohio State University.

Dad and Papa came to get me the first part of June for summer vacation. We loaded the car with all my things that I had in my dorm room at *Williams Hall*. I would be heading back to Northwest Indiana to spend time with my family and friends before stepping on the Ohio State campus. Dad knew someone at the local Burger King restaurant who got me a job there. It wasn't my first choice of a summer job but at the time, it was my only choice. For those of you who have ever worked at a fast food restaurant, it is not the easiest job in the world.

College kids always need a job and spending money while they are in school. I was no different in that regard. Grammy and Papa always gave me cash while I was at Ball State but I needed to start making my own money. I had worked previous jobs at the Griffith Car Wash and at Camp Lutherwald, and I was now going to try my luck at Burger King. The problem was that I really wasn't cut out for the fast food industry. I struggled working there and eventually I only worked two hours a day at best. The other workers at Burger King just couldn't believe how many mistakes I made working there. I once made a hamburger for a customer that fell apart as I was putting it into the bag.

The customer looked at me and said, *"What the heck are you doing? You expect me to eat that!"*

Ok... so I couldn't make a Whopper sandwich. What was so wrong with that? My boss told me that I could gain more hours by painting the Burger King playground equipment during the day. That was a fancy way of saying that they didn't want me making hamburgers for the customers.

I did that for a couple of weeks until Papa found me a job as a pool lifeguard at the apartment complex that he and Grammy were living at in the 1980's. The apartment complex was known as the Mansards and it was located in Griffith. Of course, Griffith was the first town we lived in after our move back to Indiana from Arizona in 1976.

I worked at the Mansards by lifeguarding as well as maintaining all the pools in the summer of 1987. I believe at the time there were eight pools that I was in-charge of in the complex. It was probably the best summer job I had while I was in college.

There were many days that I would go to the Mansards and watch people swim while I just sat in a chair. Since I really didn't have to save anyone from drowning, I would pass my time thinking about the upcoming school year at Ohio State and what new friends I would meet in my first year there. After work, I would often go over to Rick's house to lift weights or just hang out passing the time in the summer. I really didn't want a girlfriend knowing that I would be leaving in early September for Columbus, Ohio.

That was the plan anyways. You can never plan for when a new relationship is going to enter into your life. I had always set my sights on meeting a Buckeye girl from Ohio. However, it would be a Hoosier girl from the town of Munster that I would fall in love with in the summer of 1987. I just wasn't planning on that happening but it just did.

I had known her for a while ever since I dated Brenna during my senior year at Merrillville. Her name was Cindy, and she went to the same high school as Brenna did. I believe I first met Cindy the night I almost got into a fight with Ted over the end of my relationship with Brenna back in February of 1986. Cindy happened to be on the dance team with Brenna at the time. She was two years younger than me.

I didn't mean for the relationship to happen. She was an attractive blonde-haired and blue-eyed girl with an unbelievable smile. I fell in love with her immediately. I knew she was younger than me and still in high school, but that didn't seem to matter much.

There was just something about Cindy that made me fall in love with her. I am not sure Cindy felt the same way at the time, mainly because she still had a year left of high school. There was no doubt that I was in love with her, but that still was not going to deter me from going to Ohio State. I had already been accepted there. Dad and I were scheduled to visit OSU for 'orientation day' in late June. I would now get to see the campus for the first time as a student and not just as a football fan.

We headed out for Columbus for a scheduled orientation on Monday, June 22, 1987. Dad and I left Sunday night, and stayed in the *Holiday Inn Hotel* right off of Lane Avenue in Columbus. It was the same hotel that we always stayed at for football games during our trips to Columbus. We had been to Ohio State for football games as well as my camp experience in 1983, but this was now to register for classes as an Ohio State student. I was very excited to be there but my mind was always shifting away to Cindy. How would this relationship work?

Would she find another boyfriend once I left for school? Did she love me as much as I loved her? Yes… I said, "Love." I had fallen for the other girls that I dated but I really believed that Cindy would be the girl who I would someday marry, have a big house with, and a couple of kids. I may have said that to Anne years earlier but Cindy was my 'dream girl.' It's funny to think about your future when you are only nineteen years old.

My dream of going to Ohio State had come true and maybe someday marrying Cindy would happen as well. She did talk about applying to Ohio State at the conclusion of her senior year at Munster High School. Maybe things were meant to be between us. Dad kept saying forget the girl and focus on Ohio State.

Easier said than done.

The next day, after dad and I ate breakfast at the local *IHOP* pancake house on the main strip of the university known as High Street, we headed out to find a parking spot on campus. The only problem was that all the spots were taken. We had an 8 am appointment to meet my Ohio State advisor and schedule my fall classes. My dad was getting nervous and very frustrated that we couldn't find a parking spot.

If you know my dad, he wants everything to go perfectly, and to make sure that we were on time. It's funny and a warm memory now, but he was really mad that we couldn't find a parking spot on the Ohio State campus! Finally after fifteen minutes of searching, we found a spot in a parking garage close to Ohio Stadium where the Buckeyes played football.

We finally went into the academic building to schedule my classes and pick up my student identification card. Back then, you had to stand in long lines to schedule your classes and speak with your advisor. I was getting frustrated. I wanted to go over to St. John Arena to get my football season ticket pass to all the Ohio State football games. Dad was standing near-by as I was waiting in line for academic scheduling.

I said to him, *"Dad, if we don't get over to the ticket office soon, they will be closed and I won't get my student season pass!"*

Dad glared at me for a second and said, *"You will get the football tickets!! Relax! You are here to be a student!"*

He was yelling at me in front of all the other students as well as all the advisors who were assisting with scheduling. I was a little embarrassed but the message was loud and clear. I was there first and foremost to be a student at The Ohio State University, and not just because I was a fan of the football team. It's a warm memory now but it wasn't then.

After I got my classes as well as housing assignment, we were off to St. John Arena to sign up for my Ohio State season football pass. During my orientation visit that June, I found out that I would be staying at a dorm known as *Morrill Tower.* Dad and I went to visit the dorm, and were surprised that every floor was co-ed. That meant that the boys as well as the girls would be housed on the same floor in the student housing unit.

I would be sharing a dorm suite with fifteen other students. This would be a lot different than my experience at Ball State where Mike "D" Demakas and I shared one room. Morrill Tower was right next

309

to Ohio Stadium so my walk to watch the Buckeyes play would not be far.

Before we left the campus after orientation day, dad wanted to stop at *Conrads College Gifts* right next to the Holiday Inn on Lane Avenue. He told me to wait in the car. He came out of the store with one little bag with a bumper sticker inside.

The bumper sticker read, *"My son and my money both attend Ohio State!"* With that purchase, we headed back to Northwest Indiana for the rest of summer vacation.

I really hated my job at the Burger King but I knew that I needed extra money for college. I was only getting a shift of two hours a day and very little pay. I think the only reason they kept me around was because of the softball league that Burger King was involved in that summer.

The rest of my summer was going to be a lot more fun. I would spend my days by the pool watching people swim, go lift weights at Rick's house, and spend my nights with Cindy. I knew the summer was going to come to an end by August. Cindy would resume high school by starting her senior year at Munster. Rick would be in his second year at Purdue Calumet University, and Mike "D" Demakas would be heading back to Ball State. My friend Brian Portlock was also going to go to work full-time. He eventually made a career move into the Air Force. Life was about to change again. I just didn't realize what was about to happen.

Life is always full of surprises as well as disappointments.

Chapter 26

Hello Columbus!

Ohio State didn't start school until the second week of September in 1987. My sisters Nikki and Erin were now both in high school. Nikki was set to start her junior year and Erin her sophomore year at Merrillville. It was nice to see them for a couple more weeks before my big moment of stepping on the Ohio State campus. I didn't realize how quickly my sisters had grown up, and that they were both actually in high school.

Nikki and Erin understood my dream of going to Ohio State, and that I would be away from them for an extended period of time. Maybe they didn't want me around that much anyways.

They needed to experience high school for themselves, and all the peaks and valleys that go along with it. As for me, I was packing my bags for the ultimate destination to Ohio State for the start for the school year.

I got to see the Buckeyes one last time on TV before I departed for Columbus. They beat West Virginia by the score of 24-3. Ohio State didn't play that well mainly because they were missing their star wide receiver, Cris Carter. Cris was under investigation for possibly taking money from a sports agent and was ruled ineligible to play during the 1987 season.

I was absolutely crushed when I heard the news about him. This was the same person that I went to football camp with in 1983. Now his football career was over at Ohio State. I would not get to see him play in person.

The day after the Ohio State/West Virginia game, Dad and mom would help me pack my things for the journey to Columbus, Ohio. Cindy told me that she would be waiting for my return during Christmas break. I kissed her goodbye. As our car approached the Indiana/Ohio state line, I could see the sign which read, *"Welcome to Ohio."*

I made the comment to my mom that I was going to my new home. She looked back at me and just smiled. I had chills running down my spine. I was really going to attend Ohio State!! It reminded me of the first time I went to an Ohio State game with my parents in 1979.

It had come full circle now.

In a few short days, I would be starting classes at the school that I dearly loved since I was a little boy. I kept thanking mom and dad for sending me to Ohio State and believing that I could actually end up there. I could have gone to a lot of different schools to get a college degree. It wouldn't have been the same though. Many parents may not have let their kid go to an out- of- state school just to fulfill a dream. However, that was not the case with my parents.

Maybe it was because my dad left Northwest Indiana with all of us in the early 1970's so he could fulfill his own dream of attending the University of Arizona. My dad as well as my mom always believed that Nikki, Erin, and I should be given the opportunity to achieve our goals, aspirations, and dreams in life. I always remember some of my friends saying that their parents would never have let them go to a school just to say they fulfilled a dream. I felt thankful and blessed that my parents didn't take that stance. They could have told me that I had to stay at Ball State or go to a local college. They let me go to Ohio State. I am forever grateful.

Thank you, mom and dad.

When we arrived on the Ohio State campus, there were student assistants helping us move all my luggage and belongings into the dorm room at *Morrill Tower*. I didn't know anyone in my dorm or at Ohio State for that matter. It wasn't like the year before when I was moving into Williams Hall at Ball State University with my friend, Mike "D" Demakas.

This was like starting a whole new life. There was a banner in the front of Morrill Tower which stated, *"Welcome New Buckeyes!"* No longer could people say that I was just a fan of the school. I was now a student at The Ohio State University. I was finally *'home.'*

Once I got settled into my new living quarters, I walked with my parents to their car. I hugged both of them and thanked them for the opportunity. Mom had tears running down her face. This was a proud moment for her. She had been through a lot in her life. Mainly her health problems with breast cancer. My dad just had this happy expression on his face. He knew that I had just achieved something really special.

Before their car pulled away from the *Morrill Tower* parking lot to head back to Northwest Indiana... I walked up the stairs, turned to them, and waved goodbye. I was now an official Ohio State Buckeye!

The first friend that I met in the dorm was Mike Klein. It was like I had known him my entire life. No sooner did I have my things unpacked, Mike told me Ohio Stadium was open. The students could go inside during the week and play on the football field.

What!?

Not knowing Mike for more than a couple of hours, we raced out of Morrill Tower, and down to Ohio Stadium to play football catch. I hadn't been on the field in Ohio Stadium since the Earle Bruce Football Camp back in 1983. Four years later, I was racing around inside Ohio Stadium like a little kid again. I think all my new friends at Ohio State thought that I was a little bit crazy.

Most of them lived in Ohio, and may not have thought it was as big of a deal to attend Ohio State as I did. I was never so happy in my life! The only thing that made me a little homesick was missing my girlfriend, Cindy.

We left the summer saying that we shouldn't get too serious due to the fact that I was five hours away from her at college. I did miss Cindy a lot. I tried not to think about her while I was establishing new friends away at college. It was really tough. I knew I fell in love with her that summer.

Grammy had told me that if it was 'meant to be then she would still be around when I came home for holiday breaks as well as in the summer months.' Grammy also told me that I fell in love with *love*, and not really with Cindy. At the time, I am not sure that was really true. I really believed that this was finally the girl of my dreams.

Cindy had mentioned that she was probably going to apply to Ohio State as one of her college choices. If she enrolled at Ohio State, then we could be together forever. We could be married someday and enjoy a happy life.

Classes weren't supposed to start until Thursday that week. This meant from the time I moved in on that Sunday until Wednesday night, I had a chance to get acclimated to student life. I had my new friends take pictures of me in front of almost every academic building on the Ohio State campus.

I believe I got very little sleep within the first days of being there. Mainly, because my other fifteen suitemates would stay up late and enjoy their last days of academic freedom before classes began. I didn't care that much. I was at a place that only a few people thought was even possible.

On Wednesday, the day before classes were to start for the fall, the students had to pick up their football season ticket pass at the French Fieldhouse. French Fieldhouse is where the track & field team practiced in the winter months. It is also where the Ohio State football team practiced when the weather was bad outside.

However, in 1987, Ohio State would build a brand-new facility known as the *Woody Hayes Athletic Center*. It would become one of the best football training facilities in the country. Named after the legendary football coach Woody Hayes, the facility has an indoor practice field, weight room, training tables, coaching offices, etc...

We were to go over to the French Fieldhouse to pick up the ticket pass for the rest of Ohio State's home games in 1987. Since students were not checked into the dorms prior to the first game against West Virginia, most of them would experience their first home game against the Oregon Ducks on September 19th.

As I went into French Fieldhouse to get my season pass, I noticed a familiar person standing in the building. It was head football coach Earle Bruce! He was standing there watching all the students get their season ticket passes. When you are at Ohio State, you are going to see a lot of famous people on the campus like: Archie Griffin, Earle Bruce, Jack Nicklaus, Bobby Knight, Richard Lewis, etc...

Coach Bruce was dressed in a suit and his Fedora hat which was similar to what he wore in the Cotton Bowl game. Coach Bruce was looking right at me as if he knew me. However, I realized that I must have been staring at him the entire time and that is probably why he was looking right back at me. I looked at one of my new friends named Scott and said, *"Do you know who that is? It is Coach Bruce!"*

As if I expected Scott to share the same enthusiasm as I did about seeing the "Coach." I don't think I realized it at the time, but a lot of students were there to get a college degree and not just focus on Buckeye football. However, for the first time in my life, there was no one to argue with about how great Ohio State was or that they had the best football program in America. Everyone at Ohio State naturally liked the Buckeyes, and wanted them to succeed on the football field as well as to beat Michigan.

The night before classes started, I really couldn't sleep at all. Partly because it was going to be my first day of classes as a student. The other was because two of my dorm mates were playing *Pink Floyd* music late at night. They said that it helped them relax and get to sleep.

Well, it didn't really help me that much. It wasn't that I didn't appreciate *Pink Floyd* music. It just wasn't the type of music I grew up with when I went to those teenage dance clubs in high school.

The next day, I went to three classes on campus as well as to the library. I made it to Ohio State and now I wanted to make sure that I graduated with a college degree.

I planned on putting in a lot of study hours and preparation time as a student. This was different from when I was a student in junior high or in high school. I was only concerned about playing sports, meeting girls, and what I was doing on the weekends with my friends. In fact, the parents of one of my roommates stopped by Morrill Tower one day.

They looked at their son (Bill) and said, *"Why can't you be more like Denny, and study to get good grades?!"*

Bill just looked at me and shook his head. I don't think he or his parents realized how far I had come in life. I wasn't always focused on being a great student. That all changed now. The first game I saw as an OSU student was against the Oregon Ducks on Saturday, September 19th, 1987.

I had seats right on the running track close to the field, and in back of the Ohio State bench. The running track was still in Ohio Stadium. They had bleacher seats right behind the Ohio State team bench. It was the closest seat to the field that I ever had in a college stadium. Ohio State would go on to win that day by the score of 24-14, and move their record to a perfect 2-0.

I also watched Chris Spielman, the great Ohio State linebacker, coming to the back of the bench to get some water. He seemed to be only about ten feet from where I was sitting!

Actually, we had to stand the whole game because you couldn't see over the Ohio State players on the sidelines. It was amazing to see the team up close in a real game. Needless to say, I thought that I had died and gone to heaven. I really felt that I was now part of the university.

I was probably the last person to leave Ohio Stadium that day. In fact, I think I was! The stadium usher came up to me and said, *"You can leave now. The game is over. There will be others this year."*

He was right. Ohio State had a lot of interesting home games left on its 1987 schedule. The problem was that I didn't want to leave the stadium. I kept looking around Ohio Stadium and thinking how many great games, great players, and great coaches were part of Ohio State's football history. I was also thinking about the first home game that dad and I went to against Minnesota in 1980.

I was recounting in my head of the many times I watched Ohio State in this stadium on television, and all the great wins as well as heartbreaking losses that took place there. I know this sounds a lot like the movie, *"Rudy."*

Rudy is the kid who dreams to play for Notre Dame, and he loves everything about Notre Dame Stadium. In many ways, my story is very similar to that of Rudy Ruettiger who played for the Notre Dame "Fighting Irish" back in the 1970's.

I can relate to Rudy and his love for his school. I felt the same way about Ohio State. I would always look at my new friends and say, *"Can you believe we are students at Ohio State!?"*

Some of them would just look at me and say, *"You're strange, Bunda."*

The next week, my dad called me on the phone to ask how I liked Ohio State? I told him that I loved it. I thanked him once more for sending me to college here. He also asked if I was going to continue being a member of the Sigma Phi Epsilon fraternity at Ohio State? I was already a member of this national fraternity since I joined the chapter at Ball State.

He advised me to go over to their house, and meet the members of the Ohio State chapter of Sigma Phi Epsilon. I told him that I would think about it. My focus was on getting good grades and on Buckeye football.

That week, Ohio State was set to play the LSU Tigers on national TV in Louisiana. We had a television in the lobby of the Morrill Tower dorm to watch the game. Both LSU and Ohio State were undefeated. I knew that if the Buckeyes could win this game, they would have a great chance to go undefeated in 1987.

There had to be about forty of us students huddled around this little portable TV to watch the game. All I remember was that Ohio State was refusing to come out of the locker room prior to the game. Come to find out, Coach Bruce didn't want the Buckeye players to come out first, and then have to watch LSU Tigers come out of the locker room to a stadium pep rally.

Coach Bruce was upset because the same thing happened at the Cotton Bowl during the previous season when Texas A & M fans sang their fight song prior to the game. I had read that LSU players, particularly a running back, said that Ohio State linebacker Chris Spielman wasn't that good of a player.

What!? How could any opposing player say that about Chris Spielman?

It also appeared during the game that the LSU Tiger players were avoiding Chris by running the opposite direction away from him. Spielman did end up having eleven tackles in the game. Most of the game was a back-and-forth affair in terms of the score.

With LSU leading 10-6 in the 4th quarter, the Buckeyes drove down the field to get into field goal range. Kicker Matt Frantz came on for the Buckeyes to make the game even closer. If he made the field goal, the game would be 10-9 in LSU's favor.

I was worried because Matt had missed a crucial kick the previous year during the 1986 Michigan game which the Buckeyes lost 26-24. That is not what happened. Ohio State faked the field goal, and holder Scott Powell threw a pass to George Cooper. The whole dorm lobby was going crazy except for this one girl named Carol.

She kept asking me what my name was? She kept tapping me on the shoulder and pleading with me to tell her my name. I must have been clueless at that point. Why would she want to know my name? I just kept looking at her saying, *"How 'bout them Buckeyes!!?"*

She said, *"How about you tell me your name and what you are doing later?"*

After the Buckeyes took the lead 13-10, I along with everyone else in the Morrill Tower lobby, was standing and cheering by saying, *"Let's Go Bucks! Let's Go Bucks!!"*

We were also singing the Ohio State fight song, *"Across the Field."*

The cheers didn't last long as LSU came down and kicked a forty-yard field goal to tie the game. With about two minutes to go in the 4th quarter, the LSU Tigers once again drove down the field, and threatened to win.

Matt Franz was called on again to win the game. This time, he missed a 47 yard field goal, and the game ended in a 13-13 tie. There were no overtimes in college football like today. We all just kind of sat there stunned in the lobby. Three hours of excitement and the game ended in a tie. Carol was still smiling and winking at me.

One of my new friends said, *"I think she really likes you!"* I was in no mood to start another relationship when I had a girl waiting for me back in Indiana.

Ohio State would win the next week at Illinois by the score of 10-6. This setup a showdown at Ohio Stadium with the Indiana Hoosiers on October 10th. Being that I was from the state of Indiana, I wanted the Buckeyes to beat the Hoosiers in the worst way.

Indiana University football was not much of a threat to Ohio State because it had been thirty-six years since the last time they beat the Buckeyes. Ohio State had lost to Indiana by the score of 32-10 in 1951, which happened to coincide with Coach Woody Hayes' first year as the head coach of the Buckeyes. He told his players, as well as others, that Ohio State would not lose to Indiana again.

Indiana's head coach in 1987 was Bill Mallory. Coach Mallory had said that he attended the game with his parents the last time Indiana defeated Ohio State back in 1951. Was there going to be a connection between him and the last time Ohio State lost to the Hoosiers?

I awoke that morning to a rainy day in Columbus, Ohio. Not that rain would deter me from going to an Ohio State football game. I ate my breakfast in the *Morrill Tower Commons,* and walked over to Ohio Stadium afterwards. I always wanted to get there early to watch the team warm-up, and watch Ohio State's Marching Band make their grand entrance into the stadium.

The Indiana Hoosiers were always considered a basketball school, and hadn't had much success over the years playing college football. This day would be different. Indiana took a 10-0 lead before Ohio State started to make their move to tie the game 10-10 right before halftime.

The Hoosiers scored 21 points in the second half to defeat Ohio State by the score of 31-10. I sat there stunned in my seat. I looked across the field at the Indiana fan section who were cheering loudly once the final seconds ticked off the clock. This game certainly comes to mind as one of the worst moments as a fan on that fateful October day back in 1987.

It was the second home game I witnessed as a student that season. It also happened to be against a team from a state that most of my years I spent growing up in. I am not proud of what I did next after the game concluded. Sometimes my emotions got the best of me. It wasn't life or death but it sure seemed that way.

Since my seats were near the field, I got up and went over to where the Indiana fans were sitting. I started screaming as well as cursing at them. I had no right to do so because it wasn't their fault that their Indiana Hoosiers team just clobbered my school. I had never been a polite fan when Ohio State lost in football. I am not sure I was the only Ohio State fan yelling at the Indiana fan base however, but I was definitely one of them.

They kept chanting things like, *"Overrated!"* and *"Indiana Hoosiers!"*

I mean I was really mad! I am surprised to this day that I wasn't escorted out of the stadium by OSU security or the Columbus police. I still have the program of the Ohio State/Indiana game in 1987 as a reminder of that terrible day.

As I write this book in 2020, that game in 1987 was the last time Indiana would beat Ohio State in Ohio Stadium. I was there to witness it and experience what many consider one of the biggest losses in Ohio State football history. After the game was over, Coach Earle Bruce called in the *"Darkest Day"* in Ohio State football history.

The Buckeyes have obviously lost some heartbreaking games in its history, but this one seems to stick out more than a lot of the other games. It may have been Coach Bruce's comments after the game. How it was the 'darkest day' or the fact that this game led to other defeats in 1987.

I also had friends who attended Indiana University, so this game was always personal. Many of them wanted to reiterate to me that Ohio State lost to the Hoosiers. The next week, I traveled back to Indiana with some friends to watch Ohio State defeat the Purdue Boilermakers in West, Lafayette. The Buckeyes would win 20-17. My friends and I would spend the night at my parent's house in Merrillville. I was hoping I would see my girlfriend, Cindy.

She seemed to be moving on from our relationship at least for now. I really loved her and wanted our romance to work. I knew the distance of me being in Ohio and Cindy being in Northwest Indiana, would be a problem. The other issue was that she was still in high school and I was in my second year of college.

I tried to put her out of my mind but that was impossible. She was the only girl that I cared about in my life. Even though this 'Carol girl' in my dorm really liked me. As far as my other friends that I had accumulated at Harrison Junior High and Merrillville High School, it seemed they had all moved on in life.

It was something that I knew since high school graduation in 1986. Many of these friends and acquaintances I would never see again. Your friends are your friends. Rick Keneson, Mike "D" Demakas, and Brian Portlock would always remain my close friends. As I returned to campus that Sunday night, I was prepared to continue to study and work really hard on my college courses. I was also excited about the rest of the Ohio State football season. Grammy and Papa would drive me back to school like they would do many times, and stay at the *Holiday Inn* on Lane Avenue.

There was something strange on campus that week. Earle Bruce had always been criticized by the fans as well as the media outlets for losses as the Ohio State coach. I was starting to realize that living in Columbus, Ohio was much different than living in Northwest Indiana.

Most people in Columbus loved the Buckeyes and hated to see them lose in anything. Lose multiple games as an Ohio State player or as a coach, and life could be really tough in the central part of Ohio.

The Buckeyes did beat Minnesota on October 24th by the score of 42-9. That may have eased the tension for a while but I could hear what people were saying on campus. I really believe that the Indiana loss a few weeks earlier, and Cris Carter being ruled ineligible for the 1987 season, made things tough for Coach Earle Bruce.

I learned that Indiana had pulled off another upset that day as they beat Michigan 14-10. It was the first time in Indiana's football history that they had beaten both Ohio State as well as Michigan in the same season.

It was Michigan State that everyone was worried about the following week. If Ohio State could just beat the Michigan State Spartans on Halloween day, it would be an important win for the season. Easier said than done.

My good friend Dave Alexander from Ball State was coming into town to see me and to take in the game against the Spartans. Dave and I became good friends our first year in college at *Williams Hall* at Ball State. He was also part of the Sigma Phi Epsilon fraternity there.

I had convinced him to become an Ohio State fan that first year in college when he helped me prepare a speech for one of my communication classes. Dave had bought a "Chris Spielman" jersey so he could wear it to the game against Michigan State.

It was a sunny afternoon in Columbus. The crowd was about as loud as I ever heard it in Ohio Stadium. It got even louder when the Buckeyes scored first on a touchdown pass to wide receiver, Everett Ross.

It was the first play of the game which went for seventy-nine yards. Ohio State would lead 7-0. Michigan State would counter with a touchdown run by their quarterback Bobby McAllister, and two field goals to lead 13-7 at halftime.

Michigan State had this offensive lineman who was one of the biggest players that I had ever seen in person. His name was Tony Mandarich. He was over 6 feet 6 inches tall! Tony really stood out when he took the field. I told my friend Dave that I felt sorry for the Ohio State player who had to line up against him.

There was no more scoring in the second half. Ohio State would lose their second home game of the season by the score of 13-7. Ohio State's defense really played well but the offense was still struggling to score points.

Dave was really upset that the Buckeyes lost that day even though he went to Ball State. It was also the first time that Coach Earle Bruce lost to Michigan State since he took over the Ohio State program back in 1979.

The Buckeyes were now 5-2-1 on the season and a lot of people walked out of Ohio Stadium upset that day. It was the first time since 1951 that Ohio State lost to both Indiana and Michigan State in the same season.

Many older fans kept saying things like, *"Earle Bruce must go!"* Or, *"We need a coach who can win the big game!" "The Ohio State Chokeyes!"*

I even heard one fan say that he wasn't going to any more Ohio State games ever again! There were others who were saying that they were sick and tired of coming to games only to watch the Buckeyes lose. What!? I couldn't believe my ears.

First of all, Ohio State doesn't lose many games. Second of all, Earle Bruce was the winningest coach in the Big Ten during his tenure at Ohio State. Why would the university want to fire him after just a couple of defeats? There were things I didn't quite understand while I was a first-year student at Ohio State.

I wasn't aware that there were some people who just didn't like Earle Bruce as a coach for the Buckeyes. I would later learn that it would have more to do than just his won/lost record. Dave left Columbus after the weekend was spoiled by the Michigan State Spartans.

He wasn't just there to see the football game. Dave wanted to see the "social" side of Ohio State by visiting the famous tailgate at the Holiday Inn known as *Hineygate* as well as the main part of campus simply known as *High Street.*

High Street had plenty of bars and restaurants on campus. Three of the most famous 'establishments' were *Papa Joes, Mean Mr. Mustard's,* and the *Newport.* I believe Dave and I hit all three of those places that night as well as many others. The legal drinking age in Columbus, Ohio in the 1980's was nineteen.

As popular as it may have been to drink a beer in college, it was more important to meet girls. After the weekend, Dave said that he would come back to visit me to take in more Ohio State football games.

After that Halloween weekend in October of 1987, I never saw or heard from Dave Alexander again. We were really great friends. He had come home with me the previous year to watch Merrillville beat Hobart and came to visit me my first year at Ohio State.

Just like high school, there are people who you cross paths with, and become friends with, that you will never see again. If Ohio State fans and students thought the loss to Michigan State was bad, they hadn't seen anything yet. The scene was about to get really ugly in Columbus, Ohio.

Would things get better?

Chapter 27

DEBS

The next week on campus, I saw students as well as fans wearing buttons on their shirts and coats that said, *"DEBS"*. It stood for 'DUMP EARLE BRUCE SOON.'

Maybe it was time to get a new coach at Ohio State, I thought. Even though Earle Bruce was one of my favorite coaches, I bought a pin to go along with what everyone else was doing. I had no idea the significance of that pin which I still have to this day. That pin is a constant reminder of what happened in November of 1987, and the impact it had on Ohio State Buckeye football.

I have often said that there are moments or days in your life that you will never forget. I can always recall my accident in 1976, the first time I kissed a girl, my high school touchdown catch, the day Woody Hayes died, and now the moment Earle Bruce was fired as football coach at Ohio State.

I remember the lead-up to the situation quite well. My dad and his friends had planned a trip to Ohio State for the game against the Iowa Hawkeyes. It was November 14th, 1987. Dad was coming in to see me as well as view the football game. He brought along his friends Joe "Smokey" Olis and Woodrow "Woody" Feeler.

Joe and Woody were two of my dad's closest friends. Woody was the police officer who drove me to the skating rink back when I was at Miller Elementary School in the late 1970's.

Dad, Woody, and Joe taught in the same school corporation as well as coached various sports together. Little did anyone know that it would be one of the most remembered Ohio State football games in history, but not in a good way.

Dad and his friends arrived on Friday evening in Columbus to take in the campus life. I think all three of them skipped teaching school that day to come to Ohio State for the big game. They probably took a "sick day leave" from their work.

Little did their principal (Who was their boss) know that they were at Ohio State University going to campus bars and a football game. Just like Dave Alexander a few weeks earlier, I would take them to the many campus places on High Street during Friday nights to experience college life.

It wasn't as if they didn't know what campus life was about because all three of them obviously went to college. Ohio State was different. They all wanted to experience the big-time atmosphere, especially during a weekend the Buckeyes played a football game. I kept apologizing to dad, Woody, and Joe for all the drunk and obnoxious college students who were bumping into them in the campus bars.

Joe Olis looked at me startled and said, *"What are you talking about? This is great! This is our kind of bar!"*

I couldn't believe what I was hearing!

They actually liked the smell of stale beer, drunk college students everywhere, vomit on the floor, and the constant noise in these college establishments. It was if the three of them were reliving their youthful days partying on a college campus. I was stunned for a second at Joe Olis' response but more so when they started joining in on the fun with all the college kids.

My dad and his friends started chanting, *"Let's Go Bucks! ~Lets Go Bucks!"* with the rest of them in the bar.

I didn't realize how much fun my dad and his friends could be once they were away from home. If any of you have ever seen the film, *"Back to School"* starring Rodney Dangerfield, hanging out with my dad

327

and his buddies was just like that movie. They didn't seem to care that they were all middle age men in a campus bar with students who were much younger than them.

Yes… dad and his friends were there to see the Ohio State/ Iowa game the next day, but they were also on campus to have a good time.

One drunk Ohio State student came up to Woody Feeler and wanted to make a monetary bet with him. The student looked at Woody and said, *"I bet I can drink your bottle of beer quicker than you can drink my bucket of Rum 151"*, as he was slurring his words.

Woody made the exchange with the student while everyone in the bar gathered around and cheered them on! To my amazement as well as the others there, Woody finished the student's bucket of booze before the kid could finish the bottle of beer. Woody won the bet and walked away a few dollars richer.

I was absolutely stunned at what I had witnessed. Only on a college campus do you see things like that. It would be the first of many trips that dad would bring his friends to Ohio State for football weekends.

Some people never want to grow up. That was dad and his friends any time they visited Ohio State. They would sing the Ohio State 'fight song' long into the night while enjoying adult beverages.

The next morning, it was a bright sunny day in Columbus, Ohio. After breakfast, we all headed to the "Hiney Gate" tailgate party right outside the *Holiday Inn* on Lane Ave. The "Danger Brothers" band was playing on the stage in front of hundreds of Ohio State fans prior to the game. A lot of Buckeye fans as well as some of the fans from Iowa went to the tailgate party to eat, drink, and have a great time.

They also served these tin buckets filled with beer to all the above-age fans. The sponsors of the tailgate party were also handing out those pins which said, *"DUMP EARLE BRUCE SOON."* Dad got one too and clipped it to his shirt that afternoon.

As we headed to Ohio Stadium with thousands of others who were there to watch the Buckeyes, I could hear people talking about

Coach Earle Bruce. They hoped that he would be fired. I heard some Ohio State fans saying that they wish the Buckeyes would lose against Iowa so his firing would come sooner rather than later. I couldn't believe what I was hearing!

Who in their right mind would want Ohio State to lose unless you cheered for another team? I admit that I get very upset when the Buckeyes lose a game but I would never cheer against them! Besides my own family, I love Ohio State more than anything else in the world. Were these real fans saying these things before an important game?

Little did I know...

The unthinkable happened that Saturday afternoon. Ohio State actually trailed Iowa 22-21 in the fourth quarter when running back Carlos Snow put the Buckeyes in the lead with a touchdown. Ohio State went for a two-point conversion but missed it when Buckeye Jay Koch was stopped short of the goal line. Still, Ohio State had regained the lead and was now winning by the score of 27-22.

Iowa had one last chance to win the game. With about sixteen seconds and the crowd going crazy, the Hawkeyes drove down the field. All Ohio State had to do was make sure Iowa didn't score a last second touchdown. I could go back to the Hineygate party at the Holiday Inn with dad and his friends to celebrate the big win.

The unthinkable happened.

Again, all Ohio State had to do was stop them once. When the Iowa quarterback dropped back to pass he threw the football to Marv Cook at the ten yard line. Marv raced in for the touchdown. With the extra point, Iowa would win 29-27. Ohio State was faced with its third loss in a row and fourth overall on the season. It was also the third time that I saw Ohio State lose in Ohio Stadium that year.

It was not what I expected being a first year student at Ohio State. I walked out of the stadium dejected. Maybe it was time for Earle Bruce to go as the Ohio State football coach. The Buckeyes' record was now 5-4-1 with Michigan as the next opponent. Dad, Woody, and Joe left Columbus that Sunday morning to head back to Northwest Indiana.

Besides the game, all three of them enjoyed the campus experience and were planning on coming back to the *Ohio State Football Coaches Clinic* in the spring. What everyone was expecting would eventually become reality of *DEBS*.

"*Dump Earle Bruce Soon*"

On Monday, November 16th, 1987 I was walking back to Morrill Tower from class when I first heard the news that Earle Bruce was fired as the football coach at Ohio State. I couldn't believe what I was hearing from other students. We all heard the rumors that Earle was going to be let go as coach.

My emotions ranged from being angry, sad, and even bitter. I was intrigued on who could possibly replace Earle Bruce as coach? I skipped my late afternoon class on Monday to watch Channel 10 news in Columbus. I was glued to all the reports on the 'Earle Bruce firing.'

Many people thought he was fired because he lacked a certain image that the university wanted him to portray as the football coach. Many believed that Coach Bruce didn't have enough personality and he didn't appeal to the public. That couldn't be furthest from the truth. In my mind, Coach Bruce was Ohio State Buckeye football.

If you ever heard Earle talk... he was about as motivating, passionate, and captivating of an individual that you would ever meet. All the students and fans knew why Coach Bruce was fired at Ohio State. He was fired for losing four games that season in 1987.

Being a student at Ohio State at the time, I got a "firsthand" view of how important Buckeye football was and how much the coach is scrutinized for every move he makes within the program.

There were many stories that Coach Bruce and OSU President Edward Jennings didn't get along with each other. There were other stories that the Ohio State Board of Trustees put a lot of pressure on President Jennings to fire Coach Bruce for his record.

There were many people who believed that Earle didn't socialize with some of the prominent businesspeople in Columbus, Ohio. I have read all the stories and books regarding Coach Bruce's firing of

November of 1987. I have drawn my own conclusions as to why he was fired.

I believe the university wanted someone who was more than a football coach. They wanted someone who would make commercials, play golf with the business leaders in Columbus, and be an outgoing spokesperson for the university. Earle Bruce was a football coach and a great one!

For someone who was criticized a lot in the newspapers, on television, and in the opinion section of the *Buckeye Sports Bulletin,* Earle seemed to get a lot of supporters when he was fired. A lot of my fellow classmates at Ohio State started wearing shirts which read, *"Save Earle."*

There were also Ohio State flags hanging everywhere with the word, *"Spoiled"* written on them. There was an opinion poll taken where roughly 90% of people living in Columbus, Ohio said that Coach Bruce shouldn't have been fired. I remember students chanting in the center of campus known as the Oval.

They kept shouting, *"Keep Earle as coach and dump Ed Jennings as the university president!"*

I mean it really became an ugly scene on campus for a while. This was a lot different than going to Ball State University. At Ball State, I am not sure students cared if the football team won or lost. At Ohio State, it is part of the culture of the university.

There were demonstrations on campus where students were handing out fliers and asking others to sign a petition to keep Earle Bruce as head coach of the Buckeyes. All the while, Ohio State still had to play their last game against the Michigan Wolverines.

It has always been the biggest game of the year for anyone who is associated with Ohio State. The students, fans, alumni, and even the casual viewer, all took interest in "The Game." The game would show how tough Coach Bruce and Ohio State football players were. It would be another life-lesson on never giving up in life.

Rick Bay, the Ohio State Athletic Director, also resigned in protest over the way Coach Bruce was fired. I read that he wanted no part in the firing. He supported Earle. Rick Bay thought that it was unfair how the coach was being treated by the university.

Earle had a great record in the Big Ten Conference as well as overall. Even in one of my communication classes, the professor asked us our opinion if Coach Bruce should still be the coach at Ohio State? He had us take a secret ballot vote in class.

When the professor read the results, NOT one student felt Coach Bruce should have been fired. Not one; You could really feel the tension around the Ohio State campus that week.

Some of my high school friends even reached out to me asking if I was embarrassed of being a student at Ohio State? I kind of took offense to those comments. No matter how difficult the situation was at Ohio State...this was still my team and my school.

Ohio State would travel to Ann Arbor, Michigan to play on November 21st, 1987. To my surprise, Coach Bruce was on the sidelines for the Buckeyes. Prior to the game, the whole team made a single line behind him for the coin toss at the 50-yard line.

Every player on the team took off their helmet and had headbands on their heads which said the word, "Earle." For someone who was criticized throughout the year as a coach, he obviously was loved by his own players. There was no way that Ohio State was going to lose the game to Michigan.

However, it didn't start out that way.

Michigan led 13-0 in the second quarter but the Buckeyes were not going to quit. I kept thinking of what Coach Bruce said at the football camp back in 1983. To paraphrase his quote one more time... He said, *"In life when you get knocked down, you get back up again. If you stay down in life, that is sad."*

A couple days before the Michigan game, there was a plane flying over campus with a banner that said, *"Keep Earle, Fire Jennings."* In my opinion, if Ohio State went 11-0 or even 10-1 in the 1987 football season, Coach Bruce wouldn't have been fired from the university. I also believe that if he would have won the National

Championship back in 1979, he wouldn't have been removed from his position.

So, my first year at Ohio State was filled with controversy over the firing of Coach Earle Bruce and watching my university take sides over the issue. I would often see President Jennings on campus. I would want to say something to him about why he fired Earle Bruce.

I never did but the whole situation still bothers me to this day. I didn't realize it at the time but Coach Bruce's firing would have a direct impact on me personally. It would lead to a career decision in my own life.

Some things are just meant to be, I guess.

Chapter 28

Could I be Dreaming

On New Year's Eve, December 31, 1987, John Cooper was named the new football coach at Ohio State. I really didn't know much about Coach Cooper. The only thing that I knew about him was that he had beaten Michigan the previous year in the Rose Bowl while he was the coach at Arizona State.

This may have been one of the reasons why Ohio State decided to hire him. Everyone on campus was excited that the Buckeyes had a new football coach. It's funny but a lot of students had forgotten what happened with Earle Bruce and the controversy which surrounded his firing.

When I returned from class to my dorm room in March, a friend of mine showed me an article in the Ohio State school newspaper known as the *Lantern*. Ohio State football was looking for an OSU student to be a recruiting guide for the program.

The recruiting guide would be responsible for helping the coaches with potential high school recruits who were considering playing for the Buckeyes. The job entailed showing the football recruits around campus, talking to them about academics, discussing college life at Ohio State, and the tradition of the football program.

My friend just smiled at me and said,

"This job is perfect for you. You need to apply!"

There was a name and number to contact for the recruiting guide job. I called and made an appointment with a secretary by the name of Corrine. I was scheduled to meet the newly hired recruiting coordinator for Ohio State football, Steve Pederson.

I had been nervous before while playing sports, meeting girls, studying for tests, etc.... but I was now going to go face to face with a new assistant coach who Coach John Cooper hired on his staff. I had interviewed for jobs before like the Griffith Car Wash and my counselor job at Camp Lutherwald, but this was different. Corrine told me on the phone to report to Coach Cooper's office in St. John Arena on March 12th,1988 at 3 pm.

St. John Arena was where the Buckeye basketball team played before they built the new *Schottenstein Center* in the late 1990's. The main football offices were located on the second floor of the arena.

Was I really applying for a job with Ohio State football? Could I be dreaming? Was another dream about to come true? Maybe the fate of Earle Bruce being fired had brought me to this point. Who knew?

I left my dorm room at Morrill Tower about 2 pm to make sure I was not late for the appointment. Understand that St. John Arena was not that far from the Morrill Tower dorm and might have only been a ten-minute walk.

When I got there, it took me about five minutes to find an open door to get into the arena. I obviously knew my way around because I had already been inside St. John Arena for a few Ohio State basketball games that winter.

A worker in the arena said, *"Can I help you?"*

I told him that I was here to interview for a football job with the recruiting coordinator, Steve Pederson. I told him the interview was at 3 pm.

"Little early, aren't you?" he said.

The worker could tell I was nervous. He said that I could look around the hallways of the arena until my interview was to take place. He then said,

"Hey kid... welcome to Ohio State football!"

Just that comment alone put chills up and down my spine. Was I really part of a football program that was perceived as one of the best in the nation? I mean, after all, I am just a little known student on campus. How could I possibly contribute to the Buckeyes?

As I walked around the hallway or concourse as you would call it, there were pictures of all Ohio State football teams who had won conference and national championships. There were also photos of famous Ohio State players and coaches like Archie Griffin and Woody Hayes. The custodial worker just looked at me and smiled. It was as if he was watching a little kid in a candy store.

As I walked up the steps to the second floor, I was greeted by Corrine. To my surprise, she was a young lady maybe around late twenties, with long blonde hair, attractive, and a great smile. I don't know what I was thinking at the time, but I had this idea that secretaries were these old ladies who sat at typewriters all day long.

I quickly found out that Corrine really didn't go by the title of "secretary" but more of an 'assistant to the recruiting coordinator.' There were other students who they had to interview so the process would only take about fifteen minutes.

How was I going to sell myself as the best candidate for the job in fifteen minutes?

Steve Pederson came out of his office and introduced himself. He wasn't wearing an Ohio State coaching shirt but instead a blue shirt and tie. He looked more like a corporate businessman than a football coach. Just like Corrine, Steve was a young person, maybe around the age of thirty.

He shook my hand and said, *"Hi, I'm Steve Pederson, the recruiting coordinator for Ohio State football."*

He may have asked multiple questions but there was one question that Steve asked which stood out. He said, *"Tell me what you know about Ohio State football?"*

Really? That was the question? I don't think I stopped talking for the whole fifteen minutes of the interview.

I went on and on about my knowledge of Ohio State football, as well as how I grew up a big fan, and wanted to play for the Buckeyes.

Steve and another coach kind of just looked at each other. *"Hire this guy. He knows a lot about Ohio State football."*

With that, Steve told me that I had the job. I would be helping him and Corrine in the football office. I would also have weekend responsibilities by eating lunch with the football recruits and their families within the tower of Ohio Stadium on game day.

My job would start in August. I would have to come back to campus a few weeks earlier than other students. Steve was one of the most personable people that I had met in my lifetime. I was also introduced to Head Coach (John) Cooper that day. He seemed really nice as well.

When I left St. John Arena, I could hardly wait to tell all my friends as well as family members that I was going to work for the Ohio State Football Department as a recruiting guide!

Was I dreaming? This was like a dream come true.

At that point, I really started thinking about being a college football coach myself. Maybe someday I could coach at Ohio State just like Woody Hayes, Earle Bruce, and now John Cooper. Before my job with the football program, there were other things that I wanted to accomplish that spring of 1988.

New friends at a familiar fraternity would lead to an exciting end to my first year at Ohio State.

My dad had talked to me about joining the Sigma Phi Epsilon fraternity at Ohio State. Technically, I was already a Sig Ep member due to joining the fraternity back at Ball State during my freshman year. I hadn't really met any of the members of the fraternity at Ohio State but I thought maybe I should go over there to introduce myself.

There was a campus-wide intramural track meet which was to take place in Ohio Stadium in April. The running track was still in Ohio Stadium back in the late 1980's, so it was really neat that I was going to participate in an event inside the stadium.

There were fraternities, regular students, and even a few well-known football players, who participated in the track meet that day. I hadn't run in a competitive track meet since my high school days.

In the intramural track & field meet, I chose to run the 200 and 400 meter dashes as well as compete in the long jump. I won all three events, and broke an intramural record in the 200-meter dash at that time. I beat two OSU football players to win the event.

A couple of my new fraternity brothers were there to witness my accomplishments. They told me that I should run for the Sigma Phi Epsilon fraternity next year. Many of them also told me to stop by the fraternity house later that day. To my surprise, they welcomed me with open arms.

They were discussing plans for what they called, *"Greek Week,"* at Ohio State. Greek Week was a week-long event where all the boy fraternities and girl sororities on campus competed in events to see who would win a trophy.

Each fraternity was paired with a sorority in multiple competitions ranging from sports, a singing competition, obstacle courses, trivia, etc… This was really a big deal to all who were part of fraternity/sorority life at Ohio State.

I went to the meeting at the Sigma Phi Epsilon house later in the day to meet all the members of the fraternity. They were all in the basement of the house sitting in a huge circle. One of the fraternity brothers, Randy, introduced me to everyone. There had to be over 150 members there that day.

As I sat there listening to them talk about the business matters of the fraternity, and the upcoming "Greek Week," I could tell there was a negative vibe in the room. One of the fraternity members said to everyone, *"We don't stand a chance against the other fraternities, especially Phi Delta Theta in the Greek Week competition!"*

Everyone kind of shook their heads as to agree with his statement. Now I had only known these fraternity brothers for maybe about an hour or so, but I couldn't believe what I was hearing! It was as if they were giving up on winning before the traditional competition of "Greek Week" had started.

My fraternity brothers at Ball State had the opposite approach. They were always positive that they were going to win any competition against the other fraternities. As I looked around the basement room at all the members, I stood up from my chair and gave them the 'pep talk' of their lives! I had never really given speeches or pep talks before.

"This is your chance to be great! This is your chance to do something special! Get fired up! No fraternity can beat us if we believe in ourselves!"

For a second, each fraternity member looked stunned at me as if to think… *Who is this person?* All of a sudden, they stood up in unison and started clapping and cheering!! They started giving "high fives" and hugging me as if I just gave the greatest speech since Woody Hayes delivered one to the Ohio State players prior to a game with Michigan.

At that moment, I became a member of Sigma Phi Epsilon fraternity at Ohio State. It wasn't as if I forgot all my fraternity brothers at Ball State, but I was about ready to meet some more life-long friends now at Ohio State. The Sigma Phi Epsilon members even let me give speeches to incoming freshmen who wanted to join or pledge the fraternity.

One of my fraternity brothers said, *"Bunda, you are the spark this fraternity needed!"*

That made me really happy and I planned on moving into the fraternity house in the fall of 1988. I would also be starting my new job as an OSU football recruiting guide working for Steve Pederson.

By the way, we did win "Greek Week" that year against all the other fraternities. It just goes to show you that if you put your mind to do something, you can achieve great results. There was only one problem at the end of my first year at Ohio State. It had nothing to do with school, health, or my family.

Mom was doing fine. She had put her breast cancer in remission by the spring of 1988. It was a phone call I received in my dorm room that I wish wouldn't have happened. It was from Cindy. She wanted to know if I was coming back to Northwest Indiana for the summer.

I said that I was, and planned to work again at the *Mansards Apartment Complex* as a pool guard. Cindy said that she missed me and was wondering if we could get back together as boyfriend and girlfriend. I told her that we really needed to take things slow. Maybe we could just be friends at the start of the summer. She seemed to agree with my comments.

Was I dreaming? Was everything in my life starting to really come together? Only time would tell...

Chapter 29
Time and Change

My life was really going well heading into the summer of 1988. I had completed my first year at Ohio State, made a bunch of new friends, was now part of Sigma Phi Epsilon fraternity, and just got hired as a recruiting guide for Buckeye football. I was also home for the summer to spend time with family and friends. It would be my second summer working for the Mansards Apartments as a pool attendant.

Life couldn't be happier going into the summer. There were surprises too.

Grammy and Papa decided to move to Palm Springs, California by the summer of 1988 to enjoy their retirement years. It must have been hard for them to move away from Nikki, Erin, and I to another state. I knew they were only a phone call away but things wouldn't be the same. They were struggling financially, and needed to create a change in their own lives. I just didn't realize all the money problems they were having. Throughout the years, my family hasn't talked about it much. There were rumors that Papa tried to 'double his money' by taking some financial risks in the stock market. Knowing my grandfather, he was just trying to make money so all of his family would be financially secure. He lost it all. If you knew him, Papa was a very prideful man. He never put himself above others. He was the nicest person I ever knew. I always looked up to him. However, him and Grammy needed a fresh start to life. They needed a change.

However, sometimes change is good. Nikki was about to become a senior, and Erin a junior, at Merrillville High School. It was nice to be around them again. Rick was working in a sports shop at the Southlake Mall during the beginning of the summer. Brian Portlock was working at Azar's Big Boy Restaurant. He was getting ready to embark on a career in the Air Force.

As far as Mike "D" Demakas, I really didn't see him much in the summer of 1988. I guess my move to Ohio State caused us to lose touch for a while. We weren't mad at each other but just had gone our separate ways for the time being.

I started my summer job at the Mansards working with two good friends, Steve Stum and Jeff Pfiefer. My job was to put chlorine in all the pools, check the chemicals, and make sure no one was drowning while swimming. A very easy summer job and not stressful either.

Then there was the issue of my ex-girlfriend, Cindy. At least that is what I thought about her at the time. After all, I was a college student at Ohio State. She had just completed her senior year at Munster High School. She hadn't yet picked a college to attend. Cindy told me that she was going to apply to Ohio State at some point in June.

I said to her, *"It's getting a little late to pick a college, isn't it?"*

For some reason, she had also chosen to apply to the University of Mississippi or *Ole Miss* as it was called. Cindy had expensive taste. She really never let cost stand in her way of doing something or going somewhere. Cindy even told me that she planned on flying to London, England for her birthday. In many ways, I couldn't relate to her. I was just an average kid from Merrillville.

Regardless, there was just something that I liked about her. Again, it may have been her blonde hair and blue eyes that attracted me to her, or possibly her smile. I knew that if I saw Cindy again that we couldn't just be friends. It would take one kiss from her that would change a friendship into a summer romance.

Could this possibly be the girl that I had been searching for my entire life?

343

Cindy and I went out on a date Friday night the first week of June in 1988. I had just completed my courses at Ohio State for the spring, and wouldn't be starting my job with Ohio State football until August.

We went to a miniature golf course not too far from her house to get reacquainted with each other. She brought a friend along named Jean. Rick came miniature golfing with us as well. It was a great night and all of us had a lot of fun. I noticed Cindy smiling at me the entire time that we were playing miniature golf. I wasn't paying much attention to her at the time.

I was trying to beat Rick in the miniature golf game. Rick and I have always been competitive in anything that we have done in life. I don't care if it was miniature golf or who could eat popcorn the fastest. To this day, we still compete against each other in sports. That is what best friends do. I knew I wouldn't have to compete against him for Cindy. She just kept staring at me and smiling the entire night. I knew something was about ready to happen.

I was tempted to tell Cindy that I just wanted to be friends and nothing more. It was not going to happen. I drove her home that night and walked her up to the door. She smiled and leaned into me. Cindy's words were almost a whisper.

She said, *"Kiss me. Please kiss me."*

As Cindy closed the door to her house, she said something to me. It wasn't until I got to my car that I realized she said the words…

"I love you."

As I started my summer job at the Mansards, Rick had told me that he had lost his own job at the sports store in the Southlake Mall known as *"Athletes in Motion."* They told him that he was not cut out to be a salesman, and he should look for another job. I am not sure that is why he lost his job.

The sports store wanted to hire a Merrillville basketball player to work there because he was a well-known person in the community. They had to get rid of Rick to get this other kid a job. Rick is my best friend. I had the perfect opportunity for him. He would work with me at the Mansards during the summer of 1988!

I talked to the people in-charge of the Mansards, and Rick was hired the next day. Cindy, on the other hand, had been working at a Christian bookstore in the beginning of the summer but wasn't making much money. I would get her a job working at the Mansards as well.

In one week, I got my best friend as well as my girlfriend hired at the Mansards. It was shaping up to be a very memorable experience. For a brief time, working for the Ohio State football that upcoming fall was in the back of my mind.

Cindy and I started getting really serious about our relationship. I was definitely falling in love with her and I knew she was the girl of my dreams. My family really seemed to like her as well. I had plenty of opportunities to date other girls that summer but Cindy was the only one on my mind. She even said that we should make our relationship official by 'making love' while her parents weren't home. She once again said those words…

"I love you."

I even went to a summer party where my old friend, Steve Civanich, tried to set me up with a girl named, "Reggie." I think her real name was Regina. However, I didn't want anything to do with her that night. I called Cindy on the phone to come get me from the party and drive me home. All my friends kept saying that I must really be in love with Cindy. Especially not wanting to date other girls as good-looking as someone like Reggie.

I even took Cindy to my cousin Suzanne's wedding that summer to meet the rest of my extended family of cousins, aunts, and uncles. I was for sure that this would be the girl who I would eventually marry, have kids with, live in a big house, and take fancy vacations.

I could tell that Rick really didn't like Cindy as a person. There may have been times when he told me she was not the right girl for me. Sometimes you should listen to the advice of your best friend. In this case, I was completely in love with Cindy. I really didn't care what other people thought about her. We spent a magical summer together in 1988. We were coworkers at the Mansards. We shared our dreams as well as ambitions. We were meant to be.

"I love you."

Cindy still hadn't made up her mind on where she was going to college or at least that is what she was telling me. I knew that the summer would come to an end at some point. Life could possibly change. I didn't want to believe in my mind that she would go to a different school or that our long-distance relationship wouldn't last.

I was still holding out hope that Cindy would surprise me with the good news that she would be attending The Ohio State University. If that did happen, I knew our relationship would go to a different level. I would eventually want to marry her.

When late July came around, I noticed a change in our relationship. Cindy was making a lot of excuses on why she couldn't go out with me on a date, especially on Friday and Saturday nights. Rick, as well as my other friends, suspected that Cindy had found someone new. They also believed she was going to break-up with me. I didn't want to believe any of my friends until the night Cindy sprung the devastating news on me.

We had just gone out to a restaurant for dinner and went back to her house to sit on the patio porch. After we kissed for a few minutes, she turned away and shook her head.

I said to her, *"What is wrong?"*

Cindy paused for a moment and stared me right in the eyes. She said, *"We have lived a fantasy life this summer. It needs to end. I have decided that I am going to the University of Mississippi."*

I was completely devastated by her comments. It may have been the longest car ride home of my life from her house. This was similar to the night when Brenna broke it off with me during my senior year of high school. Many ways, this was completely different. More than any other girl up to this point, I was completely in love and devoted to Cindy. We had 'made love.'

I cried all the way home that night. The idea of being with the girl of my dreams seemed to have ended. That is at least what I thought. If life was a big, long roller-coaster, then I was on it!

I was due back to Columbus, Ohio in a few weeks to start my football job with Steve Pederson. For days, I tried to call her on the phone or even go back over to her house. She even told me that her mom had grounded her from going anywhere outside of the home. I believe this was all a plan to avoid seeing me.

Didn't she love me as much as I loved her?

When I tell you that I went through a deep depression in my life, I wouldn't be lying to you. If you look up the meaning of depression, you will find a definition similar to this: *"A mood disorder that causes a persistent feeling of sadness, and a loss of interest. It can interfere with your daily functioning."*

I was never diagnosed with depression, but I really believe I was suffering from a form of it due to the break-up with Cindy. No matter what Rick or anyone else said, it didn't cheer me up. Grammy even called me on the phone from Palm Springs, California and told me... *"I fell in love with the idea of love, and not Cindy."*

That was Grammy's way of cheering me up but that really didn't seem to work either. I don't take the concept of depression lightly, and people suffer many different types of mental illness. The effects can be short term as well as long term. It can be debilitating and devastating. The mental health industry has come a long way in diagnosis and treatment of depression throughout the years.

As I write this book, I really believe that the traumatic break-up in 1988 still has had an impact on my life today. There were many times that I thought that I wanted my life to end. I was no longer interested in life or what it had to offer. I also didn't really want to go back to Ohio State in the fall. There were many days that I would sit outside and just stare 'off into space.' I was completely numb with the breakup. Moving on would prove to be very difficult. I felt completely lost in my life.

As the summer was coming to an end, I was just going through the motions with my job at the Mansards. I would show up and physically do the work, but I wasn't there mentally. Many times, I would just want to get through the day, go home, and sleep my depression away. When I woke up, my sadness would still be there. Was this all a bad dream? I needed something to pull me through this tough time of losing Cindy as a girlfriend.

As I was eating lunch one day, the house phone rang in the kitchen. Mom answered the phone, and said the call was for me. Maybe Cindy reconsidered and wanted to get back together, I thought.

I raced to the phone and excitedly said, *"Hello!"*

It wasn't Cindy. It was Steve Pederson from the Ohio State football office. It was exciting to talk to Steve but I was really hoping the voice on the other end of the phone line was Cindy. Steve asked me if I could report for my job on Monday, August 29th, 1988. I needed to start helping with recruiting and other football-related items.

I was now in-charge of the Mansards pools since my boss Jeff Pfiefer had gone back to school to play college football. I approached Rick and told him that I would be leaving early to go back to Ohio State. He would have to take over for me, and finish out the summer by closing down all the pools for the season. Rick was now in-charge of a job that I got him earlier in the summer.

I packed my bags for Columbus. Dad drove me back to school. I didn't have my own car yet so he had to make the trip back and forth from Ohio State. That would eventually change once I got my first car from my parents... a *1977 Monte Carlo*.

I would be moving into the Sigma Phi Epsilon house before many of my fraternity brothers would arrive. I am not sure that dad and I talked much during that five hour car drive to Columbus, Ohio. Even if he was talking to me about life, sports, or politics to pass the time, I wasn't really listening. He never knew that I was silently suffering from depression.

Dean, who would be my roommate, met dad and I at the fraternity house on Waldeck Avenue to help me move in. As I moved into my fraternity, my parents had also made their move to a new house in Merrillville. It was sad to leave the old house on Johnson Street. Many of my childhood memories were there.

Our house would flood a lot when it rained, so my parents got tired of the water in our basement. The move was good for them. They needed change in their lives as well. In 1988, Grammy and Papa had moved to Palm Springs, my parents moved to a different house in Merrillville, and I would be moving out of the dorms into the Sig Ep fraternity house. As they say… life moves on and stops for no one. *Time and change.*

Dad, and my new roommate Dean, helped me move into the fraternity house on that Sunday, August 28th. The next day, I would start my job working for Steve Pederson in the Ohio State football office.

I don't think I slept at all that night. I had come such a long way. From my traumatic accident in 1976, making new friends each time we moved during my childhood, to learning life lessons from the coaches of the sports I participated in, the many girlfriend relationships, and people telling me that I was not good enough to go to college at Ohio State. I was here now and taking the next step in my journey. Still upset about Cindy, it affected me emotionally and mentally. August 29th, 1988 would be another day that would change my life forever.

Would Cindy now be completely out of my life?

Steve Pederson told me to be at the Woody Hayes Athletic Center by 8 am to meet the coaches. He was to go over instructions of what exactly I would be doing for the football program. The Woody Hayes Athletic Center was a new building where the football team practiced, lifted weights, and had team meetings.

I had never been in there before, so naturally I was very excited to see the inside of what the Ohio State football program really looked like. I only had one major problem. The Woody Hayes facility was on the other side of campus off of Olentangy River Road. It may have been over a two mile walk to get there from my fraternity house.

I got up extra early to make sure that I would be on time. There was no one at the fraternity house or no food available until the following week. Most of my fraternity brothers wouldn't arrive until a week later. I went over to a place known as *Buckeye Donuts* to get something to eat before I made my journey across campus to the football facility.

I had two powdered donuts with a little carton of milk that day. Since most students hadn't returned to campus yet, it was a very quiet walk to the Woody Hayes Center. Thoughts kept popping into my head as I made the journey to the football complex. What if I wasn't cut out to do the job that Steve Pederson wanted me to do? What if I made a lot of mistakes? What if no one liked me in the football office?

I believe that a lot of people have these feelings when they start a new job, especially one that they have been dreaming about their entire life. I was extremely nervous about being introduced to the other coaches on staff.

After all, who am I compared to them? I was just your average college student who loved Ohio State Buckeye football. These were coaches who were employed by the university to win football games, and return the Buckeyes back to the 'glory years.' I am sure the coaches had other things to do that day besides meet a college student who was going to work in the office.

As I approached the building, I was greeted by Steve Pederson. He gave me a quick tour of the Woody Hayes facility. Most of the coaches had just got done with their early morning workouts, so they were showering to get ready for their day. Steve once again introduced me to Head Coach John Cooper. I am sure Coach Cooper wouldn't remember me today. It was a thrill of a lifetime to meet the new head coach at Ohio State.

John had coached at Arizona State and had beaten Michigan in the 1987 Rose Bowl. Many people may have thought that is one of the reasons he was picked to replace Earle Bruce as coach of the Buckeyes. I had other notions why Coach Cooper was hired as the new coach.

First, he was a friendly person and very energetic. He was the type of person that if I was still playing football back in 1988, I would want as my coach. I tried to learn as much about Coach Cooper before I was hired as a recruiting guide. I know that he was a strong family-type of person.

He once said, *"You hire me, and you're really hiring my family."* That comment always appealed to me. Also, the fact that he had beaten Michigan at his previous job. This was not Arizona State, and the pressure to win would be much greater at Ohio State. In many places, college football is seen as a social event. At Ohio State, it is viewed more of a life or death situation. At least the Buckeye fans treat it that way. Don't believe me? I'll explain in more detail during the next chapter.

Steve would drive me to the main football offices in St. John Arena where I first interviewed for the job the previous spring. I was going to be helping Corrine. He said that I could sit at his desk and work on a recruiting program from his computer. At the time, I had no idea what I was doing or the experience to work on a computer.

Steve wanted me to input player names, the high school each player was from, each player's football position, their heights & weights, and possible academic major. I did this for all the high school seniors in Ohio and around the country.

Steve said that he had to go back to the Woody Hayes facility with the other coaches, and would be back to check on me later. The list was over 650 potential student-athletes who we were considering playing football for the Buckeyes. By December, that list would be cut down to about 100 players that the staff would invite in for a campus visit.

Of those potential 100 recruits, the Buckeyes could only offer 25 scholarships in any given year. So I had to input over 650 recruits into a computer database and only 25 would be coming to play for Ohio State the following year? It reminded me of when I was at football camp in 1983.

I am sure all those players back then had dreams and aspirations of playing football for the Ohio State Buckeyes just like I did. Very few have the opportunity to get a scholarship. I did feel like I was contributing to helping some of these players realize their own dreams of playing for Ohio State.

Steve also had a map of the United States and Ohio on his office wall. We had three types of push pins that we would stick into the map where a recruit was from. There were gold, blue, and red pins. The gold pins represented kids that we were most likely to recruit and offer a scholarship. If, for whatever reason, we didn't get that high school recruit, we would look at the other choices.

Steve was one of the most organized people that I have ever met in my life. He taught me a lot about being prepared, organized, and professional. He evaluated everything. From a recruit's athletic ability to their academic success, and more importantly, their character evaluation.

We were after the top 25 student-athletes who would fit the mold of an Ohio State Buckeye. It wasn't easy. Michigan, Iowa, Wisconsin, Notre Dame, and other schools were after the same players. Steve Pederson was the best in the business.

He also came up with the idea of *"25 Reasons on Why to Become an Ohio State Buckeye."*

Each week, Steve would send a letter to a recruit explaining why they should make their college destination to Ohio State. It was a brilliant idea. I asked him why 25 reasons instead of just 10 or 15? Why was the number 25?

Going into the 1988 season, Ohio State had won 25 Big Ten Conference Championships. It was a way to set Ohio State apart from other schools. Steve was trying to do something that other colleges recruiting against us were not doing. It was a unique concept to get a high school student-athlete to think about Ohio State every week by sending him a letter in the mail.

For example, in week #1, a recruit would receive a letter about head football coach, John Cooper. In week #2, the same recruit would receive a letter about the traditions of Ohio State football. In week #3, the letter would be about our strength and conditioning program, and how it was the best in the country.

Each letter specifically talked about an aspect of Ohio State football. I was amazed at how much time, effort, and detail went into recruiting players to come to Ohio State. I just thought that kids came to football camp much like I did in 1983, and were either offered a scholarship or not. I will say it again, Steve was the best in the business at what he did as the Ohio State Recruiting Coordinator.

There was no reason to believe that we wouldn't get the best players to come to Ohio State on an annual basis. I was just happy that he let me help out in the recruiting office. I felt that I was contributing to build something special. It also took my mind off of Cindy for a while.

Steve would have me cut out clippings from all the newspapers of player's performances from their high school games on Friday nights. I would send the newspaper article to the player through the mail the following week along with a note from the football office. I would also answer the phones while Steve wasn't in the office.

It would go something like this… *"Hello, Ohio State football office… this is Dennis Bunda."* Wow! I was actually answering the telephone for Ohio State football! I would often look over at Steve's assistant, Corrine after I got off the phone with a high school coach. She would just smile at me. Corrine knew that this was a really big deal. I was living a boy's dream.

I was a student at The Ohio State University and now working for the recruiting coordinator for the Buckeyes football program. I really believed that life couldn't get much better at this point. That was wishful thinking. It was about to get worse again.

Even though I was working in the recruiting office, I still had my mind on the girl. I was still very much in love with Cindy and missed her very much. She was now attending college at the University of Mississippi, and was going to meet new people. My depression grew every day when I thought about her or that she could possibly meet another boy at school.

When working in the office, I was often too busy to think about how much I missed Cindy. There were the times that I was away from Ohio State football or in my fraternity room by myself, when I became sad and depressed. Ohio State is a big school with a lot of girls. It was just that I was in love with one girl, and she didn't go there. I knew that I would meet other girls, but they wouldn't be Cindy.

I absolutely loved her. I would do anything to continue our relationship. I didn't think I would ever see her again. Little did I know...

As the school year approached in 1988, so did Ohio State's first game of the year with the Syracuse Orangemen. Ironically, it would be the same opponent that Ohio State opened up with in 1979 when Earle Bruce was making his debut as coach of the Buckeyes. Now it was John Cooper's turn as the head coach.

Syracuse had a good team led by a player named Daryl Johnston. They were coming into the game with Ohio State having already defeated the Temple Owls the week before by the score of 31-21. Before the contest, Steve, Corrine, and I greeted all the football recruits and their families in the recruiting room in Ohio Stadium.

The recruiting area was right above the locker room where the football team was getting dressed and ready to play the game with Syracuse. It was my first glance at meeting and spending time with high school seniors and juniors who possibly would someday be playing for the Buckeyes. I talked with them about what a great school Ohio State was as well as the football tradition. I remember one parent looking at me and saying,

"Why should my son pick Ohio State over Michigan?"

After going on and on about the great academics and the football tradition, the parent smiled at me. She said, *"My son is going to Ohio State!"* At that point, I felt I was contributing to the program.

It was a hot and sunny day on September 10th, 1988. I walked all the recruits and their parents inside Ohio Stadium to their seats for the game. The Buckeyes would win by the score of 26-9, and end Syracuse's streak of winning fourteen games in a row. While working for the football program, I always got a free game program.

On the cover of the program that day was a picture of John Cooper standing in his office with a football in the background. It was a commemorative football from the Rose Bowl game when he beat Michigan while coaching at Arizona State.

Ohio State pretty much played flawless that day against Syracuse and held them to just three field goals. At that point, I thought Ohio State would win the rest of their games just like they did when Earle Bruce coached his first year with the Buckeyes back in 1979.

Most of the preseason publications and experts had picked Ohio State to finish no higher than fourth in the Big Ten Conference. I just didn't realize how turbulent the football season was about to become in 1988. This would also be true in my own personal life.

If anyone was waiting for the 'proverbial bomb' to drop on the Ohio State football expectations, it happened the following week against the Pittsburgh Panthers at their stadium by the score of 42-10.

I didn't travel with the team to away games and never really asked Steve if I could. A few of my fraternity brothers and I went to a campus bar on Lane Avenue known as the *Varsity Club* to watch the game. I was stunned that the Buckeyes lost by that many points. What a difference a week makes!

Against Syracuse, Ohio State had no fumbles, no interceptions, and no penalties. However against Pittsburgh, the Buckeyes committed seven penalties, one interception, and four fumbles. I know after the game Coach Cooper got a heavy dose of criticism, especially from the Ohio State fans and alumni. A lot of people were upset that the Buckeyes lost the game but it wasn't even close.

Ohio State hadn't given up that many points in a game since 1980 when they played Illinois. The only difference was that they won that game 49-42. I got a view firsthand of how people could act when Ohio State lost. I was one of them a year before, but I was now working as a student-assistant for Ohio State football in the recruiting office.

A lot of fans were telling Coach Cooper to go back to Arizona, and bring back Earle Bruce as coach. There were other fans who were upset that John Cooper made a lot of TV commercials instead of coaching the team.

I heard one fan say, *"They wouldn't have lost the game if Coach Cooper wasn't so busy making TV commercials!"*

Working in the Ohio State football recruiting office, I knew the truth. Every fan thought that Coach Cooper was spending valuable practice time making hot tub and grocery store commercials instead of coaching football.

Little did anyone know that a lot of those commercials were made prior to the season.

Steve let me view practice a few times in 1988 to watch the Buckeyes. I can tell you that Coach Cooper was not making commercials, and he was in fact coaching the team. A lot of people thought that Coach Cooper let his assistant coaches do all the coaching, and he was just a spokesperson for Ohio State football.

Any time I was allowed to be in practice, I never saw it that way. Coach Cooper was always involved in practice. I also felt involved with the program.

Steve once asked me, *"What do you think of that player over there sitting with his parents? Do you think he can play for us?"*

I said, *"He looks a little skinny to play football for the Buckeyes. I am not sure he could play here. Steve… he is 6'7" but he is only about 215 pounds."*

Steve just smiled at me. He said that they were probably going to offer him a scholarship. That player's name was Alan Kline. He ended up being a really good player for Ohio State. Obviously, Steve and the rest of the coaches knew a heck of a lot more than me about recruiting!

Alan also ended up being an Ohio State football captain and an all-conference performer.

I do remember John Cooper once saying something on the lines of… *"If you can't recruit, you can't coach."*

He and the rest of the Ohio State staff were really good at getting players to come to Ohio State. It would build a solid foundation for future years.

During the game with LSU on September 24th, 1988, it really got exciting when the Buckeyes came from behind for a dramatic 36-33 victory. Most Ohio State fans had left the game early thinking that the Buckeyes would lose. As Ohio State was mounting a comeback, I could see over the top of Ohio Stadium where people were sprinting in the parking lot to get back in the stadium to watch the conclusion. I am not sure they were allowed back in. They missed what I believe was one of the best comebacks ever in Ohio Stadium.

I would turn twenty-one years old in a few short days. What could be more exciting than celebrating your birthday while at Ohio State? Surprises were coming my way behind every door.

I just didn't know what was on the other side.

Chapter 30

I Will Always Love You

The next week would be a moment in time that I would never forget in my life. I was turning 21 years old on Tuesday September 27th, 1988. My fraternity brothers were planning on having a birthday party for me at the house. The only problem was that they were not going to be serving cake and ice cream. My fraternity brothers were going to be serving drinks of the adult-kind, and nothing like *Kool-Aid* or *Country Time Lemonade*.

There were many problems with having a Tuesday night party at the fraternity house. I had classes the next day and my responsibilities at the football office. I also had a major math exam. Even though I insisted that we move the party to a Saturday night after the upcoming football game with the University of Illinois, my fraternity brothers would not listen.

They wanted to celebrate my birthday on Tuesday. It was tough to convince 150 fraternity brothers to cancel an event on your behalf. They also told me that they planned on inviting sorority girls over to celebrate the occasion. Sorority girls? How could I say no to that?

There must have been over 500 people in the fraternity house that night to celebrate my birthday. Most of the people at the party, I had no idea who they even were. Also, I am sure they could care less that it was my birthday. They were all there to have fun and enjoy the college experience.

I kept thinking I should be over in the main campus library known as *The William Oxley Thompson Memorial Library*. It was located on the Oval which was the center of the Ohio State University campus. I felt guilty that I was at a party on a Tuesday night when I should have been studying at the library for my math exam.

My mom and dad were helping pay for my tuition to go to Ohio State, and realize a dream. This was how I was going to repay them by being at a fraternity party on a Tuesday night? My dad was working his job as a teacher as well as some other supervision jobs at his school to help pay for all my school expenses.

I had an idea! I would slip out of the backdoor of the fraternity house without anyone seeing me.

I would go to the library for a few hours to study for the difficult math test. My fraternity brothers would never know that I was gone. I could then return after I studied for my big test. What a brilliant idea! I grabbed my book bag and headed off to the library in the middle of the night.

I sat there for three hours studying everything I needed to know for the test the next day. I had never studied like this when I was in high school. I was really prepared to get a good grade on this test which was scheduled for 8 am the next morning.

Once I finished at the library, I headed back to the fraternity to get some sleep before my math test. No such luck! To my surprise, the fraternity party was still going on with more people there than when I left to go study! I am not sure that any of my fraternity brothers realized that I had been gone for three hours at the library nor do I think they cared.

They were there to have a good time and it gave them a good reason to throw a party. I did appreciate them throwing a "big time" party on my behalf, however. If you were wondering… Yes, I did end up doing well on the test the next day. It went back to what former Ohio State Head Football Coach Woody Hayes used to say about hard work.

He said, *"Nothing in this world that comes easy is worth a damn."* Coach Hayes also said, *"Hard work never killed a person. It's the partying and socializing, late hours and the like, that affect so many people."*

Even though Woody had coached his last game in 1978, he was still worshipped by many alumni, fans, and students on the Ohio State campus. I still idolized the man, and took everything he said to heart. Preparation and hard work were two things that Coach Woody Hayes was known for, and instilled in his players.

I started realizing that if I worked hard enough that I was eventually going to graduate from Ohio State. I do often wonder what the party was like the three hours I was gone. I don't think many of my fraternity brothers remembered it either.

I had another surprise waiting for me that Friday before the football game with the University of Illinois. My fraternity brother, Mike Clark, had asked what time I would be back at the house from my classes and my job at the Ohio State Football Office? I asked him why he was asking me that question?

Mike told me that he had an even bigger surprise than the party in which the fraternity threw for me on Tuesday night. I told him that I couldn't go to another party on Friday night due to my responsibilities the next morning for the Ohio State football game versus Illinois. Mike was adamant that it wouldn't interfere with my football responsibilities on Saturday nor was it another party at the fraternity house.

What could it be, I thought? Maybe all the fraternity brothers were chipping in to buy me a new Ohio State football jersey. Could they be buying me another Ohio State hat similar to the one that I had tossed into the crowd while celebrating the big win against LSU the week before? Nothing prepared me for what I was about ready to see when I came back to the fraternity house from my classes and job that day. It is something that I still think about to this day.

I sensed something strange when I came back from my Friday obligations at the football office at St. John Arena. I was really looking forward to the game the next day and all the excitement that came with it. I opened the door to my bedroom on the second floor of the *Sigma Phi Epsilon* fraternity house to find a girl sitting there on my couch.

This wasn't any girl, however. It was Cindy! I look startled and dumbfounded that she was sitting on my bedroom couch at the fraternity house.

"What are you doing here?" I said.

She looked at me with her beautiful smile and said, *"Nice to see you too, Denny."*

Cindy had come all the way up to Columbus, Ohio from the University of Mississippi where she was in her first year as a freshman. I couldn't believe my eyes that she had flown up to see me at Ohio State! I thought that we had ended our relationship with each other prior to the start of the school year. Cindy rushed over to me and hugged me with tears running down her face.

We started to kiss. I was falling in love with her all over again. Cindy told me that she got in contact with Mike Clark about coming up to see me that weekend for my birthday. Mike picked Cindy up at *Port Columbus Airport,* and drove her to the Ohio State campus.

Keep in mind, I was still trying to get over her, and I was in a depression about our romantic breakup that summer. Seeing Cindy again brought back all the feelings as well as hardships. I was truly in love with her and thought maybe our relationship was going to last forever.

All I wanted to do was kiss and hold her in my arms. At this point, I was hoping the weekend would never end. I was determined to make this relationship work, even though she went to a different college. It just felt that our relationship was meant to be.

I had another problem that weekend of October 1st. How was I supposed to spend time with Cindy when I had football recruiting duties during the weekend? I just couldn't let Cindy just sit in my fraternity house while I was helping with the Ohio State football recruits.

The Ohio State Buckeyes and the University of Illinois *"Fighting Illini"* were playing for a traditional prize that weekend known as the

Illibuck Trophy. The game was sold-out as usual with over 90,000 expected to be in attendance that day.

Cindy really wanted to go to the game and see why I loved Ohio State football so much. Throughout our time together, she could never understand my fascination with the team. How could I get Cindy into the game?

I did the unthinkable that afternoon. I called Steve Pederson at the football office, and told him that I had a new recruiting guide that could help us out on Saturday. I didn't tell Steve, or his assistant Corrine, that Cindy was my girlfriend or that she didn't even attend Ohio State.

Both of them said to bring Cindy to the recruiting tower of Ohio Stadium and they would give her a name badge for the game. Steve didn't ask many questions about her mainly because he was so preoccupied with getting the best student-athletes to come to Ohio State. I felt bad that I wasn't honest with him or Corrine. If they only knew that she was my girlfriend and a student at Mississippi.

When Saturday morning arrived, Cindy and I went to the McDonald's on High Street to get breakfast before we headed to meet Steve and the rest of the recruiting guides at Ohio Stadium. I don't think I ate much that morning. I kept staring at her. My mind wasn't on the game either that day. She was all that I could think about while we sat there in the McDonald's.

She kept saying, *"You know I will always love you, don't you?"*

I nodded at Cindy. I told her that there were no other girls in my life. She was my one and only sweetheart. I told her someday that I wanted to marry her. She just smiled at me.

As we approached the recruiting room in Ohio Stadium, I introduced Cindy to Steve and Corrine, as well as the rest of the student recruiting guides, scheduled to work that morning. This was prior to the 1:30 pm kickoff against Illinois. I was hoping Steve wouldn't find out who Cindy was, or that I would have to explain to him the details behind our relationship.

Cindy actually fit in really well by meeting the other OSU coaches, the high school student-athletes, and their parents. She was having a conversation with the parents of these potential student recruits like she actually knew what she was talking about in regard to Ohio State, and its football program. I was amazed at how friendly she was towards everyone that day. Maybe being around me for a while, she picked up a thing or two about Ohio State football.

After we took the recruits and their parents to their seats in Ohio Stadium, Cindy and I sat together at the 50-yard line to watch the Buckeyes take on the Illinois Illini. Maybe the team was as unfocused as I was that day because the Buckeyes fell to Illinois by the score of 31-12.

This may have been one of the few times that I didn't care if Ohio State lost a football game. Part of the reason Ohio State lost that day was because a player was dismissed from the team for taking money from an agent. Two others were not playing due to injuries.

After the game, Cindy and I went out to dinner and back to the fraternity house for a quiet evening. I told her how much I was in love with her. I wanted our relationship to work out, even though she went to the University of Mississippi. That is when she told me the bad news. My recollection of what Cindy said to me that night still stings to this day.

She said, *"Denny, I really love you too. I will always love you. However, I met someone in Mississippi and his name is Ben."*

I was completely at a loss for words. Why did she fly on an airplane to Columbus, Ohio to tell me this? Could Cindy have just called me on the phone, and told me she was now seeing another person named Ben? Besides, I thought that we decided to go our own separate ways once college started back up in the fall. I asked her that very question. Cindy took a moment to gather her thoughts and responded to my question.

She said, *"I wanted to tell you in person that it is all over between us. I thought calling you on the phone would have been inappropriate and I wanted to say goodbye in person."*

Why did Cindy act like she was still in love with me during the beginning of the weekend? Why did she kiss me? She proceeded to tell me how wonderful Ben was, and how they shared the same interests in life. I am not sure what it feels like to get kicked in the stomach by a mule, but I have a pretty good idea. The emotions of losing her again was more than I could handle. I was absolutely crushed.

The next morning, I borrowed a fraternity brother's car. I drove Cindy back to *Port Columbus Airport*. I helped her with the luggage. We waited for Cindy's airplane flight back to Mississippi. Ben would be waiting for her return.

Cindy looked at me and said, *"Maybe we can get together someday, and have dinner when we are both back in Northwest Indiana."*

I didn't say a word. Tears were running down my face.

She said, *"I will always love you."*

As I watched her plane leave Columbus that day, I wondered if that would ever happen. I also wondered if Ben was going to be as good of a boyfriend as I was to Cindy. As I got back in the car, I had more tears running down my face.

I cried all the way back to the fraternity house. The song, *"One of These Nights"*, by the *Eagles* was playing on the radio. It was one of the worst days in my life. There are many times I hear that song on the radio, and recall how painful that day was for me. I would never see or talk to Cindy ever again.

I will always love her.

Chapter 31

Picking up the Pieces

To take my mind off the once again painful breakup with Cindy, my fraternity brothers Mike Clark and Dave Weber suggested that we should travel down to Bloomington, Indiana for the following weekend game with the Indiana Hoosiers. I got a few tickets from the football office. We headed down there on Friday, October 7th.

Indiana had beaten the Buckeyes the year before in Columbus by the score of 31-10. Many of the Ohio State players were talking about revenge against the Hoosiers. I looked up a few of my high school friends who went to Indiana University and asked if we could stay with them during the weekend.

One of my great friends named Tim Bianco, who grew up with me on Johnson Street during our youthful years in Merrillville, said that we could stay with him. One night was going to be enough because the following day the Buckeyes would lose the football game.

Before the game started, I remember seeing a banner hanging over the wall of Indiana's Memorial Stadium that said, *"Dark Day #2."* Earle Bruce had called the previous year's loss to Indiana the *darkest day* in Ohio State football history.

The loss in 1988 may have proved to be even more devastating than the one Indiana handed the Buckeyes in Columbus the year before. Dave, Mike, and I sat in a row of seats with all the Ohio State coaches wives in Memorial Stadium. The Hoosiers had a tailback named Anthony Thompson who ran right, ran left, and ran through the Ohio State defense to a 41-7 humiliating defeat for the Buckeyes.

All the while, the Indiana fans were really heckling all the Ohio State fans. It really got bad during the game and even worse after the final seconds ticked off the clock. All the Hoosier fans stormed the field that day and tore down the goal posts. It was only the second time they had beaten Ohio State since 1951.

They also hadn't beaten Ohio State in Bloomington since 1904. I read that Indiana's coach wasn't surprised by the score, and he knew they could dominate the game against the Buckeyes. I do remember the game in 1988 but the aftermath proved to be much worse. It's one thing for fans and students to cheer for their team but to create vandalism after the game was a whole new level of fandom or being fanatical.

As we left Memorial Stadium to get our luggage to go back to Columbus, it was as if my friend Tim had forgotten that we were guests of his for the weekend. Along with the other Indiana fans, Tim was cheering and taunting all the Ohio State fans who were leaving Bloomington that day. I can't say that I blame him because it was a big deal for Indiana to beat Ohio State.

When we got into the car to leave the IU campus that day, a few Indiana students ripped the side window off of our vehicle! There was glass shattered everywhere. There may have been ten Indiana students surrounding the car. They were also rocking our car back and forth. One of the IU students said,

"Hey Buckeyes! How about fighting us Hoosier students!?" That may have been the wrong thing to say.

Mike decided to get out of the passenger-side front seat, and try to take on these ten individuals who obviously had a lot of adult beverages to drink before and during the game. Mike was a black belt in Karate, and knew a lot about the martial arts. I have never seen students run so fast to get away from him as he started kicking and punching at them.

Indiana may have won that day, but my fraternity brother won that day as well by clearing out ten Indiana Hoosier students! By the way, Indiana hasn't beaten Ohio State since that game back in 1988. If it isn't the most lopsided football rivalry in the Big Ten conference, it is pretty close. Ohio State's all-time record against the Indiana Hoosiers is 76-12-5 as I write this book in 2020.

Ohio State's nightmarish season wasn't over yet. The following week, the Buckeyes would lose once again. This time to the Purdue Boilermakers by the score of 31-26. It would be the Buckeyes third defeat in a row. Purdue hadn't beaten Ohio State in Ohio Stadium since 1967.

It started getting really restless in Columbus. I am sure Coach Cooper was feeling the pressure of winning football games. I was trying to do my little part by helping Steve Pederson in the recruiting office as well as on game day with potential recruits who would someday play for Ohio State. I knew that the fortunes of the football program would change, but it just wouldn't be this season.

In terms of my own football career, I started playing intramural football during the week with my fraternity brothers. I hadn't played football since my last game as a high school senior during the 1985 season. I didn't really play intramurals at Ball State, so this was my chance to show off my football skills for my fraternity. It was also a way of 'picking up the pieces' of losing Cindy for a second time.

We were really good. My fraternity brothers would say, *"Give the football to Bunda, and just let him run!!"*

I could hear one of my other friends in the fraternity utter the words, *"Boy... is he fast!"*

A lot of them asked why I didn't try out for the Ohio State football team as a non-scholarship walk-on player. I often wonder if I could have suited up for the Buckeyes, and play football for them. I was always fast enough and I could catch the football. It went back to my fifth-grade year when I beat my classmates in a game at Miller Elementary School.

I was only 150 pounds in college. I doubt Ohio State was looking for someone who weighed so little.

Besides, I was having too much fun with my fraternity and working for Steve in the football office as a recruiting guide. If there are any regrets in my life, that may be one of them. I do wonder if I could have played football or run track & field while I was at Ohio State. If I am going to be totally honest, I was always worried about my dad working all those jobs to help pay for me to attend college.

I didn't want to sacrifice my academics. I knew that both my parents were helping me with some of my school bills. Do I think I would have been a starter for the Buckeyes? No, I don't think I would have even seen any playing time. I probably would have sat on the bench, and watched the game like the fans as well as students in Ohio Stadium.

Although, you never know!

With that being said, I had to settle for catching touchdown passes against other fraternities on Thursday nights at the intramural fields. Even with the breakup with Cindy, I was enjoying myself as a full time student at THE Ohio State University.

Going into the 1988 season, Ohio State hadn't had a losing season since 1966. The Buckeyes had always won more games than they had lost. It was shaping up to be a losing season for Ohio State. After the Indiana and Purdue losses, the Buckeyes would travel up to Minnesota and win 13-6.

The winning streak didn't last long however as they would fall to the Michigan State Spartans in East Lansing. This would be the team's fourth loss in the last five games.

There were a lot of people writing letters in the editorial section of the newspapers saying that John Cooper was a 'mistake' as coach. There were people saying, *"Dump Cooper, Bring Back Earle!"*

These were the same fans who wanted Earle Bruce removed the year before but now wanted him back as the coach. I did not have the same opinion as other fans as well as students on campus. I knew that Coach Cooper was going to turn around the fortunes of the team. My opportunities with the program may not have happened if Coach John Cooper wasn't the head coach of the Buckeyes.

On Friday, November 4th, I walked into the football offices at St. John Arena to hear some exciting news. Steve Pederson told me that Steve Snapp, *the Sports Information Director at Ohio State*, was looking for someone to be a "spotter" for the Ohio State/ Wisconsin game on Saturday.

I looked at him and said, *"What does a spotter do?"*

Steve told me that I would have to sit up in the Wisconsin radio network with the opposing team's broadcasters. I would give them information about individual Ohio State players, game statistics, keeping track of who enters the game, and interesting information about the team.

In other words, I would be providing game day information to the Wisconsin radio broadcast team. I would also be sitting in their radio booth section within the Ohio Stadium press box. Steve Pederson informed Steve Snapp that I would be perfect for the job.

They both told me that there would only be one problem. I couldn't cheer for the Buckeyes while I was in the press box. I would have to be a neutral spectator.

The radio station was known as "WIBA" and they would be in booth #5 of Ohio Stadium. Steve told me that I would report to gate 19 or 28, and head right up to the press box two hours before the game on Saturday morning.

Mom and dad planned on coming in for the Wisconsin game with their good friends, Mike and Connie Weiss along with Woody and Donna Feeler. Once again, my parents would be celebrating their wedding anniversary at an Ohio State game. I don't think they knew of another way to celebrate their years of marriage other than going to a college football game.

Tom Manning, one of my dad's coworker at Calumet High School, would also be there as one of the officials for the game. This would be the one time where I wouldn't have to entertain recruits or eat lunch with their families. Ohio State gave me a press box pass to go up to the booth in Ohio Stadium. I was given a headset and an Ohio State vs. Wisconsin note sheet with information about the game.

The Wisconsin "WIBA" radio station announcers were very nice to me. They asked me questions about the Buckeyes and what I thought of the season. I felt really important sitting in the radio booth. They told me that my job would be to provide them information about certain players, coaches, or stats which didn't appear on their game notes.

They would be able to hear me through the headset, and then relay the information to all the people listening to the game on the radio. The Wisconsin announcers also said that they would interview me at halftime, and get my thoughts on the first half of the game. There was to be another person they would interview at halftime.

They informed me that Archie Griffin would be coming into the booth to do a halftime interview with the network. What!? Archie Griffin the only two-time Heisman trophy winner and star running back of all those great Ohio State teams in the 1970's?!

Going back to the first time that I saw Ohio State play a football game on television against Michigan in 1975, Archie Griffin was always one of my favorite players. Now, he would be in the same radio booth as I was during the game!?

I listened to him talk about Woody Hayes, his two Heisman Trophies, and playing for the Buckeyes in the 1970's. It was like I was a kid again. Not only was Archie Griffin a great player but it was well-known that he was one of the nicest people on the Ohio State campus.

He was now the assistant athletic director at Ohio State, and was still revered on campus as a major hero. As I sat there listening to him, I couldn't believe that I had come this far in my life. A kid growing up loving the Ohio State Buckeyes. Now I am in a radio booth high above Ohio Stadium listening to the Wisconsin radio announcers interview Archie Griffin! I didn't realize at the time but Steve Pederson had more surprises for me in the future.

On that rainy and cold day, Ohio State would beat Wisconsin by the score of 34-12. I felt bad for my parents and their friends for braving the weather while I sat in the Ohio Stadium press box. It was nice for them to once again celebrate their anniversary at an Ohio State game.

After the game, my parents and their friends took a picture together at my fraternity house. Mike and Connie's son Craig had remained my friend since our earlier days growing up in Tucson, Arizona. In the course of a lifetime, it is amazing how many people have an impact on your own personal life.

Mike and Connie Weiss were close personal friends with my parents and shared the same struggles as we did during those early years in Arizona. We also had stayed at their house in Middletown, Ohio when dad and I went to see the Buckeyes play Minnesota in 1980. I had read once 'that life is a collection of moments that define who we are as people.'

I will never forget that day in November of 1988 when I got to sit in the Ohio Stadium press box, and my parents got to share one final moment with their good friends, Mike and Connie Weiss. It would be the last time that I would see them as well. Mike would die of a massive heart attack in 1989.

As the 1988 football season was coming to an end, Ohio State would tie Iowa 24-24 in a game that the Buckeyes should have won. Ohio State was leading 24-21 when Iowa kicked a field goal with about sixteen seconds left to go in the game at Iowa City. All that remained for Ohio State was their annual showdown with the Michigan Wolverines.

Michigan would be the favorites in the game. They only lost twice in 1988 to Notre Dame and Miami. No one was giving the Buckeyes much of a chance. Records don't matter when Ohio State and Michigan play football. For the record, anyone who thought that Coach John Cooper didn't take the Michigan game seriously is sadly mistaken.

There was a sign in the locker room which read, *"What have you done to beat Michigan?"*

Again, Coach Cooper knew how important this game was to the university, its fans, its alumni, and to the state of Ohio. You can't possibly be part of this rivalry and not know the significance of beating Michigan.

Coach Woody Hayes once said, *"The mark of a great Buckeye is to rise to the occasion."*

Ohio State would definitely have to play their best game to beat the Michigan Wolverines in 1988.

I acquired one ticket for my dad to come to the game that weekend to see if Ohio State could pull off the big upset. The day before the game, I actually walked into Ohio Stadium, and sat in the seat of where my dad would be the next day.

I looked around the empty stadium. I was thinking of all the great games that had been played there against Michigan. For me, it would be the first time that I would actually get to see Ohio State play the Wolverines in person.

I had only seen Ohio State play Michigan on television. I was imagining what the next day would be like with over 90,000 fans screaming, cheering, and yelling during the game. I would still have my recruiting guide responsibilities to do, but after that, I would be joining my fraternity brothers in Section 13 of C deck in Ohio Stadium.

I could have been a radio spotter again for this game but declined the offer. There was no way I could be up in the press box, and not cheer for the Buckeyes. This was the biggest game of the year!

The day started like most home games in 1988. I gave dad his ticket and told him that I would see him after the game. I reported for my duties as a recruiting guide to have lunch with the potential recruits in the tower of Ohio Stadium. Steve Pederson said that we were going to take the recruits on the field during warm-ups so they could feel what the atmosphere was like during an Ohio State home game, especially one against Michigan.

I escorted quite a few high school recruits down to the Ohio State sidelines about forty minutes before the kickoff of the game. Michigan's team just got done warming up and was running right past us on their way to the visiting locker room. Some of their coaches said things to a few of our recruits who they were also recruiting to come to Michigan.

They yelled statements like, *"Hey come to Michigan...don't go to Ohio State!"*

I always felt that was kind of rude and disrespectful to do when we were the ones hosting the recruits. Nevertheless, all is fair in love and war, and especially in the Ohio State/Michigan rivalry.

The Michigan Marching Band was also on the field prior to the game. They were doing their pregame routine before the Ohio State Marching Band was to come out to do their own performance. I had my back turned talking to one of our recruits as the Michigan Marching Band was coming off the field playing their fight song, *"The Victors."*

Due to the fact that I wasn't paying attention, one of their tuba players knocked me right in the head with his instrument. Without hesitation, I shoved the Michigan band player right in the arm, and screamed a few words at him which I can't repeat. I knew I shouldn't have done that. I am glad Steve Pederson didn't see me shouting at a Michigan band member. I was caught up in the emotions of the game and the intensity of the rivalry.

One of the high school recruits looked at me and said, *"Wow! This rivalry is really intense!"*

As we escorted the recruits and their families to their seats on the 50-yard line, the game was about to begin. I raced up to the C deck level in Ohio Stadium to watch the game with my fraternity. As a fan and student, this was the moment of a lifetime. To watch the Ohio State/Michigan game in person.

From an Ohio State fan's standpoint, the game didn't start out the way anyone was hoping it would against Michigan. The Wolverines ran up and down the field to a 20-0 halftime lead. I remember Michigan having a great runner that year by the name of Leroy Hoard. Whenever he ran the football, it took a lot of Ohio State players to tackle him.

The Wolverines also had a great field goal kicker by the name of Mike Gillette who kicked a 56-yard field goal right before halftime. No one thought Ohio State would have a chance even before the game started. More importantly, why would anyone think that the Buckeyes would come back from a twenty-point deficit after halftime?

In this rivalry game, anything is possible.

The Buckeyes played probably the best second half of football that I have ever seen them play before. It was if the players had enough of being embarrassed in Ohio Stadium by their hated rival. After trailing by twenty points, Ohio State made it a six-point game with two touchdown runs.

In the 4th quarter, Bobby Olive made almost the same spectacular catch that he made in the LSU game earlier in the year. I flung my hat in celebration once again. It was the second hat that I lost that season due to spectacular plays by the Buckeyes.

I was trying to look across the field to where my dad was sitting to see if he was cheering as loudly as I was. With over 90,000 people in the stadium that day, it was hard to see him.

Was this game going to end just like the LSU game earlier in the year?

The Buckeyes would add a field goal with just a little over nine minutes to play. Michigan would once again regain the lead with a touchdown run by Leroy Hoard to make the score 27-24.

The Buckeyes moved down the field, and scored a touchdown by Bill Matlock with about two minutes to go in the game. Ohio State would now lead again by the score of 31-27. No one was sitting at this point. If I had thought the game with LSU was one of the loudest crowds ever in Ohio Stadium, I was very much mistaken. I looked around and saw all the Buckeye fans cheering and smiling. If the Buckeyes could win this game, it would erase all the other bad games we had in 1988.

There are games, coaches, and players who I will never forget as long as I live. I wish the player that I would have remembered most from this 1988 game was an Ohio State player. That was not the case.

The player I remember most was John Kolesar from Michigan. He had beaten the Buckeyes in 1985, and was set to do it again three years later. John was from Westlake, Ohio but decided to play for Coach Bo Schembechler and the Michigan Wolverines.

John Kolesar quoted after the game as saying, *"It seemed like a fairy tale."*

Michigan won the game 34-31, and I will never forget how I felt. For me, it wasn't a fairy tale ending at all but more like an absolute nightmare. It was the first time that I saw Ohio State play Michigan in person, and it ended in a loss for the Buckeyes. I was in no mood to be around anyone.

Michigan had just won the conference title and now they were going to play in the Rose Bowl. For Ohio State, the season would end with a 4-6-1 record and no bowl game. Therefore, my first two years as a student at Ohio State, the Buckeyes would not play in a bowl game at the conclusion of the season. It was one of the worst ever stretches in Ohio State football history, and I happened to be a student at the time.

I also almost got in a fight with one of my fraternity brothers that night after the game. He was joking with me about Ohio State losing to Michigan.

He kept saying things like, *"Go Blue!"* and *"Let's Go Michigan!"*

He happened to be from Michigan but attended Ohio State as a student. I couldn't believe he was a student at Ohio State but actually cheered for Michigan! Why would anyone do that? We had to be separated because I was really close to punching him in the face. In the heat of anger, I said some things to him that I maybe shouldn't have.

I actually told my other fraternity brothers that I wanted him kicked out of the house for rooting for Michigan. Again, I just couldn't believe that someone could cheer for Michigan while they attended college at Ohio State! I guess he couldn't believe that someone like me could take football so seriously.

He never said anything to me again about the game or about the rivalry. I never did apologize to him nor did he apologize to me. We kind of went our own separate ways.

My Saturdays in the winter were filled with helping Steve Pederson host potential recruits who would someday consider Ohio State as their college destination.

We would show the recruits the *Woody Hayes Athletic Center*, have them visit with academic advisors, walk the campus, and visit with current members of the team. Steve even wrote me a note on an Ohio State football postcard.

It read:

Dennis,

Thanks for your help in the Buckeyes "Return to Glory." We look forward to another great year.

~Steve

I have to admit that I really didn't have a big of a role with the football team. It was the coaches, players, and support staff who made Ohio State a great football program. Steve Pederson always made me feel part of the process. That I was doing special things to help make the Buckeyes a great team as well as program.

I guess I did visit with a lot of high school players who would eventually play for the Buckeyes. I would tell their parents what a great academic school Ohio State was to attend and that their son would get a great education. It was just nice being around the coaches even if a lot of them had no idea who I was.

Little did many of them know that I actually sat at their football desks while they were away from the office. I would answer phones and take messages from high school coaches or others who wanted to talk to the Ohio State staff.

On occasion, I would answer the phone to some irate fan who couldn't understand why we didn't run a certain play or why we couldn't tackle very well. Of all the coaches, it was Steve Pederson who I was often amazed by because of his professionalism. I really believed that of all the people on John Cooper's staff, it was him who was going to turn the Ohio State football fortunes around in 1989. I was just hoping that would also be true in my own personal life.

I was picking up the pieces in my own life and a return to my own 'personal glory.'

Chapter 32

Go on Vacation and Hope not to Come Back on Probation!

I got surprising news from my parents in March of 1989. I was going to see Grammy and Papa in Palm Springs, California for spring break. The airlines had cheap rates and I wouldn't have to spend any money on a hotel. I called Rick on the phone to see if he had the same break as I did in March.

Purdue Calumet, where Rick went to school, had the same vacation dates. I would be flying out a few days earlier from Port Columbus Airport in Ohio. It would be the same airport that I said goodbye to Cindy for the last time. Rick, on the other hand, would be flying out of Chicago to Palm Springs.

Most of my fraternity brothers were heading to Fort Lauderdale or Daytona Beach, Florida for spring break. They asked me to join them. They couldn't understand why I was going to California. What could possibly be there? First, I would be able to see my grandparents since they moved out there in 1988. Second, it seemed as if everyone was going to Florida for spring break, so why not try something new? It was also a time to reconnect with my best friend, Rick.

During the college years, we really didn't get to see much of each other except for working at the Mansards in the summertime. I guess we didn't realize it at the time, but Palm Springs, California would prove to be a really big spring break destination for college students.

I left Columbus, Ohio on a plane Saturday, March 18th, 1989 for spring break. For whatever reason, I dressed up in a tie and nice shirt for the flight out to California. It was the first time that I flew on an airplane by myself. I actually had to catch another flight in Minneapolis to Palm Springs because the flight I was on from Columbus only went to Minnesota. I called my parents when I reached the airport in Minneapolis to tell them that I arrived safely, and I would be catching another flight to Palm Springs in an hour or two.

Being in the airport by myself made me feel really grownup and important. I was just this middle class kid from Merrillville, Indiana. I had never really traveled alone. Life was the ultimate experience.

By the time I reached Palm Springs, California it was mid-afternoon. I could see Grammy and Papa waiting for me by the airport building gates known as the concourse. I hugged both of them. Tears were rolling down Grammy's face.

They were very happy to see me because I was their only grandson. They had been a big part of my life growing up. Both of them watched me in my many sports activities as well as fulfill a dream of attending Ohio State. They always gleamed with pride of all my accomplishments.

Grammy would always write me letters while I was in college with a little extra spending money included in an envelope. I was always grateful for everything that they did for me. Even though they loved Palm Springs, I knew the move for them was difficult. They were glad that I was there to see them. However, as much as I wanted to hang out with them during my week-long vacation in Palm Springs, I think both of them knew that I wanted to be around kids from different colleges.

Papa suggested that I go to a place where one of Grammy's cousins worked in the *Palm Desert Mall*. Her name was Marilyn, but we all called her "Teta." Teta worked at a jewelry store in the mall. It also had a college spring break establishment known as the *"Green Onion."*

Since the breakup with Cindy, I really didn't really have a girlfriend. The *"Green Onion"* would be the perfect place to meet students from other college campuses, and more importantly... girls! Papa and Grammy understood that I wanted to have fun during my week-long break from college.

Rick wasn't to arrive in Palm Springs for a couple of days, so I decided to hang out at the *"Green Onion"* with the other college students. I was amazed that none of them were from mid-western schools like Ohio State, Purdue, Indiana, Notre Dame, or Illinois. The kids that I met were from San Diego State, UCLA, Arizona, Arizona State, Cal Berkeley, and USC.

Going down the main streets of Palm Springs, there were palm trees and college students everywhere! There must not have been a dress code because many of the girls were in bikinis or cut-off t-shirts. Guys were walking around with shorts but not wearing any shirts at all. It was really wild! Papa just smirked at me as he drove me to the *"Green Onion."* I mean everyone is young just once so why not experience it!

I went into the Palm Desert Mall and greeted Teta. It had been a long time since I saw her in person. She had moved out there prior to my grandparents arrival in 1988. She gave me a few dollars to spend and I was off to the college hangout inside the shopping mall.

It was nice talking with kids from other schools and seeing what they liked about their university or college. Of course, I spent most of my time bragging about where I went to college and all the great things it was known for. I am sure a few of the girls who were from schools like USC or UCLA just rolled their eyes at me as if to think... Who cares!

Most people were there just to have a good time, meet people, and drink beer. I have to admit that I was pleasantly surprised at how beautiful the girls were out in Palm Springs. I had never seen so many blonde-haired and blue eyed girls in my life. Since I wasn't dating anyone at the time, I was hoping that maybe I could find the girl of my dreams.

It was as if I almost forgot that Rick was supposed to arrive in a few short days. If I found a girl to date, I may not have cared if he was on his way to Palm Springs or not. When Rick did arrive a few days later, I think he was amazed at how much different Palm Springs was from the Midwest.

The scenery, the lifestyle, and carefree attitude was so much different from what we were used to growing up in Merrillville. Rick even bought a spring break shirt that read, *"Come on vacation and leave on probation."*

Not that we were planning on getting into any trouble. After all, we were staying rent-free at my grandparents' place for the entire week. We did plan on having a lot of fun while we were there. Rick and I never had been on spring break before as college students, so we were going to make the most of it.

We decided that we were going to sign up for the spring break games which were going on during the week. One of the games was a three on three basketball tournament. Since there were only two of us, we asked this student from *Orange Coast College* to play on our team.

There was another event I entered known as the 100-meter dash. I knew that I had a great chance at contending in that event since I was a track runner in high school, and set an intramural record at Ohio State the previous spring.

It cost money to sign up for the events but Papa was quick to give us the cash so we could have our fun. I believe it was a chance for Grammy and Papa to see me competing in sports again. I knew that they had always liked coming to my high school events when I was playing football and running track at Merrillville.

There was a rumor that week if you won your event or competition in the Palm Springs games, the sponsoring company would fly you back for free the following week to go up against the winners of Daytona Beach, Florida. I don't know if it was true or not, but I was going to try to win the events that Rick and I signed up for during the week. Even though the games were just for fun, we were going to be competitive.

Before the three on three basketball tournament, the announcer of the spring break games would announce who you were to the crowd along with what college you attended. He first announced the kid on our team from Orange Coast College. He received the loudest cheers. Rick was introduced next from Purdue Calumet, and people just looked around as if to ask, *"Where is that located? "*

When it was my turn to be introduced... the announcer said, *"From The Ohio State University...Dennis Bunda!"*

I got a chorus of boos like you wouldn't believe!! I mean they were really booing me. I didn't realize that people out west didn't like Ohio State that much. Maybe it was because schools like UCLA and USC had played us in previous Rose Bowl games or because it wasn't a California university.

We did end up winning the first round basketball game. We were due back the next day to play a team from Mt. San Jacinto College in California. The problem was that our third player from Orange Coast College didn't show up for the basketball game.

Rick and I stuck playing these three players from a community college who looked like they were really good athletes. They didn't disappoint! Even though Rick and I took an early lead, one of the Mt. San Jacinto players looked at his other two teammates and said,

"Let's turn it on!"

When I mean Rick and I got beat in the game, that may have been the understatement of the year. They absolutely destroyed us in the basketball game. Throughout the years, I have often joked with Rick that if he would have played better and caught some of my passes, we would have won the game. That couldn't have been any further from the truth.

The three players from Mt. San Jacinto obviously played college basketball. I still had another spring break game that I could do well in. It was the 100 meter dash. I actually won my first race and was scheduled to run again in the finals later in the afternoon.

That wouldn't happen...

Rick and I had a few hours until my big race so we decided to get something to eat. A funny thing happened. We saw a double-decker bus with a lot of college students riding on it down the main street of Palm Springs.

We decided to board the bus and have fun with the other college kids. I never showed up for the finals of the 100 meter dash spring break finals. I lost track of time on this double-decker bus which was touring around Palm Springs. We were having too much fun!

I think that really upset Papa. I believe he thought that I had an excellent chance to come back the following week and win the competition. It would give him and Grammy more time to spend with me. It would be another regret in my life.

During the evenings in Palm Springs, Rick and I would go to this college hangout known as the *"Pompeii Nightclub."* Papa would be our designated driver to the club so we could have a few adult beverages.

Rick spent most of his time inside Pompeii watching the Michigan Wolverines play in the 1989 NCAA basketball tournament. I, on the other hand, was socializing with all the college girls and having the time of my life.

I believe Michigan had just beaten North Carolina in the tournament that night. Rick turned to me to give me a "high-five" in response to Michigan's big win. I looked at him and said, *"I don't give high fives to anything revolving around Michigan!"*

Rick looked at me kind of startled. If to think that I should have celebrated with him. I am his best friend. I just couldn't do it! Michigan is Ohio State's rival in every sport. The Wolverines did go on to win the NCAA Basketball Championship in 1989.

Rick would buy a t-shirt commemorating their big accomplishment. In the picture section of this book, you will see Rick wearing that same exact shirt. After spring break 1989, I never returned to see my grandparents while they lived in Palm Springs, California.

They did return to Indiana a few years later due to Grammy's health problems. As Rick and I left on separate airline flights, I could

385

see them crying and waving goodbye to me as the plane was taking off from the ground.

They had such a big impact on my life. I just didn't realize it back then. I wish I could have told them how much I appreciated both of them. Rick and I would see each other again during the summer months of 1989. We both got jobs at a hardware store known as *"Handy Andy"* in Merrillville.

The Mansards' pools were no longer hiring for the summer. Rick's mom got us jobs at the hardware store. I really believe that the Mansards didn't want us to work there anymore because we were always having too much fun. It didn't matter though. As long as Rick and I were working together during the summer.

I didn't know one thing about the hardware business but it didn't matter. There were great people working there who taught me about flooring, doors & windows, appliances, and electrical. I didn't realize that learning about home improvement during a summer job would help me later in life.

My sister, Nikki was ready to start her college years at Purdue University.

Even though it wasn't Ohio State, I was very happy for her to be going to college at such a prestigious university. Nikki would be entering her freshman year majoring in elementary education. My sister Erin would be starting her senior year at Merrillville High School in 1989. My two sisters had grown up. I missed a lot of it by being away myself. They were no longer young kids playing out in the yard, but young women who had their own dreams and ambitions in life.

That summer of 1989, a song by Don Henley called, *"The End of the Innocence"* hit the radio airwaves. The first couple of lyrics are: *"Remember when the days were long, and rolled beneath a deep blue sky, didn't have a care in the world with mommy and daddy standin' by."*

It became one of my favorite songs that summer but it also meant that life was about to change again. Time and change are part of life, and you have to take the good times with the bad times. Life is a collection of moments. Happy times may come and go, but the memories we have stay with us forever.

There is a quote by life-changing speaker and bestselling author, Steve Maraboli *"Letting go means to come to the realization that some people are part of your history, but not part of your destiny."*

I just didn't realize that my destiny was right around the corner.

Chapter 33

Dreams Do Come True and the Magical Encounter

Throughout the years, people have always asked me what my favorite time was as a student at Ohio State. That has always been an easy question to answer.

The school year of 1989-1990 would be the most memorable time that I would have at Ohio State. No... we didn't beat Michigan or upset any other highly ranked opponent. In fact, the season ended with an 8-4 record, and a loss to Auburn in the Hall of Fame Bowl by the score of 31-14.

The Hall of Fame game, even though a loss, was the first time that the Buckeyes were in a bowl game since I first got accepted to go to school at Ohio State. The Buckeyes also made the NCAA basketball tournament during the year. I got to see the Ohio State basketball team beat schools like Indiana, Louisville, and Michigan all in St. John Arena as I sat one row up from the court.

Those were all great moments but not the reason why the 1989-90 school year would be a dream come true or a magical time in my life. There would be other reasons to make this my best year at Ohio State.

Rick and I finished the summer at *Handy Andy Home Improvement Center* by enjoying every minute working together. Rick would continue to work there while he went to school at Purdue Calumet.

I asked the supervisors if I could come back during winter break to help sell Christmas trees to earn some extra money. They told me that I was always welcome back to work at their store. I had remembered what Woody Hayes said about *"You Win with People."*

There was no question that the staff at Handy Andy Home Improvement Center played a significant role in shaping who I am today. To think that they almost didn't hire me that summer because I really messed up the interview! I came across as arrogant and a "know it all" during the process. What was I thinking? It took Rick's mom to convince them that I was a hard worker, and I would do a great job.

Going into the 1989 school year, a lot of my work ethic was established because of my summer job at Handy Andy. They showed me how to be accountable for myself, to be a hard worker, to show up on time, and give one-hundred percent effort every day. I am not saying that I wasn't a hard worker before, but it established the fact that I still needed to work on those areas in my life.

I want to say thank you to all my friends and colleagues at the Handy Andy Home Improvement Center. They also helped shape who I am today as a person.

As usual, I would have to report in mid-August to get ready for work as a recruiting guide with Steve Pederson and Corrine for Ohio State football. I was really excited for the season mainly because the Buckeyes were predicted to be much better than John Cooper's initial season.

In 1989, it also marked the *'Centennial of 100 years of football'* at The Ohio State University. It was also known as *"The Return to Glory"* based on the fact that the Buckeyes went 4-6-1 in 1988. It was the worst season for Ohio State football since 1966.

With the freshmen coming into the program, there was this air of excitement in Columbus, Ohio. Coach Cooper and Steve Pederson recruited a freshman linebacker by the name of Alonzo Spellman.

Alonzo was about 6-6 in height and 265 pounds, with a shoe-size of 18. Physically, he was one of the most intimidating players that I have ever seen in person. He quickly became one of my favorite players on the team. With players like Alonzo, there was no question Ohio State was on their way to a 'return to glory.'

As for me, I wanted a 'return to glory' in my own personal life. I had gone through so much. The breakup with Cindy as well as my mom's continuous battle with breast cancer. That's not to diminish what people go through in their own lives. I understand that they go through a lot of personal struggles. I can relate to everyone who has had major adversities.

Many of them have money problems, issues with drug and alcohol addiction, pressures with a job, poor health, and relationship conflicts. All of those problems can change your perspective and mess with your 'mental state of mind.'

Again, I was never diagnosed with depression. I often hid the way I was feeling to my family and friends. Many of them never knew that I was secretly suffering inside. That I spent a lot of time being lonely and sad. There were many times people would be talking to me and I wouldn't be hearing what they were saying.

I thought that having depression would be considered a weakness. I believed those who knew me would think differently, if I told them what was going on in my life. I didn't want to tell anyone that I was suffering from depression. At home and at school, there were many nights I would go to sleep hoping that I would not wake up in the morning.

There is a lot more known about mental health nowadays then back in 1989. Therefore, I didn't really say anything. I thought that these feelings would somehow disappear. They never did, however. Rick knew that I had a very difficult time after the breakup with Cindy. To what extent, I don't know. I am not sure that he really could tell that I was suffering with complete sadness and depression.

I still thought about Cindy and her new relationship with Ben. I often wondered if she was happy and in love with him, like the way we were a year earlier. I would be leaving to go back to school and my football job with Steve Pederson in August. I knew that I had a lot to look forward to in the 1989-90 school year. Due to my mental state of mind, I am not sure that I was fully excited about the return to Ohio State.

Dad had bought me a *1977 Monte Carlo* car from a colleague he worked with at his school, and I was able to drive myself back to Columbus. I did miss the days when Grammy and Papa would take me back to Ohio State and the great conversations, we had on the way there.

Of course, that was not going to happen now that they were living in Palm Springs, California. Dad was now the head football coach at Calumet High School starting that fall. I would get to see him coach his first football game against Valparaiso High School on August 25th prior to my departure for Columbus. It was always one of his dreams to be a head football coach.

A few days before dad's first game as Calumet's head coach, one of his friends, who was an assistant coach on his staff, was struck and killed by a car while walking across the street. It happened by a pizza place known as *the Flamingo*.

It was Bob Mizura, who we all called *"Beero."* I was really shaken by the news because he had always been a great friend to my dad. *"Beero"* always came around the house to see my family. He gave me my first football lesson in the basement on Johnson Street. It was another setback in life that I would have to overcome.

I convinced my dad to tell the press box announcer to have a 'moment of silence' for Bob Mizura prior to the game with the Valparaiso Vikings. The game was played at Valparaiso but they didn't have any problem with the 'moment of silence' request.

Dad's team played their hearts out that night but lost to the Vikings by the score of 31-7. It would be one of the few times that I would see my dad coach a high school football game. I am glad that I got to be there to see his debut. I just wish "Beero" was there coaching as well.

As I departed for Columbus, I said goodbye to everyone. I told them that I would see them around Thanksgiving. I left on Monday,

August 28th to start the school year at Ohio State. I had no idea that this year would change my life forever in more ways than one.

My feelings were real. I am not afraid to share them with you. I didn't really want to live anymore. There may have been five or six times that I thought about crashing my car and ending it all. As I drove down the highway towards Columbus, my perspective completely changed. I am not sure why. I was real close to 'ending it all' by killing myself. There was just something inside of me that said that I needed to live. That I had a purpose in life. That there was something waiting for me at Ohio State. At the time, I had no idea what it was. I was ready for the final two years of my journey at Ohio State. I knew there would be more obstacles in my way, but I was ready for the challenges that laid ahead.

Year of 1989-1990:

Since Ohio State was still on what they called the quarter system, we didn't start classes until mid-September. The Buckeyes wouldn't play their first game until September 16th against the Oklahoma State Cowboys. This would be the last year that Ohio Stadium had a football surface known as *Astro Turf*. Beginning in 1990, Ohio Stadium would go back to a grass surface until 2007 when they would again change the surface to what is now called "Field Turf."

My school year, and the Ohio State football season, started off in a great way. I had thought that I was going to major in television and radio broadcasting when I first arrived on campus. By the fall of 1989, I had changed my mind to majoring in Organizational Communication and Business Marketing. At that point, I had no idea what I was going to do with my life, or the career options that I had available to me. I had taken a couple of business classes that kind of interested me.

Working for the Ohio State football department and Steve Pederson was a great way to learn about business and how an organization works. My academic advisor at Ohio State changed my major and my classes so I could graduate with an Organizational Communications degree.

I was also living in the Sigma Phi Epsilon fraternity house again during the 1989-90 school year. My fraternity brothers had nominated me to give speeches and 'pep talks' to all the freshmen who were considering joining our fraternity. It is known as "Rush Week."

Rush week consisted of events and gatherings which allowed members to get to know the prospects who were considering joining Sigma Phi Epsilon. I was perfect for that role because I was a Communication major as well as my experience working with Steve Pederson as a recruiting guide.

I know my fraternity brothers like Dusty Wiseman, Jerry Williams, Mike Clark, and Eric Kertz knew that I was the right person to help recruit new members to our fraternity. In terms of Ohio State football, I was once again set to help host recruits for the opening game versus Oklahoma State.

The Buckeyes would win the game against the Oklahoma State Cowboys by the score of 37-13 on September 16th, 1989. The next week would be a different story...

The only problem with watching Ohio State play USC the next week was my fraternity duties at Sigma Phi Epsilon. We were scheduled to host a bunch of freshmen who were considering joining our fraternity house. Wouldn't you know it... the game was scheduled to start at 3:30, which was the same time we would be hosting all these freshmen at the fraternity house.

I was really mad at Mike Clark. He was the president of our fraternity. I kept trying to turn on the game in the basement to watch the Buckeyes play the USC Trojans. Mike kept turning off the game every time I was trying to see what was going on. Didn't he know how important Ohio State football was to me and the other fraternity brothers?

How could he not want to watch the football game? Mike Clark was one of the smartest people we had in the fraternity. He was also a very organized and serious person. He said, *"Dennis... we have a job to do today, and that is to get potential recruits to join our fraternity."*

Mike said that watching the game would have to wait. What!? Anyone who knows me...knows that I don't miss Ohio State football games whether they are on TV, or if I am watching them in the stadium. Needless to say, it was a miserable day for two reasons. I only got to see glimpses of the games and the Buckeyes got ambushed by the score of 42-3.

By October 28th, 1989, I also watched part of another game because the Sig Eps had an intramural football game against another fraternity that afternoon. It was one of the few times that I was sure the Buckeyes would lose a game. Ohio State had a 4-2 record on the year.

All of us in the fraternity house were stunned when Minnesota jumped out to a 31-0 lead. Up to that point, I had always watched an Ohio State football game from the beginning until the end, whether it was on television or in-person. I knew that my fraternity had a better chance to defeat the rival fraternity Phi Delta Theta than Ohio State had defeating Minnesota that afternoon.

Still to this day, when people ask me about that game or the exciting ending, I simply cringe at the memory. A lot of my family and friends would say, *"You didn't see the exciting ending to the game? What kind of fan are you?"* Ohio State came back and won...41-37.

Don't get me wrong. I don't regret playing football with my fraternity brothers that day. I do regret that the intramural football game was scheduled for the same time as an Ohio State game on television. The only time that I have seen the finish to the *"Miracle in Minneapolis"* has been on TV replays and videotapes. We did win the intramural game that day if that counts for something!

The next week, mom and dad were wondering if I was coming home to celebrate their wedding anniversary. It also happened to coincide with the fact that Ohio State was playing Northwestern up in Evanston, Illinois that weekend. I asked my parents if I could bring some of my friends home to go to the game that Saturday. Mom wasn't planning on going to the game.

Eric Kertz, one of my fraternity brothers, was sick with a possible case of bronchitis. He got up Saturday morning and wasn't feeling very well at all. He was coughing and had a slight temperature. My mom told Eric that there was no way he was going to the game up at Northwestern until he took some medicine. Eric kept insisting to mom that he was ok, and wouldn't need any medicine. She wasn't going to take 'no' for an answer. Mom followed Eric out of the house and spoon-fed him Robitussin cough medicine.

Every time I see Eric, I remind him of that story.

He always responds by saying, *"Your mom would haven't let me go to the game without taking cough syrup and aspirin!"*

Eric was right!

My mom always put other people before herself, and cared for others as if they were her own children. She was always the favorite "mom" with all of my friends. She would make them laugh, cheer them up when they were sad, give them advice, or just listen to their problems. Even with her on-going battle with breast cancer, she never seemed to be in a bad mood or let her illness get in the way of happiness. Mom was one of a kind.

Notwithstanding Eric's sickness, we all ventured up to Evanston, Illinois to watch the Buckeyes defeat the Northwestern Wildcats by the score of 52-27.

It was another cold but sunny day up in Evanston. It always seemed to be cold and windy whenever Ohio State played up there. A lot of my friends had never been to Chicago before, so we took them to a restaurant after the game in the downtown area.

As I sat there enjoying being around my college friends like Jerry Williams, Eric Kertz, and Chris Durley, I wondered how many of them I would keep in contact with once our days were over at Ohio State. College is such a wonderful and memorable experience. It wasn't just going to the football games, classes, or being involved with the fraternity either.

It was the many times that I walked around the campus admiring how beautiful Ohio State actually was as a school. There are many historical buildings and landmarks on the campus itself.

Mom's favorite place at Ohio State wasn't Ohio Stadium, the Ohio Union, or even the fraternity house where I stayed most of my college years. It was a place known as "Mirror Lake." It is actually a pond on the Ohio State campus that has a lot of tradition to it. Many students go there to study, relax, or even to kiss their significant other.

Many alumni visit Mirror Lake as a time to remember their years as a college student at The Ohio State University. During November when we play Michigan in football, students would jump into Mirror Lake to get ready for the battle with the Wolverines. Many people say that the tradition started in the late 1960's. Since I knew how much my mother loved Mirror Lake, I sent her a postcard of this historic place on campus.

It read:

Dear Mom,

"I got this postcard because I know you like Mirror Lake. I'm very lucky to have a mom like you. Throughout the years, you have always been there for me. To make sure I had a hot breakfast every morning before school, and always picking up my friends and I after football practice. I will always treasure the many things you have done for me. Thank you."

Love Always Your Son,

Denny

I knew someday that mom would need me to be there for her. It was inevitable that her breast cancer would soon return, and possibly spread to other parts of her body. It seemed so unfair that a person who loved life as much as she did would be stricken with this disease.

I often tried to put it out of my mind or hoped that it would clear up on its own, but that was just wishful thinking. I knew that mom faced an uphill battle with cancer. Mirror Lake was a special place to her. I still can see her reflection off of the 'pond.'

It is a fond memory now.

Ohio State went on to defeat Iowa the following week by the score of 28-0. With this win, I really wanted to skip the next week's game against Wisconsin and get ready for the Buckeyes to play Michigan. I was still mad at last year's loss and the fact that one of my fraternity brothers was actually cheering for Michigan!

I had waited a whole year for the revenge against the Wolverines. The problem was the game in 1989 would be played up in Ann Arbor, Michigan and the Wolverines would once again have a great team.

That answer would have to wait another week. The game with Michigan wouldn't be the most memorable game of 1989, or even during my time as a student at Ohio State. In fact, throughout the years, there may have not been a more significant game in my life or one I remember most, than the upcoming game with the Wisconsin Badgers. It is still one of the best moments in my life.

There was nothing unusual about the game itself. Ohio State was 7-2 on the season and Wisconsin was going in the opposite direction at 2-7. For most people, this would be just a regular game in Ohio Stadium.

A game that probably most people would have forgotten about as the years have gone by. For me, the memory is etched in my mind. It is the game that would eventually change my career course and what I wanted to do in life. I was a Communication major but really didn't have any idea about what I actually wanted to do. This game against Wisconsin would change my life forever…

On Monday November 13th, 1989, I finished my classes for the day and headed for St. John Arena to help Corrine and Steve with football recruiting responsibilities. Steve happened to be in a meeting with John Cooper and the other coaches when I walked into his office. Corrine was sitting at her desk organizing the itinerary schedule for the upcoming game against Wisconsin.

We had a lot of high school recruits coming in for the weekend to visit. Corrine looked up at me from her computer screen and the stacked papers on her desk. After staring at me for a couple of seconds with a grin on her face, she asked me a simple question that would change my life forever.

Corrine simply said, *"What is your dream in life?"*

For most people, the answer may have included such responses as: fame, fortune, career, or meeting the girl of their dreams. I guess all those would have been appropriate responses to her question, and they wouldn't have been wrong answers. I wanted all those things in life just like a lot of people do.

Grammy used to say that money isn't everything but it sure does help. That wasn't on the top of my list. Neither was fame or a career. In terms of the girl of my dreams, that was no longer an option.

For a long time, I believed Cindy was the girl of my dreams. I often thought we would eventually marry and have a good life together. With her meeting Ben, I had lost hope that I would ever find a girl. My answer to Corrine's question probably shocked her.

She may have thought that I would give an aforementioned response to her inquiry. As I looked at her, I simply said the first thing that came out of my mouth. I told her that I wanted to come out of the locker room and run into Ohio Stadium with the Ohio State Buckeyes football team before a game.

"Really?" she said.

I told her that I had loved the Ohio State Buckeyes ever since I saw them on television in 1975. My whole life was about reaching goals and dreams that people thought I was incapable of doing. I had often wondered what it would be like to run on the field with the Ohio State Buckeyes in front of a sold-out crowd.

It was only a dream of course and nothing to be taken seriously. Running out of the tunnel into Ohio Stadium was reserved for the team as well as the coaches, not for fans or student helpers, like myself. I surely didn't expect Corrine to take me seriously about running onto the field before a game.

She kept smiling at me, and saying, *"That is really interesting."*

I didn't think anything about our conversation other than we were passing the time. I was stuffing envelopes with information to send to high school recruits on why they should become an Ohio State Buckeye. It was Steve Pederson's *"25 reasons on why to come to Ohio State."*

I thought that I had already fulfilled the dream of becoming a student at Ohio State and now working as a recruiting guide for the football program. I had no idea that there would be more in store for me on that Saturday against Wisconsin.

When November 18th arrived, I reported to the recruiting tower in Ohio Stadium.

I would sit with the families and recruits to discuss the Ohio State campus, academics and of course, the Buckeye football program. Again, nothing really unusual about this Saturday. It seemed like most game days that I worked before. What happened next would change my life forever.

I hadn't seen much of Steve Pederson that morning. I did see Corrine a lot. We were both entertaining the guests prior to the game. All of a sudden, Steve appeared from the stairwell that led down to the locker room from the recruiting tower in Ohio Stadium. By that time, Corrine was standing by his side with a huge smile on her face.

Steve waved and pointed for me to come their way from across the room. I excused myself from the families and recruits who I was talking to about how great Ohio State was as a school. I went up to Steve and Corrine to see why they wanted to talk to me.

Steve looked at me and said, *"You are done with your responsibilities for the day."*

What!? I told him that I had more families to talk to about our football program and what a great university Ohio State was. Corrine said with an excited voice, *"You are running on the field with the team today!"* I stood there totally shocked. She had told Steve Pederson about our conversation in the office earlier in the week.

Steve then took me down to the locker room a few minutes before the team was to take the field prior to the game with the Wisconsin Badgers. I watched the players put on their scarlet jerseys and shiny silver helmets to get ready for the game. As the team lined up in the tunnel to take the field, Steve told me to stand by some of the coaches.

One of them said, *"Make sure you run out of there fast so you don't get knocked down by one of our players!"*

I looked at the coach and said, *"You don't have to worry about that, Coach! I was a state finalist in track at Merrillville High School!"*

Like he really cared. I had waited all my life for a moment like this. I kept thinking about what Coach Armontrout had told me years earlier about 'if you don't chase your dreams that you will never catch them.'

The moment was now. As the press box announcer introduced the team to the Ohio Stadium crowd, Coach Cooper gave the signal to take the field. There were fans reaching out over the side of the stadium wall to 'High Five' us as we took the field. I ran as fast as I could into Ohio Stadium to the roar of the crowd. Was this really happening? It was a moment in time that I would never forget. *It was a magical moment.*

The amount of excitement and adrenaline overwhelmed me as I reached the Ohio State sidelines. I was completely out of breath unlike any time before in my life. I had run the 400-meter dash at Merrillville and held the school record at the time, but never had felt anything like this before.

My dad happened to be at the game watching me take the field. My fraternity brothers were there too. As I looked around the gigantic stadium, I realized how far I had come in life. This was my team and my school.

When Will Smith stated in the movie, *Hitch*... *"Life is not the amount of breaths you take, it's the moments that take your breath away"* he wasn't kidding.

This was certainly one of the greatest moments in my life. I never fully thanked Steve Pederson for helping me realize one of my dreams by running out of the field with the Buckeyes. I would like to personally thank him now as I write this book.

Thank you, Steve!

We did win the game that day by the score of 42-22. It was Ohio State's sixth straight win in a row heading into the rivalry game with Michigan. I don't remember much about the actual game itself.

Besides going to my first game against Illinois in 1979, or my first game watching the Buckeyes in Ohio Stadium in 1980 with dad, this game would always be my most treasured memory.

It is the first thing that I tell people when they ask me about my favorite Ohio State experiences of all-time. I realize how important people are in my life, and the many opportunities that have been given to me throughout the years. Like Woody Hayes said… *"You Win with People."*

I had great people in my life who supported me on my journey to Ohio State.

The next week was the big game with Michigan. Steve had a couple of extra tickets that he gave for dad and I to go up to the game in Ann Arbor, Michigan. I believe I had to pay for the tickets as he couldn't just give them away for free.

I came home for Thanksgiving on November 23rd and a day later we were heading off to Ann Arbor, Michigan. I was really excited about this game and believed that Ohio State could somehow pull off the upset against the third- ranked Michigan Wolverines. Dad and I stayed in a hotel near Toledo, and the next day ate breakfast at a restaurant known as *"Le Peep."*

As we got to Michigan Stadium, it was clear that we were outnumbered by the fans rooting for the Michigan Wolverines. I had gone to games in which Ohio State played teams in their stadium, but never one of this magnitude. This game would also mark the last time in which Michigan's coach Bo Schembechler would coach a game in which the Wolverines played Ohio State.

It would also be the 86th meeting between the two schools, and I would be there in the Michigan Stadium to watch it that day. This game was to see which team was going to the Rose Bowl as the Big Ten Conference Champions. If Michigan won, then they would represent the conference in the Rose Bowl.

On the other hand, Ohio State would only go to the Rose Bowl if they beat the Wolverines, and Illinois would lose to Northwestern later in the day. In other words, the game between Ohio State and Michigan would be bigger than ever. I still couldn't believe that just a week earlier I was running on the field with the team against Wisconsin. This time, I got to watch Ohio State as well as Michigan run on the field prior to the game.

The Michigan team came out of the tunnel, jumped up, and hit a banner that said, *"Go Blue, M Club Supports You."*

While reading about the history of the rival between both schools, I remembered hearing that the Ohio State team tried to rip down this Michigan banner prior to the game in 1973. The two schools really don't like each other but there was mutual respect for the rivalry.

Even though Ohio State trailed 14-3 at halftime, the Buckeyes would close the gap to 21-18 with only about seven minutes to play in the game. Ohio State actually had a chance to win but an interception as well as a last-minute touchdown by Michigan sealed the Buckeyes' fate.

Ohio State would lose to the Wolverines by the score of 28-18 in 1989.

That is not to say that the other games were not important but there was something special about beating Michigan. With the win in 1989, Michigan was now headed to play USC in the Rose Bowl, and Ohio State was going to play Auburn in the Hall of Fame Bowl. For me, it was back to school to finish out the term, and meet with my advisor on graduation requirements.

I thought I would be able to graduate college in four years but that wasn't going to be possible. Since I transferred to Ohio State from Ball State, some of my classes didn't count towards my graduation degree requirements. I walked out of my advisor's office very dejected one day.

A lot of the people I knew back in Merrillville were set to graduate from college and start their careers by 1990. My advisor also told me that I would have to take a few more classes than usual to graduate by the spring of 1991. In other words, I was behind getting my college degree.

One of my fraternity brothers cheered me up that day by saying, *"Look on the bright side. You can be a college student for one more year and enjoy fraternity life as well as Ohio State football!"*

I guess that was one way of looking at things. I had thought maybe that I would want to work in an office wearing a suit and tie being a businessman. On the other hand, running out of the tunnel with the football team onto Ohio Stadium had me thinking that maybe someday I would want to be a college football coach.

Therefore, I told Steve that I would like to be a football coach. I really didn't know the amount of time these coaches put into their jobs but it seemed like a lot of fun. Steve arranged it so I could work with Ohio State assistant coach Gene Huey on occasion. Coach Huey was the wide receivers coach, and was going into his third year on staff with the Buckeye football program.

Although he may not remember me much, Coach Huey allowed me to sit and watch football films with him. There were times he would be watching game films of Ohio State opponents or films of high school players who would potentially play for the Buckeyes. There were a few nights that he would order food to be delivered to the Woody Hayes Center as we watched football films. It was then that I realized how much work football coaches put into their jobs, and how many hours they are away from their own families.

When I returned home for Christmas break, I told my parents that I would have to go one more year at Ohio State. That some of my classes I took at Ball State didn't transfer over to the Ohio State degree requirements. I knew money was going to be tight because Nikki was now going to Purdue University, and Erin would soon be in college the following year.

For those of you who may not know… having three kids in college at the same time is tough for most families. I was always worried that my parents would tell me that I would have to come home because the money would not be there for me to go back to school.

Dad was always positive. He said that all I needed to worry about were my grades.

He would worry about the financial situation.

I just needed to get through a year and half left of college.

Ohio State had lost the Hall of Fame Bowl on January 1, 1990 to the Auburn Tigers by the score of 31-14. The Buckeyes would end the season with a 8-4 record. Many Buckeye fans were longing for the days when we had *"9-3 Earle Bruce"* as coach and beating Michigan on a somewhat regular basis.

John Cooper was now 12-10-1 in two years at Ohio State and had a 0-2 record vs. Michigan. I kept telling anyone who would listen to me, that the Buckeyes were destined for greatness under Coach Cooper. Although the score may not have indicated it, the Buckeyes played a good game against Auburn.

As the game ended, it was also time for me to go back to Ohio State and figure how I was going to graduate with a year and half remaining of college.

I would still help out in the football office. Though my concentration was now on passing my classes and fulfilling another dream of graduating from the school which I loved so dearly.

When February rolled around in 1990, I knew there was something wrong with me. I felt sick and tired much like I did in 1984 when I was diagnosed with mononucleosis. I would go to class and just cough the entire time I was in there.

I went to the *John Wilce Health Center* on the Ohio State campus to get checked out for my sickness. The doctor ran some tests and told me that I had bacterial pneumonia. I had symptoms like shortness of breath, a high fever, chest pains, and a terrible cough. He said that it could take up to a couple of months to clear up my illness.

If the symptoms got worse, I might have to be admitted to the hospital. I phoned my parents and told them that I was really sick with pneumonia. Dad immediately took off work, and said that he would drive to Columbus to be with me. Mom couldn't make the trip. She had to make sure that Erin was taken care of back at home.

Mom may have also felt that Erin would have thrown a bunch of house parties if she was left at home in Merrillville! Nikki and I were mischievous in high school, but Erin was on a whole different level.

When dad arrived in Columbus, he had a little surprise for me. He had actually picked up Nikki from Purdue University to come see me at Ohio State. If you know my sister Nikki, she always put other people's needs before her own. She was a 'spitting image' of mom.

Nikki had sent care packages to me while I was in college by using her own money. She would also give her own plasma to pay for things. She was always helping other people in need. Dad and Nikki spent a few days with me at a local hotel to make sure that I felt better before they left for Indiana. Nikki may have missed a few classes to come see me but that was my sister. I was still attending classes but struggling to get better by the time both her and dad left Columbus.

I assured both of them that I would call them if I needed them to come back and tend to me. In my mind, having pneumonia was worse than when I was sick with mononucleosis back in the fall of 1984.

During February through April of 1990, I had lost twenty pounds, was out of shape, and really wasn't doing well health-wise. My dating life with girls went from zero to well… zero.

I really wasn't looking to get into a relationship again after the breakup with Cindy. There were a few girls who wanted to establish a relationship with me but I didn't want to go through the turmoil again.

Mentally, I was starting to get over the fact that Cindy and I would never be a couple again. I really needed to focus on graduating from Ohio State by the spring of 1991. Besides, I had my fraternity brothers and friends to hang out with during the weekends. Who needed a girlfriend anyways? Sometimes 'magical encounters' happen when you least expect them.

Ohio State was getting ready to host its annual football coaching clinic in the French Fieldhouse as well as in St. John Arena. *(Nowadays, the coaching clinic is held in the Woody Hayes Center)*

Dad was planning on making a second trip to Columbus for the coaching clinic along with some of his friends like Joe "Smokey" Olis and Mark Agerter. He was also there to make sure that I had fully recovered from my battle with pneumonia. I was scheduled to work at the football clinic during Thursday and Friday on April 26th and 27th.

Dad was going to stay the whole weekend, including taking in the Ohio State spring scrimmage game that Saturday. He, along with the rest of the Buckeye followers, were interested to see if Ohio State would be a better team in 1990.

The spring scrimmage was a chance to see how the team looked going into the fall season. My focus was entirely on the weekend with my dad and his friends as well as the responsibilities of the clinic.

"Life is what happens to us while we are making other plans." In an instant, my life would change. I never knew...

Since dad and his friends were down for the annual Ohio State football clinic and the spring game, they wanted to stop by the fraternity house for a Friday evening party. Sigma Phi Epsilon was hosting a get-together with the Phi Mu sorority girls on campus. There were many times we invited girl sororities over for parties and socialization.

No big deal. Just your regular Friday night co-ed party. Dad always liked the fraternity since he was a Sig Ep back in college during the 1960's. It also gave him an excuse to relive his 'college days' by going to a fraternity party, and having fun with younger people.

Dad always said that his college years were some of his best years in his life. All my fraternity brothers liked my dad and thought that he was a lot of fun. I didn't doubt it because he always seemed to be the "life of the party."

In many ways, I don't think dad ever let go of his college experience. Maybe because when dad went back to complete his college degree, he had already met the girl of his dreams. He also had three kids. His experience was much different than mine. Dad may have missed out on all the socialization that went with college life due to his family obligations.

Here was his chance to relive it. He was also about to be part of a magical moment in my own college experience. When the weekend started, he just didn't know it. Nor did I. Life is full of little surprises...

On Friday, April 27th, I wasn't feeling particularly well due to getting over my battle with pneumonia. I was at the fraternity party but not doing much socialization. There were a ton of girls there and many of them were very pretty.

Dad told me to get a few more beers for his friends out on the porch of the fraternity house. We had a baby pool of ice-cold beer sitting outside for all our guests to enjoy. As I was reaching down to get a few beers for my dad's friends, I heard this voice say,

"Hi Dennis, how are you doing?"

The voice was Becky, a girlfriend of one of my fraternity brothers named Chris. I looked up from the baby pool of beer and said, *"I didn't realize someone could notice who I was from my backside!"*

Becky laughed. She said that she came to the party with a friend she was rooming with in the dorms. Nothing unusual. A lot of people brought friends to a fraternity party. The more people there... the bigger the party!

I went back inside to give the beers to dad and all of his friends, thinking nothing of the conversation I had with Becky by the pool of beer. A few minutes went by. I felt a tap on my shoulder. It was my fraternity brother, Chris.

He said, *"Becky's friend saw you outside leaning over the baby pool of beer and wants to meet you!"*

I was stunned. Who would want to meet me right now? I had dropped twenty pounds due to the pneumonia and I wasn't really trying to meet a new girl. The heartbreak of losing Cindy was still on my mind. I didn't want to get into a new relationship. I asked Chris and Becky which girl they were talking about at the party?

As college kids were walking back and forth blocking my view, Chris pointed in the direction where the girl was standing. I looked over to the area and saw this beautiful girl wearing a blue shirt with a white skirt. She was absolutely stunning. Chris started shoving me in her directions telling me to go meet her. I am usually not a person lost for words but I didn't know what to say to this girl.

As I got closer to her, I could feel my heart racing through my chest and my body shaking. What should I say to her? The only thing that I could think of was asking this girl for a piece of gum. Yeah... that was a great conversation starter! I was absolutely nervous around her like no other girl that I had ever met before.

"What is your name?" I asked.

She said, *"Kelly Thomas."*

I could see my dad and his friends staring over at us as we were getting acquainted. I asked her a few more questions about her hometown, her college major, and what she liked to do. Was this love at first sight? Did I really want to start over again with a new girl, and all the problems that went with a relationship? Somehow I knew this would be different.

I walked Kelly back to her dorm that night across the Ohio State campus. We talked for a while and I held her hand the whole time. She was a very beautiful girl but very quiet. I asked her if I could kiss her goodnight, and she said... "YES."

I didn't realize it at the time, but Ms. Kelly Thomas would soon become Mrs. Kelly Bunda. There is a famous movie known as the *"Bucket List,"* starring Jack Nicholson and Morgan Freeman.

One of the wishes that Jack Nicholson's character has in the movie is to *"Kiss the most beautiful girl in the world."*

I believe I achieved that wish on Friday, April 27th, 1990. I had accomplished my goals and dreams of attending Ohio State, having a small role with the Ohio State football program, and meeting the girl that I would someday marry. There were a lot of parallels between us.

She was from Northwest Ohio and I was from Northwest Indiana. She has two younger brothers and I have two younger sisters. Her mom was born on Aug 19th and my mom was born on April 19th. Her dad was born on December 25th and my dad was born on March 25th. Oh yeah...Kelly's birthday is on March 27th and mine is on September 27th. You could say it was a perfect match.

My senior year at Ohio State we were inseparable as a couple. I moved out of the fraternity house and into an apartment complex close to the Ohio State campus known as *University Village*.

I may have lived there my senior year but most of my time was spent with Kelly.

In 1990, Ohio State would go through another average football season by their standards with a record of 7-4-1. We lost to Michigan again by the score of 16-13.

The game I remember most that year was the one against the USC Trojans in a rainstorm. With 2:36 to go, the officials called the game due to heavy rain as well as thunder and lightning around the Columbus area.

A lot of the fans were really upset that the game was called off because they felt the Buckeyes could stage another miraculous comeback much like the one against Minnesota a year earlier. The game ended with the Trojans winning 35-26.

My mom would finally get to meet Kelly in person for a game against Northwestern on November 3rd. It was another weekend that mom and dad would celebrate their anniversary at an Ohio State football game. We went out to eat after the game.

I told my mom, *"Kelly was the girl that I wanted to marry someday. She was my dream girl."*

My mom smiled at me. *"I knew the moment I saw her."*

Chapter 34

Destiny Road

I graduated from The Ohio State University by the spring of 1991. My whole family came down to see the big moment on Friday, June 14th at the commencement ceremony in Ohio Stadium. Kelly's family was there too.

As I walked across the stage to receive my college degree, I realized I had achieved my dream. It all went back to that fateful day on November 22nd, 1975 when I first saw Ohio State play Michigan on television.

There were so many obstacles that I had to overcome to fulfill this dream. There were many moments where I felt like giving up or that I wasn't good enough to attend such a great university.

I had many people tell me it was ok to be average. That going to college wasn't for everyone. I could have stayed at Ball State University and graduated from there. I also could have accepted the offer to attend Franklin College or North Central to run track and play football back in 1986.

"If you don't chase your dreams...you will never catch them."

For me, Ohio State stands for more than a sports team or an institution of higher learning. It was a place that allowed me to grow as a person. It was a place that taught me the meaning of hard work, dedication, excellence, and striving to achieve your goals. Ohio State also means "Family" to me.

Some of my best memories are with my dad at football games, walking by Mirror Lake with mom, the many life-long friendships, and of course meeting my future wife... Ms. Kelly Thomas.

It has been quite a journey going back to that moment in time when I was first introduced to Ohio State. People always ask me what my favorite moment was besides meeting my future wife on campus. That is an easy question to answer.

It is the day that I received my college degree in Ohio Stadium. It was the same stadium that I cheered the Buckeyes on while watching them on television or in person. It is the same stadium that I went to football camp back in 1983. It is the same stadium where I played football catch with my friends from Morrill Tower. It was also the stadium that I got to run out of the tunnel and onto the field with the Ohio State Buckeyes.

I have great pride in the fact that I graduated from The Ohio State University. There is not a day that goes by that I don't look at that college degree on my office wall. It is a reminder of how important that was for me as well as for my family.

Dreams really do come true!

Kelly graduated from Ohio State in 1992 with a degree in Elementary Education. In the summer of 1992, we were married in the state of Ohio in front of our family and friends. Many of them were my groomsman at the wedding. Great friends like Mike "D" Demakas, Jerry Williams, Eric Kertz, Chris Durley, Dusty Wiseman, and of course my best man and friend...Rick Keneson. My high school friend, Cheri Kelley, was also at the wedding. Coach Armontrout came to celebrate this special occasion.

As I write this book, Kelly and I have been married for over 28 years and have two wonderful children. Our son attends Ohio State as a student, and there is hope that maybe our daughter will attend there too.

I am a schoolteacher and coach now. Ohio State was able to help me get my first coaching job at Columbus South High School working for the legendary coach, Don Eppert in 1991.

411

From there, I went on to coach at Valparaiso University in 1992. I have now been with Crown Point School Corporation in Northwest Indiana as a teacher/coach since 1994. Crown Point is the same school I caught a touchdown pass against while I played for Merrillville back in 1985. There is not a day that goes by that I don't look at that football field as I am getting ready for the school day. It is another reminder of how far I have come in life.

There have been many people who have had a significant impact on my life. Some of them I have lost contact with throughout the years. Some of them have found their own dreams and ambitions. Some of them have gone through hardships and difficulties. Some of them would be gone forever.

Cindy would pass away from a terminal illness in 1994. She was only 23 years old. My good friend Craig Weiss, who I spent a lot of my early childhood life with in Arizona, lost his life in an automobile accident in 2003. I did get to see him one last time when he visited Kelly and I while he was in Northwest Indiana in 1994. We talked about growing up in Arizona as we enjoyed an afternoon of golf. I miss him every day.

Brian Portlock is retired from the Air Force and now lives a good life in South Carolina. He comes into town to see me once a year, and has always been one of my best friends. He has his children and grandchildren to keep him company.

Mike "D" Demakas is now an assistant principal of a middle school, and resides in Texas with his wife and son. Just like Brian, "D" has remained a big part of my life and one of my best friends. We always get together at Christmas time for dinner with our wives. "D" and I always reminisce about growing up in Merrillville and playing high school sports for the Pirates.

Mike "Bucky" Randall now lives in Florida, and is a proud parent and recently became a grandparent. Steve Civanich is now very successful in his career and doing extremely well in life. My fraternity brothers Jerry Williams, Eric Kertz, and Dusty Williams were all part of my wedding, and still reside in Columbus.

Recently, I reconnected with my friends Mark Hamilton and Chip Ashley. They are both doing well. I took my high school friend Dave Scott to see some Ohio State football games in Columbus. I think he now understands my obsession with the Buckeyes.

There is always my best friend, Rick. We have now been best friends since meeting each other at Miller Elementary School back in 1978. He has always been there when I have needed him the most.

Rick has actually served as one of my assistant coaches for football, basketball, and track & field during my career as a coach. There isn't a day that goes by that we are not talking about our days at Harrison Junior High or the many memories that defined us at Merrillville High School.

Coach Armontrout passed away from cancer in 2018. The many life lessons that he taught me are ones which I teach young people today. Of course, the main one is 'chasing your dreams and catching them.'

Coach "A" actually served as my assistant coach while I was the head track & field coach at Crown Point High School for seven years. I would still listen in to his conversations with the Crown Point sprinters and the many life lessons he was teaching them. I can still hear "Coach A" telling them that… *"Can't never did anything. If you say you can, you have a chance."*

On January 23rd, 2010, I returned to Merrillville High School for a varsity basketball game. The school honored Coach Armontrout at halftime. Merrillville renamed their track & field complex after him. I was the one who presented Coach Armontrout with the dedication plaque.

I can still hear the cheers that night and see the smile on his face. I will never forget that moment or the impact he had on my life. Thanks Coach Armontrout for the memories and always believing in me. Steve Pederson went on to be a very successful athletic director at the college level as well as in private business.

I owe him a lot for mentoring me throughout my time at Ohio State. He helped me realize one of my dreams of running on the field with the Buckeyes. Thanks Steve for allowing me to be part of the Ohio State football program. I am forever grateful.

Grammy would pass away in December of 1998 and Papa would follow shortly in January of 2000. They were two of the best grandparents a person could possibly have in life. I go back to the summer day in 1985.

I shared my dreams with them while I was working a summer job at Camp Lutherwald. I remember the moment like it was yesterday. As Grammy, Papa, and I were on a sailboat ride, I shared my quest of going to Ohio State. I can still hear Grammy saying, *"Feller, you can do it! Don't let anything get in your way!"*

They never gave up on me or let me give up on myself. I miss them a lot.

This is where it gets really difficult. I realize that life doesn't last forever, and we need to appreciate the time we have with those who have helped us on our journey. I don't know if there was anyone who enjoyed life, and all it had to offer, more than my mom.

Life isn't always fair and sometimes can be very cruel. Mom lost her battle with breast cancer on April 16th, 2003. Mom was almost a twenty year survivor since she was first diagnosed with the disease during my sophomore year in high school back in 1983. She died three days before her 57th birthday, and six days before my daughter was born.

My daughter's middle name is Gayle after my mother. I only have one real regret with mom's passing. She never got to see or hold my daughter. Mom did however get to spend time with my son. He was only four years old at the time of her death.

When my mom passed away, a lot of my friends attended the funeral. As the eulogy was being read about her life, I looked in the back of the church. I saw many of those friends crying. It was then that I realized how important she was to so many people. It goes back to the day I spent with her in the coffee shop as she was talking to a person she didn't even know.

However, mom didn't have to know you for her to have an impact on your life. For me, her impact on my own life was immeasurable. She was always there for me.

Thank you, mom and I miss you!

As for what Coach Hayes said about *"Paying Forward,"* I was recently a keynote speaker at a breast cancer banquet known as the *"Gayla of Life"* in honor of my mother. Whenever I am asked to donate money or speak on behalf of breast cancer awareness, I don't hesitate to help the cause. It is a disease that has affected so many people.

As for the rest of my family, everyone is doing extremely well. My sisters Nikki and Erin both went into the education field. Nikki is now a middle school principal and Erin is a middle school guidance counselor. Dad is fully retired from his job at Calumet High School, and still goes to as many Ohio State football games as he can.

I recently took him to an Ohio State football game against the University of Cincinnati in 2019. Most of the game, I sat there and observed dad enjoy himself watching the Buckeyes play in Ohio Stadium.

It took me back to the first game he and I saw at Ohio State on September 20th, 1980. For a second, I was a kid again enjoying watching a game with my father. He was the one who allowed me to go to Ohio State.

Dad simply could have said 'no' and told me that I would have to go to a smaller school, or one that offered a track & field scholarship. He didn't do that though. He allowed me to live my dream and go to Ohio State. I do thank him, but not nearly as much as I should. Dad always believed that is where I should go to school because it was meant to be my destiny. More importantly, he taught me to never give up.

Thank you, dad, for your guidance and inspiration!

Nowadays, Kelly and I have a great life together with our two wonderful kids. We have made two major home purchases during our marriage, and hope to make another one soon. This time to Columbus, Ohio to be closer to where we first met...Ohio State.

How about you? What are your dreams and ambitions in life? Has anyone ever told you that you couldn't achieve something? Do you have major obstacles and life events which are holding you back?

Don't let anything stand in your way! It is so easy to just accept who you are, instead of searching for who you want to be. In life, you usually only have a few opportunities to live out what you were meant to do.

Maybe your dream isn't to go to Ohio State. Maybe it is to go to another college like Notre Dame, Michigan, Indiana, or Purdue. Maybe it's to become a doctor, lawyer, steel worker, electrician, pilot, or a teacher.

We all have dreams in life, and dreams do come true. As actor Jeremy Irons once was quoted, *"We all have our time machines. Some take us back, they're called memories. Some take us forward, they're called dreams."*

If you dream it...you can accomplish it. I lived out my dream— Ohio State!

~*The End*~.

Coach Dennis Bunda
December 2020

Author Dennis Bunda is a 1986 graduate of Merrillville (Indiana) High School and a 1991 graduate of The Ohio State University. He has a degree in Organizational Communication and Marketing. He also has an education endorsement in the areas of U.S. Government, U.S. History, and World History.

Dennis has been an educator as well as a coach for over thirty years at the college, high school, and middle school levels.

He has been a presentational speaker for sports coaching clinics as well as for breast cancer awareness. Dennis resides with his family in Northwest Indiana.

CPSIA information can be obtained
at www.ICGtesting.com
Printed in the USA
BVHW090218261021
619844BV00020B/1428